In Over Our Heads _____

In Over Our Heads

The Mental Demands of Modern Life

Robert Kegan

Harvard University Press

Cambridge, Massachusetts

London, England

Quotation on pages 115–116 from OUT OF CANAAN by Mary Stewart Hammond. Reprinted with the permission of W. W. Norton & Company, Inc. Originally appeared in
The New Yorker. Copyright © 1991 by Mary Stewart Hammond.

LIBRARY OF CONGRESS CATALOGING-IN-PUBLICATION DATA

Kegan, Robert.
    In over our heads : the mental demands of modern life / Robert
Kegan.
        p.   cm.
    Includes bibliographical references and index.
    ISBN 0–674–44587–2 (cloth)
    ISBN 0–674–44588–0 (pbk.)
    1. Cognition and culture.   2. Adulthood—Psychological aspects.
3. Adjustment (Psychology)—History—20th century.   4. Civilization,
Modern—20th century—Psychological aspects.   5. Conduct of life.
I. Title
BF311.K37   1994
155.2'4—dc20   93–46971
                    CIP

For Barbara, Lucia, and Joshua

the home team

with love

Acknowledgments ⸺⸺⸺⸺⸺⸺⸺⸺⸺

For nearly a generation now I have drawn energy and inspiration from my connections to several communities of unending conversation and support. For their many gifts of mind and heart I thank my colleagues at the Clinical-Developmental Institute, faculty colleagues at the Harvard Graduate School of Education and the Massachusetts School of Professional Psychology, and especially students of both these schools who, by the way they listened and responded, helped shape the ideas in this book.

My collaboration with Laura Rogers led to the original conception of a methodology for my perspective. Lisa Lahey, Emily Souvaine, Robert Goodman, Sally Felix, and I formed a team, now many years ago, to create and develop "the subject-object interview." That work transformed a psychological perspective from a set of theoretical ideas into an empirically operational approach to the study of persons as makers of meaning. I am grateful to the many researchers and theorists since who, by the broad and varied sweep of their use of this perspective, have encouraged me to work on so large a canvas as the present book.

I thank my colleagues and friends who generously agreed, and even asked, to read earlier drafts of this book in part or in full. Every one of these people made the book better: Walter Abrams, Michael Basseches, Maria Broderick, Ann Fleck-Henderson, Robert Goodman, Joseph Guido, Lorraine Heilbrunn, Ann Higgins, Gina Higgins, Lisa Lahey, Carolyn Liesy, Sharon Parks, Laura Rogers, Richard Shulik, Elizabeth Speicher, William Torbert, and Barbara Wolf.

Both the schools where I teach assisted me institutionally. I especially appreciate M.S.P.P.'s explicit support for my writing, in general, and for my undertaking and completing this book, in particular.

No one could ask for more intelligent, graceful, or steadfast administrative support than I received throughout this project from Mary Jo White, who prepared the manuscript.

At the Harvard University Press I benefited from Angela von der Lippe's belief and patience, and from Linda Howe's talented regard for the rhythm and meaning of every line.

Long after his death, I am still moved by the kindness and commitment of my teacher and friend, Larry Kohlberg.

For fourteen years I have found my colleagueship and friendship with Lisa Lahey to be joyously stimulating and renewing. Much of this book was nurtured by her gifted capacities to attend and encourage.

My dear partner, Barbara, and my children good-naturedly kept a running total of their contributions to, and sacrifices for, this protracted project. It's a long list, but really only a fraction of what they have done for me. I have happily dedicated this book to each of them in deep appreciation for the distinctly different love each of them has shown me.

Contents

In Over Our Heads ─────────────────

Prologue _____

As I imagine readers beginning this book, I am reminded of a story about Jascha Heifetz on tour. Apparently he had been scheduled to perform in a town where there had been a major snowstorm, and when he came on stage he looked out onto an audience of exactly eight people. "Well, this is kind of silly," Heifetz was reported to have said. "Why don't you all just come back to my hotel room with me and we'll have a drink?" "Oh, no," called out someone in a very disappointed voice. "I've come hundreds of miles just to hear you. C'mon, Jascha, sing *something!*"

Although I am not a singer or a violinist, I always feel something of this uncertainty about just what people might be expecting in the opening moments of a sustained encounter with ideas. For that reason, I would like to use this prologue to welcome readers into the long story that is this book, to prepare them to join me in it, and to lay in some supplies for our journey. For, having written all of three books in twenty years, I have learned that although the writer is the one who starts the book, the reader is the one who finishes it. I won't know how this one is going to come out until I learn what readers make of it.

In my twenties I wrote a book about a collection of modern novels that intrigued me.[1] I was thrilled that someone wanted to publish it and took pride in its appearance. Its completion was the nearest I could come to making something for others' pleasure with my own hands. As it turned out, my feeling that I had completed it was righter than I knew. I never heard a word from a single person who had read the book, which quickly went out of print, and I came to feel that I had the distinction of being the only person to have read it. I started it and I ended it.

In my thirties I wrote *The Evolving Self*,[2] proposing a view of human being as meaning-making and exploring the inner experience and outer

1

contours of our transformations in consciousness throughout the lifespan. Although the book was published over a decade ago, it is still rare for two weeks to go by without someone putting pen to paper to write me about it. Some years ago, when I proudly told my father that it was being translated into German and Korean, he said, "That's great! Now when is it going to be translated into *English?*" And in truth, these fortnightly letters from readers occasionally have a similar theme:

> Dear Dr. Kegan,
>   We had to read your book in our psychology class. I can't believe the publishers let the thing out in this condition. No one in our class understands what you are saying. Not even our teacher, and he assigned it! Who are you trying to impress with all those big words? I got so mad reading your book I wanted to come to Boston and break your teeth.
> Sincerely,
> [writer's name]

I appreciated the "sincerely."

But most of the letters have not been of this sort. And what is most satisfying about them is their ongoing invention in the context the book creates. Far from swallowing whole what the book offers up, these readers clearly found a way to stay in relation to it and were letting me in on their own continuing experience with it. This ongoing remaking of the book both inspired me and left me feeling completely uninterested in writing another book unless I had the same kind of opportunity to offer.

So here I am again, hoping to have made something that will be a context for readers' ongoing invention. It is meaning-making and the evolution of consciousness that preoccupies me, but this time as these relate to the culture's claims on our minds. This book comes to what I believe are important discoveries and offers a new way of seeing ourselves, this time in relation to the demands of our environment. It neither expects its arguments to be swallowed whole nor hopes that they will be. I have written it in the same strange two-toned voice that one moment draws its authority from analytic criteria, the next from aesthetic ones. I respect both these sources and frankly suspect all writing that is all one or the other. In either mode, I've tried my best to write more accessibly. I am in my forties now and I want to keep my teeth.

As these thoughts would suggest, my core professional identity is that of teacher. Although this book draws on my experiences as a researcher, a theorist, a therapist, a director of an institute on lifelong education, and a consultant to work life and professional development, the binding theme is teaching. Writing creates a context for learning, and although this book is about consciousness and culture, perhaps the quickest way to grasp its passion is through the educational metaphors of "curriculum" and "school."

After twenty-five years of teaching, I realize what I have come to see as its greatest reward: it allows me to live much of my life in a state of sympathetic friendliness. I suppose the impulse to throw a sympathetic arm around the burdened shoulders of a hard-working neighbor will be regarded as a generous one. And I suppose the gradual training of one's sympathies in the effective friendliness that marks good teaching will be seen as a valuable resource. But I doubt that anyone benefits quite as much as teachers themselves. What animates this book is my impulse to throw a sympathetic arm of disciplined friendliness across the burdened shoulders of contemporary culture. If the reader is willing to look at contemporary culture as a kind of "school" and the complex set of tasks and expectations placed upon us in modern life as the "curriculum" of that school, then this book is really a generalized form of the friendly sympathy the teacher extends to the student feeling the discouragement, fear, anger, helplessness, confusion, or dissociation that can go along with the experience of not succeeding in one's studies.

We extend a generalized form of this friendly sympathy to the young all the time in real schools, school systems, national educational associations, and even graduate schools of education when we turn our attention to the curriculum itself and ask: What is it, really, that we are asking of our students here? Are these expectations sensible, fair, or appropriate? What capacities is this curriculum assuming and are these assumptions warranted? One of the great benefits of research programs that describe the evolving complexity of the child's mind is that they have led school people to consider whether curricula for a given age are appropriate to the child's expected mental capacities. Everything from reading readiness to when to teach the Constitution or the concept of number has been informed by this knowledge. As researchers have extended this work to the study of how children's mental capacities enable and constrain their social and emotional understanding, school people have in turn considered the appropriateness of curricula aimed at broader aspects of a child's life. When should a Catholic child make her first confession? Well, when can she really understand what "right" and "wrong" mean so that ideas about doing better and resisting temptation can make any sense? Is it appropriate for an exasperated preschool teacher to expect her charges to think about how she feels when they ask her to do six things at once? Well, not if she actually expects them to understand what she means and alter their behavior accordingly.

Such considerations of our expectations, the mental demands we make of our children, have been extended beyond the school to the wider culture itself. Perhaps the best example is our general concern about whether we are putting too much pressure on our children and giving them responsibilities before they are ready for them. These include the responsibility to fend for themselves after school because their parents are working, to care for or make decisions about even younger siblings, to work hard and get ahead in school lest they fall behind in the race for academic success in which they are unwittingly or unwillingly entered. The specter that presents itself is of childhood lost, or as David Elkind puts it, "a hurried childhood."[3] It feels somehow unnatural—a kind of violation of nature—not to give childhood its due, its proper freedom from too much responsibility and the need for self-protection or self-promotion.

This sharp sense of childhood's due comes from the widespread view of childhood as an era distinct from adulthood. However natural and obvious it may seem to us, this view is actually a relatively recent one, as Philippe Ariès has taught us.[4] Only a few centuries ago, as demonstrated in cultural creations as diverse as oil paintings depicting children as miniature adults and labor practices permitting ten-year-olds in factories, children seemed not to be granted so distinct a status. What, after all, is the true nature of the wrong we suspect we might be doing to children by hurrying them? We are responsive to an alarm about the hurried child because, whether we know it or not, we already believe that the mind of a child is different from the mind of an adult. We can feel an immediate sympathy, a wish to protect, or a feeling of outrage in response to the specter of little people being asked or expected to handle tasks beyond their capacities. "That's just too much to ask!" something inside us says. We don't know which to feel worse about, the children who collapse under the pressure or the ones who bravely carry on, feeling all the while overwhelmed, lonely, and confused in ways they cannot themselves decry or understand. Yet it does not occur to us to write books about how these children might better cope with the stress of their lives. Instead we write, as Elkind did, books that remind us that children are only children. They have their limits. There are depths beyond which they cannot go. Take them there and they will be in over their heads. Leave them there and even the most resilient of them will only be able to tread water in perilous exhaustion.

But if in the last few hundred years we have succeeded in recognizing a qualitative distinction between the mind of the child and the mind of the adult, it may still remain for us to discover that adulthood itself is not an end state but a vast evolutionary expanse encompassing a variety of capacities of mind. And if we have been able to extend a disciplined sympathy to children, evoked by our analytic exploration of their capacity to meet the challenges of the various curricula we create for them, it remains for us to extend the same disciplined sympathy to adult experience. *It remains for us to look at the curriculum of modern life in relation to the capacities of the adult mind.* That is what this book is about.

Most adults become partners in an intimate relationship they seek to sustain over many years. Most adults parent children. Most adults take up paid employment. Many adults pursue their own expansion through schooling or psychotherapy. All adults in contemporary America share citizenship with people whose skin color, gender, age, social position, sexual orientation, and physical capacity differ from their own. These activities present us with a vast variety of expectations, prescriptions, claims, and demands. Even the ever-accelerating flow of information to our eyes and to our ears—information competing for our attention, our allegiance, and our money—makes a claim on us to *do* something with it, and, even before that, to *decide* about it, since there is no possible way we can do even a fraction of what we are asked.

These expectations are chronicled, and even shaped, in the growing collection of cultural documents academics call (with no irony) "literatures": "the marriage literature," "the management literature," "the adult education literature," and the like. After reading widely in these literatures I have come to two conclusions: First, the expectations upon us that run throughout these literatures demand something more than mere behavior, the acquisition of specific skills, or the mastery of particular knowledge. They make demands on our minds, on *how* we know, on the complexity of our consciousness. The "information highway" we plan for the next century, for example, may geometrically increase the amount of information, the ways it can be sent, and the number of its recipients. But our experience on this highway may be one of exhaustion (a new kind of "rat race" or "gridlock") rather than admiration for the ease and speed of a new kind of transport if we are unable to assert our own authority over the information. No additional amount of information coming into our minds will enable us to assume this authority; only a qualitative change in the complexity of our minds will.

Second, for the most part, these literatures do not talk to each other, take no account of each other, have nothing to do with each other. People who write, teach, and shape the discourse about management apparently do not read the literature about intimacy. The people who create the leadership literature do not read the parenting literature. All these people are trained in different professions, each with distinct identities, modes of analysis, heroes and heroines, and ways of framing the questions that need answering. Even if each of these professions is itself doing a good job, there is no place to look to consider what is being asked of the adult as a whole. An adult is not only a worker, only a spouse, only a parent. An adult may be all of these things. The result—if we continue the metaphor of the culture as school—is that we may have a school in which each of the departments is passionately engaged in its demands upon its students, but no one is considering the students' overall experience, their actual course of study and the meaning for them of the curriculum as a whole.

This book takes the first observation as the key to the second. It submits the expectations of a variety of literatures on adult life to a common analysis of the demands they make upon adult minds. My intention is to make the experience of contemporary adulthood more coherent than we have thought possible by showing that the demands upon us are more cohesive than we have realized. While each of our professions shares the common goal of enhancing the individual and collective life of real adults, what we need is a new way of seeing in order to end the compromised pursuit of this goal by disconnected, noncommunicating sources of authority and exhortation.

In order for us to look at what it is we are asking of our minds in this new way, we need an analytic tool. We need a way of discerning the mental complexity inherent in social expectations. We need a way of looking at human development that considers not only people's changing agendas but their changing capacities. I am not assuming that readers of this book will have read *The Evolving Self*, but those who have will see that I am taking the theory first presented there—a philosophy-laden theory, a theory of the psychological evolution of meaning-systems or ways of knowing, in short, a theory of the development of consciousness—and using it as an analytic tool to examine contemporary culture. It will enable us to consider the fit, or lack of fit, between the demands our cultural curriculum makes on our consciousness on the one hand, and our mental capacities as "students" in this ongoing school on the other.

The theory has matured in the ten years since *The Evolving Self*. Readers, graduate students in my classes at Harvard and the Massachusetts School of Professional Psychology, dissertation writers and researchers at these and other schools throughout the world, and a small group of precious friends and collaborative colleagues over the years are responsible for these changes. The development of a reliable instrument for studying these structures of mind (the "Subject-Object Interview"), the production of a research manual explaining how to use the instrument and analyze its data,[5] the empirical work the instrument has enabled, including the many studies of adult development I refer to in this book, have also contributed to its maturity.

The theory's central premises and distinctions remain unchanged, but they are clearer and better supported. The principles of mental organization according to which emotional, cognitive, interpersonal, and intrapersonal experiencing is constellated are much more thoroughly spelled out. The similarities in form between our thinking and feeling, between our relationship to parts of ourselves and our relationship to others, are explicated here rather than merely claimed. What the theory addresses and what it does not have become clearer. What the theory addresses: the forms of meaning-regulation, the *trans*formation of consciousness, the internal experience of these processes, the role of the environment in this activity, are less confused with what it does not: personality types, the preoccupying concerns or central motivations of a given order of consciousness, personality "style" or "voice."

Those familiar with the theory will see that I have not shied away from the most familiar challenges to constructive-developmental psychology but have turned directly toward them. In a day when we are becoming increasingly aware of issues of diversity and the way systems of knowledge are inevitably susceptible to being used as a means to gain advantage or maintain power, it may seem anachronistic to be speaking of "adults," "evolution," "the culture," or "a theory." Which adults do I mean? Whose conception of evolution? In what sense do white people and people of color, gay people and straight people, men and women share a culture? A theory that privileges whom and valorizes what? Is the theory a Western theory? Isn't it hierarchical? Does it propose a lockstep conception of growth? Does it assume that people are consistent in their use of a single meaning system across all domains and circumstances of experience? Isn't a theory of structures passé in a "poststructuralist" age? These questions are directly and enthusiastically addressed here. This book reflects the influence over the last ten years of several intellectual currents, especially the study of gender differences, the diversity movement, and the postmodern critique of knowledge creation. It also reflects my hope that my line of thinking may, in turn, be of use to the fuller flow of each of these intellectual currents.

To those readers for whom this is a first meeting, I extend welcome to an intellectual discipline I have come to think of as "the psychology of admiration." The root of admiration is *wonder*, as the Latin (*mirar*, to wonder) suggests. And "wonder" is as two-sided, as dialectical, as ambisexual as human beings themselves. "Wonder" is "wondering *at*" and "wondering *about*." "Wondering at" is watching and reverencing; "wondering about" is asking and reckoning. "Wondering at" is Eastern, receptive, contemplation as an end in itself; "wondering about" is Western, acting upon, a means to an end. "Wondering at" is aesthetic, the inspiration of the humanities, *anima*, blessed by a feminine god; "wondering about" is analytic, the inspiration of the sciences, *animus*, blessed by a masculine god. The mode of attending to our lives that we are about to enter in these pages does not champion or choose one of these ways over the other. It does not favor the analytic or the aesthetic. It does not regard science as evil or as a savior. It does not castigate or canonize the stirrings of the human heart. It is dedicated instead to drawing deeply from both of these kinds of wisdom. If we may continue to make use of the prevailing metaphor of *school*, we might consider that the lifeblood of wholesome teaching consists in just this two-sided way of admiring. An educating intention that is too exclusively wondering about inspires a measuring mentality in which teaching standards, national examinations, and a canonical approach to curriculum predominate. But a way of teaching that is imbalanced toward *wondering at* replaces awe with zeal, and is reminiscent of the passion of Miss Jean Brodie celebrating the courage of her students—which courage is then as easily offered up to the cause of the Loyalists as to that of the Republicans in the Spanish Civil War regardless of their respective allegiances to fascism and democracy.

If as a culture we have grown disenchanted with the capacity of science to save us from ourselves, we might do well to consider that science will serve us well if we will only treat it as a servant and be its conscientious master. If we are currently charmed by calls to recover our humanism, sounded in various intellectual quarters championing our "courage" and our capacity for "caring," we might do well to remember that courage and caring, by themselves, can be as life-stealing as life-giving, that every tyrant and tyrannical movement in human history draws energy not from fear alone but from the courage and caring of its adherents.

The social sciences in contemporary culture are at a crossroads. Will they continue to be essentially a puny force, founded on no civilization of their own, borrowing from, and buffeted by the powerful civilizations of science and the humanities? Will the social sciences continue to be reminiscent of Freud's hapless infantile ego, appearing to be a player in personality but in reality swamped by the contending forces of conscience and desire? Or will the social sciences grow up and, like the mature conception of the ego, become capable of integrating the contending powers and thereby creating a third original force that can really *be* a player in human personality or contemporary culture? Such an integration in psychology would realize the fuller promise of the word itself—*psyche* and *logos,* spirit and reckoning.

In this book, I bring the psychology of admiration to the study of the relationship between two fascinating phenomena, one psychological, and one cultural. The psychological phenomenon is the evolution of consciousness, the personal unfolding of ways of organizing experience that are not simply replaced as we grow but subsumed into more complex systems of mind. In spite of the fact that the developmental trajectories of Freud and Piaget, which constitute the twin towers in the field, reach their conclusions in adolescence, most of this book is devoted to transformations of consciousness after adolescence. The cultural phenomenon is the "hidden curriculum," the idea that to the list of artifacts and arrangements a culture creates and the social sciences study we should add the claims or demands the culture makes on the minds of its constituents.

In studying the relationship between these phenomena—the fit or lack of fit between what the culture demands of our minds and our mental capacity to meet these demands—the book hopes to be a support to readers as students in this ongoing "school." But it also hopes to be a caution to readers as fellow makers of the school. All adults are not only expected of, but themselves expectors of, if only in their private and personal relations with other adults. But readers of this book almost certainly are, or will be, not only personally but professionally involved in shaping and conveying the culture's curriculum. For those of us who have another in our employ, who manage, lead, supervise, or evaluate others; who teach, advise, counsel, do therapy with, or consult to others; who publicly seek to exhort, inform, inspire, or move others to some action—we are all in the business, knowingly or unknowingly, of making mental demands. I hope to increase our sensitivity to the experience of those who are on the receiving end of this work.

I begin by considering the fit between our culture's mental demands on adolescents and their capacity to meet these demands (Part One). In essence, I argue that we unknowingly expect the contemporary teenager to develop the order of consciousness required to participate in a Traditional world. In the center of the book (Parts Two and Three) I explore the mental demands the hidden curriculum makes on adults in their private and public lives. These chapters look at parenting, partnering, work, living with diversity, adult learning, and psychotherapy. What does the literature of expertise tell us we need to do to succeed in these activities, and what implicit demands are these expectations really making on our minds? I argue that there is a remarkable commonality to the complexity of mind being called for across these non-communicating disciplines, and that together these demands create the consciousness threshold of Modernity. In the last part of the book (Part Four), I explore the mental demands implicit in the so-called Postmodern prescriptions for adult living, a leading edge in the various literatures. I argue that these expectations constitute a qualitatively even more complex order of consciousness and thus require an even greater caution on the part of those who would make these demands of others. Although I have tried to be clear and accessible, more than one prepublication reader has suggested that the book itself gradually becomes more complex as the curriculum it explores becomes more complex.

It is my hope that all those who are interested in the individual, the culture, or the historical evolution of cultural mentality will find room for reflection. The book derives its energy from its three discoveries, or more accurately, from a single discovery made in three different ways. The discovery of the mismatch for at least some portion of our lives between the complexity of the culture's "curriculum" and our capacity to grasp it awaits those with practical as well as theoretical interests in the support, education, training, or mental health of individuals. Therapists, educators, managers, and trainers may find a new clue to the sources of stress in contemporary living and a new conception of the *consciousness thresholds* individuals may have to reach in order to satisfy contemporary expectations of love and work.

The discovery of culturewide commonalities in our claims on individuals' minds awaits those with an interest in society as a whole. Policymakers and planners, curriculum designers, higher education mission-builders, civic, cultural, and institutional leaders may benefit from considering, for example, that our current cultural design requires of adults a qualitative transformation of mind every bit as fundamental as the transformation from magical thinking to concrete thinking required of the school-age child or the transformation from concrete to abstract thinking required of the adolescent.

The discovery of the mental structures inherent in Traditionalism, Modernism, and Postmodernism, and their evolutionary relationship, awaits those with an interest in the historical evolution of cultural mentality. I invite educational philosophers, intellectual historians, and philosophers of mind to join me in puzzling through the implications of the claims these cultural frames of mind make on our consciousness in light of what a mind-oriented psychology is learning about the constraints and abilities of individual development.

Teachers, therapists, managers, corporate trainers, policymakers, curriculum designers, institutional leaders, educational philosophers, intellectual historians, and philosophers of mind—this is a varied crew, certainly worthy of an ambi-admiring psychology bent on reverencing and reckoning. But my invitation is ultimately to people, not to job roles. Whoever my readers might be, I welcome the hopes, concerns, commitments, or passions that brought you to this book. I hope you will let me know how it comes out.

I

The Mental Demand of Adolescence

1

The Hidden Curriculum of Youth: *"Whaddaya Want from Me?"*

Peter and Lynn are wide awake at two in the morning, but they are not having a good time. They are having a teenager. Matty, their son, was due home two hours ago. He is sixteen, his curfew is midnight, and they have heard nothing from him. They are wide awake and angry, and most of all, they are worried.

But this is not going to be one of those nights that changes anyone's life. Nobody is going to die. Nothing of this night will be on the news. This is the ordinary night nobody writes about. Matty is going to come home in another half hour hoping his parents have long since gone to sleep so he can assure them tomorrow that he was in "only a little past twelve." When his hopes are dashed by the sight of his wide-awake parents, he will have an excuse about somebody's car and somebody else's mother and a third person who borrowed the first person's jacket with his car keys and left the party early, and maybe it's just because it's now nearly three in the morning, but the story will sound to Peter and Lynn so freshly made up that all its pieces barely know how to fit together.

Lynn won't be thinking about it now, but only six years ago—not a long time to her—she had been struck by how independent Matty had become. This clingy kid who seemed to need her so much had become a little ten-year-old fellow full of purpose and plans, in business for himself, with a sign on his bedroom door: "Adults Keep Out." A part of her missed the little boy who didn't want to be left alone, but a bigger part of her was pleased for both of them by this development. But six years later, at two-thirty in the morning, it will not occur to her to say,

"Matty, my son, I'm so impressed by the way you are able to take care of yourself, by how much you can do for yourself, by the way you just go wherever you want to and come home whenever you want to, by how little you seem to need your dad and me. You're really growing up, son. Your dad and I just wanted to stay up until two-thirty in the morning to tell you how proud we are!" No, what it will occur to Lynn to say is something more like "*This isn't a hotel here, buddy!* You can't just come and go as you please! You're a part of a family, you know! Your father and I have feelings, too! How do you think we feel when it's two in the morning and we haven't heard a thing from you? We're worried sick! For all we know you could be splattered all over the highway. How *would* we know? You don't call us! It's time you joined this family, buddy, and started *thinking about somebody other than just yourself!*"

Peter and Lynn want something more of Matty now than they wanted when he was ten. What even delighted them then, Matty's "independence," is a source of anger, worry, and frustration now when it shows up as a "lack of trustworthiness."

But what kind of thing is it Matty's parents want of him? One answer is that it is a behavior, a way of acting. They want him to stop doing certain things he does and start doing others. But a little thought reveals that it is more than behavior Peter and Lynn want from their son. In Lynn's exasperated words we can hear that she is also asking for a certain attitude in Matty. She doesn't just want him to do the right thing for whatever reason. Even if he did always get home at the appointed hour, but did so only because he wanted to avoid the certain consequences of his parents' terrible swift sword, his mother would not honestly be satisfied. No, she wants to feel that she and her husband can retire from the Parent Police and start relating to their growing-up son as a trustworthy, self-regulating member of a common team. She wants him to "behave," but she wants him to do so out of his feelings for members of the family of which he sees he is a part. So perhaps the "something" Matty's parents want from him is more than behavior; it is about feeling a certain way. They want him to feel differently about them, about his willingness to put his own needs ahead of his agreements, about his responsibility to his family. What at first seemed to be a claim for a certain outer behavior now appears to be about his inner feelings.

But where do these inner feelings come from? Or, to put it another way, what would have to change in order for Matty's feelings to change? The answer, I believe, is that Matty's feelings come from the way he understands what the world is all about, the way he knows who he is, *the way he cares about what his parents care about.* In order for Matty really to feel differently about coming in at two-thirty in the morning he would have to know all this differently. What Lynn and Peter and any other parent of teenagers like Matty really want is for Matty to change not just the way he behaves, not just the way he feels, but the way he knows—not just what he knows but the *way* he knows. So, odd as it sounds, and unlikely as it is that they would ever think about it this way, what Lynn and Peter most want at three in the morning, now that they know their son is alive and well, is for his mind to be different. They want him to alter his consciousness, to change his mind. (That, and for them all to get some sleep!)

As it turns out, Matty's parents are not the only ones who want him to change his mind. In fact, like every teenager in America, Matty is also under a rather constant barrage of expectations at school, in the community, and even with some of his friends to know the world in a way different from the now "too independent" way it took him nearly the first decade of his life to achieve. Sometimes we will hear these expectations proclaimed in public discourse by the schools, the Department of Labor, or the politicians. Most of the time these expectations are present but private—particular, subtle, and unspoken in the intimate arenas of family and neighborhood.

What do we want of Matty? Well, as I say, lots of things—lots of quite different-sounding things. Some people want Matty to be employable. Now, what does this mean? When we look into it, it is always less that they want him to know specific content or skills he can bring into the workforce ("Nah, we can teach him all that when we hire him") and much more that they want him to be someone they can count on, someone who shows up on time, someone who can get along with others, someone who can develop some loyalty to the company, someone it is worth putting in the time and money to train because when he makes a commitment he will keep it.

Other people want Matty to be a good citizen, a member of a democratic society. What does this mean? Well, for most people it does not really mean they hope he will go to the polls regularly and vote at election time. It usually means they hope he won't break into their homes when they are visiting their relatives in Florida. It means that in a society with a great deal of personal freedom, they hope Matty won't abuse that freedom.

The people who actually know Matty, his family and his friends, want a similar thing for Matty, though they express it in a way that is more personal than "good citizenship." They want him to be decent and trustworthy, someone who will hold up his end of a relationship, someone who will take them into account. They want to know that if Matty has a midnight curfew and he's going to be late they can count on him to call.

The schools want all these things from Matty and more besides. They want him to be able to think well—reflectively, abstractly, critically. They want him to understand the denotative meaning but also the connotative meaning, data and inference, instance and generalization, example and definition.

In addition to all these, we have expectations about how Matty feels. Not only clinicians and therapists and school counselors, but in many instances teenagers' parents and even their friends want them to be able to identify and share an inner psychological life. We expect teenagers to identify their inner motivations, to acknowledge internal emotional conflict, to be to some extent psychologically self-reflective, and to have some capacity for insight and productive self-consciousness.

As if this isn't enough, a lot of people want Matty to have good common sense, a whole different thing from thinking well. They want him to know that he should look before he leaps, that he should consider the longer-term consequences of choices that may seem momentarily appealing but are ultimately too costly. They want him to know the difference between reasonable risk and foolish risk. They want him to have friends but not be led around by them. They want him to have a mind of his own.

And a lot of people want that mind to have values, ideals, beliefs, principles—and not just values about good conduct that will help them feel safe knowing they are sharing the street with Matty. Because they care about Matty independent of their own welfare, they want him to have, and to feel he is ready to begin having, a meaningful life. Because the adults that surround Matty differ among themselves over what constitutes a meaningful life, which particular values, beliefs, and ideals they may want him to have will differ. In the 1960s and 1970s there were adults who wanted teens to value patriotic duty and there were those who wanted them to value the questioning of, and resistance to, authority. In the 1990s there are adults who want teens to value safe sex and those who want them to value abstinence. There are adults who want teenage girls to take on the values of traditional femininity and those who want them to value retaining the pluck and energy of their childhood voices. But although these adults may differ among themselves over which ideals they think teens should form, and no doubt they are more aware of what distinguishes them from each other than what they share, what they do share is a common claim upon adolescents to form ideals to which they feel loyal, with which they are identified, and from which they can lean toward what they imagine would be a better future for themselves and the world of which they are a part.

So, we want Matty to be employable, a good citizen, a critical thinker, emotionally self-reflective, personally trustworthy, possessed of common sense and meaningful ideals. This is a lot to want. It grows out of our concern for ourselves, our concern for others who live with Matty, and our concern for Matty himself. Will he be up to all these expectations?

To answer that we have to ask the same question we asked of his parents' disappointed expectation at two in the morning. What kind of expectation did they have? I have suggested that although it looks like an expectation about how Matty should behave, it is really an expectation about more than his outer behavior, and although it looks like an expectation about his inner feelings or attitudes, it is about even more than this, because his feelings and attitudes come from how he knows. I think the same thing can be said about every one of the expectations I have just mentioned. They are all about more than how we want teenagers to behave, more than how we want them to feel, more than what we want them to know. They are all expectations about *how* we want them to know, the *way* we want them to make meaning of their experience. They are claims on adolescents' minds.

Although we don't realize it, we have some shared expectations about what the mind of a teenager should be like. Whatever definition of "adolescence" we might cull from a textbook, the one that is operating most powerfully on the human being who happens to be going through adolescence is the hidden definition derived from the culture's claims or expectations about how an adolescent should know.

The very word *adolescence* shares an intimate relationship with the word *adult:* both come from the same Latin verb, *adolescere*, which means "to grow up." The past participle of the same word is *adultus*, "having grown up," or "grown-up." The word *adolescence*, then, suggests that by looking at what a culture asks its youth to "grow up to" we can discover that culture's definition of adulthood, the implication being that the culmination of adolescence constitutes adulthood. This may have been true once, but is it true today?

How *do* we want an adolescent's mind to change? Let's back up a bit. At some point in childhood, usually by the age of seven or eight, children undergo a qualitative change in the way they organize their thinking, their feeling, and their social relating. They move beyond a fantasy-filled construction of the world in which toy dinosaurs can plausibly transform themselves into the six-foot singing Barney, and instead come to scrutinize Steven Spielberg's *Jurassic Park* for the tiniest errors he may have allowed to creep into his depiction of *Tyrannosaurus rex*. In other words, they begin to construct a concrete world that conforms for the first time to the laws of nature, and they are interested in the limits and possibilities within that world. They read *The Guinness Book of World Records* to learn about the biggest cookie ever baked and the most expensive stationery ever printed.[1]

At the same time, they move beyond a socially egocentric construction of the world, in which they imagine that others share the same mind and views as they do, and come to recognize that people have separate minds, separate intentions, and separate vantage points. They stop engaging bewildered parents in the second half of conversations, the first half of which they have conducted in their own head ("So what did you and Richie do after *that?*" the four-year-old may ask her mother, who has no idea what her daughter is talking about). Where before their speech was a more ancillary or peripheral aspect of their social interaction, it now becomes the necessary bridge between distinct minds.[2]

At the same time, by the age of seven or eight, most children have emerged from a moment-to-moment relationship to their desires, preferences, and abilities. Younger children are neither able to delay gratification for more than a minute nor plagued on Tuesday by an experience of failure on Monday. But by the age of ten they organize their desires as things that persist through time. Issues of self-esteem have become more salient because there is a self whose abilities are not reconstituted from one moment to the next ("I'm bad at math" doesn't just mean "I'm not enjoying it at this moment").

Between the ages of five and ten, in other words, a child makes a host of discoveries that seem to have nothing to do with each other.[3] Consider, for example, these three: (1) the quantity of a liquid does not change when it is poured from one glass into another, smaller glass; (2) a person who could have no way of knowing that another person would be made unhappy by his actions cannot be said to be "mean"; (3) when I tell you "I don't like spinach," or think to myself, "I'm a Catholic girl," I mean that this is not just how I feel and think now, but that these things are ongoing, these are how I am or tend to be. Now, as different as these three discoveries are (they are about one's understanding of the physical, social, and personal worlds), it is the same principle, or way of knowing, that makes all of them possible.

In each case, the discovery arises out of the same ability to see that the phenomenon being considered (thing, other, self) has its own properties, which are elements of a class or set, and that the phenomenon (thing, other, self) is itself known as this class, which, like all classes, has durable, ongoing rules creating the idea of class membership and regulating that membership. "Liquid," for example, becomes a class that has as a member the property of *quantity*, and that property is not regulated by my perception. It may look as if there is more water in the smaller glass, but, unlike the three-year-old, who believes it has actually become more water, the ten-year-old does not regulate meaning by how something appears. "Other person" is a class that has as a member the property of *intention*, and that property is not determined by my wishes. I may be unhappy or even angry that my father unwittingly got home too late to take me to watch the little league game, but since I know his mind is separate from mine, I could not, like the three-year-old, regard him as "mean" or as "a bad daddy." "Self" is a class that has as members the properties of *preference*, *habit*, and *ability*, and—since the self is a class, something that has properties—these things are aspects of me in some ongoing way, as opposed to merely what I want to eat or do now. Hence, new ways of knowing in such disparate domains as the inanimate, the social, and the introspective may all be occasioned by a single transformation of mind. In each case, what is being demonstrated is the ability to construct a mental set, class, or category to order the things of one's experience (physical objects, other people, oneself, desires) as property-containing phenomena (see Figure 1.1).

This ability to create the mental organization I call "durable categories" changes physical objects from being principally about my momen-

THE DURABLE CATEGORY
(or Class or Set)

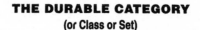

contains
elements or members.

---

(1) *Things* seen as Durable Categories

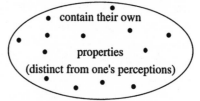

contain their own

properties
(distinct from one's perceptions)

and so are constructed as *concrete*.

---

(2) *Others* seen as Durable Categories

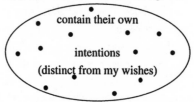

contain their own

intentions
(distinct from my wishes)

and so are constructed as having distinct points
of view and minds of their own.

---

(3) *The Self* seen as a Durable Category

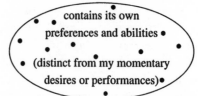

contains its own
preferences and abilities

(distinct from my momentary
desires or performances)

and so is constructed as having enduring
dispositions, ongoing needs, self-interest.

Figure 1.1 The Principle of Durable Categories

tary perceptions of them to being about their existence as property-bearing "classes" with ongoing rules about what elements may or may not be properties, irrespective of my perceptions. It changes other people from being principally about my wishes in relation to them to being about their existence as property-bearing selves distinct from me, with ongoing rules about which intentions or characteristics actually belong to this class, irrespective of my wishes. It changes my own desires from being principally about my present impulse to being about the class of my ongoing, time-enduring needs or preferences, which class or category may contain my moment-to-moment impulses or wishes. What I am suggesting is that the ability to construct a concrete world, independent points of view, and a property-bearing self is expressive of a single form of consciousness. A common organizing principle or "order of mind" is at work, the durable category. Now we can ask: How adequate would this order of mind be for Matty in meeting his parents' expectations on a Saturday night?

Whether it is a community's demand that Matty be a "good citizen" or his family's demand that he "keep us in mind," both are really aspects of a common expectation that Matty will be able to take out loyalty to or membership in a wider human community than the one defined by his own self-interest. In the private realm of personal relations we are hearing from Matty's parents a hope or an expectation that he will demonstrate to them a trustworthiness born out of their accurate sense that he not only knows what they care about but in some way shares in what they care about, that he attends to what they care about not merely to get his own needs met or to calculate the consequences of defying them, but because these are to some extent what he cares about too. They want to believe that he will care about what they care about—for example, that everyone in the family keeps his word or that everyone in the family recognizes everyone else's need to know they are all right—even to the extent of subordinating some of his own particular interests (staying out past midnight with his friends) to that shared interest. Matty's parents, in other words, want to experience themselves in real relationship *with* their son, who is fast becoming a young man. He is looking more like a young man, talking more like a young man, and demanding the greater freedoms of a young man. Although they may not exactly know it, they believe that if they are to see him more as a man than as a child, they should be able to experience him on the other side of a relationship that no longer requires them to regulate an unsocialized, self-interested creature who needs their behavioral limits and who is constantly testing whether they will effectively keep playing and keep winning a game of control. Their expectation is that Matty's own relationship to what he knows they care about will allow them to feel themselves included in shared bonds of mutual trust and concern.

This is an expectation, clearly, that goes beyond *what* Matty will know. It is an expectation about *how* he will know what he knows. Would Matty be able to meet this expectation if he knew the world through the order of mind I call "durable categories," the order of mind that first comes into being around the age of seven or eight?

If he were knowing the world through the principle of durable categories, he could certainly understand his parents' point of view, see it as distinct from his own, provide his parents with the accurate sense that he understood their point of view, and even "take on" this point of view when it cost his own point of view nothing. He could thereby confuse them into thinking that he actually identifies with their point of view: that he not only understands their sense of its importance but shares that sense. He could do all this from a durable categories order of mind. But all this is *not* their expectation.

In order for him actually to hold their point of view in a way in which he could identify with it, he would have to give up an ultimate or absolute relationship to his own point of view. In order to subordinate his own point of view to some bigger way of knowing to which he would be loyal, in order to subordinate it to some integration or co-relation between his own and his parents' point of view, in order for his sense of himself to be based more on the preservation and operation of this co-relation than on the preservation and operation of his own independent point of view—for all this to happen, Matty would have to construct his experience out of a principle that was more complex than the principle of durable categories. He would have to construct his experience out of a principle that subsumes or subordinates the principle of durable categories to a higher order principle. Instead of a principle that has elemental properties as its members, he would need a principle that had durable categories themselves as its members! (see Figure 1.2). Lynn and Peter's demand, in other words, is an unrecognized claim that Matty's principle of mental organization should be of an order qualitatively more complex than categorical knowing. It is a claim that he should be able to make categorical knowing an element of a new principle, what we might call "cross-categorical" knowing.

In other words, if we know that Matty considers staying on at the party past his curfew although he is aware that his parents want him in the house by his curfew, we still really do not know how he understands the situation in which he finds himself until we see what principle of mental organization he brings to bear on these particulars. If he makes his own point of view or his own intentions, preferences, or needs the basic context in which to decide his course of action, then his decision to stay or not to stay will be governed by one set of calculations ("Will I get caught? What will happen if I get caught? Is staying at the party worth running these risks? How can I keep from getting caught? How can I keep from being punished if I am caught?"). If he subordinates his own point of view to the relationship between his point of view and his parents' point of view, or if he subordinates the construction of self as a set of particular intentions, preferences, or needs to the construction of self identified in the relationship between his own collection of intentions, preferences, and needs (one category) and those of his parents

THE PRINCIPLE OF THE DURABLE CATEGORY
(in the Interpersonal Domain)

A HIGHER ORDER PRINCIPLE
(Durable Categories as an *element* of a *new* principle)

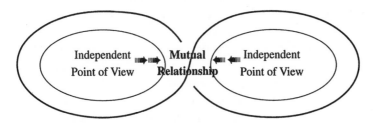

Figure 1.2 The Transformation from the Principle of Durable Categories to a Higher Order Principle

(another category), then he frames the situation as something quite different, and the decision to stay or not to stay will be governed by a whole different set of calculations ("Will my staying be damaging to the bond of trust between my parents and me? How *can* I stay? I'd feel so guilty; what will they think of me if I disregard our agreement?"). These questions betoken the existence of a different way of being *in* one's involvements with others, that of orienting not just to what will happen to me or to my wants but what will happen to my bond or connection or relationship. Relationships thus move from being extrinsically valuable to being intrinsically valuable. This different way of knowing is what Lynn and Peter expect of Matty.[4]

And Lynn and Peter are not alone. As it turns out, every one of the expectations we generally hold of teenagers makes the identical demand! The expectation that Matty will be a "good citizen" as a member of a town, a school, or any social institution that has rules for good order is an expectation not only that he will understand the institution's rules and regulations, not only that he will understand the consequences of violating them, and not only that he will keep from violating them, but that he will share in the bigger purposes of social regulation and fair treatment those rules serve. The expectation is not merely that Matty will be well contained by his fear of the consequences to him of violation, that the system will work its controlling forces on him. Were that the expectation, the principle of durable categories would be enough to allow Matty to meet it. No, the expectation is that Matty will be a fellow citizen, himself a sharer in the idea and activity of preserving the societal bonds of the commonwealth. To do this, Matty will need a way of knowing at least as complex as the cross-categorical principle.

And it is not just these more prosocial expectations that require cross-categorical knowing. All the expectations do. Wanting someone to subordinate his self-interest to the needs and value of a relationship seems like quite a different thing from wanting someone to think abstractly. But for Matty to think reflectively, inferentially, connotatively, or thematically requires that the concrete (a durable category) become an element of his principle of knowing rather than the principle of knowing itself. "Definition" is minimally a cross-categorical way of knowing because it takes the concrete example as an instance or an element of a bigger principle of knowing that includes all the concrete examples. Examples must therefore be an element or member, not the principle itself. "Inference" is a minimally cross-categorical way of knowing because it takes the category of datum or fact as an instance or element. Data must therefore be element, not principle. *Re*flective thinking requires a mental "place" to stand apart from, or outside of, a durably created idea, thought, fact, or description. The idea, thought, fact, or description is made subordinate (as figure or element) to a *super*ordinate ground or principle that is now capable of "bending back" (the literal meaning of *reflective*) its attention to focus on its own products. Each of these expectations about thinking is really an expectation for yet another expression of what it means to think abstractly.[5] But each of these expectations for "abstractness" is identical in its organizational principle to the expectations for interpersonal trustworthiness.

The expectation that adolescents experience their emotions as inner psychological states is also a demand for the subordinating or integrating of the simpler, categorical self ("I'm mad at my sister. I like BLT sandwiches. I don't like it when my father cooks my eggs too runny") into a more complex context that relates to the categorical self ("I'm much more confident. I used to be just super insecure, very self-conscious"). Thus, the expectation that adolescents be able to identify inner motivations, hold onto emotional conflict internally, be psychologically self-reflective, and have a capacity for insight all implicate the cross-categorical capacity to experience the self in relation to a given set or category rather than as the set or category itself.[6]

The construction of values, ideals, and broad beliefs also requires at least a cross-categorical principle of mental organization. Knowing that people are operating from such a principle tells us nothing about what their values or ideals will be or what they will "set their hearts on." But to construct *any* kind of generalizable value or ideal they must subordinate the factual and the actual to the bigger array of the possible or the currently contrary-to-fact.[7]

The very idea of the future as something one lives with as real in the present rather than as the-present-that-hasn't-happened-yet requires the same cross-categorical emancipation from actual/factual/present reality. The most common kind of lack of common sense we find in teenagers is often mistakenly referred to as "poor impulse control," an imprecise characterization paying too much respect to the "raging hormones" view of adolescence. The categorical order of mind is enough to handle impulse control. What we are asking here of adolescents is more complex, because it is rarely unmediated impulses that actually lead adolescents into the more foolish risks they are willing to run.

Much more often it is an embeddedness in the short-term, immediate present—a present lacking a live relation to the longer-term future.[8]

What Lynn and Peter want of their son, what his teachers want, what his neighbors want, what his potential employers want—what we adults want of teenagers—is not just a new set of behaviors or even a new collection of disparate mental abilities. What we want is a single thing: a qualitatively new way of making sense, a change of mind as dramatic as the change a child undergoes between the ages of five and ten. The common, single organizational principle at work in every expectation we have of adolescents entails the subordination and the integration of the earlier form—durable categories—into a new form capable of simultaneously relating one durable category to another. The principle of mental organization reflected in all the expectations of adolescents is this *trans-categorical* or *cross-categorical* construction (see Figure 1.3).

DURABLE CATEGORIES
(Second Order of Consciousness)

Concreteness
Point of View
Categorical Self

CROSS-CATEGORICAL MEANING-MAKING
(Third Order of Consciousness)

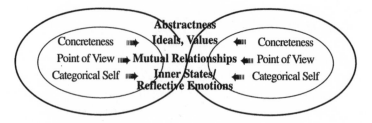

Figure 1.3 The Transformation from Durable Categories to Cross-Categorical Meaning-Making (and its products in the cognitive, sociocognitive, and intrapersonal-affective domains)

By now it should be clear that when I refer to "mind" or "mental" or "knowing" I am not referring to thinking processes alone. I am referring to the person's meaning-constructive or meaning-organizational capacities. I am referring to the selective, interpretive, executive, construing capacities that psychologists have historically associated with the "ego" or the "self." I look at people as the active organizers of their experience. "Organisms organize," the developmental psychologist William Perry once said; "and human organisms organize *meaning*."[9] This kind of "knowing," this work of the mind, is not about "cognition" alone, if what we mean by cognition is thinking divorced from feeling and social relating. It is about the organizing principle we bring to our thinking and our feelings and our relating to others and our relating to parts of ourselves.

In *The Evolving Self* I looked at psychological growth as the unselfconscious development of successively more complex principles for organizing experience. Building on the work of Piaget and those who came after him, I took the idea of such principles of mental organization and extended its "breadth" (beyond thinking to affective, interpersonal, and intrapersonal realms) and its "length" (beyond childhood and adolescence to adulthood). I have already mentioned three of these principles for organizing experience (their differing capacities are summarized in Table 1.1).

The first and least complex of these principles is the one most commonly used by young children, the principle of *independent elements*. Their attachment to the momentary, the immediate, and the atomistic makes their thinking fantastic and illogical, their feelings impulsive and fluid, their social-relating egocentric. The second of these principles is the *durable category*, the principle children usually evolve in latency, or between the ages of seven and ten. During these years, children's capacity to organize things, others, and the self as possessors of elements or properties enables their thinking to become concrete and logical, their feelings to be made up of time-enduring needs and dispositions rather than momentary impulses, and their social-relating to grant to themselves and to others a separate mind and a distinct point of view. The third of these principles, *cross-categorical knowing*, is the one we unwittingly expect of adolescents. The capacity to subordinate durable categories to the interaction between them makes their thinking abstract, their feelings a matter of inner states and self-reflexive emotion ("self-confident," "guilty," "depressed"), and their social-relating capable of

Table 1.1 Three Principles of Meaning Organization

First Principle Roughly 2 to 6 years	Second Principle Roughly 6 years to teens	Third Principle Teenage years and beyond
Logical-Cognitive Domain		
Can: recognize that objects exist independent of own sensing of them ("object permanence")	*Can:* grant to objects their own properties irrespective of one's perceptions; reason consequentially, that is, according to cause and effect; construct a narrative sequence of events; relate one point in time to another; construct fixed categories and classes into which things can be mentally placed	*Can:* reason abstractly, that is, reason about reasoning; think hypothetically and deductively; form negative classes (for example, the class of all not-crows); see relations as simultaneously reciprocal
Cannot: distinguish own perception of an object from the actual properties of the object; construct a logical relation between cause and effect	*Cannot:* reason abstractly; subordinate concrete actuality to possibility; make generalizations; discern overall patterns; form hypotheses; construct ideals	*Cannot:* systematically produce all possible combinations of relations; systematically isolate variables to test hypotheses
Social-Cognitive Domain		
Can: recognize that persons exist separate from oneself	*Can:* construct own point of view and grant to others their distinct point of view; take the role of another person; manipulate others on behalf of own goals; make deals, plans, and strategies	*Can:* be aware of shared feelings, agreements, and expectations that take primacy over individual interests
Cannot: recognize that other persons have their own purposes independent of oneself; take another person's point of view as distinct from one's own	*Cannot:* take own point of view and another's simultaneously; construct obligations and expectations to maintain mutual interpersonal relationships	*Cannot:* construct a generalized system regulative of interpersonal relationships and relationships between relationships

Intrapersonal-Affective Domain

Can: distinguish between inner sensation and outside stimulation

Cannot: distinguish one's impulses from oneself, that is, is embedded in or driven by one's impulses

Can: drive, regulate, or organize impulses to produce enduring dispositions, needs, goals; delay immediate gratification; identify enduring qualities of self according to outer social or behavioral manifestations (abilities—"fast runner"; preferences—"hate liver"; habits—"always oversleep")

Cannot: internally coordinate more than one point of view or need organization; distinguish one's needs from oneself; identify enduring qualities of the self according to inner psychological manifestations (inner motivations—"feel conflicted"; self attributions—"I have low self-esteem"; biographic sources—"My mother's worrying has influenced the way I parent")

Can: internalize another's point of view in what becomes the co-construction of personal experience, thus creating new capacity for empathy and sharing at an internal rather than merely transactive level; coordinate more than one point of view internally, thus creating emotions experienced as internal subjective states rather than social transactions

Cannot: organize own states or internal parts of self into systematic whole; distinguish self from one's relationship; see the self as the author (rather than merely the theater) of one's inner psychological life

Source: R. Kegan, "The Child behind the Mask," in W. H. Reid et al., eds., *Unmasking the Psychopath* (New York: W. W. Norton, 1986), pp. 45–77. Copyright © 1986 by W. W. Norton and Co. Adapted by permission.

loyalty and devotion to a community of people or ideas larger than the self.

These principles share several important features. First, they are not merely principles for how one thinks but for how one constructs experience more generally, including one's thinking, feeling, and social-relating. Second, they are principles for the organization (the form or complexity) of one's thinking, feeling, and social-relating, not the content of one's thinking, feeling, or social-relating. Knowing that someone is in the grip of the second principle tells us a lot about *how* he or she thinks or feels, but it doesn't really tell us anything about *what* he or she thinks or feels.

Third, a principle of mental organization has an inner logic or, more properly speaking, an "epistemologic." The root or "deep structure" of any principle of mental organization is the subject-object relationship. "Object" refers to those elements of our knowing or organizing that we can reflect on, handle, look at, be responsible for, relate to each other, take control of, internalize, assimilate, or otherwise operate upon. All these expressions suggest that the element of knowing is not the whole of us; it is distinct enough from us that we can do something with it.

"Subject" refers to those elements of our knowing or organizing that we are identified with, tied to, fused with, or embedded in. We *have* object; we *are* subject. We cannot be responsible for, in control of, or reflect upon that which is subject. Subject is immediate; object is mediate. Subject is ultimate or absolute; object is relative. When the child evolves the second principle, for example, the momentary impulse or the immediate perception then moves from being the subject of her experiencing to being the object of her experiencing. Now the durable category (not impulse but ongoing preference or need; not appearance but concrete reality) becomes the new subject of her experiencing. And this new subject governs or regulates or acts on what has become object (she controls impulses; she reflects on appearance and distinguishes it from reality). If the adolescent evolves the third principle, then *durable category* moves from being the *subject* of one's experiencing to being the *object* of one's experiencing. Now cross-categorical meaning-making (not concreteness but abstraction; not the ultimacy of self-interest but its subordination to a relationship) becomes the new *subject* of experiencing, acting upon or regulating what has become object. Each principle of mental organization differs in terms of what is subject and what is object, but every principle is constituted by a subject-object relationship.

Fourth, the different principles of mental organization are intimately related to each other. They are not just different ways of knowing, each with its preferred season. One does not simply replace the other, nor is the relation merely additive or cumulative, an accretion of skills. Rather, the relation is transformative, qualitative, and incorporative. Each successive principle subsumes or encompasses the prior principle. That which was subject becomes object to the next principle. The new principle is a higher order principle (more complex, more inclusive) that makes the prior principle into an element or tool of its system. A geometric analogy for the relation between these three principles might be that of the *point*, the *line*, and the *plane*: each subsequent geometric form contains the previous one. A line is a "metapoint" in a sense; it contains an infinite number of points, but as elements subordinated to the more complex organizational principle of the line, where earlier the point was itself an organizational principle. Similarly, a plane is a "metaline," an organizational principle containing line as an element.

We can see this analogy almost literally at work by considering how people might make use of the three principles to explain a movie such as *Star Wars*, which had broad age-appeal because it was no doubt interesting to moviegoers with a variety of organizational principles. Young children using the first principle demonstrate no sense of a story or of a logical connection between one part of the movie and another. Instead, they talk about a single point in time in the movie, or they talk about a single character with no indication that they understand his importance to the story ("I loved Chewbaka; he was so big and hairy"). Children using the second principle can subordinate point to line but not line to plane; they can string the events together to create a linear narrative of the story at a concrete level, but they do not organize an abstract theme of which this particular story is an expression. "What the movie is about" is the linear sequence of events that happened in the movie (as any exasperated parent knows who has asked this question, but was not prepared for the marathon recounting of the entire story that followed). It is only by making recourse to the third principle that the movie might be "about" the battle between good and evil or some such thematic abstraction in which the line of the story's plot is subordinated to a larger field or plane of consideration. In other words, the principles of mental organization are not only "natural epistemologies" (subject-object structures found in nature), they are developmentally related to each other: each one is included in the next.[10]

Fifth and finally, the suggestion that a given individual may over time come to organize her experience according to a higher order principle suggests that what we take as subject and what we take as object are not necessarily fixed for us. They are not permanent. They can change. In fact, transforming our epistemologies, liberating ourselves from that in which we were embedded, making what was subject into object so that we can "have it" rather than "be had" by it—this is the most powerful way I know to conceptualize the growth of the mind. It is a way of conceptualizing the growth of the mind that is as faithful to the self-psychology of the West as to the "wisdom literature" of the East. The roshis and lamas speak to the growth of the mind in terms of our developing ability to relate to what we were formerly attached to.[11] The experiencing that our subject-object principle enables is very close to what both East and West mean by "consciousness," and that is the way I intend the term throughout this book. In Figure 1.4 I represent these first three principles of mental organization as "orders of consciousness," highlighting all five of these features.[12] (I use the term "order" not in the sense of "sequence" but in the sense of "dimension." Each successive principle "goes meta" on the last; each is "at a whole different order" of consciousness.)

In *The Evolving Self* I explored psychological growth as the unselfconscious development of more inclusive and complex principles for organizing experience. Here I want to suggest that to the list of phenomena a culture creates and we study we should add "claims on the minds of its members." This book examines the relationship between the principles we may possess and the complexity of mind that contemporary culture unrecognizedly asks us to possess through its many claims and expectations—the mental demands of modern life. *The Evolving Self* was particularly concerned with the costs inherent in the processes of growth. This book is also concerned with a kind of psychological cost or burden, the one we must bear if the demands made of us are over our heads.

In this chapter we have seen one-half of an untold story about present-day adolescence. What gives to that which we call "adolescence" a coherence as a distinct time of life might be something more than a distinct biology or even a distinct psychology possessed by those in this age group. Surely adolescents reflect a variety of biologies and a variety

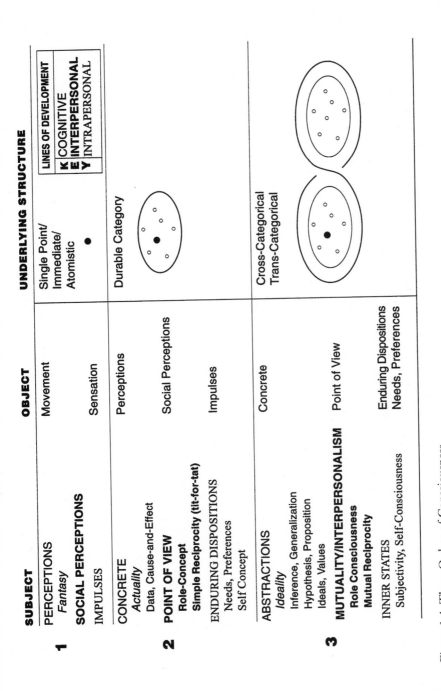

SUBJECT	OBJECT	UNDERLYING STRUCTURE	LINES OF DEVELOPMENT

UNDERLYING STRUCTURE

LINES OF DEVELOPMENT
- **K** COGNITIVE
- **E** INTERPERSONAL
- **Y** INTRAPERSONAL

1

SUBJECT

PERCEPTIONS
Fantasy

SOCIAL PERCEPTIONS

IMPULSES

OBJECT

Movement

Sensation

UNDERLYING STRUCTURE

Single Point/
Immediate/
Atomistic

2

SUBJECT

CONCRETE
Actuality
Data, Cause-and-Effect

POINT OF VIEW
Role-Concept
Simple Reciprocity (tit-for-tat)

ENDURING DISPOSITIONS
Needs, Preferences
Self Concept

OBJECT

Perceptions

Social Perceptions

Impulses

UNDERLYING STRUCTURE

Durable Category

3

SUBJECT

ABSTRACTIONS
Ideality
Inference, Generalization
Hypothesis, Proposition
Ideals, Values

MUTUALITY/INTERPERSONALISM
Role Consciousness
Mutual Reciprocity

INNER STATES
Subjectivity, Self-Consciousness

OBJECT

Concrete

Point of View

Enduring Dispositions
Needs, Preferences

UNDERLYING STRUCTURE

Cross-Categorical
Trans-Categorical

Figure 1.4 Three Orders of Consciousness

of psychologies. But something that might be true across the myriad diversities within any real group of teens is the common claim upon them for a distinct level of consciousness. In spite of all our present-day difference, in the midst of the current American experience of more *pluribus* than *unum*, lacking a self-conscious commonality of value, purpose, or persuasion, divided by geography, race, gender, and social position, it appears that there may exist, nonetheless, this odd and interesting national concert, an unwitting collective agreement about what we want from the adolescent mind. This is half of the story, the real answer to the adolescent's question, "Whaddaya want from me?" The other half has to do with whether adolescents can give us what we want.

2

Coaching the Curriculum: A Bridge Must Be Well Anchored on Either Side

That there may exist an unrecognized claim on teenagers—by parents, teachers, employers, neighbors, psychotherapists, fellow citizens, even by other teens—for a particular principle of mental organization, what I call the third order of consciousness, is only half the untold story about adolescence in contemporary culture. The other half is this: people do not generally construct the various realms of their experiencing at this order of complexity the moment they become thirteen, reach puberty, start fighting with their parents, or whenever it is we think adolescence begins. In fact, if a wide range of mind-oriented developmental studies, including my own, are to be believed, it makes more sense to conceive of the period between twelve and twenty as a time during which normal mental development consists in the gradual transformation of mind from the second to the third order. This means that it would be normal for people during perhaps much of their adolescence to be *unable* to meet the expectations the adult culture holds out for them! If the two halves of this story make for a problematic whole, how do we understand adolescents who consistently do not meet these expectations?

The answer to this will depend on the answer to the first question in the last chapter: What sort of thing is it that adults expect of adolescents? If we think of these expectations as primarily about *behavior*, then the adolescent who cannot meet them will be seen as misbehaving or incompetent, someone who will not or cannot do what he or she should. If we think of these expectations as primarily about *feelings*, then the adolescent who cannot meet them will be seen as disturbed or emotionally ill. The problem with both of these ways of thinking is that, unwittingly, they project onto the adolescent a way of knowing that is just like that of an adolescent who is meeting the expectations, except that the disappointing adolescent is somehow running this mind incompetently or the mind is somehow disturbed. As a result, the disappointing adolescent is seen as a loser, an incompetent person, and one who, by reason of stubbornness, inability, or illness, is unable to come through for us, evoking our pity or hostility.

But there may be something wrong and even dangerous in this way of thinking. What we see as the disappointing adolescent's "misbehavior" or "illness" might reflect more on our erroneous attribution to that adolescent of this third order, cross-categorical way of knowing. If the adolescent does not yet construct this way of knowing, the difficulty might be more a matter of not understanding the rules of the game than one of an unwillingness to play, a refusal to play, or an inability to play a game he or she nonetheless does understand. These disappointing adolescents may be in over their heads, and their situation is all the more dangerous for being misunderstood by those adults whose expectations they are disappointing. We all feel much less sympathetic toward people we think have let us down because they choose to than toward people we think have let us down because they are unable to do otherwise.

Consider, for example, an extreme instance of the disappointing adolescent, the person who is known clinically as "sociopathic" or as having an "antisocial personality," and who is known to us as a con-man (or con-woman), an operator, a delinquent.[1] We used to call such people "psychopaths," a term often confused in the public mind with "psychotic" and "paranoid," conjuring images of delusionary killers like "Son of Sam" or Jeffrey Dahmer. But sociopaths are not insane and are seldom killers. More commonly, they break the hearts of those who love them, cause family members to sleep with car keys or credit cards under the pillow, cause parents to take out second mortgages to repair the trail of personal wreckage their children leave in their wake. Such people fail in a big way to meet all the expectations society holds out for adolescents.

And such people to this day, professionals will agree, are not well understood. One of the most poignant lines in a classic text on the subject, Hervey Cleckley's elegant and humble book-long observation,[2] is his statement toward the end that such people "do not make the ordinary meaning of human experience." What puzzled Cleckley more than fifty years ago is still puzzling us today.

But whatever else may be going on in the psychology of sociopaths, when we look into the form of their meaning-making, at every turn we tend to find the signature of the second order of mind. "Before I sentence you," one judge said to the adolescent who was standing in front of him, "I just have to ask you: How can you steal from people who trusted you so?" "But Your Honor," came the sincere reply, "it's very hard to steal money from people if they *don't* trust you." Another judge had before him a young fellow who repeatedly ordered meals in restaurants, ate them, and then was unable to pay for them. The judge sought to inquire into the motives of the unhappy man before him. "Tell me," he said, "what's going on with you? I mean, why do you do this?" The young man thought for a moment and then answered earnestly, "Well, Judge, I go in and order the meals because I'm hungry. And then I don't pay for them because I don't have any money." The judges were seeking, no doubt, some report of inner states, maybe even of inner conflict, at least some verbal consequence of self-reflection. But perhaps they did not receive it because there was no "self" organized in such a way that "reflection" would lead to a report of internal conversation. Psychological states, experienced and expressed as such, grow out of a coordination of points of view within the self. If these youths were constrained by the second order of mind, "self-reflection" would amount to a narration of logically sequential behaviors, which is just what the judges got.

The ability to construct one's own point of view and to recognize that others are constructing their own as well, coupled with the *inability* to coordinate these points of view, to construct the self or the other not only in terms of one's own point of view but in terms of the relation of one point of view to another—this simultaneous achievement and constraint allows one to take others into account to the extent of providing them with the sense that they are understood, although one's intent has mainly to do with the pursuit of one's own goals and purposes. If other people are expecting otherwise, they will see this behavior as selfish, callous, manipulative, deceptive, or even dishonest.

Cognitively, clinicians describe the sociopath as often both highly intelligent and pathetically naive: capable of extraordinarily intricate plotting and of holding a variety of pieces of information in his head at once, but at the same time unable to engage in long-term planning. In description after description clinicians call the sociopath's thinking unusual but not psychotic and without a thought disorder in the usual sense of the word. But what if the sociopath's "thought disorder in the non-usual sense" is essentially the order of thinking of categorical consciousness, here expressed cognitively by concrete operations? Concrete thinking, governed by the durable category, is simultaneously capable of holding several pieces of information together and incapable of subordinating the category of the actual to the cross-categorical realm of the possible, which is required for the construction of long-range plans, patterns, or generalizations. It is not enough to say that some sociopaths are highly intelligent; studies should look more carefully into the form of this intelligence. Brilliant ten-year-olds, for example, have higher IQs and are more apt to appear to us as "highly intelligent" than normal thirty-five-year-olds, even though the former may not be able to think abstractly and the latter can. If we talk further with the brilliant ten-year-old and the normal thirty-five-year-old, we will come to see that, yes, the ten-year-old is very intelligent, but also very naive, exactly what we say of the person diagnosed as sociopathic. In my view, the delicious essence of the famous exchange between bank robber Willy Sutton and a newspaper reporter is that everyone else thought his answer funny, although Sutton was completely sincere:

> "Why do you rob all these banks, Willy?"
> "Because that's where they keep the money."

Meanwhile, sociopathic adolescents don't look like ten-year-olds to us. They don't have the bodies or life-trappings of a ten-year-old. We see them as adolescents (as we should); we want to hold them to the expectations we have of adolescence (as we should); and we assume that their mental equipment is currently able to understand these expectations (as we should *not*). Without realizing we are doing it, we assume that sociopathic adolescents possess a cross-categorical order of consciousness. We thus come to feel, and say, not just that their sense of morality is inadequate to our expectation that they be responsible, but that they are amoral; not just that we feel exploited by them, but that they are willfully manipulative; not just that their inner emotional lives seem to lack the complexity we expect, but that they are hollow.

In actuality, the sociopath is not without a morality; he is simply without the one we want. Roxanne was an inmate in a women's correctional institution.[3] She had prostituted herself, shoplifted, picked pockets, stolen other people's welfare checks, and used other people's credit cards. She felt that stealing was generally wrong ("stealing is the worst thing I do"), except when it was necessary to meet her needs. She felt that people who shoplift for the fun of it are definitely wrong, and that "people who sleep around a lot are whores" ("It's wrong if you're not getting paid for it"). When she was asked if it would be fair for someone else facing the same kind of needs to steal her checks, she says, "No. That wouldn't be fair." As Blakeney and Blakeney say, the morality seems to be that "it is right for me to take someone's check *because I need it*, and it is wrong for someone to take my check *because I need it*," a position that is at least consistent if not mutually reciprocal.

Is the sociopath's inner world really hollow? Or do we empathically "try on" the sociopath's inner experience and find that it doesn't fill *us* up? What we try on may be accurate, but the place where we "put" it may not be. The sociopath may not feel hollow at all. The sociopath may have recourse to the same order of consciousness as that of a normal ten-year-old. Most sensitive parents realize their ten-year-old children would be tempted to sell them for a cold drink on a hot day, but they do not think of the rather shortsighted self-interestedness of their children as a sign of "hollowness." Indeed, latency-age children (Erikson's "industrial children," who he says are "on the make"[4]) are *full* of plans and goals and organized wants. While they are quite ready, however sweetly, to make use of anyone or anything that can be pressed into service as a tool on behalf of accomplishing these ends, we do not think to call them hollow. Their inner world may be concrete. It may be more filled with persons-as-tools than persons-as-sharable-psychologies. But to the child or the sociopath it is not empty or hollow. If a caterpillar doesn't know its future has wings, it hardly experiences itself as landbound.

Adolescents who are diagnosed as sociopathic (or, in current parlance, as "having antisocial personality") may stand at an extreme in terms of their incapacity to meet our cultural expectations. Of course, most adolescents are not sociopathic whatever their order of consciousness. But the sociopath's circumstances—being unable to put the world together at the required order of complexity, being in over his head, being inadequately understood by us—may all reflect, in magnified proportions, circumstances any adolescent could face for some part of his or her teen years. The mismatch between external epistemological demand and internal epistemological capacity is characteristic of some portion of every person's adolescence. Is it necessarily a bad thing for the mental demands of one's environment to outstrip the present state of one's mental equipment?

If I were asked to stand on one leg, like Hillel, and summarize my reading of centuries of wise reflection on what is required of an environment for it to facilitate the growth of its members, I would say this: people grow best where they continuously experience an ingenious blend of support and challenge; the rest is commentary. Environments that are weighted too heavily in the direction of challenge without adequate support are toxic; they promote defensiveness and constriction. Those weighted too heavily toward support without adequate challenge are ultimately boring; they promote devitalization. Both kinds of imbalance lead to withdrawal or dissociation from the context. In contrast, the balance of support and challenge leads to vital engagement.

Were we to look at contemporary culture itself as a kind of "school," and were we to evaluate the effectiveness of the environment we create for the growth of all its constituents, I believe we might be surprised by our assessment of both ingredients. We will soon be turning to consider how modern-day adults are faring in our culture-as-school, but even if we confine ourselves for the moment to the adolescent "student," I think we could conclude that our culture deserves high marks when it comes to providing adolescents with a continuous experience of challenge. At home, at work, in school, and even in many of their peer relationships, adolescents experience a continuous demand for cross-categorical consciousness. Without any national figure or agency directing it, our culture may thus design a curriculum that is admirable on the grounds of its extensiveness (it cuts across all important arenas of an adolescent's life), its intellectual consistency or coherence (the order of complexity being demanded in the various "courses" of this "curriculum" is the same), and its difficulty (the order of complexity is neither so far beyond adolescents' capacity as to be unrecognizable or unattainable nor so firmly within their current grasp as to be boring.) The challenge of a curriculum is greatly impaired if it is confined to a small aspect of the student's life, or if it is inconsistent in the order of complexity it demands, or if it is too far out of, or too easily within, reach. On these grounds our culture-as-school may deserve the highest grade when it comes to the criterion of providing challenge.

But how well are we doing on the criterion of support? How extensive is it? And how well matched is it to the evolution of consciousness called for by the curriculum? If, as a culture, we expect people to operate out of the third order of consciousness as soon as they enter adolescence, then we are designing a "school" with an admirably challenging curriculum but a shameful lack of the sympathetic coaching appropriate to the gradual outgrowing of a way of knowing the world. The experience of challenge without support is painful. It can generate feelings of anger, helplessness, futility, or dissociation, all of which can be heard in the familiar adolescent plaint, "Whaddaya *want* from me?"

To answer my earlier question, it is *not* necessarily a bad thing that adolescents are in over their heads. In fact, it may be just what is called for *provided they also experience effective support.* Such supports constitute a holding environment that provides both welcoming acknowledgment to exactly who the person is right now as he or she is, and fosters the person's psychological evolution. As such, a holding environment is a tricky transitional culture, an evolutionary bridge, a context for crossing over. It fosters developmental transformation, or the process by which the whole ("how I am") becomes gradually a part ("how I was") of a new whole ("how I am now").

One natural source of this facilitation normally is a new kind of peer

"This song is dedicated to our parents, and is in the form of a plea for more adequate supervision."

Drawing by Koren; © 1991 The New Yorker Magazine, Inc.

whom most youth find at some time in adolescence. This relationship differs from the latency friendships of doing/exchanging/comparing/competing/compromising and signals instead the first bloom of co-constructing, co-experiencing interpersonalism. Whether these are Sullivan's "chum relationships"[5] or involve a more unilateral fascination with someone deemed especially admirable, such relationships, by virtue of the individual's identification with the other, are facilitators of a kind of trick nature plays on the second order of consciousness, for it must seem to one at first as if no view separate from one's own has "really" gotten inside. But the other-who-is-just-like-the-self is a "transitional object," both part of the old way of knowing and part of the new. In taking the other into account one is simultaneously continuing the categorical embeddedness in a single point of view (since the other's point of view is the *same* as one's own, a feature of identification) *and* bringing another's point of view into the process of constructing the self's point of view. Working from the direction that this is someone one considers very like oneself, and whom one wants to continue considering like oneself, one responds to one's inevitable discoveries of slight differences between the two views in ways quite different from making the other into the antagonistic holder of a competing point of view. On the contrary, one tries instead to *restore* one's sense of an identity between the two views by finding some way to bring the views back into line. Such radical mental "behavior," dislodging one's identity with one's own categorical point of view, can lead to a whole different order of consciousness!

But can we afford to leave to adolescents' peers the job of providing the supports that adolescents need? Our culture enhances itself as a school for adolescents each time it more effectively endows another frequented arena of adolescent activity with supports for the transformation from second to third order consciousness. The great religions of traditional cultures, a paradigmatic example of one kind of effective culture-as-school, make use of all the regularly frequented arenas of ordinary human conduct to induct and inspire their members in the faith. How we eat, do business, make love, honor our mother and our father—supposedly *private* domains—are not handed over to independent, idiosyncratic, and variably meaningful rule. The contexts for education are not shrunk down to the narrow confines of periodically attended church or school. On the contrary, the regularly frequented arenas of human conduct provide the most important opportunities for teaching. The effective culture-as-school takes over these arenas and bends them to its curricular purposes. The actual schools in which our culture teaches adolescents, the families in which it raises them, the values for sexual conduct into which it inducts them—if these are organized to be at once immediately meaningful to, and ultimately disruptive of, categorical consciousness, then they become powerfully educative vessels in support of the culture's challenging curriculum.

What are some examples of how we can help adolescent contexts foster our culture's hidden curricular purposes rather than leave their design to local, idiosyncratic circumstance? In *The Evolving Self* I told a story about three adolescents, all of whom had sufficiently disappointed the expectations of their culture that it was deemed necessary to take institutional action. Roxanne, the young woman who stole checks, was sent to a prison, Terry to a psychiatric hospital, and Richard to a job-training program. Although these various types of response seem to distinguish the three as "criminal," "sick," and "unemployable," it is possible that they have much more in common than not, since each is in need of support for the same transformation of mind. As it happened, only Richard was helped to make that transformation, not because job-training programs are inherently preferable to psychiatric or correctional programs, but because the particular job-training program in which Richard found himself was job-training-plus-something-more, a medium that both welcomed categorical consciousness and nurtured the seeds of its productive undoing.

Roxanne's correctional program, guided by behavioral theory, consisted in a token economy in which inmates' behavior, like that of B. F. Skinner's pigeons, was shaped through token rewards into increasingly "responsible" activity. The pigeons in correctional institutions can probably be expected to come to know as much about social relations as the birds come to know about bowling—essentially, that certain behaviors will lead to certain payoffs. Although the program is highly acknowledging of, and sensible to, categorical knowing, it does nothing to promote the development of cross-categorical knowing: in shaping the superficial behaviors of good citizenship without any self-conscious attention to the organization of the person giving rise to these behaviors, the behavior modification approach comes close to the notion that the living of one's life is comparable to an activity like bowling, where the behavior is identical to the thing itself. That inmates in such programs return to their former lives, former crimes, and sometimes even their former prisons with no less frequency than other inmates[6] is testimony either to the greater complexity of a game like life or to the possibility that, however different the discharged inmate's behavior has come to look, he or she remains in some fundamental way unchanged.

If a program can fail to provide the necessary evolutionary support by neglecting to build a bridge out of and beyond the old world, it can also fail by expecting its charges to take up immediate residence in the new world. This was the case with Terry's milieu therapy unit, which required of patients the ability to speak reflectively in group meetings of their psychological motivations and internal conflicts. Terry's tendency to talk instead about what other people were or were not doing in relation to what she wanted to do was seen by staff as "resistance," as refusal to do "the work of the ward," from which she was eventually exiled.

In contrast to programs that were in essence either insufficiently challenging to the adolescent's order of mind or too far beyond it, Richard's job-training program artfully recognized and welcomed categorical knowing and then quite deliberately created the circumstances for its productive undoing. In Richard's program,

> The values of cooperation, mutuality, joint decision-making, taking responsibility and sharing are *not* placed in the foreground. What Richard saw when he first arrived was a half-finished boat in a boatworks; a letter from a buyer offering several thousand dollars for the boat when it was done; competent adults who knew how to finish the boat and who were willing to teach people like himself how to build them. Richard was engaged by the program . . . because he was first of all communicated with at the most fundamental level of his meaning-making, which was, at this point in his development, oriented to personal control, personal enhancement (even aggrandizement), and the display of, and acquisition of, personal competence. At the powerful, subtle levels his inability to be *inter*personal [or cross-categorical] was not only *not* being tagged as a problem, but the strengths and motivations of his [categorical] instrumentalism were being recognized. Once hooked, of course, it was only a matter of time before he came to see that there were limits to his way of making meaning. Learning to build the boat eventually became quite a different matter than he first surmised, involving not just new acquisitions for the person he had "always" been, but an actual reconstitution of who he is.[7]

The program's insistence that the trainees work in groups, their need to learn each other's skills and limitations as well as their own, to hold the other in mind even as they pursue their own ends, naturally promotes a cross-categorical way of knowing. The boatworks-plus-something-more held in waiting a cooperative community ready to receive the gradually more cross-categorical knower when he or she was ready to join it. Two years into the program Richard told us, "It used to be when I screwed up I worried that I was gonna get it. Now when I screw up I worry that other people are going to worry."

The artful features of Richard's boatworks are often replicated by athletic coaches of adolescent teams, a form of teacher-student relationship or "classroom design" that should be spread far more widely throughout the junior and senior high school, beyond the gym and playing field and right into intramural physics scrimmages, the interschool math league, or the history olympics. The emphasis here is not on competition and rivalry as the main event but as a means to the purpose and performance of teams. Guided first by a concern for a developmental process rather than a victorious product, the basketball coach, like the master boat builder, can stand in the doorway of an alluring and valuable activity welcoming adolescents to a bounty of opportunity for increased personal competence, self-display, self-aggrandizement, and personal reward. Only later, once hooked, will the same adolescents discover, if artfully coached, that in order to get what they want for themselves they must learn, gradually and with understandable ambivalence, the need to take out membership in a community of interest greater than one, to subordinate their own welfare to the welfare of the team, even, eventually, to feel a loyalty to and identification with the team, so that its success is experienced as their own success and their failures are assessed in terms not of their personal cost but of the cost to the team ("It used to be when I screwed up . . .").

But in order for teachers, be they basketball or biology teachers, to value, for example, the opportunity to induct young people into a team, they would need a better understanding of the common enterprise in which they are engaged. Such a re-visioning of the enterprise of adolescent education, to which we now turn briefly, would constitute a valuable reattuning of the curriculum of the school to the hidden curriculum of the culture.

To one extent or another most school faculties have factions. The junior and senior high school I taught at did, and from my experience as a teacher and a consultant in the twenty-five years since, I would hazard that nearly every faculty has its subgroups doing battle with each other in subtle but ongoing ways. The tensions that divide a group of teachers supposedly engaged in a common enterprise are not wholly a matter of differing personalities, generations, or gender. Much of the disagreement is downright philosophical, or ideological. The faculty members have different beliefs about what, fundamentally, they should be up to in the teaching of the young. Sometimes these differing beliefs are discussed outright; more often they are expressed indirectly through a faculty member's actions and reactions; too often they are experienced as unwelcome and unpleasant personal conflicts. But potentially they amount to a fascinating lived conversation between equally respectable parties who care deeply about the outcome of a philosophical conflict because it has real implications for their own lives and the lives of their students.

If we were to place these differing ideological positions on a continuum, at one end we might find a fundamentalist curricular philosophy I'll call "Back to Basics" and at the other end a humanist philosophy I'll call the "Whole Child." The curricular vision of "Back to Basics" stresses the acquisition and mastery of a generic set of cognitive skills that will equip the learner for later life tasks, and an ever-increasing fund of knowledge about the culture, past and present, in which he or she lives. In caricatured (by those who are critical of this vision) form, "Back to Basics" is an attention to rote learning, memorization, and the uncritical inculcation of the culture's historical values. It is possible, however, to hold the vision in a more sophisticated form that orients to the realization of an increasingly complex set of cognitive skills, including the capacity for reflective and critical thought. From this point of view, "Back to Basics" is less a naive fundamentalism than a stand against neglecting the need for a solid educational foundation out of misguided deference either to faddish pursuits of "relevance" or to a particular set of values not necessarily shared by the full range of students' families in a pluralistic society.

The vision of the "Whole Child," in contrast, declares that cognitive development is a valuable but only partial curricular agenda that must include equal respect for the student's emotional and social development. It too has a common caricature in the hands of its antagonists: intrusive, quasipsychiatric forays into the feelings and valuing of students (to which their families might properly say, "This is none of your business"), and social-engineering according to the blueprint of one faction of society, which feels it has the right to define mental health and good social order for everyone else. But it is also possible to see in the curricular vision of the "Whole Child" an old-fashioned and long-esteemed conviction that good schooling should nurture "the wit *and character*" of the young,[8] that if we are not to become captives of our own increasingly mechanized society, the young must not only be smart, they must also be capable of conviction and self-defined purpose.

The way these competing visions get discussed in educational circles is often historical or sequential: "Back to Basics" became a dominant vision in the late 1950s and early 1960s in reaction to presumed Soviet scientific accomplishments symbolized by the launching of *Sputnik*. The "Whole Child" ideology arose in the late 1960s and early 1970s as a pedagogical expression of the more general cultural rediscovery of humanism and romanticism in reaction to the manifest contradictions within the public and private institutions of a democratic society. Then, in the late 1970s and throughout the 1980s, the pendulum again swung "Back to Basics" for reasons that depend largely on one's view of recent history. Some would argue that the reascendance of this vision is made necessary by the inevitable costs of conceiving of schooling as a solution to social problems and made possible by the relative amelioration of those problems—reduced racial, ethnic, and gender discrimination; ending the war in Vietnam. Others would argue that the reascendance of the "Back to Basics" vision is a defensive reaction to the deeply disturbing and still largely unanswered questions raised by the cultural critique of the 1960s. It remains to be seen whether the 1990s will come to be characterized by yet another swing of the same pendulum or by some synthesis of these polarizing influences. In any case, the problem with thinking of these ideologies primarily in linear, historical terms is that the reality of life within contemporary school faculties gets occluded. In real faculties at any one time these competing ideologies are coexistent, if unsynthesized. A teacher today experiences the tension between them within her faculty, and perhaps even within herself.

Although these tensions are no one's fault, they are costly. They tie up energies both within a faculty, in which teachers of one persuasion may actually believe that teachers of the other are ill-serving the young, and within a teacher's relationship to herself, in which she may feel at times constrained or even paralyzed by her recognition of the competing wisdoms expressed in each view. These tensions tie up energies that could be put to better use in achieving the shared purposes of the school if only some integrating vision of those purposes might be found.

I would suggest that such an integrating vision may be found in an unrecognized curriculum: the culture's widespread demand for a common transformation of mind during adolescence. Interestingly, both "Back to Basics" and the "Whole Child" are compatible with this hidden curriculum, although each can also undermine it. A new curricular vision tied to sympathetic coaching for the gradual growth of the mind from categorical to cross-categorical consciousness need not award victory to either "side" but could instead clarify a common enterprise hospitable to both. Such a vision recognizes and indeed celebrates the inevitable diversity of teacher temperament, personal preference, and educational ideology, but it also goes beyond an eclectic spirit of uncritical tolerance. It provides a way for very different kinds of teachers to look across the faculty room at each other and think, "That guy has an entirely different way of going about it than I do, but we are both pulling in the same direction."

If five lamps are lit in a large living room, how many sources of light are there? We might say that there are five sources of light. Perhaps the maker of each lamp, genuinely committed to bringing us into the light, will be partial to his own and bid us to come to that source. Or at best, some generous spirit of eclectic relativism may obtain, and the lamp-makers may concede that there is a benefit to our being exposed to each of the lamps, each separate source having little to do with the other except that, like the food groups of a well-balanced diet, each has a partial contribution to make to a well-rounded, beneficial whole. But quite a different answer to the question of how many sources of light there are in the room is possible—namely, that there is only one source. All five lamps work because they are plugged into sockets drawing power from the home's electrical system. In this view, each lamp is neither a contender for the best source of light nor a mere part of a whole. Each lamp is powered by the whole, expressive of the whole. And if the lamp-maker's mission is not first of all to bring us to the light of his particular lamp but to bring us to the light of this single source, then he can delight equally in the way his particular lamp makes use of this source and in the way other lamps he would never think to create do also. His relationship to the other lamp-makers is neither rivalrous nor laissez-faire, but co-conspiratorial: the lamp-makers breathe together.

In like manner, the ultimate goal of any school leader is to get the faculty to breathe together, but it cannot be done by firing the trouble-makers, burying the conflicts, or hiring a crew to make all the lamps in the same way. It can only be done by identifying a mission that pays the greatest respect to the diverse lamp designs while at the same time keeping in the foreground the common source of power to which the different designers share loyalty.

The development of the student's mind is such a mission; the vital forces of mental development (an energy no educator brings to the school or classroom or student, but rather finds there) are the common source. But such a vision does not transform a school if it lives only rhetorically or is espoused in the abstract, even an abstract disguised as parable.

It lives in the nitty-gritty operations of the classroom and in the school as a whole. It lives through faculty members' views—be they "Back to Basics" or "Whole Child" advocates—about whether the way we teach "plugs into" the developmental source. Let us consider, for example, two junior high English teachers, each teaching a unit on the short story. Teacher A and Teacher B couldn't be more different in their temperaments, life styles, or educational philosophies. Teacher A fought in the Korean War, still wears a crew cut, and remembers with fondness the days when "students would never think of talking back to their teachers." Teacher B refused to serve in his generation's war, only recently cut off his ponytail, and remembers with fondness the days when "kids cared more about causes than designer clothes." Teacher A sees English class, first of all, as a place to teach kids how to read and write intelligently. He uses the short story as a vehicle to teach the kids both, challenging them to get as much meaning out of the story as the author put into it and taking the story apart to show the kids how it is made. Teacher B sees English class, first of all, as a place to engage the valuing side of his students. He respects good reading and writing, and wants to see it in his students, but he feels that the overall school curric-ulum is already weighted much more heavily on the cognitive side and that English class is an opportunity to teach about values and social re-lations. He uses the short story as a vehicle to engage the kids' philoso-phies and enhance their ability to respect each other in spite of the fact that they may disagree.

Now, we might ask of Teachers A and B: Are they good teachers? Is one better than the other? Are they collaborating or competing? Do they respect each other? Do they experience each other as true colleagues, breathing together, or do they at best put up with each other? The answer to all these questions is that we do not yet have enough information to know. We know that one teacher is partial to "Back to Basics" and the other to the "Whole Child," but this doesn't tell us who is the better teacher. We know that the two have dramatically different educational philosophies, but this doesn't necessarily tell us that they are pulling in different directions.

So let's get more information. The short story each is teaching today is O. Henry's "Gift of the Magi." Teacher A on this particular morning wants to get across the concept of irony to his seventh graders. He asks for a definition, and the first student responds, "Like when the husband sold his watch to get his wife the combs for her hair, but then she had sold her hair to get him a chain for his watch—that's irony." Now how does Teacher A respond to this? One sort of Teacher A might respond, "Well, that's not really a *definition* of anything. That's an *example*. Depending on what you think that example means, it might even be a correct example of irony, but it's certainly not a definition. Now, can someone give me a definition of irony, not an example?" The probable sequence of events might go something like this: (1) Students volunteer a few more examples of irony, which the teacher does not accept as definitions of irony; (2) there is eventual silence on the part of the class; (3) the teacher, having stumped the class, defines the term irony, possibly writing the definition on the blackboard for the students to copy into their notebooks, memorize, and file away for the exam. And perhaps, from this Teacher A's perspective, he successfully created a heightened readiness and interest in learning a concept before he provided the answer.

Now, another sort of teacher, Teacher A', might respond differently: "Well, that's a terrific example of irony, all right. Let's put that one up on the blackboard and circle it. Okay, can someone give me another example of irony? It doesn't have to be from the story, it can be anything." The probable sequence of events goes like this: (1) the students will offer many more *examples* of irony ("It was ironic that Samantha Smith, that girl who went to Russia for world peace, then died in a plane accident"; "It was ironic that Dennis Eckersley, who used to pitch for the Red Sox, was the one who ended up beating the Red Sox for the pennant"; and so on). Teacher A' salutes each example, puts it up on the board, and draws a circle around it; (2) the teacher says, "Let's stop and take a look at all these great examples of irony." He then draws one big circle enclosing all the separate circles. "Now can anyone tell me what *irony* is in a way that would be true for all these examples?"; (3) at this point, the students collectively struggle toward a generalization that can be checked against all the particulars.

Both Teacher A and Teacher A' are Back-to-Basics-oriented. Both want to teach about a cognitive concept, and both know how to teach. Each is able to foster a process that creates the "teachable moment." The difference is that Teacher A creates a teachable moment in order to teach rote learning, memorization, an increasing fund of knowledge. What is Teacher A' doing with the teachable moment? He is engaging the developing mind of his students, their evolving orders of consciousness. How? Rather than demonstrate to the students their inability to generalize, to make the concept concrete so they can then handle it by memorizing, Teacher A' directly engages their growing edge, which is expressed in their inability to move smoothly from the concrete to the abstract (which subtends the concrete). Both teachers' requests (to define) exceed the limits of the categorical order of mind. The difference between an example and a definition is precisely the difference between a concrete fact, a second order way of knowing, and abstract generalization, a third order way of knowing. By welcoming the concrete as a route to the abstract, Teacher A' creates a teachable moment that involves an epistemological stretch just a little beyond most of his students. He invites his students to take the concrete examples as *objects* and create a new knowledge structure that will contain all these objects. This new knowledge structure, which they collectively struggle to create, will express itself as the capacity to *define* (rather than merely to *exemplify*), but of course it is the much bigger capacity for cross-categorical consciousness.

Now let us turn to Teacher B. He's teaching O. Henry too, but he's not teaching the concept of irony. On this particular morning, as the students are engaged in heated controversy, the learning goal on his mind has to do with the very way the students listen to each other—or, more precisely, the way they do not. He is struck by the way they interrupt each other and by the way that, even when they take turns, they seem to ignore completely or distort what the previous speaker has said in order to return to the point they favor. Teacher B does not think about this as just a classroom management issue that must be resolved in order to get the kids back on track for learning. He regards this as part of the track, an opportunity for learning, an opportunity for teaching them important lessons about respect, good listening, and learning from others.

Now, how does Teacher B teach this? One sort of Teacher B may elect any of the following approaches: (1) he establishes rules for proper conduct in conversations, along with consequences for violating the rules (for example, he announces, "If you interrupt, you can't speak again for fifteen minutes"; or he gives each student three tokens, and since they must spend one each time they speak, no student can speak more than three times); (2) he stops the discussion and gives a sincere, eloquent, hortatory speech about the need for the students to treat each other better; or (3) he stops the discussion and runs a brief "therapy group" in which students are encouraged to talk about how they feel when they are interrupted or ignored.

Another sort of teacher, Teacher B′, might teach the lesson this way. He lets the conversation/debate proceed, but he institutes one new requirement: before any speaker may make her point, she must restate the preceding speaker's point with sufficient accuracy that the preceding speaker agrees it has been adequately restated. At first the students try to fulfill the agreement by restating the point in the straw man fashion they are prepared to attack. But they do not get the chance to attack, because, amid the laughter and the hooting, the preceding speaker objects, requiring them to restate the opposing view in a nondistorting, noneditorialized fashion, however maddening it may be to do so.

Again, both Teacher B and Teacher B′ share a "Whole Child" philosophy. They want their class to affect the students' social as well as intellectual development. And, again, both know how to teach. But *what* they know how to teach differs. The first Teacher B, who establishes rules for respectful behavior, may actually possess, whether he knows it or not, a theory of education in relation to social development that bears remarkable similarity to that of Teacher A, who teaches the rote learning of concepts. Although Teacher A directs the teaching to controlling the internal operations of the mind and Teacher B to the external operations of the body, both essentially see good teaching as being about the effective shaping of (inner or outer) behavior. The second Teacher B, who preaches a sermon, directs his teaching to winning souls, converting the junior high heathen. The third Teacher B, who runs the therapy-type discussion group, directs his teaching to the healing of the psyche. All three kinds of Teacher B are coming out of a "Whole Child" agenda. But in contrast to "teaching social development" from the stance of behavioral engineer, secular minister, or amateur psychiatrist, only Teacher B′ pursues the same agenda in a way that regards good teaching as being about the growth of the students' minds. All the teachers have a vision or a metaphor that animates their teaching, but in contrast to the actions of control, conversion, or healing, only Teacher B′ supports a motion or *telos* that does not get its start from him. What is the teaching motion for Teacher B′?

Teacher B′ is supporting a motion that comes from his students and their own vitality rather than from himself. He is supporting their natural epistemological development as it expresses itself in the realm of social understanding. And what makes him a *good* teacher of the mind is that he has devised a way to engage both the strengths and the limits of the students' current epistemological predicament. He engages them "where they are" but invites them to step beyond that limit. How? The little rule Teacher B′ adds to the "game" of class conversation ingeniously transcends mere classroom management and joins the students' natural consciousness curriculum. Their categorical capacity to take another's perspective allows them to stand in a classmate's shoes and restate the classmate's position; but their incapacity either to hold multiple points of view simultaneously or to integrate them means that when the student does stand in his classmate's shoes he experiences the temporary surrender of his own preferred view. He will not necessarily enjoy doing this, as the initial attempts to distort tendentiously the other's view demonstrates, but out of the desire to express the view he favors he will accept the unwelcome route. The trick is that this unwelcome route, first seen as a mere means to an end, has the promise of becoming an end in itself, since the continuous consideration of another's view in an uncooptive fashion, which requires a continuous stepping outside of one's own view, is a definite move toward making one's own view *object* rather than *subject* and toward considering its relation to other views. This approach, like that of Teacher A′, again supports the growth of cross-categorical consciousness.

Teachers A, A′, B, and B′ thus demonstrate two important points with respect to the ideological factions that divide faculties. First, in the context of a curricular vision of the growth of mind, the distinction between better and poorer teaching has nothing whatever to do with the distinction between fundamentalist and humanist visions! On the contrary, as Table 2.1 indicates, the examples help us to suggest what stronger and weaker teaching might look like in each of the approaches.

Second, as the "Developmental" column in Table 2.1 also indicates, as different as teachers in the two factions might be, were each to practice his or her vision in the context of supporting the growth of the mind, the bigger truth is the complementary and collaborative nature of their teaching venture, not its antagonism. The "prime" teachers in the examples just given, A′ and B′, may be of different generations, political persuasions, and life styles, but the "deep structures" of their practice, their attention to enhancing the structures and processes of their students' meaning-making, are remarkably similar however disparate their practices may appear on the surface.

School leaders, hoping to develop faculties that breathe together, may understandably throw up their hands as they confront, among faculty, differences in those qualities that greatly influence the nature of a teacher's engagement of her students—differences of temperament, social and interpersonal style, preference or comfort about which aspects of a child's mind one seeks to engage. But these differences do not need to defeat the hope of a co-conspiratorial faculty. The more that teachers can be "prime teachers," whatever their ideology, the greater likelihood they will come to see that their fellow prime teachers, whatever their ideology, are joined with them in a common pursuit. Teacher B′ may never want to use an O. Henry story to teach the concept of "irony" as Teacher A′ does. But joined in a common curriculum, these teachers know much more than that they are on the same team; they know that each in his own way is trying to accomplish the very same thing.

It is important for our culture to exercise a more powerful grasp on actual schooling as a context to support and foster (not just promote and expect) its consciousness curriculum for youth. But an effective culture, as I have said, does not shrink its educating to a single locale. It reaches its teaching hand into every frequented arena. It would be uncourageous and, at this point in history, especially dangerous, for me to end this chapter without giving thought to another arena of adolescent life as salient and regularly frequented—I refer to adolescent sexuality. Is this really a part of the culture-as-school that should be included in our assessment? Is an adolescent's sex life the business of anyone other than that adolescent? Is the conduct of an adolescent's sexuality built, or at

Table 2.1 Nondevelopmental and Developmental Approaches to Fundamentalist and Humanist Curricular Visions

Curricular Vision	Developmental Approaches	Nondevelopmental Approaches
Fundamentalist (back to basics)	Support for cognitive construction	Shaping of cognitive behavior
	Exercise of cognitive structures	Rote learning, information transfer
	Opportunities for the relativizing (objectifying) of cognitive structures	Increase in fund of knowledge
	Support for the integration of relativized structures into new structures	Teaching of cognitive skills as distinct and separate operations, and building up of the number of such skills
Humanist (the whole child)	Support for social, affective, and intrapersonal constructions	Shaping of social and emotional behavior
	Exercises of social, affective, and intrapersonal structures	Preachment, suasion, social pressures, and secular conversion
	Opportunities for the relativizing (objectifying) of social, affective, and intrapersonal structures	Quasitherapeutic supports and interventions
	Support for the integration of relativized structures into new structures	Teaching of each social or emotional skill as a distinct and separate operation, and building up of the number of such skills

Source: R. Kegan, "Minding the Curriculum," in A. Garrod, ed., *Approaches to Moral Development* (New York: Teachers College Press, 1993).

least influenced, by the culture in which it takes place? Does the hidden consciousness curriculum extend to adolescents' sexuality, and if so, are we not then bound to evaluate whether the culture takes any responsibility for *supporting* the curriculum it espouses? I believe the answer to all these questions is "Yes."

The sexuality of adolescents seems to show up in adult consciousness as either a focus of lurid fantasy (as depicted in the advertising and entertainment of popular culture) or a social "problem" in need of our conscientious concern and solution. This unfortunate splitting of desire and responsibility on our part will do adolescents no good, since it is precisely the live connection between the two that they themselves need to learn.

The concerns we have about the sexual conduct of our culture's teenagers have never been more real or of such crisis proportions. The possibility of sexually transmitted diseases now includes the literally life-and-death risk of contracting HIV, the bubonic plague of the modern age. Teen pregnancy and births to teens are on the increase, despite greater support for the use of contraceptives and more widespread sex education. Less dramatic, less statistically documented, but no less legitimately worrisome are the injuries to heart and spirit of exploitative, self-involved, uncompassionate passion.

So there is a lot to be legitimately worried about, even alarmed about. But these concerns will count for little if they are not joined to our acknowledgment that, however newly arrived, however ambivalent they may be at finding themselves there, adolescents have entered a human realm, the allure of which we ourselves find unabating. They have entered a realm whose pleasure, power, warmth, heat, sweetness, stimulation, delight, and satisfaction our finest poets do not tire of trying to name. The more our worries about teen sexuality increase, the more the whole subject shows up for us as a "social problem" and the further we are removed from our understanding of what teen sexuality is to teens themselves. Sexuality to teens is not first of all a "problem" in need of a solution. Our anxieties about their sexuality (organized around themes of *danger* and *risk*) are not at all the same as their anxieties (organized around themes of their own *acceptability* and *competence*). Our unacknowledged prurience and projection about the pleasures of teen sexuality bear little relation to their pleasures in sexuality. (When a sixteen-year-old Brooke Shields is used to sell Calvin Klein blue jeans, and the camera pans slowly along her long legs while she recites suggestive lines such as "Nothing comes between me and my Calvins" and "If my Calvins could talk I'd be in big trouble," this strikes me less as an expression of a sixteen-year-old's sexuality than as a copywriter's fantasy about adolescent sexuality.)

Let me suggest, then, two ingredients that must be present in any valuable new approach to our culture's concern for adolescents as sexual people: First, the approach will recognize from beginning to end that sex to teenagers opens a world of extraordinary allure, unexplored possibility, and scary but thrilling and companionable adventure. (Sex is what God gives to teenagers when the appeal of Disneyland starts to fade.) And second, the approach will recognize that adolescence is *not* synonymous with the third order of consciousness; rather it is a period in need of support for the gradual evolution of mind from the second to the third order of consciousness. Exactly what this new approach will be I cannot predict, but I guarantee that it will have these two qualities, which means that it will be sure to make many people uncomfortable: (1) it will treat sex as fun, friendly, tender, wet, warm, and wild; and (2) it will not assume from the start that teens are "responsible." When we find ourselves uncomfortable with the odd sound of such an approach, we would do well to be aware of how comfortable we are with the success of our current approaches. As I say, I cannot predict exactly what the new approach will actually be, but if for nothing more than concrete example, I will offer my candidate for a new cultural norm for adolescent sexuality at the dawn of a new century.

The current norms for teen sexuality we are trying as a culture to promote are either "abstinence" (which in translation essentially means "limit sexual activity to what you can do with your clothes on, hands above the waist, buttons buttoned, zippers zipped") or "safe sex" (which in translation means "if you are going to have intercourse, make sure the young man is wearing a condom"). These new norms are of course in conflict with each other, but what they share is that each is possessed of a certain undeniable wisdom, neither is proving particularly successful at being adopted, and each fails my test by omitting one of the two crucial ingredients.

The "abstinence" norm's biggest failing is that it denies how irresistible sexual experience is. Now, I never met a denial I couldn't feel sympathy for. There is always a very good reason why it would be more pleasant to assume that the denied reality is not real. The denial of teens' interest in sexuality is *not* the province of obviously out-of-touch, repressed, or parochial people alone. Sophisticated, urbane, progressive professionals in high schools and private schools frequently are alarmed by crises that require them to face a picture of teen sexual activity quite different from the one they have been carrying around in their heads. The expectation of abstinence is unrealistic because it asks adolescents to put on hold, disable, or disengage a qualitatively new medium for connecting to and experiencing the world. It is one thing to ask people to forego a feature of their diets—for example, to stop eating high cholesterol oils or high-fat meats. It is quite another thing to ask people to stop eating altogether.

The "safe sex" norm's biggest failing is that it unwarrantedly assumes an order of consciousness capable of such responsibility, far-sightedness, and future-mindedness. Given how infrequently even college-age youth make use of the condoms and dental dams passed out during freshman orientation week, is it not wildly unrealistic to believe that sexually active twelve-, thirteen-, fourteen-, fifteen-, sixteen-, and seventeen-year-olds are going to have the presence of mind to involve these devices regularly in their sexual activity when these devices are completely unnecessary to, and unenhancing of, the only real goals and interests they have in mind at the moment?[9] This may be as big a denial on the part of "safe-sex" proponents as is the denial of sexuality's irresistibility on the part of "abstinence" proponents. As I said, I have never met a denial I couldn't sympathize with. It is frightening, but I think necessary, to consider that not only is a great proportion of teens' sexual behavior and judgment compromised by alcohol, spontaneity, susceptibility to a partner's pressure, and silencing embarrassment about the technical details of sex, but *even when that judgment is completely free to do its best work*, it is constrained by an order of consciousness that considers the future as the present-that-hasn't-happened-yet rather than as something real, right now, and commanding of their attention.

Discussing norms for adolescent behavior is not the same as discussing the means by which the norms are promoted or taught. How we shall engage adolescents on the subject of sexual behavior is not, at the moment, my topic. I am addressing the former issue. However directly or nondirectly, didactically or nondidactically, dialogically or unilaterally, mutually puzzling or authoritatively we present ourselves to teens on the subject of sexual behavior, there must, at bottom, be some set of convictions or values we hold on the matter. Adolescents need to hear from us, or sense in us, a place where we stand. In suggesting a new, third norm for adolescent sexuality, I am not now addressing adolescents. I am addressing us adults, the keepers of the cultural school. I am addressing our need to clarify among ourselves not how we teach our lesson but what our lesson should be.

In our culture, for whatever reason, we have come to equate sexuality with the act of genital intercourse. The vast variety of sexually pleasuring acts in which the penis does not enter the vagina are referred to professionally as "foreplay," as if they are mere appetizers and unacceptable as the main course. The meaning of "going all the way" suggests that the only complete realization of a sexual experience is intercourse. When adolescents today, and many adults as well, use the expression, "having sex," they mean that the penis went inside the vagina. The term "sexually active teenager" means *not* that the teens fondle each other's genitals or bring each other to climax with their hands or mouth. Apparently these acts do *not* constitute being sexually active. Only if the penis enters the vagina is a heterosexual couple said to be "sexually active." Yet there is nothing ordained by biology or divinity that says this is what sexuality should be. It is wholly a cultural invention. And it is even an odd one for this day and age, when sexuality is no longer fused with procreation. The reduction of sexuality to genital intercourse has come home to haunt us as we see it reflected in the sexual behavior of our adolescents.

All norms draw a line. In contrast to a norm that draws a line between behaviors which are or are not associated with sexual pleasure ("abstinence") or a norm that draws the line between protected intercourse and unprotected intercourse ("safe sex"), I suggest a norm that permits as wide a range of sexual pleasure as adolescents feel comfortable sharing, but that draws the line between sexuality with intercourse and sexuality without it.

In contrast to the stance of "abstinence" ("limit sexual activity to what you can do with your clothes on, hands above the waist, buttons buttoned, zippers zipped") and the stance of "safe sex" ("if you are going to have intercourse, make sure the young man is wearing a condom"), I would suggest that there are merits to a stance more like this:

> Adolescents have become sexual people. It's only natural that this powerful new way of experiencing and expressing themselves is going to be an important addition to the ways they relate to others and to themselves. Their sexuality might naturally become one of the ways

they explore a variety of important personal interests, needs, concerns, and issues, including their developing sense of themselves as a man or a woman, their wish to feel attractive, accepted, or loved by another of their own age, their need to express their fondness, affection, attraction to, or love for another of their own age, and, of course, their desire to experience and share the physical pleasures of sexuality. Their sexuality is an understandable and natural way of expressing or pursuing any and all of these. Some percentage, in every culture at every time in history, will naturally feel drawn sexually to those of the same sex; most will be attracted to those of the opposite sex.

How adolescents will express this new capacity will be shaped to a large extent by interaction between the "curriculum" of their culture and the way they understand that curriculum. As makers of that curriculum we must be aware that the wish to exercise this new capacity is irresistible and that the ways adolescents will understand our curriculum will vary. If our curricular aims (that people express their sexuality respectfully and responsibly, with concern for the other's feelings and with regard to the future implications of present acts) are somewhat over the heads of the entering "student," then we must build a transitional or bridging context for younger sexuality that is both *meaningful* to those who will not yet understand that curriculum and *facilitative* of a transformation of mind so that they will come to understand that curriculum. We cannot simply stand on our favored side of the bridge and worry or fume about the many who have not yet passed over. A bridge must be well anchored on both sides, with as much respect for where it begins as for where it ends.

A bridging context might somehow convey a message such as this one concerning the particulars of how sexuality among teens is expressed: So what, you may ask, do we think is okay and not okay for you to actually do? What does your culture tell you? First, your culture tells you that you should not do anything more than you want to or feel comfortable doing, and obviously that may involve some trial and error on your part. But within the limits of your comfort, and the comfort of your partner, your culture says that what you actually do is almost entirely up to you. As you will see, there is a continuum of sexual arousal and satisfaction that begins with the slightest degree of excitation and ends, for both young men and women, with the unusually intense satisfaction and release of orgasm. Obviously your own comfort and imagination, and those of your partner, will suggest a variety of ways you can touch (and even talk to) each other that will lead to your both becoming more and more aroused. If the question "How far can we go?" refers to this continuum of arousal, your culture's answer is, "You may go just as far as your comfort and that of your partner permit." If "all the way" means experiencing the climactic end of this continuum—you or your partner, or both of you, having an orgasm—then your culture is saying, "When you are ready to go 'all the way' you can; this is not prohibited behavior." Nor does your culture seek to impose a limit on the number of partners you may have, whether the relationship is casual or committed, whether you are in only one sexual relationship at a time or have multiple partners. That is all your choice. Of course, your culture does not condone lying to your partners about your true feelings for them or your sexual conduct with others, but that is a particular instance of the more general cultural norm against lying and deceit, which applies to, but is not peculiar to, norms of sexual behavior. The only line your culture wishes to draw regarding your sexual behavior is that until such time as you are ready to enter into a serious relationship, you do not engage in intercourse. Bluntly put, the penis does not enter the vagina or anus. A serious relationship is marked by a different intention toward each other (for example, to remain together, or to decline other sexual relationships, or to be held by one's community as a couple, or to create a family), and by a different order of responsibility for each other (including, for example, responsibility for one's sexual relationship through the practice of protected intercourse). Your culture makes a distinction between sexual relationships marked by this seriousness of commitment and those that are not. It values both. Each may have its proper time. The culture does not reserve a greater degree of sexual pleasure for one kind of relationship over the other—both kinds may engage in fully pleasurable sexual expression. It simply reserves one form of sexual expression, intercourse, as an exclusive marker of the more serious relationship.

Now, before I consider whether it is psychologically plausible that such a norm actually could be adopted by adolescents at the dawn of the twenty-first century, let me quickly make note of the array of concerns that would be significantly affected if just this single norm were made viable:

1. The incidence of sexually transmitted diseases—especially contracting the most frightening of these, HIV, the virus that currently leads inexorably to AIDS—while not eliminated would be dramatically reduced, and without the intermediation of prophylactic devices. Is oral sex a risk-free sexual practice? According to experts and the best evidence on HIV transmission, it is not absolutely risk-free. It certainly involves a higher risk than protected intercourse. But is this really the

relevant comparison? Given the unlikelihood of the universal use of condoms by twelve- to eighteen-year-olds, the more realistic comparison is between the safety of oral sex and that of *un*protected intercourse. Oral sex is a much less risky sexual practice than unprotected intercourse. Faced with our concern about a deadly virus, if we could choose whether adolescents would practice only safe sex or only oral sex, of course we would choose the former. But if the former is not realistic, the latter is enormously preferable to the current situation of widespread unprotected intercourse.

2. The incidence of unplanned pregnancy would be greatly reduced, and without the need for contraceptive devices, because the single prohibition affects not only those who would have intercourse without regard to pregnancy but also those countless teens who now employ ineffective prevention methods such as "withdrawal" or having intercourse during "safe" times of the month.

3. Shifting the focus, purpose, conclusion, or even the very meaning of shared sexual intimacy away from genital penetration and toward the feelings and, if desired, the sexual satisfaction each partner is giving and receiving may eventually promote the mutuality, reciprocity, sensitivity, thoughtfulness, and even technical skillfulness of adolescent sexual activity. It offers a much greater likelihood that youthful sexuality would be an arena in which one would come to understand the other's sexuality; that each partner would keep the other, as well as him or herself, in mind; that each partner would make the other's experience, as well as his or her own, central to what shared sexual activity is about.

4. The new norm redraws a distinction that many value and are concerned has been lost between premarital and marital intimacy or, at least, between casual and committed relationship; and, in its own fashion, it reasserts the sanctity of the family, which many feel has been profaned. It fosters the idea that one conducts oneself differently in committed relationships such as those that bear or care for children.

Thus, by drawing this single new line, the culture addresses its own concerns about disease, unwanted pregnancy, emotional insensitivity, and the decay of the institutions of marriage and family. It addresses issues dear to a variety of positions on the political spectrum. It speaks to the concerns of advocates of both the current contesting norms, incorporating features of each (although I am sure it will please neither, since it is neither as "safe" nor as "abstinent" as either would want).

But is it plausible that a new norm of fully pleasurable sex without intercourse could actually be internalized by teens of the future? (I am thinking now of *tomorrow's* teens, of those who are today young children or not yet born). My answer is that the greater barrier to its being internalized rests in the minds of adults who themselves equate sexuality with intercourse, not in the minds and bodies of teenagers whose motives and interest in sexuality carry no necessary demand for the particular act of genital penetration. Nothing that calls adolescents to sexual expression *requires* genital penetration for its satisfaction. Not the motive to feel loved or lovable, to be taken care of or care for, to give or receive pleasure, to win or confer a valuable prize, to make another person jealous, to hold a boyfriend or girlfriend, to establish one's identity as a sexual person, to satisfy curiosity about another person's body, to fill the gaps in the conversation, to become more separate from one's parents, to experience physical tenderness, to have something to do on Saturday night, to have an orgasm, to have an orgasm with another person, to create and sustain an intimate relationship—not one of these *requires* the act of intercourse for its satisfaction. (In fact the *only* motive I can think of that does is the motive to have a baby, which does exist among some adolescents, usually disadvantaged girls who do not consider having a child a further burden but view it as an opportunity to assume a preferable social role and have an object to love. But this is more an instance of a claim to readiness for a "serious relationship," challengeable or not, than of needing intercourse to be part of one's noncommitted sexuality.)

Fully pleasurable sex without intercourse, implausible though it may sound in our current cultural climate, is actually quite responsive to both the irresistibility of sexuality and the inevitable variation in adolescents' consciousness capacities. More than this, it represents a way for the builders of the culture, acting as more responsible keepers of "school" in relation to the hidden consciousness curriculum, to foster the arena of sexual behavior as yet another supportive context for the gradual evolution from the second to the third order of mind. How?

Consider that efforts to get teens to abstain from drug use by "just saying no" or to "stay in school" by appealing to the importance, down the road, of a high school diploma, are not likely to be too compelling to adolescents organizing reality at the second order of mind. Adolescents of categorical consciousness do not "say yes" to drugs primarily because of peer pressure but because of their own interest in the experience they derive from getting high. If I construct the world out of the short-term, quid pro quo logic of categorical consciousness, you are proposing that I give up something I value in return for exactly nothing. Why would I want to do that? There is no short-term reward for giving up getting high. You want me to give up something I like and you leave me with nothing but the internally or externally depressing condition I was seeking to escape in the first place. Stay in school? Why? If I don't like school, if I am humiliated or bored there, what is the short-term pay-off? There is none. Appeals to the long-term consequences of drug abuse or of dropping out of school are not compelling when the future is constructed as the present-that-hasn't-happened-yet.

Now consider that the norm of fully pleasurable sex without inter-course does not require cross-categorical knowing to be immediately meaningful and that it is not first of all about privation. Like the basket-ball coach who has in mind basketball-plus-something-more, or the master boat builder who has in mind a boatworks-plus-something-more, the culture advocating a provisional or bridging context for ado-lescent sexuality would stand in welcome in the doorway of an alluring and valuable activity offering the prospect of highly attractive personal reward. It is only when one is drawn into this unusual *kind* of team, or boatworks, or sexual behavior, that one comes gradually to learn that the increase one sought might amount to a change not just in what one "gets" but in who one is. This is the more Zenlike or Eastern approach to one's curricular goals, an approach that moves with rather than against the natural direction of the student, but in doing so uses the student's own momentum as a resource for his or her transformation.

In sanctioning a provisional or transitional arena for youthful sexual-ity, the culture, like Richard's boatworks, would *not* be setting as the price of admission the ability immediately to understand and identify with a set of prosocial values. Nor would values such as "act respectfully and responsibly, with concern for the other's feelings, and with regard to the future implications of present acts" even be what teens "see" first when they "enter." What they would see first is an alluring opportunity for self-enhancement and the pursuit of their own ends. What they would perceive their culture seeming to say sex was all about is precisely what it would seem to them to be about. The fact that there is a rule involved would not be fatal to this student-curriculum match in mean-ingfulness. The fact that the master boat builders tell their young charges they have to show up on time does not sour the adolescents on the meaningfulness of the boatworks. It is a small enough price to pay, and it doesn't reduce the number of goodies available. The "no intercourse" rule is no different. As I have said, not a single motive that draws an adolescent into sexual experience requires the act of intercourse. That it sounds strange to say the rule does not reduce the number of available goodies might only be a sign of how embedded we are in the equation of sexuality with intercourse.

"But doesn't the very act of excluding something," some may object, "make it that much more alluring? Adolescents are going to want to have intercourse all the more if you try to reserve it to some later time in one's life." Actually, it is not true that reserving something until later in life automatically makes it more appealing. Adolescents do not want the long-term, day in and day out responsibilities of childcare, for example (but they do want to earn money babysitting); they do not want to carry a monthly mortgage (but they do want a room of their own); they do not want to have to sustain themselves economically (but they would like an allowance or a part-time job). There are many activities already reserved for later in life that are not made one bit more alluring by being so. What adolescents of categorical consciousness want is not actually a function of whether adults reserve it for later; it's a function of whether it meets their immediate needs. The culture reserves the commitment to full-time employment until later in life, but in doing so it doesn't make this activity more alluring. Teens may want the culture to provide more part-time jobs so they can generate more spendable cash, but they have no heightened need for full-time employment. Aside from the money, they may have a need to "try on" the experience of work, but they have no real need to take on the full trappings of employment. Teens may want to have sexual experience, may feel the *need* for sexual experience, but, odd as it sounds, they may have no real *need* for genital penetration *unless the culture builds a dazzling shrine to it.* If we continue to believe that the climax of sex is genital penetration, rather than that the climax of sex is climax, then it is true that in trying to get adolescents to forego intercourse until they are more responsible we will simply make intercourse even more alluring. But it will not be because the act of reserving something until later in life automatically makes it more desirable. It will be because we are being dishonest and disingenuous, and adolescents will know it.

Every healthy culture must create provisional environments for its youth.[10] The practice of unprotected sexual intercourse among teens does not create a safe, wholesome arena for provisionally experiencing and expressing one's sexuality. The norm of safer sex creates a wholesome provisional arena, but it also creates a barrier to entry that is beyond the mental reach of practically all adolescents during at least some portion of their teen years. The norm of abstinence creates no provisional environment at all. The norm of fully pleasurable sex without intercourse creates a safer environment with an "entry fee" whose cost the adults in the culture can reduce to affordability. Given our own initiation to sexuality in an "intercourse-centric" culture, it takes an act of imagination to consider what happens to sexuality when this center is shifted. If we placed orgasm rather than intercourse at the end of the sexual continuum adolescents would correctly see that the arena of provisional sexuality the third norm creates is one that offers them a full range of expression. We would not be saying (or meaning), "You can go almost 'all the way' but not quite."

I do not pretend that adolescents who are closer to the second order of consciousness than the third will suddenly be less exploitative or more responsible because they practice their sexuality within this provisional context. I fully expect them to be as captive of their short-term interests as ever. That is one reason a provisional environment is provisional; people can make poor choices and be mistaken at less cost. Teens of both sexes will continue to make use of each other for their own ends. Some will still want to "score"—there is no way to abstain from categorical consciousness. But there is a way to make its expression less dangerous. Exploitation of one sort or another will continue. But it could continue with less actual intercourse, less HIV transmission, less unplanned pregnancy.

And it could continue in a context that is actually more conducive to overturning categorical consciousness. A well-schooled culture is a tricky culture. It not only creates environments that are intensely meaningful to the current way its members construct their experience, it also increases the likelihood that interacting with this environment will disturb this very way of constructing reality and promote its transformation. When the goal or aim or end of sex is shifted from the purely bodily cooperation of fitting one's genitals together to a goal aimed at pleasure, sensation, and satisfaction, the form of cooperation also shifts by necessarily requiring fitting minds together as well as bodies. I am called to think about you, what feels good to you, what you need, at the same time I am thinking about me, what feels good to me, what I need. This is just the sort of activity that comes to relativize categorical consciousness and promote the cross-categorical consciousness that makes the values of mutual respect and responsibility more meaningful.

At this point the adolescent is ready to pass out of the provisional environment into a new realm of sexual practice, a realm that not only sanctions intercourse but warrants that those who have intercourse—be they more mature teenagers or adults—*if they wish this to be a part of their sexual expression*, are responsible enough to do so in a way that abjures the risks of disease, unplanned pregnancy, and exploitation. The idea is not that genital penetration is somehow itself the acme of mature sexual expression, or that this is what people should do when they are more mature (women whose partners are women, for example, would be the first to attest to this), but only that if intercourse is part of one's sexual expression it should occur in relationships where partners have the capacity to love each other responsibly.

Promoting a new cultural norm is hard work, to be sure. Discouraged, we may say, "How can we get people to change their behavior?" But it is not impossible. Were I to have said fifty years ago that Americans as a group would radically reduce their smoking or significantly alter their diets to reduce fat intake, my prediction might have seemed as incredible then as this suggestion may seem now. Not a single food company in America sat down and said, "Gee, our customers don't know it, but our products aren't really that healthy for them. Even though these consumers are making us rich, let's see if we can sour them on our existing products. Let's promote an altogether new health consciousness in them and then design a new set of more wholesome products for them to buy." The great corporate engines didn't throw themselves into reverse. They were thrown by the one market force more powerful than the conglomerate producer: the shifting cultural values of consumers themselves.

Why did our smoking habits and food choices change? It takes a compelling, simple, and clear signal to effect a change like this one, preferably a signal of alarm. More people stopped smoking and eating so much fat because they came to believe if they did not it would kill them. The threat of death is a compelling signal. And it is the threat of death, above all, that fuels our culturewide concern about adolescent sexuality.

Who can be moved by this threat of death? Not the adolescent of categorical consciousness, for whom the future is not a part of the present. So why spend time trying to create fear where there is none? I would spend it trying to mobilize fear where it is already present or latent, in the minds and hearts of parents capable of assuming the responsibilities that are ours as keepers of the cultural curriculum. It is we adults, not adolescents, who are failing to create the wholesome provisional experimental spaces adolescence needs to make mistakes and learn safely. I admire those relatively few adults who, by actively promoting the norms of safe sex or abstinence, are without doubt seeking to assume some responsibility for this important aspect of our culture-as-school.

Promoting a new cultural norm is very hard work, daunting, slow, incremental, fraught with failure amid only intermittent success. But if we are to take up the work of promoting the internalization of a new norm, then let us elect one, unlike abstinence or safe sex, that reflects the realities as well as our concerns. Let us elect one that reflects the realities of the irresistibility of sex and the consciousness constraints of adolescence. And let us elect one that makes of this important and highly frequented arena of adolescent activity a hospitable environment for the mental growth our culture requires of people of this age. When it comes to sexuality and adolescents it may be that the way we will "get *them* to change" their behavior tomorrow will depend on our changing the way *we* think today.

II

The Mental Demand of Private Life: Parenting and Partnering

3

Parenting: Minding Our Children

Peter and Lynn are wide awake in bed at one in the morning, but they are not having a good time. They are having an argument. Or rather, just now they are *not* having an argument. Lying there silently, side by side, unable to get on with anything else, unwilling to reengage their angry and hurtful conversation, they look like a horizontal version of two standing strangers forced to wait together in close quarters for an overdue bus or elevator. For Peter these situations are even physically painful. He is someone who finds himself with an upset stomach when his wife is angry with her boss or her dentist or the jeweler who misrepaired her digital watch. For himself to be the object of Lynn's unhappiness is almost incapacitating. He feels nervous to the point of nausea. At the same time, he is mad at Lynn and, more particularly, he is hurt by what he sees as her stubborn and selfish disapproval of his spontaneous invitation to his parents to join the two of them on their summer vacation next month in northern Vermont.

"I can't believe you just went ahead and asked them without talking to me about it first," he remembers her saying, which left him both hurt that she had not supported the generous spirit of his gesture, and embarrassed that perhaps he had blundered badly. "We spent months working out a plan for us to have some time without the kids and you go and invite your parents." Peter had so many simultaneous reactions to this statement he could only feel them crashing into each other: First, he *had* loved the picture of the two of them walking hand-in-hand by the water, a picture that gave him a feeling he missed deeply, the feeling

73

he thought they both had in the earlier years of their relationship. But he had *also* felt bad about not taking the kids along and didn't know why he and Lynn couldn't feel that way with the kids there too. So, he had never had quite Lynn's enthusiasm for that part of the summer plan anyway. And then, insinuating itself into this older conflict, which Lynn's words had resurrected, there was the current conflict they were actually fighting over now.

"You make it sound as if I planned to invite them and carried this all out behind your back. First of all, I don't really even want them to come, and second, you know when it gets right down to it they probably won't."

At this Lynn makes her familiar gesture of exasperation, hands hurried into the air, and then, as if forgetting their purpose, falling from their own weight.

"Look," Peter says, "I was in the middle of telling them about our summer plans and they sounded so forlorn and abandoned I thought it would be really nice for them to join us—I just wanted to cheer them up. Maybe they could just come after we've been there a while and we could have some time to ourselves."

"But the whole point of the trip was to have some time to ourselves and now we're back to figuring out how to have some time to ourselves!"

"I know, I know, but you should have heard them. Look, Lynnie, these are my *parents*. They really aren't bad company and these are their last years and you know how they love to see us and, really, is it so much to have them along when it will make them so happy?"

"'After all they've done for me the least I can do is invite them to join us in Vermont.'"

"Well," Peter says, a little sorry to hear his exact sentiment intoned in a less than wholeheartedly embracing voice, "I do feel kind of like that."

"Next you'll be suggesting we bring the kids along too—after all, *they'd* enjoy it, and your parents would be even happier to see their grandchildren than they'd be to see us."

"Good idea! Why not!" Peter says in a spiteful tone, suggesting that he finds the suggestion as preposterous as Lynn intended when in fact he doesn't really find it so preposterous at all.

"Look, Peter," says Lynn—and Peter feels humiliated by the instructive note in her voice, in part because he suspects what she is about to say will really be instructive—"I'm not sure we're getting anywhere. I love our children. I love you. I even love your parents and you know I do. What I don't get is how our precious week together in Vermont, which I thought we both agreed should be a time just for us, gets turned into a gift to your deserving parents. And sort of without batting an eye! I mean if you'd said originally, when we were making summer plans, 'I want to do something wonderful for my parents,' I could even see how we might come up with the very plan you proposed."

"But I'm telling you I didn't *have* any plan. It just came up in the conversation and I could see they were feeling so bad."

"But I thought you *did* have a plan, Peter. You had *our* plan, our plan to go off together for a week."

This is where Peter stopped talking. His attention was drawn inside to the beginning signals of The Bad Feeling.

"And that's what upsets me the most, Peter, how quickly our plan vanishes if your parents—or the kids, it could be the kids, too!—if any of them says 'Boo!' You asked your parents because you couldn't help it."

Yes, it was surrounding him now, The Bad Feeling. He was right in the middle of it ("How could she think that?"), that impossible feeling ("She makes it sound as if I don't care about us. I just hate that she's saying that!"), that impossible feeling of having to "be" in several places all at the same time ("Doesn't she know how terribly much I want to recapture that walking-by-the-water-hand-in-hand feeling? Why, I think I'm even more committed to our trip than she is! How can she say this?"), that feeling of being ripped apart, or being pulled in different directions, the feeling of wanting everyone you love to be happy, of even feeling you could *make* them all happy—if only they would cooperate and somehow didn't need it all at once.

When compared to the categorial meaning-making of childhood and early adolescence, the accomplishment of the third order of mind is a spectacular transformation, admired by developmental researchers and parents of adolescents alike. Nearly twenty years of living may go into the gradual evolution of a mental capacity that enables one to think abstractly, identify a complex internal psychological life, orient to the welfare of a human relationship, construct values and ideals self-consciously known as such, and subordinate one's own interests on behalf of one's greater loyalty to maintaining bonds of friendship, or team or group participation.[1]

But as extraordinary as this mental capacity may be, the question now arises, "Would third order consciousness equip one to meet the demands, not of adolescent life, but of adult life in America?" There is no reason why, in and of itself, this order of consciousness should prove insufficient to meet the demands of any of several perfectly reasonable ways cultures *could* construct and *have* constructed adult life. It is a dignifiable, sophisticated, and socially responsive way of organizing experience. It is the culmination of "adolescence" (etymologically, "becoming grown up"), and so, by rights, it should constitute a respectable form of adulthood. The third order of consciousness amounts to the psychological threshold for what sociologists call "socialization": we become truly a part of society (rather than its ward or charge) when society has become truly a part of us. Our capacity to internalize, and identify with, the values and beliefs of our social "surround"—as these may be communicated by family, peer group, state, religion, ethnic clan, geographic region, or social position—makes us inductable into the commonweal.

But the question before us is whether the third order would equip us to meet the actual demands of adult life as these exist in present-day America. I am not asking, "Is there something wrong with third order consciousness?" or, worse yet, "Is there something wrong with contemporary adults who organize their experience according to this principle?," I am inquiring into the "goodness of fit" between the mental demands of modern life and the third order of consciousness. In the next six chapters I invite us to explore these mental demands as they occur in the arenas of parenting, partnering, working, living in a diverse culture, being in therapy, and learning in school. By bringing these non-communicating discourses of expertise and expectation together, and by subjecting them to a single gradually building analysis of their demands on our minds, I hope to generate sufficient thrust to move us temporarily beyond our "gravitational field." When a rocket gets far enough into space it begins to send back pictures that let us see the curve of the Earth, the boundary or shape of the wet, blue planet with which we otherwise tend to be fused. I am trying in this book to gain a glimpse of the psychological curve of modern life. And why? Being able to take the whole Earth as an object of attention has led us to a greater sympathy for it, for its fragility, its vulnerability, and its need of our support. Might glimpsing the psychological curve of the modern world likewise provoke in us a greater sympathy for our condition or move us to do better at providing the supports we need to sustain ourselves?

Peter has long since developed the third order of mind, and its complex form can be found throughout the contours of his life. Like the biology of an aging lake, its common distinguishing features are evident in a broad-gauged view of its ecosystem or in a single drop of its water under a microscope. Indeed, every aspect of the third order's capacity can be found in the tiny drop of Peter's life that is this late-night battle in bed: the ability to think abstractly, identify a complex internal psychological life, orient to the welfare of a human relationship, construct values and ideals self-consciously known as such, subordinate one's own interests on behalf of one's greater loyalty to maintaining bonds of friendship, team, or group participation. But the funny thing is that the same abilities that looked like (and indeed were) such a splendid accomplishment when found in the mind of a seventeen-year-old adolescent look much less heroic or successful in the mind of a perfectly normal thirty-six-year-old husband having an argument with his wife in bed at one in the morning. Indeed, the very capacities we would have celebrated had we found them in Peter twenty years ago now seem to be the very source of his unhappiness.

Peter may be in some difficulty, but I do not say this as a criticism of him. If his difficulty lies, as it may, in his inability to master the hidden curriculum of his culture's "school," whose problem is this? Whose fault is it? It would be a cruel school indeed that would think first to blame the student for his or her inability to master its curriculum. We are going to meet many bright, conscientious, well-intentioned, and dignifiable adults over the next several chapters who are nonetheless having their own difficulties with the hidden curriculum of modern life. The first question I raise in response to these difficulties is not "What is their problem?," as if this is a matter of individual limitations, but rather, "What is the fit or match between the way they are making sense and the way their culture is *demanding* they make sense?" A sympathetic and humane school, confronted with struggling students, doesn't blame the students but seeks to provide supports to aid them in mastering the curriculum. But in order for us to provide such supports effectively we need a better understanding of what exact process or purpose we are trying to support. Our generous intention to be helpful would not be enough. We would need to better understand our own curriculum, make what is hidden unhidden, and learn what it actually takes to master it.

In the previous chapters we learned that Peter and Lynn's teenage son, Matty, knowingly and unknowingly finds himself amid a host of expectations all visited upon him by simple virtue of his being a teenager. So also Peter, knowingly and unknowingly, lives amid an even more daunting set of demands just for being an adult in present-day America. At the moment he is experiencing his wife as the source of these demands. They concern the private sphere of his family life, saturating his roles as spouse, parent, and the adult child of his own parents. But Lynn is actually the tip of an iceberg of expectation, and the sphere of family life is but one big iceberg in a sea of such icebergs, a sea in which Peter—bright, conscientious, even privileged though he may be—may well be nonetheless over his head.

If we confine ourselves for the moment to the sphere of family life and the activities of parenting and partnering, a dense, rich set of expectations or demands is conveyed through the public voices of our culture's experts and authorities, who are not shy in spelling out the requirements for the successful exercise of these adult roles. Though sometimes abstract sounding and lifeless in their form, these public prescriptions resonate to the passionate particulars of real-life conflicts and disappointments such as Peter's and Lynn's.

Consider just a few of the expectations from the contemporary literature of expertise on parenting and partnering.

(1) As parents, we adults are expected to be the leaders of the family: to take charge, to assume responsibility, to institute a vision and induct family members into it, to look out for the development of the children, to take stands, and to embody and express some theory, ideology, or overall set of values by which the family operates.

Despite the fact that we are told in first grade that the most powerful leadership job on Earth is the presidency of the United States, we all come to know that our parents, who have us at considerably closer range over a longer period of time, nearly always have more influence on who we are and who we become than the occupant of the Oval Office. The responsibilities, and the license, of parenting make it truly one of the most powerful jobs on Earth, and since most of us do become parents, it may be for many adults, whether we know it or not, our most significant leadership experience.

When I ask parents what they think are the most important things a ten-year-old needs from his or her parents (besides the basics of food, shelter, and clothing), the lists that are generated are usually of this sort:

1. Love
2. Understanding
3. Flexibility
4. Openness
5. Warmth
6. Humor
7. Open-mindedness
8. Ability to listen
9. Respect for the child's individuality
10. Taking an interest in what interests the child

Surely this is a list to warm anyone's heart. But is this the whole story of effective parenting, of effective leadership as a parent? I sometimes ask parents what their lists would really mean in action. "What should we do," I might say, "if we discover our ten-year-old is stealing from the corner drugstore?" The answers: "Find out why." "Talk with him [her]." "Love the child harder." "A child who steals is a child who needs something; find out what she [he] needs and give it to her [him]." Eventually some brave soul in the back of the room says, usually a little defiantly, "I'd scream and yell at my kid so he knew I was angry." "Really?" I say in horror, as the others in the group shrink away from the Neanderthal in their midst. "You'd actually get *angry?* What about 'open-mindedness,' 'understanding,' and 'respecting the child's individuality'?"

What the list is missing is a child's need for parents who can exercise power on behalf of convictions, exert control, be righteously indignant, even express moral outrage (a virtue lauded by the Greeks and in woefully short supply at every level of modern American life). *Power, authority, control* are words that make people uncomfortable, especially in a context such as parenting, which is first of all about love. But perhaps effective parental loving of a ten-year-old must include competent executive functioning, a child's sure sense that someone is in charge who believes in something and will stand for those beliefs. Why might this be? Developmentally, children from the age of six or seven until adolescence are in the process of learning to take charge of their own impulses, to exercise control over themselves so that they can pursue their own goals with a new measure of independence and self-suffi-ciency, so that they can take pleasure in the competent exercise of social roles (child, peer, pupil) and participation in social institutions. A child at this age may be greatly in need of inclusion and recognition in social institutions that he or she experiences as fair, committed to some shared purposes, and, above all, led by persons who are models of the executive command that is first on the child's own psychological agenda.

The most intimate institution in which the child participates is the family, and the most visceral and instructive lessons the child receives in effective self-leadership come from the ways she or he experiences being led. In a family with an eight-year-old someone must be clearly in charge, and it had better not be the eight-year-old. Power, authority, and control make many of us uncomfortable, in part because we have seen so many arbitrary and abusive exercises of power (especially at the governmental and corporate levels) that we come to feel that all exercise of power must be intrinsically arbitrary or deleterious. But what if, on the contrary, the exercise of power as a parent is itself intrinsic to effective loving and effective leadership? And just what order of consciousness is necessary to fulfill this exercise?

(2) As parents, we adults are expected to manage boundaries effectively: to recognize and preserve distinctions in membership to different subgroups within the family and to recognize and preserve the distinction between family and nonfamily membership. Young children are no less a part of the family than their adult parents, but they do occupy different roles than their parents in ways that matter substantively to the governance of the family, to family members' access to information, to the assigning of responsibility for family functions, and to the regulation and initiation of extrafamily involvements.

Effective boundary management in a family with young children seems to require the simultaneous exercises of inclusion and exclusion: providing children with the sure and certain sense that they are fundamentally a part of a durable human group that is deeply committed to them and at the same time, and just as surely and certainly, excluding them from the burdens of adult participation in this group to protect their need to live as children within it. We fail in these boundary-managing duties whenever we make children into adults (for example, by having them share the palpable or psychological burdens of our leadership) or make ourselves into children (for example, by acting as if we are free of the leadership responsibility we delegate to them; by not claiming our greater authority, competency, or entitlement to lead; or by suggesting we could operate as peerlike confidants of our children apart from our roles as their parents). Is there a consciousness threshold that must be reached to meet *this* expectation successfully?

(3) As parents, we adults are expected to be able to set limits, a special instance of which is largely implicated in the earlier task of managing boundaries. When we refuse to allow our children to assume worries over the family finances, become the surrogate parent of a younger sibling, or seek to right some family wrong by their misbehavior or over-determined conscientiousness, we preserve the boundaries between parents and children by setting limits on the children. When we resist the temptation to derive from our children the emotional sustenance we lacked as children or are disappointed not to find in our spouses, deny ourselves the apparent solutions to family leadership problems that may exist in the willing energies of our young, or correct our tendency to communicate to our partners through our children the difficult feelings that must be delivered to our partners directly, we are preserving boundaries between parent and child by setting limits on ourselves.

But as parents we adults are called upon to set limits on behalf of a whole host of things that matter to us, not just preserving boundaries. In fact, one way we institute our vision, agenda, or overall plan for the family (the first expectation on the list) is by putting our foot down in the presence of anything that violates cherished elements of that vision. Our limit-setting may disappoint others and even enrage them—including especially the beloved others who may not only be members of our family but those on whose very behalf we are acting when we are disappointing and enraging them. However much we love them and do not want to see them unhappy or in pain, much less be the very *cause* of that unhappiness or pain, we may nonetheless feel called upon to inflict such misery on behalf of our children's safety, our commitment to protect the weaker from the arbitrary abuses of the stronger, the conviction that cooperation and sharing is preferable to obstinacy or selfishness, or myriad other values and beliefs. Would third order consciousness, the mental achievement we expect in adolescence, necessarily enable us to take such actions?

Institute a vision of leadership. Maintain boundaries. Set limits. While a surprisingly vast set of parental activities and conundrums are implicated in these three kinds of expectations, these are not of course the whole story of parenting or of the expectations we place on ourselves as parents. But even just these three are enough for now.[2] Let's include the realm of *partnering* and consider a few more fundamental expectations derivable from a separate literature, this time on marriage and intimacy. (I would remind the reader that I am not prescribing or even necessarily endorsing these expectations; rather, I am taking an inventory of what is expected of us.)

(1) As adults, in our intimate partnerships we are called upon by those who study successful and unsuccessful couples to have developed sufficient psychological independence so that we do not see the other as an "organizer of the self."[3] We are charged, rather, to develop "a well-differentiated and clearly defined sense of self"[4] or a "separate identity"[5] distinct from our mate's. Women who do counseling with lesbian couples write of the need of partners to foster intimacy by providing each other with "increased distance, personal space, and individual autonomy."[6] Given our tradition in this country (only recently countered and even then by relatively few) for women in heterosexual couples to "take the name" of their husbands when they marry, it could be presumed that this general expectation would necessarily be more difficult for women to meet than for men, but as we will see, such a presumption, as in the case of Peter and Lynn, may be quite unwarranted.

(2) A related but distinct expectation is that, as adults, in our intimate partnerships we are called upon to transcend an idealized, romanticized approach to love and closeness in favor of the recognition that a marriage is a partnership between two distinct individuals who do not share one mind, heart, and soul. Partners, we are told, will inevitably experience differences and conflicts, which differences need not signal the failure of their closeness or bond but rather the reality of their distinctness. Corollary to this expectation is the idea that successful couples do not give up the pursuit of closeness in their intimate relationship but reconstruct the very definition of what closeness is about. Rilke's words may suggest something of this postromantic conception of closeness: "Once the realization is accepted that even between the closest human beings infinite distances continue to exist, a wonderful living side by side can grow up, if they succeed in loving the distance between them which makes it possible for each to see the other whole against the sky."[7]

(3) Reminiscent of the discussion of the demand for limit-setting as parents is the expectation upon us as intimate partners in the family to set limits in order to preserve the couple as a distinct subgroup in the family with a purpose all its own, separate from the children and from

the grandparents or in-laws. Successful couples, we are told, take action to keep their relationship from becoming only about their roles as parents or as the adult children of their own parents. They recognize that to sustain their marriage, they must give time to this relationship apart from the compelling and demanding activities arising from other important roles inside and outside the family. Limits must be placed, then, on children not merely to preserve their opportunity to have a childhood (a parenting expectation) but also to allow the partners to have a partnership that is about something more than just their parenting. The parents of the parents, for all the love they may have to bring into the family, must not be allowed to overrun it, or be used as allies in indirect communication between the partners. This entails limits, then, on one's children, oneself, one's own parents, and even, on occasion, one's parents-in-law. (Peter's seeming inability to disappoint his own parents on behalf of preserving the couple's private vacation time, which has left Lynn feeling inadequately cared for or protected, may be an example of his failure to fulfill this expectation for limit-setting.) Finally, we are called upon to set limits on our involvements *outside* the family—on work, friendships and leisure-time activities that we do not pursue as a couple, civic involvements, and the myriad forms of self-expansion such as higher education, psychotherapy, or self-help support. Any or all of these can deprive a couple of even the minimum time necessary to sustain itself, let alone to thrive.

(4) Then, too, in growing recognition that adulthood is not an end-state in development but is itself a time of potential development, we are called upon as adults, in our intimate partnerships, to support our partner's development. This is apparently a demand quite different from the one we face as leaders of the family who are called upon to support the growth of our children. Yet there are also similarities.

Unlike the demands of our parenting role, the charge to support our partner's development does not assume that we occupy a place of greater wisdom, maturity, or foresight than the person we are seeking to support. We may have had little or no hand in creating the future toward which the developing person seeks to move. We are called rather to "sign on" to the other's plan or aspiration and to aid our partner in the accomplishment of his or her goals. This is all quite unlike our parenting support in which, however much we recognize the independence of our children, we also bear some responsibility for at least collaborating in the construction of the future, a future that must, to some extent, involve passage over terrain we as longer-lived parents have already traversed, however different the trip may be for our children.

At the same time, partnering support *does* involve the same challenge to our loyalties that we face as parents: are we more loyal to the person our partner or our child is and has become, or to the persons they *may* become in consequence of the ongoing process of growth and transformation? If the challenge is similar in nature, it may be even more difficult in fact when the person we are seeking to support is our partner. With our children, a powerful predisposition exists for us to recognize and even celebrate the idea that our children will grow and change, achieve hallmarks that proclaim such changes, and become people in some ways different from who they were. "When you are bigger," we say to our children, "you can, you might, you must, you should, you will." "When they are bigger," we say to ourselves about our children, "they can, they might, they must, they should, they will." As powerfully as this way of thinking operates on our minds, an opposite way of thinking operates for our view of adults, including those we marry or live with. We marry when we believe we are "grown up," and we marry persons we believe to *be* "grown up." Who would want to marry someone not "mature enough" to get married? We marry a person because we feel deeply drawn to that person as he or she is right now. We consider that it would be good to live a long time, even the rest of our lives, with that person. We do not think about our spouses in terms of "when he is bigger," yet the reality of psychological development in adulthood is that he may get "bigger." Supporting our children to achieve greater degrees of independence or a greater capacity to be a responsible, caring member of the family means helping them to leave behind what has largely come to be experienced as a confining dependence or an unrewarding self-involvement. Although we may have some mixed feelings about how our children are "growing up too quickly," these are mostly welcome leave-takings. Supporting our partner's development might be an altogether more complicated affair if we have come to rely upon, indeed, feel most at home with, the person as he or she is.

(5) Heading many lists and the goal of much professional work with, and advice to, couples is the expectation that we learn to communicate well. A host of subtasks are implicated in this general expectation, including that we speak to each other directly, not require of our partners the ability to read our minds, and learn to stand our ground and make

known our unhappy or critical feelings but in a way that is productive and does not induce our partner to become defensive or to counter attack. We are told that we must "convert complaint to request," "fight hard but fair," eschew "'You'-messages" in favor of "'I'-messages." We are told that, in sending our communications, we must not dump "our own stuff" in our partner's lap, and that, in receiving communications, we should learn, perhaps, to cross our legs.

(6) Let us conclude with an expectation deriving from the recognition that as adults we carry long histories with us into our present-day involvements, including our history of previous intimate relationships and family experience in our families of origin. Forming intimate partnerships in adulthood, especially those that create a new family, inevitably resurrects feelings from our first family, feelings about which we may be partially or completely unaware. An intimate relationship is like the original "field of dreams": "if you build one they will come." "They," as in the movie *Field of Dreams*, are the ghosts of our past, those restless figures from our earlier life still roaming our world because they have not been properly buried.

As adults, in our partnering relationships, we are called upon, by those who study what distinguishes successful from unsuccessful partnering, to have an awareness of the way our personal history inclines or directs us. This is an expectation that we understand the "stories," "scripts," "dramas," or "myths" we internalized when we were too young to think about such things but old enough to have such things be about the way we think. The idea here is that when we are not aware of these "stories" they continue to author us, and not merely our past but our present and future as well. When we are unaware of these "dramas" we may unknowingly cast our spouses into roles and act with them on the stage of our relationship according to a script they have no way of understanding. For a truly mind-boggling image of the typically reciprocal inability of each partner to meet this expectation, we could imagine a marriage in which the partners are sharing one stage, and each is casting the other in a role derived from a script neither the "caster" nor the "castee" knows they are enacting! The "myths" we are charged to be aware of so that we might have them rather than be had by them may involve the quite private and idiosyncratic "wisdom" peculiar to each person's family history or the more public and systemic myths shared by the bigger group (ethnic, religious, class) of which that family was a part. Myths might even be societally shared constructions cutting across these subgroups, such as the myth of male entitlement to hierarchic superiority that so permeates American culture. What underlies the metaphor of "story," "drama," or "myth" is the category of passionate assumptions taken as true, conveyed by the vehicle of plot line, script, or ethos, and held by the person without awareness that these "truths" are not *the* truth, but only *a* truth, collectively come to by the real but merely human people with whom one has lived. We are expected, as adults, to see through to the partial, or assumptive, nature of these "truths" lest we subject our partners to a dogma of which we are unaware we are orthodox adherents.

So now, just focusing on the roles of adult family life, we have identified a set of expectations or demands that exist at every level of culture, from the abstract prescriptions of the culture's expertise to the demands of a disappointed spouse at one o'clock in the morning.[8] To recap, it appears that in our roles as parent and partner we are expected to

1. Take charge of the family; establish rules and roles; institute a vision of family purpose.
2. Support the ongoing growth of the young, including their growth within and away from the family.
3. Manage boundaries (inside and outside the family).
4. Set limits on children and on oneself to preserve and protect childhood.
5. Be psychologically independent from, but closely connected to, our spouses.
6. Replace an idealized, romanticized approach to love and closeness with a new conception of love and closeness.
7. Set limits on children, in-laws, oneself, and extrafamily involvements to preserve the couple.
8. Support our partner's development.
9. Communicate well, directly, and fairly.
10. Have an awareness of the way our personal history inclines or directs us.

Now, what does it mean that we ask all this of ourselves? Anyone upon reading such a list could be daunted by its sheer size, but we do not approach anything like a realistic sense of what is being expected until we move from a quantitative to a qualitative consideration of the list. What *manner* of thing are these expectations? I ask, just as I asked in the first chapter of the list of expectations we hold for adolescents. There I suggested that the expectations appear to be claims for certain behaviors or *feelings* or *attitudes* that would generate the behaviors. But as I also suggested, just as the behaviors may be generated by feelings or attitudes, the feelings and attitudes are generated by the very way we understand the situations in which we find ourselves. And I suggested that the expectations are really expectations for us to *know* or *mean* a certain way, that they amount to claims on our minds.

What order of consciousness might actually be demanded of us in order to meet these expectations? What is the likelihood that our own consciousness will match well with this demand? I think the answers to both of these questions are fascinating, unexpected, disturbing, potentially liberating, and filled with implications for understanding why modern American life feels as it does.

Let us begin with the expectations of parenting. Consider the following:

Alice is a single parent of ten-year-old Ann and seven-year-old Jenny. Separated from their father for little more than a year, Alice is disturbed by a conversation she has had with Ann. In the midst of comfortably answering Ann's questions about the origin of babies, prompted by their seeing a pregnant woman at the supermarket, Alice is caught off-guard by Ann's question, "Have you had sex with anyone since Daddy left?" What concerns her is that although she *has* had sexual relations since her separation, she told her daughter that she had not. Why does this concern her? "I've been upset about it ever since it happened. I lied to my own daughter. I believe very strongly in being open and honest. I want my daughter to tell me the truth and here I am lying to her. I don't want to lie but I am worried that if I tell her the truth she will dislike me and turn away from me. I want my daughter to approve of me, and I worry about her reaction."

Meanwhile, Jenny, Ann's younger sister, is disturbed about something else. She is very close to her sister, but they are quite different. Ann is smart but disorganized and unpunctual, and always makes Jenny wait for her. Jenny, on the other hand, is a hard worker, very neat, and always tries to be on time. Every morning Ann and Jenny get ready to go to school together, eat breakfast together, and usually walk together to the bus. Jenny has no trouble getting up in the morning and is always ready when her mother puts breakfast on the table. Ann is exactly the opposite. She finds it difficult to get out of bed and arrives at breakfast late; she is barely ready to leave for school when Jenny is ready and waiting. The same problem arises almost every morning—Jenny is ready to go and Ann is still in the bathroom brushing her teeth or at the table gobbling down her breakfast. Jenny yells at Ann to hurry up. Ann yells to wait a minute, and Alice tells Jenny to go on and yells at Ann to hurry or she will miss the bus. Jenny has never left without Ann but usually ends up crying. Often they have to run to the bus and make the driver wait. If they miss the bus because Ann is late, Alice must drive both children to school.[9]

Finally, Ann has her own concern, which has to do neither with her mother's sex life nor her sister's frustration. Three Fridays each month Ann and her sister spend the weekend at her father's. Relations between her mother and her father have become quite strained, primarily around money. They have not yet come to a legal agreement, and the girls' father has been paying their mother a monthly amount for support that Alice feels is too little to meet their needs. Knowing how smart her older daughter is, that she has already picked up on the financial dispute, and that her estranged husband is far more sympathetic to the daughters' requests than his wife's, Alice has gradually moved from talking with Ann *about* the problem ("We can't buy that, Sweetie, because your Dad doesn't give us enough money") to inadvertently coaching her daughter as to how she might suggest to her father that they need more money. While Ann initially found it interesting to talk to her Mom about such grown-up things, she now feels very uncomfortable whenever her mother brings up the topic because she has found that her Dad does not like to talk about it, and she doesn't want to tell her mother, when she returns, that she's never told him anything about the money.

"Happy families are all alike," Tolstoy said, "but every unhappy family is unhappy in its own way." While it feels a bit presumptuous to disagree with Tolstoy, I do admit to wondering if there might not be a little more regularity to at least some forms of family unhappiness than he suspected. These vignettes do not depict a seriously disturbed family. Nothing is happening that would make the state intervene. If life in Alice's family is not exactly normal, it is certainly commonplace. But if the family is unexceptional, it is also unarguably unhappy, and, many would suggest, potentially unwholesome. Alice, Ann, and Jenny are running a series of risks that may or may not come to cost them dearly. Let us consider each of their unhappinesses in turn.

However admirable Alice's genuine upset at her violation of her own conviction about the importance of "openness and honesty" in family relations, is it possible that this value is insufficient as a guide when it comes to young children's requests for the intimate details of their parents' private life? In not being forthcoming with her daughter about her sex life, she feels guilty about keeping a secret from her. This sense she has of being in bad faith with Ann suggests she may not make a distinction between secrecy (in which one feels that the withholding of information is a violation of trust or an action of alienation from another) and privacy (in which one feels that the withholding of information is perfectly appropriate and even, at times, an act of solidarity with, or protection toward, another). Alice seems not to ask herself whether her ten-year-old daughter has any business knowing about her sex life. She considers that the most important reason not to tell her has to do with preserving her daughter's respect or approval of her, rather than preserving her daughter's freedom from the burdens of information she does not need.

But clearly Alice is not a thoughtless or unprincipled mother. She takes her ideals seriously and is plagued by her lie. She is genuinely perplexed at how she can remain loyal both to her ideal of honesty and to the image of acceptability she wants to maintain in her daughter's eyes. Alice's difficulty here could be talked about in terms of the behaviors she needs to enact, or skills she needs to learn, or attitudes she needs to acquire—any or all of which would help her with a problem like the one she encountered with Ann in the supermarket. But at bottom her problem may have to do with consciousness, specifically, with the mismatch between her own order of consciousness and that required to master the "parenting curriculum" she faces. In her ability to regulate her activity according to an ideal, and in the way her daughter's view of her figures in her own self-concept, she demonstrates the complex order of mind I call cross-categorical constructing. But her apparent captivity within this ideal as a guide to how she should feel and behave and her apparent captivity within the relationship with her daughter as the very context from which to feel or behave in matters concerning the relationship suggest that cross-categorical constructing may also be the limit of her current order of mind. What would be required for Alice herself to feel that she has no need to answer her daughter's request for such private information directly?

Rather than have her behavior regulated by and held to the standard of a value, ideal, or belief, she would have to be able to subordinate a perfectly respectable ideal (like "openness and honesty") to a bigger theory or ideology that can regulate the ideal. Why after all is it important to be open and honest? If it is because this is "just the way I was brought up myself," or "this is the value shared by the people I admire" or "with whom I feel bound" or "to whom I feel loyal," then one has no way to stand outside of the value without feeling in violation of one's fidelities. But if it is because the value reflects or derives from a deeper, internal set of convictions, then it is from the context of this set of convictions that I can regulate my activity, not the confines of this single value.

Alice might then be able to say to herself: "Hmmm. My daughter is asking me a perfectly sensible question, which it occurs to me I don't want to answer. I was enjoying this rather frank conversation my daughter and I were having about sex because I liked the fact she felt she could ask me about these personal things. I value frank conversation, open communication, and, for that matter, telling the truth, all of which I've been consistent with up until now. But now she has asked me about my own sex life and I'm becoming aware that some other values I wasn't even considering have been brought into play. Like what? Well, for one, I feel this is a time of great change and worry and loss for her, with her parents splitting up, and I don't want to bring more of all that into her life unnecessarily. I'm not sure what she thinks sex really means, but she knows this is something I shared with her daddy and for me to tell her that I'm sharing it with someone else, especially when I'm not seriously involved with anyone at the moment, could be very upsetting or get her fantasizing about a new daddy when none is on the scene." Or the "other values I wasn't even considering" might implicate a different angle of vision on the particulars, a vision concerned with not burdening one's children with information that may be too stimulating; or a vision dedicated to protecting the children's relationship with *each* parent from damage even when the relationship between the parents themselves is damaged; or a vision animated by the conviction that children do not always want the answer to the questions they ask.

But notice that these bigger "visions" are not just values. They are "values *about* values." They are systems by which we can choose among our values when they conflict. "Truthfulness" is a value, a generalization across concrete particulars, a cross-categorical structure, an expression of the third order of mind. "A child's right to a childhood" or "a parent's duty to protect that right" can amount to something significantly more than a generalization across concrete particulars. It may be more like a generalization across abstractions, across values, including the value "truthfulness" but also including a myriad of others.

The ability thus to subordinate, regulate, and indeed create (rather than be created by) our values and ideals—the ability to take values and ideals as the object rather than the subject of our knowing—must necessarily be an expression of a fourth order of consciousness, evinced here in the mental making of an ideology or explicit system of belief.

Let me suggest another way to put what would be required for Alice herself to feel that she has no need to answer her daughter's request for such private information directly. Rather than have her feeling and behavior in her relationship to Ann confined to the context of the relationship itself, Alice could stand somewhat *outside* the relationship, where she could make judgments about its demands without feeling that in doing so she had fundamentally violated the relationship itself. Were she able to do this, Alice might then be able to think to herself something like this: "Hmmm. Ann is framing this in terms of 'Have I had sex since the separation or have I not?' but I think the more appropriate frame is, 'Would this be information it would be helpful for her to have access to (or would it not)?' and that's the context in which I'm going to answer her." In reframing the question, Alice would no longer believe she had no answer to give. In the original frame Alice feels there is no answer she can give, at least none with which she feels comfortable, because she is not comfortable lying and she is not comfortable disclosing the truth. Viewed from the original frame, my suggestion to Alice that she could say neither that she has or has not had sex can only appear to her as no answer at all. Reframing the question, however, creates this response as an answer, an answer to a question from her young daughter Alice is willing to entertain. Viewed from the original frame, my suggestion can only appear as a rupture, a suspension, or an abandoning of her ongoing connection to her daughter, however temporary or small in scale. But with the question reframed, *whatever* Alice's decision about the usefulness of the information to her ten-year-old daughter, her response would issue from, rather than being an abandonment of, her relationship to her daughter. It is just that the "relationship to her daughter" would now have its origins in a mental context that is larger than her daughter's own expectations or claims upon her.

This larger context involves her own "relationship to the relationship," a context into which her daughter's claims can be placed and evaluated. Out of this context Alice might refuse to meet certain of her daughter's claims (including, by the way, some Ann holds far more dearly than a mere request for information: to sleep over at a friend's for a third straight night, to have her mother buy her a whole new wardrobe because her clothes don't have the right designer label, or to take the subway downtown by herself because she "is too" old enough), refusals that may inspire Ann's grief or wrath, refusals that may even cause her to claim that Alice *has* violated the bonds of the relationship. But the interesting and important thing to note is that neither Alice's refusal nor Ann's claim that Alice has breached the relationship will by themselves constitute an actual breach from Alice's new point of view. In sparing her daughter information she feels will only be a burden to her, Alice will feel not that she has turned *from* the relationship but that she has only strengthened it all the more.

In establishing this larger context in which the relationship would go on, in creating a *relationship to the relationship*, Alice would again be demonstrating a qualitatively more complex order of consciousness than cross-categorical knowing. She would be creating a mental structure that subtends, subordinates, acts upon, directs, and actually generates the meaning of her relationships. This mental structure, which gathers cross-categorical constructions into a complex or integrated system, I call the fourth order of mind. Its subject-object architecture and other features are depicted in Figure 3.1.

Alice's apparent inability at present to establish this larger context for her relationships to her ideals and to her daughter may be the source of her unhappiness in the first vignette about her lie to Ann. But this same inability may also be the source of her daughters' unhappiness in the other two vignettes. Indeed, the unhappiness of this and many "unhappy families" may have its origins in a source far more common and patterned than Tolstoy ever imagined.

Jenny's unhappiness has to do with the way her beloved sister, Ann, keeps making her late, or nearly late, for school, in spite of the fact that Jenny gets up early and is always ready. If she could do it, little Jenny would get up even earlier and do whatever Ann needed so that Ann would be ready on time, so much does she adore her big sister and so important is it to her to be on time. But Jenny cannot make her sister be more punctual and this is a constant source of agony to her. Whose problem is this? Nearly everyone I have talked to about this vignette (more than a thousand people by now) agrees that it is certainly not little Jenny's problem, that it is somehow Ann's problem, but that most of all it is their mother's problem; it is incumbent upon her, more than anyone else, to do something for Jenny's sake and for Ann's. All well and good. The mother must do something, but what? And that is where the agreement ends. Katherine Kaufmann posed the question "How would you handle this problem?" and asked mothers to jot down their answers.[10] Consider the difference between these two typical responses:

A.
I would stay in Ann's room to make sure she was awake. I would make sure the lights were on or that the curtains were open and perhaps turn a radio on to create some noise. After she was fully awake, I'd have her get dressed while I was still there. Tell her to then go downstairs and eat breakfast. Leave for school.

B.
I would not allow the situation to go on any longer—clearly, Ann must be made to deal with the consequences of her tardiness. I would insist that Jenny not wait for her sister, but rather urge her to go along to the bus by herself. If Ann can't manage to get to breakfast on time—no breakfast; if she misses the bus, she should walk to school. I know this sounds harsh, but I don't mean it as punishment. It sounds as if she has too long been allowed to make people wait for her. This is not good for her. Also, the burden seems to be on Jenny to urge Ann to hurry—and it really shouldn't be her dilemma. I'd want Jenny to know it's not her fault if Ann is late. Parental intervention is obviously needed here!

We don't have to vilify or enshrine either of these hurried, top-of-the-head responses to Kaufmann's question, but the contrast is an interesting one. Person A's solution would be well within Alice's current grasp, though it would seem to earn more points for selfless conscientiousness than successful family leadership. It's hard to find in Person A's solution a limit-setting, development-facilitating, boundary-managing, stand-taking, vision-embodying leader (unless we consider that the vision has to do with avoiding conflict and effecting change by moving with rather than against a person's natural direction; but even then the vision is more about the successful management of people's behavior than about leadership). In any case, Person B's response *seems* to be operating at a whole different level, or at least, Person B much more explicitly demonstrates the structure behind her solution. Person B does

	SUBJECT	OBJECT	UNDERLYING STRUCTURE	LINES OF DEVELOPMENT
				K COGNITIVE
				E INTERPERSONAL
				Y INTRAPERSONAL
1	PERCEPTIONS *Fantasy* **SOCIAL PERCEPTIONS** IMPULSES	Movement Sensation	Single Point/ Immediate/ Atomistic ● Durable Category	
2	CONCRETE *Actuality* Data, Cause-and-Effect **POINT OF VIEW** **Role-Concept** **Simple Reciprocity (tit-for-tat)** ENDURING DISPOSITIONS Needs, Preferences Self Concept	Perceptions Social Perceptions Impulses		
3	ABSTRACTIONS *Ideality* Inference, Generalization Hypothesis, Proposition Ideals, Values **MUTUALITY/INTERPERSONALISM** **Role Consciousness** **Mutual Reciprocity** INNER STATES Subjectivity, Self-Consciousness	Concrete Point of View Enduring Dispositions Needs, Preferences	Cross-Categorical Trans-Categorical	

SUBJECT	OBJECT	UNDERLYING STRUCTURE
ABSTRACT SYSTEMS *Ideology* Formulation, Authorization Relations between Abstractions	Abstractions	System/Complex
4 **INSTITUTION** **Relationship-Regulating Forms** **Multiple-Role Consciousness**	Mutuality Interpersonalism	
SELF-AUTHORSHIP Self-Regulation, Self-Formation Identity, Autonomy, Individuation	Inner States Subjectivity Self-Consciousness	

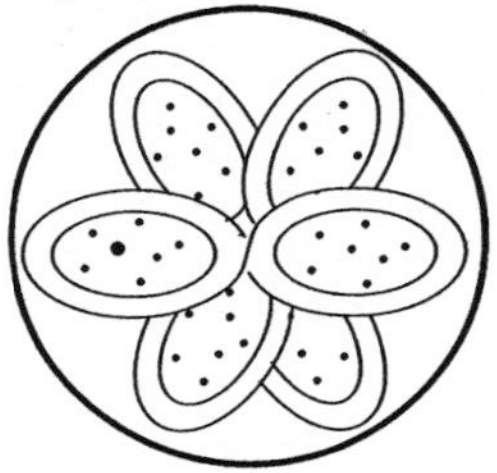

Figure 3.1 Four Orders of Consciousness

not just plunge us back into the relationship of Alice and Ann and give new guidance about how that relationship should go. Person B establishes a way of *relating the relationships*, holding onto Alice-Ann, Alice-Jenny, and Jenny-Ann simultaneously. Person B seems to have an overarching theory about how the family should run that defines the roles of each member, assigns various responsibilities to these roles, and identifies breaches of these assignments. It also sees that the leader's role involves an oversight function to correct the breaches. While Person A's Alice would be tremendously responsible (cajoling Ann through each step of her morning), she would not be responsible for Ann's responsibility. She would be truly heroic once in the role of helper but nonexistent in the superordinate activity of creating the roles in the first place or overseeing their operation.

Our self-conscious adherence to the responsibilities of our social roles and our identification with them are third order accomplishments. They betoken cross-categorical structures of mind. For Alice to intervene in little Jenny's unhappiness from the context implied by Person B's response, she would need to grasp not only the cross-categorical exercise of role but also the fourth order capacity to create and regulate role. Just as limit-setting *as an expression of one's relationship to one's relationships* requires fourth order consciousness, maintaining boundaries requires fourth order consciousness because it amounts to the continuous creating and recreating of roles rather than just the faithful adherence to the demands within them. If "role" is a third order construction, we can be responsible *to* our roles with third order consciousness. But we cannot be responsible *for* roles—for monitoring others' and our own responsibility to them—without a fourth order capacity to nest cross-categorical structures into a new organization of mind that subtends them.

If the lack of necessary controls in this family leaves little Jenny at risk of being a victim of Ann's tardiness, the last vignette shows that Ann herself is every bit as much a victim. In the second vignette it is clear that Alice needs to limit Ann's exploitation of Jenny *and* she needs to limit Jenny's willingness to "save" Ann by taking on her responsibilities. But in the third vignette, we see the leader's need to place limits on *herself*. Alice's inclination to bring her daughter, however subtly, into her dispute with her husband is understandable and reenacted countless times every weekend all over America. Her inability to curb her inclination places Ann's relationship to each of her parents in jeopardy.

But if at the moment Alice is organizing reality at the third order of consciousness it is important to see that her "inability to set limits" or "preserve boundaries" is not a failure of character but a matter, literally, of vision. That is, it may not be that she will not preserve boundaries but rather that she does not see a situation in which precious distinctions are being eroded. There is no reason whatever to believe that the same self-sacrificing conscientiousness and concern currently expended on behalf of preserving what she sees as precious would not be equally spent on preserving something *else* she sees as precious. "Setting limits" or "preserving boundaries" taught merely as "parenting skills," without addressing the way reality is being constructed, amounts to bringing new ideas to an old consciousness. The old consciousness will make the best use it can of the new ideas *on behalf of the old consciousness!*

In this case, the "old consciousness" is the third order of mind, and by itself it will not be enough to put the exercise of Alice's caring and concern back onto a wholesome track. That Alice *is* caring and concerned, even in making her older daughter a delegate in her conflictual communication with her husband, there can be no doubt. After all, her efforts to secure more financial support are not on behalf of indulging herself but in faithful exercise of her nurturing relationship to her two children. However admirable her devotion to this relationship, it is her inability to *have a relationship to this relationship*—and this would require the fourth order of mind—that makes her loving vulnerable to being unwittingly unwholesome. In the exercise of her loyalty to caring adequately for her daughter, she is unknowingly damaging her daughter's own bond with both her mother and her father.

How much of the psychological unhappiness parents visit upon their children is of this unwitting, devoted sort, deriving from precisely this sophisticated level of consciousness? Such a picture stands in sharp contrast to the possibly rarer, though more commonly conjured, image of the damaging parent as a nakedly self-interested exploiter, rendering his or her child a mere provider of supplies to the parent's needs, a circumstance arguably implicating the second order of consciousness, and requiring for the child a whole different sort of amelioration and protection. The troubled children Alice Miller writes about in *The Drama of the Gifted Child*[11] or the anorexics in Hilde Bruch's *The Golden Cage*[12] have parents these authors describe as loving, conscientious, and responsible. These are not the pictures of Dickensian exploitation—of the selfish use of children as conveniences or servants or personal resources by unsocialized parents who cannot form relationships of concern, trust, and responsibility. Miller and Bruch suggest pictures of parental misuse that are much more complicated. Though Miller is aware that she is breaking the "one taboo that has withstood all the recent efforts at demystification: the idealization of mother love,"[13] a careful reading of her work will show that however much she has come to be known as a "mother-basher," vilifying the psychological exploitation of children by their "narcissistically wounded" parents, the real question she is raising is not whether such parents love their children or are dedicated to them, but whether the particular form the love and dedication takes is unintentionally dangerous to the child. In describing the ways some parents make their children into providers of soothing supplies to their own internal psychological wounds, Miller is describing a kind of unwitting misuse that comes not from a failure to form relationships of trust, concern, and devotion but from the very context of such relationships.

Where Miller and I may part company is in her identification of the "mental mechanisms" that enable the emotionally exploitative parent to make use of his or her child. Miller speaks of the parents' childhood wounds, their own neglect at the hands of *their* parents, a surmised history that may very well be accurate. But then she attributes the present-day abuse by these adult parents to their currently existent unconscious "child selves," which make use of parental powers to win from their real, dependent child the kind of unfailing love and attention they themselves missed—and are still missing—as children. The mental culprit in Miller's reading, then, is an unconscious, wounded child-living-in-the-adult who, in the context of this unique opportunity to enslave another to his or her own needs, *breaks through* the competent, responsible, and sensitive adult part of the self and takes over the personality. This is the only way Miller can square her twin perceptions of such parents as emotionally exploitative and at the same time often intelligent, sensitive, and even empathic toward their children. She must create a picture of the parent as "two people."

A more parsimonious explanation, and one with quite different implications for treatment, is that the parent is not "two people" but one, and that it is actually the same admirable sophistication, acknowledged as the "adult part" of the self, that is operating in the adult's exploitative parenting. The history of a wounded childhood is reflected not in the independently coexisting "child self" but in the particular kind of third order consciousness this person is now organizing. What Miller considers the exploitative nature of the "child-self" within the parent might not represent any suspension of the "adult self" but may be completely syntonic with it and expressive of it. After all, the form of the parental exploitation is not childlike, and the parents themselves do not necessarily feel any conflict between the behaviors Miller would call exploitative and those she would consider appropriate. (These are not situations in which parents regret temporarily "losing it.") The problematic parenting Miller writes about seems to be less expressive of a childhood mentality and an oversized regard for one's own needs than of an undersized regard for one's own needs distinct from the claims of one's roles and relationships. Even Alice's injection of her daughter Ann into her dispute with her husband, which may seem a selfish abuse of her daughter's trust and loyalty, may reflect an undeviating devotion to her daughter's welfare and her own duty to adequately care and provide for her. It is the absence of a self that is independent of these duties and devotions, not the selfish neglect of them, which may permit their exercise to be at one moment in her children's best interests and at another moment not.[14]

Were she able to "have" these duties and devotions rather than "be" them, were they to shift from ground to figure, or from subject to object, in her consciousness, she would herself necessarily be something more than her conscientious exercise of her roles. Or rather, that same conscientiousness would be devoted to the very relationship between the roles that she had become. The wish to provide for her daughter more adequately, although still important to her, would become relative to a greater loyalty, such as that of not overburdening her daughter, or making her choose between her parents, or some such other expression of a consciousness that not only exercises relationships but regulates and even creates them.

The implication of such a suggestion about Alice—and about all of us who are or have been like Alice in our consciousness—is that even if our consciousness leaves us unable to handle many of the important functions of modern American parenting without support, we will never be well understood or well helped if we are seen as "unsuccessful" in the exercise of tasks that *require* a fourth order of consciousness precisely because we are not actually *engaged* in the tasks of fourth order consciousness! What Alice is doing in all these vignettes is not "failing at fourth order tasks" (setting limits, maintaining boundaries, creating and preserving roles, exercising executive leadership); what she is doing is attempting to succeed at third order tasks as she finds them in the exercise of her parenting.

Before we go much further in this exploration of the question "How adequate is third order consciousness in handling the demands of parenting and partnering?" it may be important to make explicit a companion question: "If, as now seems clear, third order consciousness may not be sufficient to meet the demands of modern parenting, does this mean that one is ill equipped to be a parent if one constructs the world according to the rules of third order consciousness?" It is important to see that the answer to this question has nothing to do with the order of consciousness of the parent and everything to do with the nature of the world in which that parent lives.

Taken by itself there is nothing wrong with bringing third order consciousness to the realm of parenting; that is, there is nothing one can say about the person for doing so. I would guess that the number of Americans with fourth order consciousness was considerably smaller one hundred years ago than it is today, but I am certainly not suggesting that parenting was less effective or successful one hundred years ago. The exercise of third order consciousness as a parent certainly does not by itself mean I am ill, crazy, developmentally delayed, or defective. It does not by itself mean I am ill equipped to be a parent, irresponsible, or necessarily less successful in my parenting than a person who exercises fourth order consciousness, nor am I necessarily a successful parent for constructing experience at the fourth order. All we can say for sure is that I will not only see the tasks and challenges of parenting *differently* if I construct the fourth order rather than the third, but I will see them more complexly. Whether this difference actually matters to my success with the parenting curriculum depends on how the culture is designed and where the culture expects fourth order constructing to come from. That is, the issue is never the student's capacity alone but the match or mismatch between the student's capacity and the tasks the student (rather than someone else) is supposed to perform.

Let me provide an extended analogy to clarify what I mean. The difference between the capacity to exercise third order consciousness and the capacity to exercise fourth order consciousness can be compared to the difference between the capacity to drive an automobile with an automatic transmission and the capacity to drive an automobile with a standard stick-shift transmission. Certainly one cannot by any stretch of the imagination be said to be a better person for being the driver of either an automatic or a stick-shift. And nothing can even be said, at least at first, about who is a better, safer, or more conscientious driver. At the same time, we cannot pretend that these capacities are merely noncomparable differences or nonrelatable expressions of human diversity (such as gender, learning style, or sexual orientation) that we would do best to recognize and respect, and that we are unable, nonarbitrarily, to compare. The fact is, there *is* a normative relation between the two drivers. One is better than the other in one quite circumstantial way: All stick-shift drivers can also drive automatic cars, but not all automatic drivers can necessarily drive stick-shift cars. Stick-shift drivers are not better people, they aren't even necessarily better drivers, but they can definitely drive certain kinds of cars that many automatic drivers cannot drive, and the opposite cannot be said. More precisely, stick-shift drivers are themselves able to take responsibility for an important feature in a car's operation—changing gear—over which drivers of automatics do not exercise responsibility. Drivers of automatics leave this operation to something external to them, namely, the engine, which has the ability to change gears automatically.

So what? Nothing necessarily. The fact that the driver of an automatic who is unable to shift the gears himself is dependent on some aspect of the bigger context in which he is operating to perform this action really doesn't matter at all so long as there are always plenty of automatic cars around and they work well. If there are always plenty of well-functioning automatic cars available, the difference between automatic and stick-shift drivers would not only not matter at all but the very distinction would probably disappear from view. We wouldn't notice it. People who have lived their whole lives in a state of unendingly available supplies of automatic cars just naturally feel that this is the way the world is, and they have no reason even to be aware of the fact that this is one of the features they assume to be true about the world. On the other hand, should the world *not* consist primarily of automatic cars, should the world be one in which, more and more, the very act of driving is assumed to consist of manually shifting the gears on one's own, *then* the characteristic of only being able to drive automatic cars, which before meant nothing, would be of extraordinary significance.

Finally, it should be clear that the difference between the two kinds of drivers is not that their cars perform differently. Both kinds of cars have to go through frequent gear changes. The difference is in who or what does the gear changing. Gear changing itself is a constant; it goes with the territory of operating a car.

So what is the point of this analogy? What I am suggesting is that certain key features of parenting—setting limits, creating roles, managing boundaries, regulating relationships, taking stands, facilitating development—may require fourth order consciousness and, at the same time, go with the territory of family operation just as gear-shifting goes with the territory of car operation. Does this mean that a parent must be able to perform at the level of fourth order consciousness in order to "operate" a family successfully? No, no more than it means that a driver must be able to shift gears in order to operate a car successfully. Does this mean that a parent who does organize reality with fourth order consciousness is necessarily a successful parent? No, no more than it means that a driver who can shift gears will always drive carefully. But what it does mean is that where cars and families are operating successfully, gears *are* being shifted and fourth order functions are being performed, somehow, by someone or something. It means that the one circumstance we'd want to avoid at all costs, put metaphorically, would be something like this: *parents who can only drive an automatic find themselves behind the wheel of a stick-shift car, and the car is loaded with children.*

How rare or how common is this worst-case possibility? This question is an extraordinarily important one, and it is not directed accusingly at the overwhelmed parent behind the wheel but rather at all of us, that we might consider together the adequacy of the supports our culture provides to meet the demands of the hidden curriculum. I will take up the answer to this question—how common it is that parents find themselves without either the internal or external equipment to perform crucial functions of parenting—more explicitly in a later chapter. But the answer is a profoundly alarming one, and it may be useful to prepare ourselves for it by considering for a moment what it really means to think about external support in a way that is quite different from how we usually conceive of it.

We usually conceive of support in terms of its quantity, the extensiveness of the network, its physical proximity, its consistency, and the intensity with which our sources of support care for us or we perceive that they do. What does it mean, then, to think of support in terms of "consciousness complexity," its borrowability as a way of ordering reality?

In her book *The Drama of the Gifted Child*, Miller asks a question that really amounts to wondering whether adults at the third order of consciousness must necessarily be at risk for unhappy or unsuccessful experiences. "Is it not possible," she asks, that such individuals "may live quite happily?" Here is her answer:

There are indeed such examples, and above all there were more in the past . . . Within a culture that was shielded from other value systems, such as that of orthodox Jewry in the ghetto, or of Negro families in the Southern states a hundred years ago, [such an] individual was not autonomous and did not have his own individual sense of identity (in our sense) that could have given him support; but he did feel supported by the group. The sense of being a "devout Jew" or a "loyal slave" gave individuals a measure of security in this world. Of course, there were some exceptions, people for whom that was not sufficient and who were strong enough to break away. Today it is hardly possible for any group to remain so isolated from others who have different values. Therefore it is necessary today for the individual to find his support within himself, if he is not to become the victim of various interests and ideologies. This strength within himself . . . thus becomes crucially important for him on the one hand, and on the other is made enormously more difficult through living in contact with various different value systems.[15]

Miller harkens to a different form of social organization she imagines was more prevalent in the past. In traditional cultures or subcultures there exists a more homogeneous fabric of value and belief, a shared sense of how the world works and how we should live in it. When we live in communities of mind as well as geography, the number of original decisions we have to make about how we conduct our lives is dramatically smaller. Whether such communities are literally religious in nature, they are all implicitly so, providing a common core of beliefs that are entered and reentered via a seamless fabric of ceremony, celebration, ritual, gesture, and symbol. Whether bound by explicitly religious loyalties or ethnic, regional, or civic ones, such communities are distinguished by a kind of homogeneity that makes the notion of "role model" pandemic. Everyone older is a role model, and the elders are unrecognizedly inspiring in that young men or young women, without even being aware they are doing it, "breathe in" the way they are to conduct themselves today and tomorrow through their inescapable association with and fealty toward those who are a generation ahead of them.

Anyone who has ever been part of such fundamentalism, and I count myself among them, knows that ultimately it is the community's collective consciousness itself that is the source of order, direction, vision, role-creation, limit-setting, boundary-management, and developmental facilitation. The very expression of its vitality and integrity is the community's capacity to regulate its parts like a single living organism, to warn those constituents who are in danger of transgressing its limits and boundaries and to rescue those who step over the line. This is the real meaning of the "ortho" in "orthodox"; it refers not to rigidity or dogmatism but to the action of correcting or straightening (like "orthodontia"). The vision or overarching theory or ideology that directs life is provided via a corporate canon or creed that exists not in some lifeless text or impotent shrine but in the body of practice, sanction, and prohibition coursing through daily life. However unique the content, style, or mood of each community's creed, what they all share at the formal epistemological level is the delivery of a fourth order consciousness that creates and regulates the relations, roles, and values with which most of the adults in the community become identified and to which they are loyal. For many, and even most, this may be the source of fourth order consciousness. It does not *and need not* come from their own minds, nor from their autonomous, "manual" shifting of the gears. It comes from their mental and spiritual participation in the common weal, the body politic, the collective direction, which in its automatic action provides for them (who have no reason even to be aware that this plentiful and continuous supply is an assumed feature of how the world works) a definite sense of their place, their time, and their song in the universe.

The Traditional Community represents one way in which the third order consciousness of individuals can be supported to resolve the fourth order tasks of adult life, such as those intrinsic to parenting. This continuous, uninterrupted provision of fourth order support in the Traditional Community is ordinarily less a matter of other people actually *telling* us how to set limits or preserve boundaries than of observable figures on the ground of our living (although such persons, to whom we are bound and loyal, would certainly be available). More often, such "information" communicates itself in the very fabric or ground of living. We see how we are supposed to handle this or that situation, and how we are "supposed to" is how we suppose we should as well. Handling this or that situation in the supposed ways is not merely the solving of this or that problem but the very expression of our atonement or in-tune-ment with our community.

I mean neither to celebrate nor to disparage the arrangements of the Traditional Community past or present. From a posttraditional perspective, any of us might condescend to such a picture in tribute to what we imagine to be our greater mental freedom, or we might longingly admire the spiritual rootedness of such a picture in dismay at our present-day drift and disunity. But whatever our feelings about the actual Traditional Community, and however much or little such actual traditional communities may still exist in pockets of contemporary culture, it is not the context in which most present-day Americans find themselves. Although it may constitute *one* form of "borrowable mind" to support third order consciousness in the regulation of fourth order tasks, the essence of today's pluralistic, privatistic, individualistic, and secular modernity is to fragment the mental monolith of Tradition.

As a result, when we, as contemporary adults, order reality according to third order consciousness, we do not find ourselves suspended in a communal medium that holds and nourishes us. Rather, though we do not know it, we are like fish out of water who must move *toward* something that will suspend us since we have not been born into and taken up by that which suspends us. The modern world is heterogeneous. The communities of mind to which we are welcomed are multiform and they contest each other. The external provision of fourth order direction is not automatic, uninterrupted, or seamless.

Although we may never think of ourselves as premodern or traditional people, if we construct reality out of the third order, in terms of our consciousness we are actually traditional people living in a modern world. The claim of modernity is the call to fourth order consciousness, heard in each demand or expectation for successful parenting or partnering and echoed in Alice Miller's words: "It is necessary today for the individual to find his support within himself." We must shift the gears ourselves, she is saying, and not be looking for cars with automatic transmissions.

What such a directive means to third order consciousness might be quite different from what it means to fourth order consciousness. "A fish out of water" evokes the image of a desperate, expiring creature cut off from what it needs to survive. But "a fish out of water" is also the story of the evolution of our species. For a land-living creature that has evolved from a seaborne one, Miller's directive may make sense. But most fish out of water are not looking for a way to evolve into a creature that can live on land. They are looking for another pond to jump into.

Support to third order consciousness in a *modern* world may be of these two exact sorts: those that provide a new pond to jump into and those that facilitate the evolution from life in the water.

I will take up the subject of support as *support to our consciousness* more explicitly later, but I wanted to foreshadow it because as we considered the nature of parental expectations—to lead the family, create roles, set limits, preserve boundaries—it was becoming clear that the answer to the question "Is third order consciousness adequate to meet the demands of parenting?" might be No, and this could seem to be saying that a parent who orders the world according to third order consciousness cannot succeed at parenting. But the second idea does not follow so simply from the first. The implication is that in his or her parenting, an adult with third order consciousness will need access to support that provides fourth order consciousness. "How widespread is this need?" and "What is the nature of the available responses?" are issues to which we will eventually turn. How important these issues are, however, depends on whether what we have concluded about parenting is true for the claims implicit in other realms of contemporary adult life.

4

Partnering: Love and Consciousness

In our consideration of parenting we picked up a piece of the Big Question, "Is third order consciousness a good match with the demands of adult life?" And we found that, for the realm of parenting, third order consciousness is *not* by itself sufficient given the expectations of contemporary culture. Now I want to consider this question in another context: "Is third order consciousness adequate to meet the demands of *partnering?*"

As I said in Chapter 3, in our roles as intimate partners we are called upon to (1) be psychologically independent of, but closely connected to, our spouses; (2) replace an idealized, romanticized approach to love and closeness with a new conception of love and closeness; (3) set limits on children, in-laws, ourselves, and extrafamilial involvements to preserve the couple; (4) support our partner's development; (5) communicate directly and fairly; and (6) have an awareness of the way our personal histories incline or direct us. How adequate is third order consciousness to meet these demands?

Consider this most famous interchange between spouses as conceived by the nineteenth-century dramatist Henrik Ibsen at the conclusion of *A Doll's House:*

> *Nora:* I mean, then I passed from Papa's hands into yours. You arranged everything the way you wanted it, so that I simply took over your taste in everything—pretended I did—I don't really know. I think it was a little of both—first one and then the other. Now I look back on it,

it's as if I've been living here like a pauper, from hand to mouth. I performed tricks for you, and you gave me food and drink. But that was how you wanted it. You and Papa have done me a great wrong. It's your fault that I have done nothing with my life.

Torvald: Nora, how can you be so unreasonable and ungrateful? Haven't you been happy here?

Nora: No; never. I used to think I was; but I haven't ever been happy.

Torvald: Not—not happy?

Nora: No. I've just had fun. You've always been very kind to me. But our home has never been anything but a playroom. I've been your doll-wife just as I used to be Papa's doll-child. And the children have been *my* dolls. I used to think it was fun when you came in and played with me, just as they think it's fun when I go in and play games with them. That's all our marriage has been, Torvald.

Torvald: There may be a little truth in what you say, though you exaggerate and romanticize. But from now on it'll be different. Playtime is over. Now the time has come for education.

Nora: Whose education? Mine or the children's?

Torvald: Both yours and the children's, my dearest Nora.

Nora: Oh, Torvald, you're not the man to educate me into being the right wife for you.

Torvald: How can you say that?

Nora: And what about me? Am I fit to educate the children?

Torvald: Nora!

Nora: Didn't you say yourself a few minutes ago that you dare not leave them in my charge?

Torvald: In a moment of excitement. Surely you don't think I meant it seriously?

Nora: Yes. You were perfectly right. I'm not fitted to educate them. There's something else I must do first. I must educate myself. And you can't help me with that. It's something I must do by myself. That's why I'm leaving you.

Torvald: [Jumps up] What did you say?

Nora: I must stand on my own feet if I am to find out the truth about myself and about life. So I can't go on living here with you any longer.

Torvald: Nora, Nora!

Nora: I'm leaving you now, at once. Christine will put me up for tonight—

Torvald: You're out of your mind! You can't do this! I forbid you!

Nora: It's no use your trying to forbid me any more. I shall take with me nothing but what is mine. I don't want anything from you, now or ever.

Torvald: What kind of madness is this?

Nora: Tomorrow I shall go home—I mean, to where I was born. It'll be easiest for me to find some kind of a job there.

Torvald: But you're blind! You've no experience of the world—

Nora: I must try to get some, Torvald.

Torvald: But to leave your home, your husband, your children! Have you thought what people will say?

Nora: I can't help that. I only know that I must do this.

Torvald: But this is monstrous! Can you neglect your most sacred duties?

Nora: What do you call my most sacred duties?

Torvald: Do I have to tell you? Your duties towards your husband, and your children.

Nora: I have another duty which is equally sacred.

Torvald: You have not. What on earth could that be?

Nora: My duty towards myself.

Torvald: First and foremost you are a wife and a mother.

Nora: I don't believe that any longer. I believe that I am first and foremost a human being, like you—or anyway, that I must try to become one. I know most people think as you do, Torvald, and I know there's something of the sort to be found in books. But I'm no longer prepared to accept what people say and what's written in books. I must think things out for myself, and try to find my own answer.

Torvald: Do you need to ask where your duty lies in your home? Haven't you an infallible guide in such matters—your religion?

Nora: Oh, Torvald, I don't really know what religion means.

Torvald: What are you saying?

Nora: I only know what Pastor Hansen told me when I went to confirmation. He explained that religion meant this and that. When I get away from all this and can think things out on my own, that's one of the questions I want to look into. I want to find out whether what Pastor Hansen said was right—or anyway, whether it is right for me.

Torvald: But it's unheard of for so young a woman to behave like this! If religion cannot guide you, let me at least appeal to your conscience. I presume you have some moral feelings left? Or—perhaps you haven't? Well, answer me.

Nora: Oh, Torvald, that isn't an easy question to answer. I simply don't know. I don't know where I am in these matters. I only know that these things mean something quite different to me from what they do to you.[1]

Clearly Nora's passionate and troubled words are a declaration of independence, if not within the marriage then without it. But it is important to consider what sort of independence they bespeak. When we are told that successful modern marriages and intimate partnerships require that each person be able to achieve "psychological independence" (without having to leave the relationship to find it, as Nora does) what does this really mean? What does it mean for each partner to have a "well-differentiated and clearly defined sense of self," for neither to see the other as an "organizer of the self"?

"Psychological independence" usually translates to "having a mind of one's own," but it is important to see that Nora is not simply saying that other people's ideas are no longer acceptable to her. She is not merely warming to some new ideas she likes better and making herself independent of the old ones held by others. And she is saying more than that she must have her own ideas instead of accepting what other people think. All these things could be taken as forms of "psychological independence." But Nora is not just coming to some different ideas of her own. She is coming to a new set of ideas *about* her ideas, about where ideas even come from, about who authorizes them, or makes them true. She is making a bid for independence not merely from someone else's ideas but from *anyone* else's ideas from a source external to her that can create and validate her ideas. Her discovery is not just that she herself has different ideas, but that she has been uncritically, unawarely identified with external sources of ideas (her husband, her church, and her culture). To be uncritically, unawarely identified with these external sources is to be *unable* to question or weigh the validity of these ideas; it is to take them as The Truth. Nora is not just rejecting the assumptions of her husband or church or culture; she is rejecting her *relationship* to these assumptions as Truths. Her discovery is not that she has different ideas, values, or beliefs, but that ideas, values, and beliefs are by their very nature assumptive.

In fact, Nora's declaration of independence does not necessarily involve championing differing or competing values and beliefs. Conceivably, she is really saying, she herself could come to the same beliefs as those held by her husband or her pastor ("I don't know where I am in these matters"). What she is separating herself from is not so much these beliefs and values as her previous stance *toward* these beliefs and values, a stance of being uncritically made up by them. The "psychologically independent" self emerging in Nora is not, then, just a "stronger" or "more confident" version of her former "psychologically dependent" self. It is not the same self now listening to its own drummer rather than stepping to the beat of another. This is a *wholly different way of constituting what the self is, how it works, what it is most about.* This is a self that has gone from being identified with and made up by the trans-categorical structures of belief, value, and role to relativizing these structures, being aware of a *stance toward* or a *relationship to* these structures, that is, of having them *as object* rather than being them *as subject.* The same conscientiousness Nora demonstrated as a "doll" in her loyalty to these values and in her fulfillment of her duties as mother and wife she now expresses through a new structure. In fact, she has not yet actually consolidated this new structure, has not yet integrated the cross-categorical structures into a coherent complex or system, because as she says, she does not yet know what she believes and needs to educate herself. But she does know she has become someone who will be the "looker at" her values, beliefs, roles, and duties. Although she now self-consciously identifies a duty "towards myself," she was, in truth, no less dutiful toward herself when she was a "doll-wife"; it is simply that *that* self was a differently constituted one. It is not merely that the "vector of loyalty" has swung from the other to the self, as if who the "other" and the "self" were remains unchanged. Nora is in the process of reconstructing the very principles by which other and self are constituted. Her declaration of independence is an expression of the evolution of consciousness from the third order to the fourth order.

And we might also note that, despite the socially constructed superiority of Torvald's position as husband and quasi-lord, despite his role as the keeper of the dolls, the one who condescends to play with her, the one whose "taste in everything [she] simply took over," in making the epistemological move Nora seems to be making she may actually be outstripping the consciousness of her husband rather than catching up to it. For, odd as it might have sounded to Torvald—and to his compatriots and peers in that culture at that time—it appears that he has no more "psychological independence" than did Nora when she was a doll! Torvald not only seems to be upset with his wife and in conflict with what she proposes, he also seems genuinely baffled. He doesn't get it. He tells her she must have lost her mind. His first reaction to her words focuses on the way her actions will look to others ("to leave your home, your husband, your children—have you thought what people will say?"). More tellingly, he reveals where he bases his validation of his own position when it is challenged by Nora: "Do you need to ask where your duty lies in your own home? Haven't you an infallible guide in such matters—your religion?"

An infallible guide outside ourselves, in which we comfortably invest authority and to which authority we pledge loyalty, fidelity, and faith—this is the essence of psychological *de*pendence. It is the essence of the premodern Traditional state of mind, and it is the essence of third order consciousness. However socially sanctioned the superiority of Torvald's role, the Traditional state of mind can only seem, once one has left it, innocent or naive. As Nora says, "Oh, Torvald, you are not the man to educate me." It may be more Torvald's *lack* of "psychological independence" than Nora's need to achieve it that makes her feel it is impossible to continue in the marriage. What Nora has broken is more than the marital vow; she has broken the spell of their mutual embeddedness in the third order. Their famous dialogue at the turn of the century is really a consciousness conversation at cross-purposes, the mind of Tradition speaking with the emerging mind of Modernity.

Is this because the turn of the century was itself a period of transition from Traditionalism to Modernity? Or is it possible, as we approach the turn of the *next* century, that such cross-conversations between Traditionalism and Modernity continue to this very day—even into the wee hours of this day, in the bedroom of Lynn and Peter?

Lynn will tell you that when she and Peter first married she was amazed at how similar they were, amazed and pleased. They had identical senses of humor, liked and detested the same politicians and movies (and for the same reasons), agreed that ketchup belonged inside the refrigerator and mustard in the cupboard. They each felt so comfortable with the other's family that when they married, the usual clichés at a wedding about being welcomed into another family seemed odd to them, referring to something that had happened long ago. That they could complete each other's sentences, start a topic the other was just about to bring up, communicate complicated thoughts in a few code words—these were the rich folds in a thick comforter Lynn would wrap around herself.

What would be harder for Lynn to determine exactly is when all this began to change. But one of the things she feels certain now makes her married life difficult is her unwelcome preoccupation with how different she and Peter are. Although she would like to hold onto the idea that she and Peter "are really one soul"—Peter's expression, and an idea she knows is still dear to him—more and more she is struck with the realization that she and Peter approach life very differently. "He's much looser with the kids; I'm a lot stricter. I like a big old house with more rooms than you know what to do with; he wants to move to something 'cozier.' I like to eat out once in a while in a fancy restaurant or bring home an extravagant bottle of wine; he says fancy restaurants are pretentious and is kind of proud about the fact that he can't tell the difference between chablis and montrachet. He likes to exercise at the end of the day in order to get refreshed; I like to take a nap. And on and on and on. Little things, big things, stupid things."

But what concerns Lynn are not so much the differences as the feelings she has about them: "On my best days I tell myself that there is nothing better about my choices and preferences, that Peter's way makes as much sense as mine. But most days are not my best days and I surprise myself sometimes with the size of my antipathy. I'm just furious with him, and it's really so unfair. What makes things worse is that I think he's more hurt on my *best* days than when I'm being critical! When I'm feeling accepting or, on occasion, even appreciative of our differences I think he's more bothered by it than when I'm carping at him! I'm priding myself on my bigness of mind by accepting that his way of doing things also makes sense, and he's getting more and more upset that I'm not fighting to regain our state of being 'one soul.' He thinks what I'm accepting is the inevitability of our drifting apart, that we will stop being so close, even stop loving each other. He looks at my acceptance as resignation! This is when I really get frustrated. Or, if I don't feel frustrated, I just start to feel really lonely in the relationship, because I have to keep a kind of secret life. I don't tell him how I feel about this or that because I know he'll take it as a sign we're not as close. And then I think, 'Well, he's right. We *are* getting less close and I *am* drifting away.' But it's so complicated. I mean, we're drifting apart, but *not* because we have differences, but because he won't *accept* that we have differences. Do you see what I mean?"

The differences dividing Lynn and Peter are not their different values, preferences, and beliefs, however long a list of such differences Lynn can generate. Although they do differ in their (cross-categorical) values, this is not really what makes Lynn feel she occupies a separate psychological world. The implication of her hard-working words is that they could continue to hold such differences and still be very "close," and that their current lack of closeness has less to do with these differing values than with their differing view of difference itself. Peter sees the route to their regained closeness in the *dissolution* of their differences, a possibility he gleans in the arguments Lynn initiates and which he prefers to what he sees as her stubbornness or resignation in beginning with the premise that each of them is entitled to their differing views. On her best days, as she puts it, Lynn has a different conception not only of difference but of closeness. The more this conception comes to feel to Lynn as if this is who she is, the less close she is going to feel to Peter, who is unable to grasp it, since this new definition of closeness, as less about the sharing of particular values and more the cooperation of independent value-generators, betokens a whole new construction of the self, a fourth order construction.

Interpersonal intimacy, as we all know, is about closeness, about the self being near to another self. The variable we usually pay most attention to here is the nearness, the varying distances between the selves. But what is often overlooked, although it is crucial to this definition, is the hidden variable of how "the self" is constructed in the first place, for this sets the terms on what it is one is getting "near to." If the self is subject to its third order constructions so that it *is* them, then the sharing of values and ideals and beliefs will in itself amount to the sharing of the self. But if the self relativizes its third order constructions so that it no longer *is* its third order constructions but *has* them, then the sharing of values and ideals and beliefs will not by itself be experienced as the ultimate intimacy of the sharing of selves, of who we *are*, nor will the *non*sharing of our values and ideals and beliefs necessarily be experienced as an ultimate rending of our intimacy. Peter definitely experiences his relationship to Lynn this way. But more and more Lynn is coming to experience closeness and its breach in a qualitatively different way. Though it is unlikely she would ever put it like this, she longs for a closeness with Peter that is based not on shared values but on their recognition of each other as persons who hold, create, and regulate values. That is who Lynn is coming to be, and unless she can feel someone "near to" that, she will not feel intimately connected. Peter regards Lynn's acceptance of their differences as an abandonment of intimacy; Lynn is coming to regard it as a necessary step toward intimacy. This is another consciousness conversation at cross-purposes, the mind of Tradition crossing the mind of Modernity in late twentieth-century America.

Peter and Lynn's predicament notwithstanding, late twentieth-century America is also reconsidering and reconstructing traditional sex roles. In the context of a history of status differences culturally ascribed to the men and women in intimate relationships, the demands upon each of us to have a distinct psychological identity, not to be psychologically defined by our partner, and the like, may be especially complicated for women or especially threatening to men, whose cultures (and often, whose mothers) have been teaching a different curriculum. At the same time, it should be clear that these demands are not, first of all, demands for particular behaviors. Behaviors that "look" independent may not be, and those that appear to be in the thrall of traditional definitions of female subservience or compliance may actually issue from personal self-definition. Mary Stewart Hammond's poem, "Making Breakfast,"[2] expresses these complications, but it also makes clear how apparently traditional behaviors (and nurturant loving) may nonetheless reflect a modern consciousness of personal authority:

> There's this ritual, like a charm, Southern women
> do after their men make love to them in the
> morning. We rush to the kitchen. As if
> possessed. Make one of those big breakfasts from
> the old days. To say thank you. When we know we
> shouldn't. Understanding the act smacks of Massa,
> looks shuffly as all getout, adds to his belly,
> which is bad for his back, and will probably give
> him cancer, cardiac arrest, and a stroke. So, you
> do have to wonder these days as you get out the
> fatback, knead the dough, adjust the flame for a
> slow boil, flick water on the cast-iron skillet to
> check if it's ready and the kitchen gets steamy
> and close and smelling to high heaven, if this
> isn't an act of aggressive hostility and/or a
> symptom of regressed tractability. Although on
> the days we don't I am careful about broiling his
> meats instead of deep-fat frying them for a couple
> of hours, dipped in flour, serving them smothered
> in cream gravy made from the drippings, and, in
> fact, I won't even do that anymore period, no
> matter what he does to deserve it, and, besides,
> we are going on eighteen years, so it's not as if
> we eat breakfast as often as we used to, and when

we do I now should serve him oatmeal after? But
if this drive harkens to days when death, like
woolly mammoths and Visigoth hordes and rebellious
kinsmen, waited outside us, then it's healthy, if
primitive, to cook Southern. Consider it an extra
precaution. I look at his face, that weak-kneed,
that buffalo-eyed, Samson-after-his-haircut face,
all of him burnished with grits and sausage and
fried apples and biscuits and my power, and adrift
outside himself, and the sight makes me feel all
over again like what I thank him for except
bigger, slower, lasting, as if, hog-tied, the hunk
of him were risen with the splotchy butterfly on
my chest, which, contrary to medical opinion, does
not fade but lifts off into the atmosphere,
coupling, going on ahead.

If it is clear that the demands upon us to achieve "psychological independence" and overcome a "romantic approach to closeness" in our marriages really amount to yet another kind of fourth order claim, it should come as no surprise that the same is true of the requirement to set limits on behalf of preserving our couplehood. We have already seen that the complications of limit-setting place a fourth order burden upon us as parents. The nature of what is required epistemologically when it is the couple we are standing for rather than our children cannot be different. Our parents, our partners, our children, our friends, our co-workers, our employers—all of these familiars can make moves, choices, or demands, which, usually unwittingly, do pose a threat to the continued authority, integrity, or vitality of our couplehood. It is commonplace in psychological writing to see these persons, however much we care for them or know they care for us, as at times dangers or threats to the couple. But in fact, my parents, children, friends, and colleagues are not a threat to my marriage. It is my construction of my relationships to these people, the loyalties I feel to these connections, that is the source of possible threat. The people are not the threat, nor is it even really *these* people upon whom I must set limits. Rather, it is my own loyalties to them, to the relationships I value with them, upon which I must set limits. As such, the epistemological demand in limit-setting compels me to stand *in relationship to* these bonds and loyalties, to be myself "bigger" than they are so that if I need to I can act *upon* them. By now it should be clear that this is a demand to relativize cross-categorical structures of knowing and hence at least a fourth order claim.

We need only return to the one A.M. argument of Peter and Lynn at the beginning of Chapter 3. "I can't believe you just went ahead and asked them without talking to me about it first," an exasperated Lynn says about her husband's invitation to his parents to join the two of them on their "second honeymoon" vacation. "We spent months working out a plan for us to have some time without the kids and you go and invite your parents." Later she says to him, "And that's what upsets me the most, Peter, how quickly our plan vanishes if your parents—or the kids, it could be the kids, too!—if any of them says 'Boo!' You asked your parents because you couldn't help it."

What is it that Lynn is really asking of Peter and what order of consciousness would he need in order to fulfill it? From her point of view there are any number of possible takes on Peter. Perhaps he just lacks strength of purpose and is too easily manipulated by people who have a stronger will. Or maybe he knows quite clearly what he wants and intends but lacks the courage to stand up to those he would have to oppose. Or maybe he has plenty of courage and plenty of will but his problem is that he loves too much and that the reach of his big heart exceeds the grasp of his finite capacity to make everyone happy. Peter's own inner experience seems closest to this last. A feeling creeps over him so familiar he has given it a name: "The Bad Feeling, that impossible feeling of having to 'be' in several places all at the same time, that feeling of being ripped apart, or being pulled in different directions, the feeling of wanting everyone you love to be happy, of even feeling you could *make* them all happy—if only they would cooperate and somehow didn't need it all at once."

What all these takes on Peter have in common, however, is that, like the characters in *The Wizard of Oz*, Peter *lacks* something. If only he had more courage, more strength of purpose, or a bigger heart, then Lynn would feel not only that her husband could make a plan for them to have some time for themselves and be committed to it, but that she could count on him to withstand the threats to it that come in the form of her husband's parents or their children—or better put, that come in the form of his love for them. If these were really the most promising routes to Lynn's feeling about Peter, then it would make sense for him to follow the yellow brick road to one of the many available contemporary wizards who could "train" him in "assertiveness," help him get over his "addiction" to "people pleasing," or take him out into the woods to drum up a reconnection with the lost strength of his natural masculinity.

I would prefer, however, to conclude that there is nothing wrong with how much Peter loves, and that he is as courageous and has as much strength of purpose as anyone might hope to have. Nor would I suggest that he is closer to the scarecrow and so in need of a bigger brain. Peter is as smart as you would expect any advanced-degree-holding professional to be. His intelligence, his love, his courage, and his will may all be operating "to the max," but they can only operate in the world as he sees it, as he *constructs* it. And the way he constructs it may no longer be a good match with the unrecognized demands that are implicit in what Lynn now needs in order to feel wholly close to him, to feel that she herself can be seen and held *by him* as she is coming to see and hold herself. This is surely not "Peter's fault," for there is nothing in itself "wrong" with how he constructs the world. The problem emerges in the context of a relationship, including the relationship between the demands we unwittingly make on each other's minds and our capacity to meet these mental demands.

If Peter is subject to cross-categorical structures of knowing, then the world he sees will be different from the one Lynn sees, which seems well along in the subordination of such structures to a system that authorizes and regulates them. Lynn makes it clear that she loves their children as much as Peter does. This is not even a story about the dreaded in-laws, for she says that she also loves Peter's parents. Lynn does not love any less than Peter, but the exercise of her loving is not founded upon her identification with her connections to those she loves. She could sympathize deeply with whatever disappointment her in-laws or her children might feel because she is placing limits upon them, but she would not necessarily feel unloving for doing so. She would not feel guilty or only guilty for doing so. She would not feel she had damaged herself in some way for doing so. But Peter feels all these things as the agent of such disappointment, and anyone who wants to measure his courage had first better consider the constraints under which he is operating in putting the world together in this way.

What Lynn is really asking of Peter, to answer the earlier question—though she has no more idea of it than she and Peter had of what they were really asking of Matty, their adolescent son—is an order of consciousness over his head.

The popular wisdom about what constitutes good rules for communication in marriage has undergone a quantum leap in just two generations. Both my parents and my in-laws have been married for fifty years, but when I ask them if they were aware of and followed any rules for good communication in their relationship, my in-laws say, "In our day we didn't *have* 'relationships.' Your generation spends a lot more time *thinking* about all this"; and my parents say, "One rule we always tried to follow was, 'Never go to bed angry.' If you had to stay up until two in the morning to talk it out you did." Peter and Lynn might be interested in this rule, although they might ask, "What do you do when you've been talking it out until two in the morning and you haven't gotten any less mad?"

Today we have further advice from a host of authorities and experts (most of whom have probably not stayed married to the same person for half a century), which addresses a question like this one, recognizing that what is important is not just *that* people talk through their conflicts but *how* they do. After a period of celebrating the importance of "getting mad" and "fighting it out," we now realize that not all fighting is necessarily wholesome and distinguish between dysfunctional and productive fighting. In a similar way, we have perhaps transcended the stereotypical idea that women do most of the "real" communicating in a marriage and that men primarily avoid and truncate efforts at communication. Books such as those by Deborah Tannen and Lillian Rubin[3] implicitly or explicitly make the point that although men and women may have different styles, what each is doing constitutes "real" communication. But what we have not done, and have yet to do, is to evaluate the order of complexity unwittingly built into modern expectations for how couples might enhance their communication, especially conflictual communication.

Let us consider one of the most commonly promulgated principles of good communication, which is taught to couples every day in workshops and counselors' offices throughout America: "Make 'I' statements, not 'you' statements." When you come upon your husband's dirty laundry strewn on the floor for the third time in a week, the experts advise you *not* to say, "You are such a slob! Can't you throw your dirty clothes in the hamper?" Instead you might say, "I don't like it when you repeatedly leave your dirty clothes all over the house," or, "I feel disrespected by the way you leave your dirty laundry all over for me to pick up, because I'm left feeling that you think I'm your maid or something."

What is the idea here? Well, if I make "I" statements the communication is about *myself* not about the *other person*, and there is less chance the other person will become defensive and respond unproductively. When I make "I" statements I am reporting on my feelings or experience, not making demands upon the other. I am not blaming the other for anything, not even how I am feeling. I do not say, "You *make* me feel such and such a way." I say essentially that "in consequence of what you do, I am feeling, or *cause myself* to feel, such and such a way." I am not holding the other responsible for anything. On the contrary, I am hoping the other will feel unpulled-upon, undemanded-of, and completely free to respond as he or she so chooses. Of course, I am also hoping that the other has sufficient regard for me or for our relationship that the report of my unhappiness will be taken seriously and that the other will give my experiences due consideration in his or her future choices. The point is that the laundry-leaving husband is now free to respond however he wishes; he is not bound to follow his wife's order or defend himself from the negative attribution she has made about his character. All well and good, and some people find such advice very useful. But as anyone who has ever worked along these lines with couples knows, some people do *not* find such advice helpful even if they are able to perform the specified behaviors! Why not?

What if such advice, without anyone's recognizing it, presumes something about how the sender and the receiver of such communication understand the communication? What if such advice has certain *kinds* of mind in mind?

Consider the following: Communication of this sort is always animated by the sender's experience of some kind of breach, however temporary, in the relationship. Something is wrong. The advice essentially suggests a more promising way to express this experience that something is wrong than the more common, unproductive responses of silence, complaint, or personal attack. But what usually goes unrecognized is the fact that the advice actually constructs the something that is wrong. The aggrieved wife responding in this way, for example, is actually reporting an injury to the way she wants to feel in the relationship, a violation of whatever size to her "theory" of how the relationship should go. She is able to identify the discrepancy between what is happening in the relationship and her own understanding—separate from her husband's or someone else's—of how the relationship should be or how she should feel in it. And she is able to identify this breach without simultaneously feeling that the relationship itself has ceased or has been severed. That is, she is able to stay in the relationship and continue having the relationship. Right now she is having it by discussing her unhappy experience of this aspect of it. Finally, she is able to have unpleasant, unwelcome feelings, caused by her husband's actions and inactions, without holding him responsible for creating these feelings in her. Instead, she sees him as responsible for his behaviors and herself as responsible for the feelings she has about those behaviors.

Twenty years of empirical study of the mental systems people use to construct reality have convinced me that the ability to construct the "something wrong" in this way is not at all automatic. We cannot assume that a person possesses it because he or she has reached a certain age, achieved a certain educational level, or attained a certain social position. It is not conferred along with a state-issued marriage license. It is instead an extraordinarily sophisticated ability that men and women of whatever age, education, or social position may or may not gradually grow into over the course of their adult years. I am convinced that there are completely different ways of experiencing the something wrong in the first place.

The fourth order way of constructing the something wrong sees it as a violation of a person's self-constructed view of how the relationship should go or should feel. The fourth order can internally process this experience in the context of a self that exists apart from the organization of the relationship, however much that self is committed to the relationship or however greatly it values the relationship.

But what if the sender of this communication, the aggrieved wife, say, constructs the world according to the third order? The breach she may feel may be less about a violation of a self that is, all the same, intact than about an interruption of the self. The breach may be less a discrepancy from, or a violation of, her own plan for the relationship and how she should feel in it than a reconstitution of what the relationship is about or how she actually feels in it. It is not even self-evident that anger is exactly what she feels. She may feel sad, lonely, incomplete, empty, devaluing of herself, or simply have some other feeling she cannot name. She may feel "done wrong to" or mistreated, not as an expression of her stand for the continuing existence of her personal standard, which has been violated, but because she is lamenting the way things have changed, the way in which her relationship (not her standard) continues to exist. The stand she may take instead may be "by her man," however sadly, like the character in Tammy Wynette's song from whom Hillary Clinton distinguished herself when discussing her marital history on national television between halves of a superbowl game. (On that remarkable occasion a hundred million people heard the future First Lady of the United States essentially declare that she did not construct her marriage at the third order of consciousness.)

The "something wrong" is set right at the fourth order through the exercise of a self-evaluating, self-governing system: the husband does or does not start putting his dirty clothes away, the meaning of which is constructed in terms of the wife's ongoing theory of her husband, herself, their relationship, and what she is willing or unwilling to live with. The husband, in other words, will do whatever he will do, and the wife will set things right for herself. At the third order—subject to the cross-categorical construction of the self, the other, and their relationship— the wife cannot actually set things right by herself. Things will be set

"If something is bothering you about our relationship, Lorraine, why don't you just spell it out."

Drawing by Eric Teitelbaum; © 1990 The New Yorker Magazine, Inc.

right when her inner psychological life is happier, but her inner psychological life is not an "object" under her control.

We should note that the very proposal to handle her unhappiness by speaking directly to her husband may be experienced differently by the two orders of consciousness, costing the person using the third order much more dearly. A person using the fourth order does not necessarily suffer a loss of closeness by experiencing herself in a snag with her husband or wishing he would conduct himself other than he does. Here our earlier discussion about Peter and Lynn's different constructions of psychological closeness comes back into play. If our sense of closeness derives from our feeling that we share one heart and mind, or at least that when we are doing our best we do, the very idea of having to ask so directly for what we want invalidates the possibility that this could be a route to setting right what has gone wrong. As people have said to me when we have discussed the "I" statement advice: "If I have to ask her for it I don't want it," and "There is nothing loving in getting something you need from your lover by having to ask him for it; if he hasn't figured out you need it, or doesn't want to give it to you badly enough, then forget about it," and "I want to be *given* love, I don't want to *take* it." Viewed from the fourth order, this will be seen as the unreasonable demand that we be able to read our partner's mind, or at the very least, that we pass some kind of exam by listening carefully enough to all the indirect little hints our partner leaves us that we can divine what gift will be most appreciated at the birthday party of life. Our preference, that we simply ask our partners what they would like and that they tell us outright, will be seen as terribly unromantic.

But what if what is romantic is not simply a matter of custom or personal taste or whether one is or is not old-fashioned? The recommendation to speak in I-statements rather than You-statements is really a particular instance of the more general claim for "direct communication" among partners. What is most "romantic" is probably that which makes us feel most "loved up." But whatever else we do once we get there, "loving up" someone cannot even begin without first meeting, holding, and engaging that person *as he or she constructs a person to be*. If "direct communication" is another fourth order claim, as it certainly appears to be, then although it may be unromantic to the third order, to the fourth order it may be the *sine qua non* of a romantic relationship. No matter how much a person lavishes attention on us, makes personal sacrifices for us, or places us at the center of his or her life, none of this can make up for that person's failure to regard us as psychologically distinct. In the end we will find the love—however real and pure and honorable—to be suffocating because it wants to wrap itself around a smaller self than the one we have become.

One last word about the suggestion that we report our feelings in I-statements rather than You-statements. This suggestion also makes a fourth order claim on the *receiver* of the communication. However perfectly we craft our I-statement, however explicit we are about not holding the other responsible for the feeling we report, whatever lengths we go to to ensure a nondefensive reception for our communication, the receiver is still apt to do and feel the very things one does and feels in response to a You-statement if that person is unable to perform the differentiations of the fourth order. Instead of saying, "You're so inconsiderate to bring me to this party and then just leave me the moment we walk through the door!" we say, "I don't like it when we go to a party and I don't see you the whole evening." Or better yet, to make my point, let us say we are honors graduates of the I-statement school and come up with a beauty like this: "Boy, I really notice that I get myself into quite a thing when you go away from me at a party. It's like I do this whole number on myself that everyone's more interesting to you than I am. I'm intrigued, and also a little appalled, to tell you the truth, to see that I do this. It's something I've really got to take a long look at." There. We have said it so that it is entirely a report of our experience. We have practically *thanked* him for this valuable opportunity. We've even made it clear that the next step is ours, not his. Even so, some people will still feel blamed, guilty, apologetic, or defensive in response!

It turns out that having the other person feel nondefensive or unindicted is not totally within our control. The requirement of "good communication" is actually a claim on both the sending and the receiving sides. Although it may sound strange to say so, the receiving end is as active a role in communication as the sending end. After all, listening is an interpretive event. How we hear what we hear will be enabled and constrained by our system of knowing. If a first requirement for good communication from the sending end is to take responsibility for what is truly our own (such as our own reactions to what the other does), perhaps a first requirement for the receiving end is not to take responsibility for what is truly the other's.

Defensiveness can only follow the act of taking responsibility (we will never feel defensive about something for which we do not feel responsible), although this prior act is commonly overlooked. Our experience, when we are being defensive, is that we are being pushed or pulled upon in some way, that we are being acted upon. The commonsense notion is that we "get defensive" when we feel "attacked" or "judged." But attacks and judgments from those we do not take seriously do not make us defensive. Although we don't usually think of it this way, the crucial element in defensiveness is the feeling of being moved to a place to which we do not want to go, so it is necessary, in order for us to feel defensive, for there to be a "force" or "power" that we reckon can move us.

Now the really interesting question is where we think that power is coming from. When we "get defensive," or feel we have been "made to feel defensive," we think the power to move us where we do not want to go comes from the other person. This determination that it comes from the other person and that we have to deal with their threatening power is *constructed*; it arises out of our *way* of constructing the world. When we are being defensive, we are constructing the experience of being pushed or pulled upon by the person we are defending against. As I have said, we can construct such an experience when the person actually is trying to push us in some way ("You must stop throwing your dirty laundry on the floor!") as well as when the person is not ("I notice I have quite a reaction to . . ."), so it is not the other's communication entirely that determines whether we are going to be defensive or not. We have a lot to do with it. Even if the person tries to push on us ("You are a slob!"), we can react nondefensively by converting the communication into the information about the other's experience it undeniably is, for which the other is responsible ("She does not like my behavior, she is angry with me . . ."). We can then choose to alter our behavior or not in accordance with our *own* purposes, standards, and convictions, for which choice we are now responsible. And, conversely, if the other person makes it very clear she is *not* pushing on us, as did the partner left alone at the party, we can construct the experience as if we are being faulted for this and then react against the other by defending ourselves, or react against ourselves by feeling guilt or remorse.

What must we do to avoid these erroneous claims of responsibility and the (other-attacking) defensiveness or the (self-attacking) guilt that ensues from it? We can heed an externally supplied directive (from spouse, friend, counselor, self-help group, or psychological pop culture) not to be "co-dependent," a "people-pleaser," or "addicted to love." If the directive comes from a valued and constant enough source (with whom we are perhaps, in another way, "co-dependent," "people-pleasing," or "addicted"), this may do the trick, but it is a lot to ask.

However, if we are to call upon something *internal*, something that is continuously available to us, in order to avoid taking responsibility for that which is not ours, we will need a mental capacity that preserves a distinction between the other person and our internalizations of the other person's point of view, between ourselves and our internalizations of the other's point of view. What does this mean?

One triumph of the third order of mind is the new way the other's point of view matters to us. Indeed, we construct our sense of self in the relationship between our own point of view and the other's. The other's point of view now matters to us intrinsically, not just extrinsically as a means of satisfying our more egocentric purposes. This is the psychological architecture of what sociology would call "socialization," in which the individual really becomes a part of society because society has really become a part of the individual. But what is a triumph of mind compared to the constraints of the past is itself a constraint compared to what may be required of us in the future. This bringing inside of the other's point of view, this co-construction of the self, is a cross-categorical capacity, the triumph and limit of the third order. The reason the third order cannot avoid internally taking responsibility for "that which is not ours" is simply because from the third order point of view it *is* ours.

According to the third order, to be in serious relationship to others entails a co-constructing of ourselves out of the relation between the categories of my perspective and their perspective (the cross-categorical subjectivity). If we are constructing reality from the third order and receive the suggestion that our partner's complaints need not make us feel angrily defensive or remorsefully guilty, we may tend to hear such advice as an invitation to be colder, more callous, even indifferent, or to take up a position of greater distance in relation to the other. This is yet another consciousness conversation at cross-purposes, however, since this suggestion need have nothing whatever to do with hardening one's heart, caring less, or becoming less close. On the contrary, the suggestion, often tendered as if it requires simply a tiny adjustment in our thinking, does not call for a change in the degree of closeness or caring in the relationship but for a qualitative reconstruction of what self and what other will even be *in* relation. How so?

When the self does not ignore its cross-categorical comminglings with the other's point of view but is bigger than these co-constructions and thus no longer identical with them, the source of its own sense of continued well-being and integrity is not limited to its life within the shared reality of the relationship. Ignoring my understanding of how the other feels would be a hardening of the heart, an armoring, a caring less. But if we neither identify with the internal registering of how the other feels nor ignore it, but are able instead to be in relationship to it, then we do not leave off caring for the other, we leave off being *made up by* our caring. We become able to do something with our caring for the other. We can move away from, look at, and decide about what our partner asks of us without feeling that we are moving away from *our partner* in doing so.

The self's new ability to be an internal judge establishes a distinction for the first time between it and its caring for the other. But does this imply a weakening of the bond with the other? If our partner makes a claim on us when we construct the self out of the third order, we are perforce *brought back* into the fold (whether we guiltily comply with or defensively react to being "brought back"). But if we construct the self out of the fourth order, and the result of our internal judging is that the other's claim or expectation or demand falls within the nature of the relationship to which we are committed, we *bring ourselves back* into the fold. Which bond seems the stronger? In being able to do such judging, which requires fourth order constructing, we free both ourselves and the other from an identification with the present nature of our bond. We can provide company to our partners in their unhappiness or discontent (even their unhappiness or discontent with us) because at some level we are aware that our closeness to them does not require us to be made up by their experience ("I am not her experience"), and at some level we are aware that the other is the maker of her own experience ("she is not made up by her experience"). This realization can be enormously liberating for both the self and the other; it is about a *new kind* of bond or connection rather than about a weakening of the current bonds or connections on behalf of some self-involved independence.

When we see that we are not made up by the other's experience, we then have the capacity not to take responsibility for what is now genuinely and for the first time not ours. And as a result, we can get just as close to the other's experience as we might like (even the other's experience of how disappointing, enraging, or disapprovable we are!) without any need to react defensively to it or be guiltily compliant with it.

When we see that the other is not made up by her experience, we can respond not only to the other's feelings but to the other as the maker or possessor of those feelings. The other is more than, or bigger than, her experience. We can do our connecting and responding to *her*, to the biggest *her*, to the her-who-experiences rather than to the experience itself. Even when the experience the other is having is a negative experience about us, we can connect to the regret, anger, or disappointment the other is feeling in having it. Our relationship to the other includes, in a powerful way, our recognition of the other's relationship to herself.

When we see that we are not made up by our experience, we do not hold the other responsible for our experience of unhappiness with her. She did not create that experience; we did. And when we see that the other is not made up by our experience, we do not hold the other responsible for failing to make us feel better when she learns of our unhappiness.

These four insights:

1. we are not made up by the other's experience
2. the other is not made up by his or her experience
3. we are not made up by our experience
4. the other is not made up by our experience

are the conceptual foundation for the ability to "avoid taking on responsibilities that are not one's own" and to "avoid assigning to others responsibilities that are not theirs." These abilities are crucial for meeting the culture's demands upon adults to be "good communicators" not only in their intimate relationships but, as we will see shortly, in their public relations, especially in the world of work. But this conceptual framework itself rests on a bigger epistemological foundation, a qualitatively different order of consciousness that constructs anew how the self or the other works and what "responsibility" means. This is a *qualitatively* different order of consciousness, because the former order of consciousness (cross-categorical structures) is transformed from whole to part, from the very system of knowing to an element in a new system, from subject to object. The four insights cannot be taught and they cannot be "learned." Tacking them on the refrigerator, or memorizing them, or chanting them in a large auditorium can only serve ends other than that of understanding them. If I construct reality at the fourth order, there is no need to keep them in front of me. If I construct reality at the third order, they make a sense that seems unfriendly or strange. Insight cannot be taught or learned, but the consciousness that gives rise to insight can be *developed*. Trying to teach insight without transforming consciousness is like trying to create apples without growing apple trees.

The demands upon us to protect the couple of which we are a part effectively and to communicate well speak to the need to sustain and nourish the life of a relationship. But what is it that brings two people together in the first place? Despite my belief that the unrecognized epistemological dimension of adult life is a promising source of clues to many mysteries, I doubt it is the answer to this one. I tend to think that we find each other in love out of some correspondence we feel with our deepest personal and primordial themes of longing, hoping, and desiring. We sense in the other some reply or refuge for our longing—to be healed, freed, deeply comforted; to be less suffocated or more closely held; to be better protected or allowed to protect; to be more intensely met or relieved from an overstimulating connection to the world. These deeply felt desires and needs animate our personal images, themes, stories, and myths. And the images, themes, stories, and myths inside our skins look for people to portray and enact them outside. Our deeply felt desires and needs, not our epistemologies, create and fuel our intimate relationships. But our epistemologies are implicated in the ways we *relate to* these primordial themes, images, stories, and myths. They are implicated in the way we care for their passionate possibilities, their promise, their life-giving powers. And they are implicated in the way we do or do not protect ourselves from their life-threatening capacity to limit, constrain, and even destroy through enactments with present-day partners of past feelings of injury and disappointment.

It may be important for marital partners to communicate well, especially when there are differences between them, but where do these differences come from? Perhaps the burden of the claim for "good communication" might be lessened somewhat if partners could better engage the very sources of their conflicts upstream, before these conflicts have even become conflicts. And one such source might well be our own deepest longings, the very source of our coming together as a couple in the first place. This leads us to the final claim upon us in our partnering: in order to be successful partners we are told we need to have an awareness of the way our personal history inclines or directs us. What sort of mental claim is this? What sort of awareness is really being called for? What order of consciousness would be necessary to meet this modern requirement?

It is one thing to see that we *have* a personal history that inclines or directs us. Not until sometime in adolescence at the earliest does any-one say, "My father always worked so hard himself; maybe that's why I feel that no matter how much I'm doing it's never enough." Or "I think the reason I love him so much is that he's just so *normal* and his family is so normal. I mean, I came from a family that *never* had dinner to-gether, and I think I always wanted things to be more regular." Why don't we hear ten-year-olds talk this way? The thought of their doing so makes us laugh, but this is only a sign of how intuitively we assign such speech to greater maturity. But our reaction does not explain why ten-year-olds don't talk this way. It certainly can't be that ten-year-olds are not smart enough. They can repeat the starting line-ups and batting averages of their favorite team, and although they don't know they know it, they can interpret the meaning of a hundred different paralin-guistic communications their parents use. What is more, they even know they have a history to the extent that they can report in astonish-ing detail the events of their day or a day they lived five years ago. If they can "figure out" others and record their own experience, why don't they ever talk this way?

What we mean by maturity in people's thinking is not a matter of how smart they are, it is a matter of the order of consciousness in which they exercise their smartness or their lack of it. Ten-year-olds don't talk like this because they don't think abstractly and they aren't literally self-conscious. They have a record of their experience, but they don't reflect on it or derive generalizable themes from it. They know what they are moved to do, but when they are made to ask themselves why, they never leave the concrete plane:

"Why do you want money?"
"Because with money you can get what you want."
"Why do you want to get what you want?"
"Because then other people can't say you can't have it."[4]

The capacity to see that we have a personal history that inclines or directs us—that our concrete experience can be tied to generalizable motives, patterns, or themes—demands the third order of conscious-ness. But is this order of consciousness sufficient for us to do something with our personal history so that we are less likely to punish our spouse for it?

Thirty-year-old William and his wife, Betty, see a couples therapist because they find that the stresses they are currently dealing with in their relationship have led to a distance between them. They both trace the major source of stress to Betty's bad back, which from time to time requires extended periods of rest. William is outwardly sympathetic, but he is also beset with far more than his share of household and parenting chores. He says, initially, that the distance in their relationship is not due to any change in his feelings toward his wife but to the sheer demand upon his time and energy. They spend less meaningful time together, he says, because he has less free time, and when he does have free time he is exhausted. But as the conversations in therapy continue, he realizes that it is very upsetting for him to experience his wife as not being up to participating fully in the family, that sometimes it makes him angry with her and sometimes it makes him frightened.

In addition, the therapy gives both William and Betty a chance to talk about their own parents' marriages and the families in which they grew up. Something that seems significant to William, Betty, and the therapist is that William's mother was frequently hospitalized during his childhood. As William talks more about what it was like to have his mother frequently and unpredictably absent, he forms an insight into how his personal history inclines or directs him to feel about his wife's back problems. He realizes that Betty's problems evoke in him a sense that she is fragile and possibly undependable, and that this feeling is nearly unbearable because it is associated with his childhood experience of being unprotected and powerless, a way of experiencing himself he hated and found excruciatingly painful. And further, let us be clear, this insight into how his personal history inclines or directs him does not exist for him merely as a possibly interesting therapist's interpretation, which intellectually makes sense but fails to register any lower in his body. For William it is an awareness that is not just cognitively plausible but emotionally true. He feels it in his guts when he thinks about it, in his lips when he talks about it, in his eyes when he listens to the therapist talk about it.

So now let us ask: Does William meet the claim upon him (and upon every one of us) to be aware of the way his personal history inclines or directs him? If we answer yes or no, we are making an assumption about what William now does with this insight, for there is no way to know if he meets this requirement until we learn what difference it makes for him to see this connection, and there is actually no way to predict what difference it *will* make for him based on what we have heard so far.

Many therapists have found themselves puzzled about why clients differ so in their ability to "make productive use" of the insights psycho-therapy can generate. In the face of their perfectly accurate assessment that two different clients are each "capable of insight," why should it be, they wonder, that for one person it leads to a real change of whatever magnitude in the way they construct their experience (an accommoda-tion, Piaget might have called it, of their meaning-making system to the insight), while for the other the present system of meaning-making is unchanged or even fortified by the insight (an assimilation of the insight to the present system)?

William might, for example, make the powerful connection we de-scribe and yet continue to hold Betty responsible for the painful feelings her need for bedrest evokes in him! And he would see it in just that way: *Her needs and behaviors create in him painful feelings.* He would know bet-ter *why* they do but would continue to construct *that* they do as her responsibility. As I have been intrigued and dismayed to discover in my own therapy practice, he might even hold her more responsible when he has come to the insight in the context of couples therapy: "You were here listening to all this. You have heard what I went through as a kid, and you *know* now how difficult this would be for me, yet you *still* have these periods when you must take to your bed."

William's third order consciousness makes it possible for him to dis-cover patterns and themes to his life history, make connections between past and present, and have insight into why he feels as he does. But his lack of a fourth order consciousness makes it impossible for him to "do something productive" with the insight, just as it is one thing to *have* an inner psychological life one can experience and report as internal (a third order capacity) and quite another to see oneself as the constructor of that inner psychological life. If one's inner experiences just "show up" there, so that the self-conscious self is an audience for its inner ex-periencing, then insight turns out to be insight into why the audience reacts as intensely to the content as it does, rather than into why or how the author writes the script or drama as he does.

The requirement that we "be aware of 'our issues,'" as it is popularly expressed, that we be aware of the way our personal history inclines or directs us, is actually an expectation to do something more. It is a claim that we be able to see the way our personal history tends to filter our reading of experience so that we do not hold others responsible for the way we feel in response to their actions or choices. Even with his in-sight, William's construction of things is: "Betty, your behavior creates painful feelings in me. I am aware that it is so painful because of its psychological similarities to my experience with my mother." But this is actually *not* the "awareness of our issues" that is called for by this cultural demand. What is expected is that we should be able to frame it something more like this: "I am aware that my being upset with Betty's behavior is greatly influenced by its similarity to my painful experiences with my mother. If I'm not careful, I'm going to confuse this situation with that situation and Betty with my mother. If I want this situation to be just this situation (because in some important ways it is *not* the same as my situation with my mother), and if I want the way I know Betty to be just about Betty (because in many ways Betty is *not* like my mother), I'm going to have to be careful."

This way of being "aware of my issues" presumes a self that is not only the *experiencer* of a reportable internal psychological life but also the *maker* of an internal psychological life. The demand for this construction of the self—as author, maker, critiquer, and *re*maker of its experience, the self as a system or complex, regulative of its parts—is again a demand for fourth order consciousness. The demand that we be in control of our issues rather than having our issues be in control of us is a demand for fourth order consciousness.

Although it isn't evident from our story so far, Lynn and Peter spend only half of their lives at home. In addition to their full-time roles as parents and spouses, each has important ongoing commitments away from the family. Both work outside the home. Each is in the midst of a significant job change at work involving increasing responsibility and recognition. Both have a big life beyond their front door—the place where we usually think we meet the world and its demands. But Lynn and Peter haven't yet gone beyond their *bedroom* door, let alone their front door, and already they are inundated with an elaborately layered set of cultural demands as parents and as partners.

However "private" these two roles of our "private lives" are supposed to be, our success in them, so the experts tell us, depends on our capacity to carry out a number of tasks that are not privately designed but are shared by every other partner and parent in our culture. But what the experts have not told us is that these tasks may represent a kind of graduate level curriculum in which we are required not only to increase our fund of knowledge (a change in *what* we know), but to transform qualitatively the very *way* we know. The order of consciousness we put together by the end of our adolescence—when we truly joined our culture, took out membership in it, became loyal to it—may not be sufficient for successfully living as modern adults.

If this is so, then even before we have looked at Lynn and Peter's life beyond their front door, what seems to me a most intriguing hypothesis has begun to insist itself upon us. This hypothesis can be expressed in terms of individual development or of the historical evolution of cultural mentality. Ontogenetically, I would put it this way: the demands of modern adult life may require a qualitative transformation in the complexity of mind every bit as fundamental as the transformation from magical thinking to concrete thinking required of the school-age child, or the transformation from concrete thinking to abstract thinking required of the adolescent. Phylogenetically, I would put it this way: the mental burden of modern life may be nothing less than the extraordinary cultural demand that each person, in adulthood, create internally an order of consciousness comparable to that which ordinarily would only be found at the level of a community's collective intelligence. This amounts to the expectation that faithful adherents themselves become priests and priestesses; or, that the acculturated become cultures unto themselves. We grieve the "loss of community" we take to be a condition of modern life in large part because it is profoundly lonely. We feel unaccompanied at the level of our own souls. Are we unaccompanied because the gods have died or abandoned us, as early modern philosophers contended, or because we feel charged to become them?

III

The Mental Demand of Public Life: Work and Self-Expansion

5

Working: On Seeking to Hire the Self-Employed

Peter and Lynn are both up early today. Hurrying through morning routines, their minds already out of the house, they are thinking of work before they even leave the bathroom. Both of them could say, "These days my work is too much with me." Different as their work is, they have noticed that in each of their jobs a similar circumstance has gotten them both stirred up.

Lynn has been at Highland Junior High School for twelve years, originally as an English teacher. Although she still teaches several classes, three years ago she also became chair of the English department. Then last year it was decided that several department chairs, including English, would be part of the principal's newly formed Leadership Council, and Lynn added that to the usual duties of leading a department. The Council, which she had initially been eager to join, was the outgrowth of Highland's decision to "go SBM," as the lingo in the school district would have it. "School-based management," as it was explained to Lynn and the rest of the faculty, meant that the responsibility and authority for running the school would no longer be vested in the single person of the principal, but shared mainly among the principal and the faculty or its representatives. There would be more work, more meetings, more to worry about for the faculty, to be sure, but they would also have a greater hand in how the school was run. This sounded good to Lynn, who reasoned that especially with such a veteran faculty (over 70 percent had been at the school for more than ten years; their average age was forty-one) Highland's teachers were up to the challenge. Appar-

137

ently Lynn's colleagues agreed, since—along with the principal and a majority of the parents association—two-thirds of the faculty had to approve the new governance structure before it could be tried, and they did.

Peter has worked at BestRest Incorporated for nineteen years. The country's third largest bedding manufacturer, it has twelve regional factories shipping to furniture and department stores in all forty-eight contiguous states. Peter began working for BestRest during the summers while he was still in college. His earnest sincerity and intelligence were immediately appealing to Anderson Wright, the plant manager, who took it upon himself to provide Peter with a "real-world business education" to go along with his classroom college education. "If you want to learn the manufacturing business, the place to begin is in the factory," Anderson said, introducing Peter to the sisal room, a noisy, messy place where box springs were filled with the hemplike material. "The very word 'manufacturing,' Peter, means 'made with the hands,'" Anderson said, "and no matter what your future in this business, you should understand the sweat and craft that go into the making of the product. We're making money here, sure, but it's no shell game. We're making money because, first and last, we're making something people *need* and we're making it *well.*"

Peter was impressed with Anderson's integrity, energy, and vision, and so were the people in the national office of BestRest. As the charismatic Anderson Wright rose to positions of greater authority he brought Peter along with him. When government regulations mandating flame-retardant fabrics threatened to mire the mattress industry nationally, it was Anderson who turned lemons into lemonade, spinning off a new product line of flame-retardant bed linens, comforters, mattress pads, and even children's pajamas. Using the same treatment equipment they had been forced to purchase for the twelve plants, he turned an enormous additional cost into a fatter bottom line. When Anderson—now a corporate vice president—became intrigued with other challenges three years ago, he put Peter in charge of this new product line with the responsibility to report directly to him. Peter enjoyed the job and the continuing close association with Anderson, whom he consulted frequently and easily. Their years together had only deepened the admiration and devotion Peter felt for Anderson.

But life has definitely become more complicated for Peter of late. The focus of Anderson's curiosity and creativity has evolved from an interest in improving how BestRest made what they sold, to expanding the line of what BestRest made, to his current interest in the way the company itself is "made." "Everybody in the company is manufacturing something, Peter," Anderson told him one day. "The people in our factories are manufacturing sleep products. Our sales force is manufacturing customers. And those of us in the front office, we're manufacturing the company itself. Ever think of it that way?" Peter said that he hadn't and thought to himself that he wasn't even sure what Anderson really meant. "We're the executives," Anderson said. "And the way we're executing is shaping the way the company works. *Our* product is the company, how we're designing this company. Every manufacturing process can stand some refining, Peter, and so can ours." It wasn't long after this that Anderson began talking about "worker participation" and "collaborative management philosophy." And at their next quarterly check-in on the newer product line, Peter finally learned what all this meant for him.

"If you're game, Peter—and I think you're ready—I want you to think of the new line as a company on its own—SafeSleep Products—and I want you to run it. I want it to be your baby and I want you to think of me more as your banker. Plans, directions, and initiatives will come from you, not from me. You'll have to come to me, sure, when you need more resources to fund your initiatives, just like you'd come to your banker, but it's your baby. I'll review your plans like a banker would, evaluate their soundness, and extend credit or not. But if I do, it's still your project that's getting funded, not mine; it's your plan that's rising or falling, not mine. It'll be your responsibility to come through, make your payments, make a go of *your* business. My responsibility is to the shareholders and owners of the 'bank.' And if I'm skeptical about extending credit or don't want to risk the bank's resources, well, it's still your baby. Tell me why I'm wrong, or tell me to stick it in my ear and find yourself a new banker. Because it's your company, Peter, whaddaya think? You wanna be president of BestRest's SafeSleep division?" Peter could hear the excitement in Anderson's voice, his pleasure in offering Peter what Anderson clearly regarded as a wonderful present. He could feel how much Anderson loved the place to which he had just moved the relationship. So Peter, without hesitation or conscious deliberation and true to his deepest commitment where Anderson was concerned, moved himself to rejoin Anderson in this new place. "I love it," said Peter, like the spouse of a newly restationed military officer, happy to be reunited with one's partner but looking around in sheer terror at the unfamiliar surroundings, wondering what life here could possibly be like.

Thus Lynn and Peter, the school teacher and the business executive who seldom feel their work has anything in common, find themselves contending with a similar circumstance at work. One job is service-oriented, the other product-oriented; one is nonprofit, the other for-profit; one involves a predominantly female environment, the other a male environment; one has an organizational "culture" distinguished by gentleness, safety, and nurture, the other a culture distinguished by competition, maneuvering, and results. Yet Lynn's and Peter's work lives are both out of equilibrium for the same reason: worker-participation initiatives have recast the issues of responsibility, ownership, and authority at work. One of the central aspirations of such initiatives is surely the revitalization and increased morale of the workforce. But no one would know that by looking at Lynn and Peter. Both are miserable and demoralized about the changes at work. Let's take a closer look to find out why.

"I can give you a typical example of why this thing is not working at Highland," Lynn says. "Probably every department chair and most of the faculty would agree that there are big flaws in the way we do faculty evaluations. First of all, except for the first-year teachers, of whom there are very few, faculty evaluations are based on two class visits by the principal. Two visits, that's it. And it's the principal who does them. They are announced visits, so teachers end up preparing for a perfor-mance, which they resent and which is a lousy basis for evaluation. The teachers don't feel that the principal gets a fair sample of what their work is like. The kids know what's going on and act weird—they're on 'good behavior' too, and completely unspontaneous. The principal writes up a generally innocuous report, which the teacher then pores over like an old Kremlinologist trying to detect the hidden meaning in some routine public communiqué. Usually there is no hidden meaning. The principal is just discharging a duty that she finds as unpleasant and unrewarding as the teachers. Nobody is learning a thing, but at least the principal can tell the central office that 'everyone's been evaluated' and she has the paperwork, neatly typed in the files, to prove it.

"I went along with this like everyone else, but by the time I'd become the English department chair I'd begun to form some very different ideas about evaluation, about everything, really. I got the idea that the school should be a Learning Place for *everyone*, that we're supposed to be experts on learning, that we could evaluate everything we're doing on the basis of whether it's prolearning or not. I know my own kids are unbelievably aware of what Peter and I do; we teach them more by modeling than by explaining. I decided that if we want kids to be learning in school it would help them if we modeled learning ourselves. It was actually some version of this that got me excited about being on the Leadership Council in the first place. When Highland was deciding whether to go to school-based management, at first I felt, 'What business do I have *administering* the school? That's management stuff, the kind of thing Peter knows about, and, to give her her due, the kind of thing Carolyn, our principal, knows about. It's not what I know about.' But then I felt, 'Well, it's good that Carolyn knows about how organizations work, and that's the special expertise she brings and why she's the principal. But I know a lot about what promotes learning and what gets in the way of it, and if I could get people to buy my idea of the school as a Learning Place, then this might be the one organization where what I know about would come in handy at the management level.' Something like that.

"Anyway, I had some different ideas about faculty evaluation. I wanted to return the emphasis to learning, not file-filling. I wanted the teachers to identify what their learning agenda was and what they needed to fulfill it. And I wanted to use my chairmanship to advocate that the administrators be interested in supporting the teachers' learning. Especially, once the teacher was tenured, as most of our faculty is, I wanted the principal to get out of the evaluation business. I felt it was better handled within the departments. I thought Carolyn was a good administrator and that that was an honorable profession—after all, I'm married to one—but that it was different from being a school teacher. I felt that she was less effective when she crossed over from her profession into mine. My feeling is that a good hospital administrator runs the hospital well, but she doesn't tell the surgeon where to cut.

"So when Carolyn proposed SBM to our faculty I admired her for being willing to let some other voices come into the leadership of the school, but I wasn't thinking, 'Good, now we're going to take over.' I don't want to take over. I don't want to be the principal. But I don't want Carolyn being the department chair either, and I felt that we had a better chance of clearing these things up in group discussions, like we'd have on the Council, than in one-on-one meetings in Carolyn's office.

"The whole thing started to fall apart for me this semester around just this issue of faculty evaluation, and it wasn't even my initiative. It's not as if we don't all know each other pretty well by now, but when Alan—he's the history chair—brought in his proposal, it was a complete surprise to me. It was not, as I think Carolyn was suggesting, some kind of conspiracy. There had already been a lot of behind-the-back grumbling about the Council by the faculty before Alan's proposal. The 'Becky and Betty' incident earlier in the year, for example, people found demoralizing.

"Without going into it at great length, two spunky ninth-grade girls—the school goes up to ninth grade—created a stir because they decided they were going to the 'Grad Prom' together as a couple. It's not even what you think. They weren't 'coming out.' They're not gay. And even if they were, Highland has a newly minted nondiscrimination policy. They weren't flouting sexual mores, they were flouting contradictions in *Highland's* mores! Although the graduation prom is a 'couples only' affair, the conventional definition of 'couple' was successfully challenged last year by two senior high school girls who were openly lesbian and were allowed to attend their prom together. Now this year, these two ninth graders, one a class officer and just a super kid, decide that it's ridiculous that they can't go to their own prom just because they don't have dates. 'We could go together if we were lesbians,' one of them says to the other laughing, and then it occurs to them that it's ridiculous that because of what is essentially the private matter of their sexuality they are unable to attend the prom together, when two girls *were* allowed to attend together.

"You can see where this is leading. They insist they have a right to attend together, and claim that the school or the prom committee have no right to inquire into the private matter of their sexuality. Just a wonderful mess! Exactly what happens with kids. They find the flaws in the system, and head right for them. Anyway, the issue was so attractive beyond the school that it became an embarrassment for Carolyn. Or she made it into an embarrassment. There were inquiries from the American Civil Liberties Union. We talked about it at length on the Council and I think the predominant position was that the kids were just pointing out that the whole 'couples only' policy can't be defended;

it no longer makes sense. Once we acknowledged that a homosexual couple was an acceptable couple, then it was no longer possible to decide who was an unacceptable couple without prying into matters that were none of our business. Most of us felt we should drop the 'couples only' rule, congratulate the kids on making an effective point, and laugh at the difficulties we are all having adjusting to a changing world. Besides, where did this 'couples only' craziness for fourteen- and fifteen-year-olds get started in the first place?

"But Carolyn felt differently. She thought the kids were making a mockery of the school's rules and traditions, that they were taking advantage of an open-minded, inclusion-oriented rule—that gay couples were legitimate couples—for their own purposes, and that those purposes included making fools of the grown-ups. Carolyn felt the last thing kids need is to be successful at making the grown-ups in charge into fools. She also objected to the idea of dropping the couple rule entirely, claiming it was a bad message to say that acknowledging diversity leads to giving up the whole idea of couples. Or something like that. I never quite understood the argument. But anyway, the point is not that Carolyn's position was unreasonable. The troubling thing was that her position was *clearly* a minority position on the Council, but because the case was briefly a tempest in a teapot and Carolyn had to respond to the world outside the school, she represented her own opinion as the school's opinion. This made the rest of us on the Council feel upset: 'Wait a minute! Who are *we*? An advisory committee to the principal?' Granted, she was in a difficult position. You always are when there's negative publicity and the local station wants to bring in television cameras. And it's even worse if you have to represent a position you do not completely agree with yourself. But, hey, that's what team management is all about. She could have represented the division within the Council. She could even have said she was not herself neutral with regard to this division. But a lot of us felt that she undermined the Council when she didn't even include the prevailing view.

"People on the Council started to have their doubts. You know, 'Oh, I guess "school-based management" means that the principal still calls all the shots, but she just consults with more people before she makes up her mind.' Some people felt they weren't interested in the time commitment or the pretense to collaboration if they were just going to be a consultative group. I felt it was bad timing and not a fair test of Carolyn's relation to the Council. School issues that make the local newspaper are scary, and the new management system is in an early phase. We're *all* getting used to it. I didn't like how Carolyn handled it, but I could see how, under pressure, she might have reverted to the more familiar and well-tested format for how the school is run. Still, you can see there were already some misgivings when Alan made his proposal about faculty evaluation.

"Alan's proposal, basically, was that the history department be allowed to run a one-year experiment on evaluation. He wanted to get the performance-anxiety, test-taking dimension out of it. He wanted people to have the option of entering supervisory relationships with him or a few other senior members of the department that would really be more consultative than supervisory. No write-ups or evaluations of the teacher by the supervisor/consultant. The supervisor/consultant would, in effect, be 'hired' by the faculty member to advance the faculty member's learning goals. The teacher could 'fire' the consultant without consequences. No visits by the principal. If the teacher wanted the consultant to visit some classes for the teacher's purposes, that could certainly be arranged, but not for the purpose of entering something in the faculty member's file. No file entries for one year. Alan proposed that he would study and document the project over the year, try to get a sense of how the faculty used it and how much and what kind of learning was going on, but all anonymously, evaluating the experiment, not the teachers. That was basically it.

"I loved the idea, of course. I was envious that I hadn't thought of it myself. It seemed like a good way of putting into operation my idea that the faculty member should run his 'evaluation,' that the evaluation should be aimed at learning, not putting on a show, that the chair could serve as a consultant and a resource to self-directed learning.

"We've now had three long discussions about this on the Council, and we still haven't had the first word about the real merits of Alan's proposal. As I now realize I should have been more aware, the issue for Carolyn had less to do with promoting faculty learning than with the precedent it sets about accountability in general and accountability to her specifically. Stop visits by the principal? Let the faculty decide what they need to learn? No evaluations for the files by *anybody?* These didn't go down easily with Carolyn. Rather than take her usual stance of speaking last in a conversation in order to give everyone a chance to weigh in on the matter, she was the first to speak after Alan made his proposal, and what she had to say pretty much silenced the rest of us.

She didn't identify any merits in the proposal. She didn't even acknowledge the implicit problems the proposal was at least trying to address. She didn't present her problems with the proposal as just *her* problems, which could still leave open for discussion whether these needed to determine the *group's* actual decision. She didn't invite anyone to help her with her problems with the proposal. She just said basically, 'This is something we can't do.'

"I'm not proud of the way I responded, but it was just such a unilateral and imperial stance for her to take, and I guess I got mad. What I said was, 'Why, Carolyn? Is it illegal what Alan is proposing?' and everyone else laughed and I could see that Carolyn was very angry. I hadn't meant it exactly the way it came out. I didn't mean she was out of line to object to the proposal. I was reacting to the way she framed it. I meant that Carolyn is the principal, and where the Council strays into areas that may violate civil ordinances or the district charter, she has every right to take a unilateral position. But where the Council is not straying into this kind of territory I didn't feel she had the right to just shut down the conversation. At the time I attributed my overreaction and sarcasm to the fact this was an especially important issue to me personally, and I resented how it was being dismissed. That didn't justify my sarcasm, but it did dignify it somehow.

"Anyhow, after that Council session Carolyn asked to meet with me in her office, and she read me the riot act: How could I do that to her? Didn't I know how much she counted on my loyalty? Didn't I realize how powerful I was as a department chair, and that to take such a doubting view when she had clearly committed herself was terribly undermining? That she thought of us as partners, that we had worked so well together all these years, and how it was even more important with SBM that we read each other's signals well and be a good team. I had to say, 'Whoa, Carolyn, time out, I'm having too many reactions to all this.'

"We ended up having a good conversation, actually, one of our best in years, but it was really difficult. I had to tell her I thought it was unfair of her to trade on my loyalty to her, that that felt like a risky business. I told her I *did* respect her, and that we *were* friends, and I *was* grateful to her for her support to me professionally over the years, but that I was sure she was not interested in a friend who was a clone or in promoting a colleague because she was a yes-man. I had to puzzle through all the different 'teams' we were on because I felt that I was still very much a team player even when I disagreed with her, although she seemed to feel I was abandoning the team if I disagreed. This got us into the whole SBM, Leadership Council thing, and whether that was itself a team, and what were the expectations about how we functioned as members of that Council. Carolyn broke down and cried and said she was finding SBM terribly hard, that she had had no idea what she was getting into, that half the time she had nightmares that the school was going to fall apart because there was more chaos than leadership, and the other half of the time she had nightmares that the school was getting along too well without her running things and that she was slowly being relieved of her job, that SBM was about gradually making the principal irrelevant.

"So I'm not sure where we are now in this great experiment, but I do feel that the superintendent's office was incredibly naive about the way they instituted SBM. A couple of explanatory meetings and a faculty discussion do not prepare you to vote on a change of governance as profound as this. When people voted for SBM they voted for their own fantasy of what a more collaboratively run school would look and feel like. People weren't voting for a messy process, perhaps a very *long* process, in which everyone involved, faculty and principal, gradually *learn* how to collaborate. I left my meeting with Carolyn feeling that I and a lot of the other faculty had been unfair in blaming her for derailing SBM. If Highland's going to be a Learning Place for everyone then Carolyn has a right to a Learning Place, too, and it's obvious to me that SBM is a challenging curriculum for Carolyn, and those of us on the Council were doing a lousy job making it a good Learning Place for her. I was expecting her to just jump right into this collaborative mode, no problem. I was feeling very impatient with her for not knowing how to do it. It was like being mad at your students in the fall for not already knowing what you're hoping they'll learn by the end of the year!

"And I realized that my sarcasm toward her in that meeting was not just about my sacred commitment to a learning approach to faculty evaluation. There was a less noble side to it. I'm not the greatest person at actually living out everything I say I believe. I run into my own roadblocks, the things I get afraid of, and deep down I think I'm quite ashamed of my own inhibitions. I don't like experiencing myself that way, and so, like most people, I find ways to make sure I do *not* experience myself that way too often—not by being less inhibited, mind you, but just by finding ways to avoid facing that I am. Anyway, I'm sure something of this gets involved in my annoyed impatience with Carolyn for not living up to the spirit of what SBM is supposed to be about. I don't like the 'me' I see in her, so I take it out on her instead, or something like that.

"So that's it. I'm not sure we're going to succeed at this thing. I don't know if Carolyn will really want to support SBM as she learns more about what it really means. I don't know if the rest of us can be good enough supports to her learning. I don't know if it's possible for everyone to readjust their expectations about the learning *process* we all have to go through to get from unilateral to collaborative leadership. I guess we can all share some of the responsibility for the fix we're in. The district may have been naive in their planning and preparation, but we're supposed to be educators ourselves, and we were naive to think you can go from not knowing to knowing with no messy learning phase in between."

Nothing has felt quite right to Peter since Anderson established Safe-Sleep as a company-within-the company and made Peter its president. In congratulatory teasing his friends and family have asked Peter if he felt any different, now that he was a president and he always said, "No, I have the same office, same desk, same secretary, and, at least as of now, the same salary. I'm running the same operation I've been running for the last three years." It was the same operation, but in truth he did not feel the same. He noticed that he did not say, "I have the same boss," even though, as far as he was concerned, Anderson Wright was still his boss. "I have the same boss," Peter thought to himself, "but my boss is not the same."

Were Peter to tell us what it *really* felt like to be "Mr. President," he might say something like this: "Honestly? It's definitely a different ballgame! What game is it? Well, let's see. I guess you could say before I was president, I was playing a game of catch. Anderson would throw things at me and I'd catch them. I'd throw things back at him and he'd catch them. A good long game of catch. And now? Now I'd say I'm a juggler. There's not one ball, there are five, and then there are ten, and then there are fifteen! People keep tossing more in to me to add to those I'm juggling. But I'm not throwing to anyone. I'm just throwing them into the air. As soon as I get them I just toss them back into the air. And my job as the juggler is to keep them all going up there, not let any of them drop to the ground.

"You couldn't believe the number of things that come across my desk. 'Anderson says to take this to you now.' 'Anderson says he's not the guy on this anymore; you are.' I bet I heard that twenty times the first month we set up SafeSleep. If it wasn't one thing, it was another. You have to deal with a lot of people's feelings about this change. Everybody thought the company concept for SafeSleep was a hot idea when Anderson proposed it, but now that we're actually doing it, a lot of people aren't so sure. I told Lynn the other night I'm not even sure *Anderson's* so sure at this point. People keep asking me how I feel about the change, but the truth is, I don't have time to think about how I feel about it because I spend half my day dealing with how everybody *else* feels about it."

"Take Ted, for example. He's one of our salespeople. I've known Ted ten years in this business. His son and my Matthew are like brothers; they grew up in each other's homes. I probably see Ted's son as much as my own. Ted's putting a lot of pressure on me not to separate him from the SafeSleep line. Ted's a mattress salesman and a damn good one. He does excellent work for his customers. His customers are furniture stores and the mattress departments of two large chains of department stores. They love him and he loves them. The SafeSleep line got its start by accident, or what Anderson called 'entrepreneurial jujitsu,' turning a weakness into a strength. New government codes mandated that we manufacture flame-retardant mattresses and it cost millions of dollars to set up the capacity. Since we had the capacity, Anderson reasoned, why not use it for other things, too? Presto! The SafeSleep line. But originally these products were just an 'extra' that the mattress salespeople offered their furniture stores. The store used them as 'sweeteners' to sell their customers our top-of-the-line mattresses. They'd throw in a king-size quilt along with the purchase of a king-size mattress and box spring. Stuff like that. Everybody was happy. The furniture store's customer liked the freebie; the store liked the mattress sale; our salespeople liked the increased mattress orders they got from the stores. And that's just the problem. Everybody was happy. 'So why are you ruining a nice thing?' Ted wants to know. 'Peter, I'm family,' he says to me. 'And Harold is not,' which is true. 'So why are you letting this guy take the bread off my table?' he says.

"I hired Harold soon after I became president of SafeSleep because Harold had sales experience in bedclothes. He was the first nonmattress salesperson in the place, and I thought we needed that for the new company. He's turned out to be a dynamo. The guy's got more ideas per square inch than I've ever seen, and most of them make sense. But they're also making some people, like Ted, mad. And I'm not so sure Anderson's very keen about him either.

"Harold's take was that BestRest was choking SafeSleep, that the best reason for setting up SafeSleep as a separate company was that its growth was stunted in the shadow of the mattress company. Furniture stores, he said, were not the place to be selling pajamas and not even the best place to sell quilts. He said our products were better than premium giveaways and should be promoted on their own merits. We should be placing them in the bed linen and pajama departments of our department stores, not the furniture and mattress departments. We should be making flame-retardant pajamas for grown-ups, not just kids. Grown-ups smoke in bed and are more likely to set themselves on fire than kids are. And on and on. It all made sense to me, but whenever you start talking about doing things differently people get worried about what it means for them. Harold said our real problem was that BestRest had a national sales force of mattress salespeople, not pajama salespeople. BestRest's customers were furniture stores, not pajama stores, that the conventions, shows, trade press, and brand recognition for BestRest are all oriented to the furniture trade, not bedclothes, white sales, or children's clothing. His view is that if SafeSleep is really going to be its own company, it needs its own *identity*, its own *purpose*, and its own *sales force* selling to its own *customers*. It has to get out of the hip pocket of BestRest.

"The problem with this is that as soon as you pull the SafeSleep line away from the mattress sales force, a guy like Ted, who has gotten a lot of mileage out of it, yells 'ouch.' I think Harold's basically right when he says that you can't establish the quality of a product by giving it away in one place and hoping to sell it somewhere else. But Ted's probably right, too, that his mattress orders will go down, at least for a while, if we pull the SafeSleep line from him, because that's what's already happened where we've begun to separate the line from the mattress business. Ted's not just worried about his volume, he's worried about his bonus benefits. He's doing one helluva job making me feel guilty, that it will be on my head to explain to both of our wives why he and Ada won't be along on this winter's 'customer cruise' since he'll be coming in under quota and won't qualify for the trip. Why doesn't he go make his *stores* feel guilty? It's their fault if they short-order him, not mine.

But the truth is, Lynn and I had dinner with Ted and Ada last week and it was not a good time. You could feel the tension. By the end of the evening, I'd gone from feeling bad that I was making them both unhappy to being angry at them for making me so miserable. What right did they have making me feel guilty? I'm trying to run a business and they're upset about the Bahamas. Give me a break!

"I consider Ted and Anderson two of my best friends and if this new job ruins both of these friendships I won't be surprised. When Anderson offered me the presidency he said it was a way to move our relationship to a whole new level, that we were becoming true colleagues, that he couldn't wait to see what would come of it. It's a whole new level all right! I guess if you never want to see a guy again you should become true colleagues with him! But I know if you ask Anderson he'll say he's just as available, that it's *me*, that *I* don't call. And that's true. I just stay away from him these days and figure that when he needs to tell me something he will. I'd leave our meetings feeling as if we'd talked a lot but I had no clearer idea where I was when I left than when I'd come in. I'd run my sense of what was going on with SafeSleep or what needed to happen by him, and I'd have no idea where he stood on any of it. Half the time I felt he couldn't care less and had lost interest in the whole thing. Then he'd make some kind of comment like 'Nobody smokes anymore,' when I'd bring up Harold's idea about an adult pajama line, and I'd spend a week trying to figure out which way the wind was blowing.

"It was very clear that he didn't want to be asked straight out what he thought we should do. It was very clear that he wanted me to have a plan. But it was also clear that he liked some plans better than others. He'd dump all over a lot of Harold's ideas. I'd leave his office and find myself down on Harold for the next three days. I'd feel that he was trying to warn me away from Harold but wouldn't come right out and say so. What I'd always liked about Anderson was that he was a straight shooter. He'd always tell you exactly what he wanted, and what he said he wanted turned out to be exactly what he really did want. You didn't have to decode him.

"I find him a lot harder to read right now and it makes me uneasy. One meeting he tells me to quit worrying about Ted and the Bahamas and start worrying about two hundred Teds and the BestRest CEO who's going to see *all* his sales numbers down when we get SafeSleep completely out of the BestRest bloodstream. I left his office totally humiliated. I felt that I'd completely missed the boat. I felt the way you feel when you buy your first car and think you've figured out exactly what your monthly costs will be, and then they come at you with six different additional items and the government wants an excise tax and you feel you just didn't know what it was really all about. I figured he thought I was doing a worthless job and was probably the wrong guy for the job anyway. And then the next time I meet him he's all enthusiastic about getting SafeSleep its own sales force and its own customer base, and I'm thinking, 'What about the CEO?' He doesn't tell me he thinks I'm doing well and he doesn't tell me I'm screwing up. The only thing I know for sure is he'd be disappointed in me somehow if I had to ask.

"We had some pretty clear ways to measure how SafeSleep was doing when I was just running it as a division reporting to him. But the bottom line is just one number now, and if we go ahead with the things Harold and I are talking about, it's not going to be the pretty number it was. Pulling the products out of the furniture stores, establishing new customer groupings, testing a market for flame-resistant sleepwear for adults, running our own ad campaign separate from BestRest—all these things are going to put us way down in the red for the short haul. How do you evaluate something like that? I want Anderson to sign on to these plans and he keeps saying, 'If this is where *you* want to put *your* chips.' I feel that he's putting me out on a limb all by myself and saying he's down on the ground cheering for me. A fat lot of help that is! When I tell him it must be nice for him to be out of it he gets annoyed and says, 'Don't think for a minute I'm out of it! You're turning Safe-Sleep from a cute afterthought into a corporate factor, and if it goes down the tubes they'll be asking me what happened.' And then I feel even less reassured because now I'm responsible for *Anderson's* not getting hurt. That's a lot of what's different about being the president. I've got to worry about Ted. I've got to worry about Anderson. The balls keep dropping into my hands and I keep throwing them back up into the air and somehow it's all supposed to keep going and no one is supposed to fall to the ground. My arms are getting awfully tired, and I'm not exactly sure what I did to deserve this wonderful job."

Peter and Lynn may both be unhappy with their current situations at work. And they may identify a similar *source* for their unhappiness: a shift toward greater employee participation. But their words suggest that they actually experience these changes quite differently. In fact, their words suggest that there are important differences in the way they experience and understand the whole enterprise of work in general.

Our culture's experts in the world of work and management are no shyer than our authorities on marriage and parenting. They have created no less daunting a literature of implicit or explicit prescription and expectation for success, mastery, or excellence. That the people who write about, and are listened to, on the subjects of management and of marriage do not refer to each other in their texts, and seem to have no awareness of each other, is not, at first, surprising. The intellectual training, professional identification, analytic language, and established frames of reference in each field are different. It is understandable that the experts act as if the differing literatures do not matter to each other. The tasks, problems, skills, and intentions they address do not seem at all similar. An employee is not a child, and it is more often a problem than a solution when she is regarded as one. The idea of effectively "managing" our spouses is as offensive as the idea of better loving our employees is inappropriate. The very exercises of devotion, loyalty, and signing on to the other's agenda that seem to define the bonds of marital partnership may be constraining and exploitative within the bonds of employment.

For these reasons, it may seem strange if I now suggest that what the literatures have in common is actually far more impressive than what distinguishes them. Like the marriage and parenting literature, the management literature demands not mere skills but a qualitative order of mental complexity. More important and more to the point, the *specific* order of complexity demanded in the workplace is precisely that which is demanded in the home and family. We would have a much better understanding of what contemporary culture really demands of its adult constituents were we to violate existing custom and bring the literatures of love and work together, look upon them as the intellectual artifacts of a single culture at a single time, and subject their aspirations and exhortations to epistemological analysis. I want to make use of the joint and separate travail of Lynn and Peter to do exactly that.

Many of the attributes encouraged by contemporary management authorities are evidenced in Lynn's account of the move to school-based management at Highland Junior High. According to my survey of a wide range of sources, we are expected, as workers:

1. *To invent or own our work* (rather than see it as owned and created by the employer).

2. *To be self-initiating, self-correcting, self-evaluating* (rather than dependent on others to frame the problems, initiate adjustments, or determine whether things are going acceptably well).

3. *To be guided by our own visions at work* (rather than be without a vision or be captive of the authority's agenda).

4. *To take responsibility for what happens to us at work externally and internally* (rather than see our present internal circumstances and future external possibilities as caused by someone else).

5. *To be accomplished masters of our particular work roles, jobs, or careers* (rather than have an apprenticing or imitating relationship to what we do).

6. *To conceive of the organization from the "outside in," as a whole; to see our relation to the whole; to see the relation of the parts to the whole* (rather than see the rest of the organization and its parts only from the perspective of our own part, from the "inside out").

Lynn's words express a degree of frustration with herself and her colleagues, but they also convey self-possession and personal authority in relation to her work. Although very few people who work in organizations have jobs they themselves have actually invented, there is still a sense in which people do or do not "make up" or invent their job, regardless of the fact that someone hired them for a prescribed position. Lynn's words evince her own deep-running possession of the design of her work. No matter how competing forces in a complex bureaucratic life inevitably move to alter or compromise her possession, she responds, perhaps unwittingly, by using such incursions as occasions for reestablishing her ownership of her work. She does this without belligerence, off-putting self-assertion, or any need to set herself against or even move further away from those who would compromise her self-possession. On the contrary, she says she and Carolyn, her employer, actually had one of their better and more intimate conversations when Lynn met with her to clarify and reassert her design of her work role. Lynn does not hold it against Carolyn when she suggests that Lynn's personal and professional debts make her beholden to her employer, but neither is Lynn confused by her own genuine feelings of gratitude and indebtedness to Carolyn, or by her own belief that her employer does have the right to expect some kind of loyalty in their relationship.

Without actually becoming involved in a fight with her boss, she nevertheless contends against the way Carolyn defines her debt and her loyalty and sets these definitions aright in a way that acknowledges she is still indebted and loyal. She makes clear she is a team player as much as ever, but that her play is governed first by the work design of which she is the author and only then by her recognition of Carolyn's own wishes, needs, or expectations. Like Ibsen's Nora, Lynn recognizes a loyalty to herself, but it is not, as in Nora's case, a loyalty so tenuously glimpsed that it can only come before her loyalties to husband and children. It seems that Lynn can hold onto her other loyalties, to employer or colleague, *in the context of* her loyalty to herself. She does not have to *leave* Carolyn to express her loyalty to herself as Nora feels she must leave Torvald.

Lynn's conversation with Carolyn does not have the character of winning or wresting back the design of her job from a controlling boss or even a strategizing adversary. Her moves in the conversation reflect her sense that she has been the owner of her work and will continue to be. When other players in the organization (in this case, Carolyn) temporarily losing sight of this fact, as inevitably they will (in this case due more to Carolyn's own temporary stresses and needs than any premeditated intention to dominate or win advantage), Lynn's moves merely remind the organization of this preexisting fact. It is not that she is necessarily conscious she is doing it. Her "ownership" of her work seems more like the capacity of an experienced bike rider to maintain her balance while riding. It is an equilibrium that is now quite natural to her. She does not work to achieve it or even think about how she is doing it. It is just who and how she is. She *does* notice when a bump in the road threatens for a moment to disrupt that balance, but then she quite automatically moves to reestablish her equilibrium. Lynn is finding work difficult these days not so much because she is having a hard time keeping her balance but because she finds herself on an especially bumpy stretch of road.

Of course, no one but the self-employed owns or invents a job. Someone invented it before she arrived, gave it to her, and can take it away. But Lynn's account demonstrates that irrespective of who invents and owns our job, we can still be the creator and owner of our work. Any distillation of the contemporary literature on work would surely begin with the claim upon us to *invent* or *own* our jobs. We are told we must come to see that "your job belongs to you," "you have some control over your work," "your job is part of who you are,"[1] "the most trustworthy source of authority comes from within the person," "treat the business as your own," "act on your own values," "stand for [your] own autonomy," "be conscious of, but uncontrolled by, the expectations of [your] bosses," "recognize fully that [you] are not in this job simply to seek [your] bosses' approval," and "the key to survival is not in [your] bosses' hands; it is in the quality and integrity of the work that [you] do; it is in the quality and integrity of the way [you] manage [your] relationships."[2] Figure 5.1, for example, is a fair representation of the experts' view of what we need to do to succeed at work.[3] The mental demand (here made upon engineers) that we own our work runs throughout the experts' list of "strategies" (even into the strategy of "followership"!).

The way Lynn resists allowing her ownership of her work to be absorbed into Carolyn's definition of loyalty is just one expression of how Lynn reestablishes the balance that now feels natural to her. We also see how she stays on this bicycle, in spite of the inevitable potholes of modern organizational life, when she comments on the difference between administrators and teachers or principals and department chairs.

Nearly all organizations are hierarchical. Positions at the top generally enjoy greater power, prestige, privilege, and salary than those lower down. The hierarchical superiority of, for example, the principal's role can easily serve to coopt or absorb the teacher's or chair's ownership of

"Well, I'm employed by them, but I'm working for me."

Drawing by Cline; © 1990 The New Yorker Magazine, Inc.

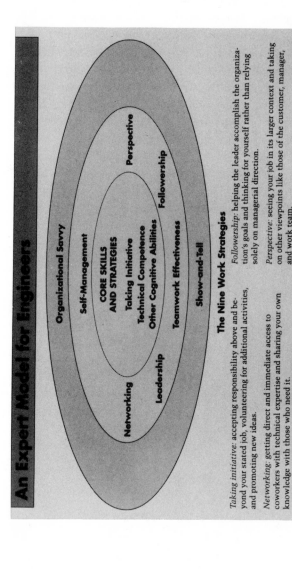

An Expert Model for Engineers

Organizational Savvy

Self-Management

CORE SKILLS AND STRATEGIES
Taking Initiative
Technical Competence
Other Cognitive Abilities

Perspective

Followership

Networking

Leadership

Teamwork Effectiveness

Show-and-Tell

The Nine Work Strategies

Taking initiative: accepting responsibility above and beyond your stated job, volunteering for additional activities, and promoting new ideas.

Networking: getting direct and immediate access to coworkers with technical expertise and sharing your own knowledge with those who need it.

Self-management: regulating your own work commitments, time, performance level, and career growth.

Teamwork effectiveness: assuming joint responsibility for work activities, coordinating efforts, and accomplishing shared goals with coworkers.

Leadership: formulating, stating, and building consensus on common goals and working to accomplish them.

Followership: helping the leader accomplish the organization's goals and thinking for yourself rather than relying solely on managerial direction.

Perspective: seeing your job in its larger context and taking on other viewpoints like those of the customer, manager, and work team.

Show-and-tell: presenting your ideas persuasively in written or oral form.

Organizational savvy: navigating the competing interests in an organization, be they individual or group, to promote cooperation, address conflicts, and get things done.

Figure 5.1 The Mental Demands at Work: An Expert Model for Engineers. Reprinted by permission of *Harvard Business Review:* An exhibit from "How Bell Labs Creates Star Performers" by R. Kelley and J. Caplan (July/August 1993). Copyright © 1993 by the President and Fellows of Harvard College; all rights reserved.

her work. But must it? When Lynn defines each role, insisting that each has its integrity, that a principal's encroachment on the teacher's role is no more acceptable to her than a teacher's encroachment on the principal's, she demonstrates the capacity to distinguish between people's *social* power in an organization and their *psychological* power to define who owns the work. She demonstrates that the question of who owns one's *work* is not necessarily determined by social organization and political advantage, by who owns one's *job*. When she says that the hospital administrator doesn't tell the surgeon where to cut, she does not deny that the administrator is the surgeon's boss, that the administrator has forms of control he or she can properly exercise over the surgeon, including removing the surgeon from the job. But she also makes it clear that whatever control the administrator exercises over the surgeon's job, it does not extend to control over the surgeon's work. Lynn thus complicates the issue of power in hierarchical relationships at work: neither the boss nor the subordinate is the sole possessor of superior power. Rather, as she constructs it, in some aspects of their relationship the boss holds the upper hand and in some aspects the subordinate holds the upper hand.

How is she able to do this? By some accounts, this capacity is associated with "professionalism." When one's work is an institutionalized profession, like law, education, or medicine, inherent codes of ethical and professional conduct require a person to serve simultaneously in the positions of "hired hand" and "master of one's fate." When I hire a lawyer, for example, he or she is working for me and is thus in some sense my subordinate; I hold power to remove this person from his or her job. At the same time, the lawyer should be governed by an internal code of conduct he or she will not be willing to violate. So however much I own the lawyer's job, the lawyer should own his or her work. But obviously, written codes of professional conduct cannot ensure a professional's capacity to adhere to the code, and not merely because humans are sinners and will fall short of the noblest aspirations of their profession. What if, for many, the failure to adhere to this code is not about the suspension of a perfectly performable skill in favor of a baser motive (say, financial gain) but about the incapacity actually to understand what is really being required in the code? What if such a code is itself an epistemological demand?

Lynn's capacity to construct two different power positions in one relationship is obviously not an ability that automatically accompanies the social identification of a particular kind of work with a "profession." We all know "professionals" who do not demonstrate such a capacity, just as we all know "nonprofessionals"—blue collar, clerical, support staff workers—who do. When then Attorney General Elliot Richardson refused Richard Nixon's appeal to employee loyalty by resigning rather than firing Watergate special prosecutor Archibald Cox, he demonstrated this capacity; he lost his job but he retained his ownership of his work. But the same capacity is also being demonstrated by the anonymous housecleaner I wrote about in *The Evolving Self*, who makes clear to her employers before she agrees to work for them that in order for her to do her work according to her own standards she has a number of requirements, including what specific cleaning equipment must be present in the house.

It may well be that the capacity Lynn demonstrates—to hold onto two different conceptions of power and authority within one work relationship—is a capacity people would want to associate with their concept of "professionalism." But then we have to realize that some lawyers are not professionals and some housecleaners are. What it means to be "professional" might have less to do with external social definition than with internal psychological capacity.

That this is so may best be seen in those contexts where whole groups of workers, blue collar and white collar, struggle to achieve ownership of their work in spite of an institutionally inferior position in the power hierarchy. Somewhere in this picture there is always someone who, while still standing in the institutionally less powerful position, is also able to *stand up* to those in the more powerful position. The sight of the factory worker Norma Rae standing bravely on a shop table with her union sign may be Hollywood's version, but I have heard enough testimony from those who have worked in and for trade unions to know that while a union can be just another source of externally derived directive, it can also provide the supports that enable people to hear and develop their own voices, to create their own internal authority.[4]

An example that is far from Hollywood, far even from the United States, comes from the research of the Taiwanese labor educator Lin-Ching Hsia.[5] Hsia studies the struggle for "fully autonomous unions," worker organizations that are not under the direction of management or ownership, in Taiwan. She tells the story of a critical moment in the life of one such union when it was still in the formative stages. The company owner (whom the employees called "Young Boss," since he was the son of the former owner and had been known to many of the workers since he was a small child playing in the factory) walked into a meeting of 250 workers without warning. Deferentially, one of the union leaders asked Young Boss if he would like to speak on the matter at hand. (The workers were discussing the differences between a to-be-established union proposed by management and a worker-initiated union proposed by some of the factory workers.) Young Boss spoke about his longtime support for the concept of a union in general, about his sense that management's proposal for how the union should be run was a good one, that he couldn't understand why they were not satisfied with it, and finally, with great emotion, about his long friendship with and affection for the workers, many of whom, he noted, had played with him in these very spaces when he was a child. Hsia writes:

> The previously enthusiastic group climate was changing into silence at that moment. No one immediately responded to his talk; the whole group kept silent for about three minutes. Then Mr. J. stood up and gave a talk which played an important function in reframing the affective relationship between a "kind patriarch" and a "nice family member" into a picture of the management-worker relationship in industrial society.

Here is what Mr. J. said (translated into English):

> We very much appreciate your willingness to communicate with us face to face . . . We can see your gesture is a caring and a protective one, but to organize a union is our workers' business. Due to your situation as a boss, your kindness and sincerity may lead to consequences that are not beneficial to our workers. It is not about you as a person but is related to your job position. Today, you are the boss, so your words will be perceived as a kind of "order." It is just hard for the workers to be able to communicate with you equally within the context we have now encountered. At this critical moment, our workers need a space in which they can organize a union all by themselves. At this moment, any "kind" suggestion may interfere with their initiatives. Although you have a "good" proposal, it needs the workers themselves to make their decision as to whether they accept it. They need the space now. And the most important thing is that our workers also have their own proposal.[6]

Hsia writes that after Mr. J.'s intervention, the workers gradually began to express their dissatisfaction and disagreement with management's proposal in the presence of Young Boss. Then, says Hsia, a dramatic example of the patriarchical relationship took place. While responding to the confrontations of several older workers, Young Boss disclosed his sadness and shock. Tears came down his cheek. "I had never in my life sensed that I was a capitalist until this moment," he said. The whole group was now affected by his tears. A few workers immediately expressed apologetic feelings. Mr. J. told me that he had experienced this as the most critical moment because he could feel that Young Boss's tears generated a kind of guilt feeling and some workers began to blame themselves. He then made another decisive intervention to reframe the touching tears by saying, "We know you must feel very hard now, because to learn how to become a modernized boss, to face the challenge, is a tough task of adjusting. This is a process we all need to face and go through . . . This is the price of learning to be a modern manager." The group tension was released to a certain degree after Mr. J.'s intervention, and the group was able to continue its discussion about the workers' proposal.[7]

Mr. J., like Lynn on the other side of the world, owns *and retains ownership of* his work. Like Lynn, Mr. J. too holds onto his bonds of affection for his employer but will not allow these bonds to coopt him. In Hsia's own terms, to do so he must stand apart from an engrained cultural definition of the relationship between owner and worker, from a tradition of deference to those who occupy a superior hierarchic position, from patriarchic tradition. As different as the culture of China is from that of the United States, Hsia makes it clear that to make such a move it is not enough for Mr. J. and his fellow workers simply to develop the courage to overcome their *fear* of those to whom they defer (as if intimidation alone is the source of their subordination). They must also overcome themselves, their own definition of the rightness of such deference. They must overcome their own pain at being the cause of Young Boss's tears. Mr. J. is teaching both his employer and his fellow workers about the distinction between our connection to persons and our connection to the roles they occupy. And, interestingly, he himself refers to the lesson he is teaching as modernism.

In a similar way, we can see whole professions that have historically been in a subdominant relationship to more powerful professions—nursing in relation to doctoring, school teaching in relation to school administration, religious education in relation to the clergy, for example—nonetheless seeking to establish and maintain the distinct integrity and self-possession of their professions. In spite of their less powerful positions within the institutions of hospital, school, or church, some members of these professions, like Mr. J. in the Taiwanese factory, are essentially seeking to reconstruct long-standing relationships and loyalties. Since the subdominant professions have been historically female and the dominant professions historically male, it is understandable that, like Mr. J., they characterize these traditional relationships as "patriarchal" and warn against "cooptation." A 1990 issue of *Nursing Outlook*, for example, features an article entitled "The Moral Failure of the Patriarchy,"[8] and, in another article, Joyce Roberts, the director of a nursing program, writes, "Collaboration between nurses and physicians has been characterized as co-optation because what nurses view as collaboration, physicians may view as supervision."[9]

What exactly is this psychological capacity that allows people to meet the demand or expectation that adults "own" their work? What allows them to retain ownership when, like Lynn, Mr. J., or the members of subdominant professions, they are in an institutionally less powerful relationship to those who would take it from them? To be clearer about this, let's take a look at Peter's work story. As in Lynn's experience, the theme of maintaining one's equilibrium seems to run through Peter's work story, too—he himself says he is trying to balance a lot of balls—but it is a different kind of equilibrium than Lynn's. Lynn seems to move automatically or unselfconsciously to reestablish her ownership of her work when Carolyn temporarily makes claims to coopt her, and we can see Peter also moving automatically and unselfconsciously to reestablish the balance with which he is most identified. In the fateful conversation in which Anderson Wright offers Peter the presidency of SafeSleep, Anderson not only reconstructs the nature of Peter's job, he reconstructs his expectations of Peter. He reconstructs how he wants to be connected to Peter or partnered with Peter, and how he wants Peter partnered with him. Peter's acceptance of the presidency is no more a conscious and deliberate choice than Lynn's setting Carolyn straight about loyalty and team membership is a conscious and deliberate choice to rearticulate her ownership of her work. Peter saw the new place to which Anderson moved the relationship and, acting to reestablish the form of equilibrium with which he is identified, he followed. He did what was called for to preserve faithfully his place within the fold.

The automatic and unselfconscious moves we make to neutralize what we experience as unbalancing forces reveal not the commitments we *have* but those that *have us*, those with which we are identified. Put another way, these moves reveal not the commitments we *have* but those we *are*, the commitments that are "subject" for us. Lynn and Peter are both committed people. When the exercise of their commitments at work is compromised, they each feel disturbed and find work "too much with us these days." In the exercise of their commitments each displays courage: it could not have been easy for Lynn to interrupt her boss's "reading [her] the riot act," nor for Peter to accept a job that left him immediately wondering what he had gotten himself into. The difference between them is not one of being committed or having the courage to act on behalf of the commitments with which they are identified. The difference lies in the commitments themselves.

It is easy to take a condescending view of Peter's work predicament. His efforts to balance the needs of his subordinates and superordinates—to keep everyone happy—leave him overwhelmed and unable to act without great difficulty because each move on behalf of repairing or sustaining one relationship is disruptive or injurious to another. So long as he was primarily a subordinate—playing catch with Anderson—this was not a problem. But now that he is the person who must call the shots, now that he is *expected* by Anderson and subordinates alike to call the shots, the world of work has changed even if his office and secretary have not. Although he seeks to continue the same job—to discern and meet Anderson's expectations—work has come to feel quite different because Anderson's new expectation is essentially that Peter call his own shots and stop meeting his expectations! Although he says it is a new ballgame, as long as Peter continues to relate to Anderson's reconstruction of their relationship as if it were *the same game but with new expectations*, he is never going to feel quite right at work. He will go on seeing Anderson's opinions and evaluations (about an adult pajama line, about the overall effect on mattress sales of separating the product line, about Peter's new associate, Harold) not as the honest reactions of an interested party but as indirect ways of telling Peter what he expects. The clearer Anderson makes it that he is not the one calling the shots, the more Peter feels either that he has become "harder to read" or that he has removed himself from having a stake in the operation. Peter surmises that Anderson has doubts about Harold, but Anderson's concerns may have less to do with Harold than with the way he sees Peter abdicating his leadership to Harold.

So what is Peter's problem? We could imagine that Lynn might thrive with a boss like Anderson, but Peter is having trouble. The management literature would see Peter as overly fearful, dependent, and willing to compromise his own beliefs or convictions for the approval of others. In *The Empowered Manager*, for example, Block writes: "If we are focussed on seeking others' approval . . . then we run the risk of sacrificing our integrity . . . for the sake of finding the most popular path."[10] The implication here is not that Peter is acting in consonance with the commitments to which he is subject but that he is actually compromising them on behalf of some overriding character weakness, the need for approval. The implication is that Peter has some other agenda or vision or way of understanding his work and his relationship to it, this other way being his integrity, which he then sacrifices or ignores or undermines. Peter's "dependency" is thus viewed as if it were an addiction to alcohol, an irresistible urge to drink to the point of drunkenness that overrides his preexisting determination to be a sober and responsible citizen. According to this view, if we could just eliminate Peter's character flaw, his addiction or dependency, his already existing "integrity" could operate undistracted.

Another common approach in the management literature is less moralistic but provides essentially the same picture of who Peter "really" is: Peter's need is not for a *cure* to his *addiction* but for a *remediation* to his *learning deficit*. What Peter lacks, according to this view, are the skills to assert himself, to claim his own space, to resist feeling guilty about the needs and demands of all these people that are swirling around him. The picture here is that Peter lacks a set of skills, which need to be "input." Peter obviously has a fine mind, but for some reason he hasn't had the chance to learn something he needs to learn to function well at work. What his mind knows needs to be increased. This is essentially an *informational* stance toward Peter's problem. The "form" of Peter, or Peter's mind, does not need to change any more than the "form" of the "addicted," dependent Peter has to change. It is just that we have to get something "bad" *out* of the form (the *addiction* view) or get something "good" *into* the form (the *learning deficit* view). Block could not state more clearly his view of how employers can help workers become more empowered than when he urges them to "create ways to push authority inside the person."[11]

An *in*formational stance leaves the form as it is and focuses on changing what people know; it is essentially a *training* model for personal change. I would contrast this with a *trans*formational stance, which places the form itself at risk for change and focuses on changes in how people know; it is essentially an *educational* model for personal change. The word *education* is built out of the Latin prefix *ex* plus the verb *ducere* ("to lead") and suggests a "leading out from." While *training* increases the fund of knowledge, *education* leads us out of or liberates us from one construction or organization of mind in favor of a larger one.

A *transformational* view of Peter's predicament rejects the notion that in juggling the balls of competing expectations he is sacrificing his integrity. Rather, it considers the integrity of the current form of mind he expresses in having to juggle the balls. It rejects the notion that Peter's "dependency" is an invasive disease or a blight upon his otherwise fine character that is in need of excision. Rather, it considers his so-called "dependency" as the perfectly respectable expression not of an appendage to how Peter is formed but of the heart of how he is formed. It considers that Peter's current integrity, with which he *is* congruent—the perfectly respectable way in which he is now formed—may be a poor match with the curriculum he faces at work. There need be no shame in this circumstance any more than there need be shame in any student who finds himself faced with a curriculum that will require his real growth for its mastery. Nor is there a lack of energy, interest, or money on the part of corporate America for helping people *be* more effective at work. What may be lacking is an adequate conception of the changes people need support in making to become more effective at work. What may be lacking is an understanding that the demand of work, the hidden curriculum of work, does not require that a new set of skills be "put in" but that a new *threshold of consciousness* be reached.

Only in a world where the management and parenting literatures do not communicate with each other would it make sense to call Peter's form of commitment "dependency" and regard it as an invasive blight on his character. According to Block, the essence of this "dependency" is the erroneous thinking that "the fundamental and most trustworthy source of knowledge is outside of oneself. There is wisdom external to ourselves that needs to be revered and respected. It is this reverence of the external authority in the organization that leads to our very strong feeling of dependency and our wish for approval."[12]

But when this "faulty" way of thinking, feeling, and revering appears fully in Lynn and Peter's son, Matty, it will not be called "dependency." Far from being regarded as an invasive blight, it will be welcomed and heralded as an important and necessary development, even as the very source of Matty's ability to meet a number of the expectations that attend adolescence. We could not have a more powerful example of how wrong many psychologists may be when they suggest that our culture does not clearly distinguish between the eras of adolescence and adulthood. This view—that adolescence is the last clearly demarcated phase of the lifespan, the point after which developmental theories lose their voice, that the definitional place where adolescence ends and adulthood begins is vague, arbitrary, or nonexistent—is clearly in need of retirement. The difference between what we ask of adolescents and what we ask of adults is as dramatic as that between our expectation for early childhood and latency or for latency and adolescence. And although we have not yet recognized it, a qualitatively different order of mind—as different as that between prelogical and concrete thinking, or between concrete and abstract thinking—is called for to meet these expectations in adulthood.

Lynn's capacity to "own" her work and retain that ownership in the face of challenges to it does not derive merely from the fact that she is a member of a profession. And Peter's discouragement over the impossibility of satisfying all his colleagues at work does not derive from his "dependency." Rather, these differing equilibria reflect a distinct order of consciousness, a different relationship between what is subject and what is object in their ways of knowing. We said that although she did not recognize it, Lynn was actually combining two relationships into one in her complex construction of her interactions with her boss, Carolyn. In one "subrelationship" she is the subordinate, recognizing and respecting the hierarchical superiority of Carolyn's position, but in another she is the one in the position of greater authority, preserving the working conditions she requires. Constructing either subrelationship would require *cross-categorical* structures of knowing. The capacity to integrate two different "subrelationships" into a single complex relationship requires the ability to take the cross-categorical structures as an *object* of knowing, minimally the fourth order of consciousness. Were one *subject* to cross-categorical structures one could *not* integrate them into some new way of knowing.

A typical evaluation of Lynn's behavior with Carolyn would be that she has "the ability to defend her boundaries." But she would not even have boundaries that needed defending were it not for her capacity to differentiate herself from cross-categorical structures rather than be subject to, or identified with, them. The "boundaries" that get reflected in our social relationships with others do not get their start in the social realm. It is not, after all, really the other person one is keeping on the other side of the boundary, it is their *claim*. The boundaries that we demonstrate in our *social* interactions reflect the *internal* boundaries we maintain psychologically. Lynn is able to limit how compelled she is by Carolyn's claim on her because she is able to regulate the cross-categorical ways of knowing within herself. Both Carolyn's expectations of Lynn (from the subrelationship in which Carolyn has superior power) and Lynn's own expectations of Carolyn (from the subrelationship in which Lynn has superior power) are regulatable by Lynn. They have a place in the more complex system to which she is subject in her way of knowing. When Carolyn temporarily tries to move a subrelationship into a position of eminence, it disrupts Lynn's equilibrium and she reestablishes it.

Peter, by contrast, would typically be described as "giving his power away" to the Andersons, Harolds, or Teds of the world, whose concerns become his concerns. This image, a frequent one in the literature on empowerment, depicts the "unempowered" person as one who by "giving away his own authority" *becomes* small by making others large. The obvious training need, then, is how to *reclaim* what one has given away. But a very different way of thinking about what may be required of effective management training for the "unempowered person" results from considering that such persons never "gave away" their power or authority because they never had it in the first place.

The disequilibrium Peter feels cannot be overcome by confining the category of "others' expectations" to its proper place within his system. The disequilibrium comes from living in—being in—the category of expectation and finding it impossible to fulfill one expectation without disappointing another. Peter not only does not take action against the moves of others to become the owner of his work, he also does not fail to "take action" in the sense that he experiences their moves as causing him to lose something he ought to protect. We have no reason to believe Peter feels that Anderson (in defining the new terms of their work relationship) or Harold (in essentially providing the directing vision for Peter's presidency of SafeSleep) is causing him to cave in or give up or abandon some part of himself, or that his comfort with their inventions is due to its congruence with his own inventions. Peter neither moves against nor accedes to "boundary violations" because he does not create these kinds of boundaries. This does not seem to be what he is up to at work. This is not where he is thrown off balance. Lynn's work is not his work. He does not regulate or subordinate the claims others make on him; rather, they regulate him.

The first issue any management training oriented to *transformation* would have to address is exactly this: what is the person having to manage psychologically? Peter has to manage preserving his loyalties to the people with whom he works. Lynn has to manage not allowing such loyalties to overrun the purposes of the bigger system of which they are a part. In a sense, the answer to "the first question for management training" is always the same: what the person has to manage psychologically is himself or herself. But what this management entails differs depending on how the self is constructed, what its central principle of cohesion, its fundamental loyalty, and its principal threat are.

If the self is derived from cross-categorical ways of knowing, as seems to be the case with Peter, the looming failure to preserve a collection of irreconcilable expectations may be experienced as a difficulty in holding *himself* together. There is no reason for Peter to experience this as "dependency," or for us to suggest that he is any less "loyal to himself" than Lynn. If Lynn does not have Peter's difficulty, it is not because her system of knowing is able to hold together this collection of expectations, but because she is able to subordinate them to some supervening principle. This supervening principle can regulate or mediate the cross-categorical structures of loyalty, relationship, expectation, value, belief, and conviction. When they conflict it can choose among them or order their priority.

These cross-categorical structures are precisely the balls Peter is trying to juggle. He is beset with five, ten, fifteen balls, each one a different loyalty, value, expectation, or conviction. He can no longer throw them to Anderson because Anderson no longer wants to catch them. A juggler in control of the juggling understands that he is really throwing the balls to *himself*. But Peter is not in control. He cannot yet throw them to himself because he does not know what to do with them, so he is trying to keep them in the air. But because he is identified with them he is "up in the air" himself, trying to keep himself and his charges from crashing to the ground. Being up in the air with them himself, he is directly and *immediately* affected by each thing that happens to them. Lynn, however, is only *mediately* affected by the loyalties, values, and expectations that are important to her at work. She eventually handles, treats, and acts upon them according to the *systemic* way of knowing with which she is identified.

The very idea of *managing*—the central preoccupation in the work literature and the schools of business—suggesting as it does the activities of handling, arranging, configuring, deciding, executing, finessing, operating, and presiding would seem to require or to imply the *authoring* capacities of the fourth order of consciousness. The greater psychological differentiation of this way of knowing is reflected in the social ability to order the parts by first distinguishing oneself from them. The greater internality of this way of knowing now creates the self—not the present social surround—as the *source* of direction and value. These capacities are called for not only in the first of the expectations upon us at work—to own or invent our labor—but in all of them.

The expectation that we be self-initiating, self-correcting, and self-evaluating rather than depend on others to frame the problems, initiate the adjustments, or determine whether things are going acceptably well, runs through much of the work literature and through the stories of Lynn and Peter. In a sense, this expectation is really an extension of owning one's work, since this is the way we might naturally behave if we truly regarded our jobs as belonging to us. Lynn and Peter's difficulties reflect two fundamental ways the work context can default on the requirement to join effective support to a challenging curriculum. In Lynn's case, the espoused philosophy of "school-based management" is indeed a call to rely more on oneself than on the boss, but at Highland Junior High School the boss is herself quite conflicted about how much she really wants her subordinates to be self-initiating.

This is quite common. In suggesting, as I am, that there is an increasing epistemological demand upon workers at all levels to be self-authoring, I am not ignoring the fact that many employers make no such demands at all much less feel conflicted about them. Some employers actually want nothing more from their employees than what the culture wants of adolescents—well-socialized, responsible, loyal workers who will conscientiously perform explicitly assigned duties, as well as pick up on, and feel claimed by, the subtler cues and hopes of their employer. But such managers are in default on what the experts and discourse shapers say the managers of high-performing or *quality* companies (a favorite word) should do. Many more employers are genuinely conflicted about the amount of self-initiating, self-correcting, or self-evaluating they really want their employees to do. They will rail against their employee's "dependency" and bemoan being made into "Big Daddy" or "Big Mama" by employees they say they wish would not act like children, coming to them for every little decision the employees could make perfectly well on their own. But then they will subtly punish or overtly undermine the efforts at self-initiation these same employees make.[13] Such conflicting messages do not make the demand for fourth order consciousness less true, but they do make it more difficult to meet. Lynn may be more ready to meet the demand than Carolyn is ready to support her in meeting it.

Anderson's reconstruction of SafeSleep as a separate company with Peter as its head and himself as its "banker" (a reframing for empowering a subordinate suggested by Block) is likewise a demand for the employee's self-initiation, but in this case it appears that Anderson is able to act congruently with the demand. When people come to him to make decisions that are in Peter's purview, he is able to resist being pulled in and thereby undermining Peter's position. When Peter himself seeks to make use of Anderson as a directional compass, he refuses to let Peter undermine his own position. But Peter's situation is also unsupported in a different way. He is obviously in over his head. Although dogs may learn to swim by being thrown into deep water, the capacity for fourth order consciousness is not an instinct; it evolves. However benign Anderson's intention, he has fulfilled only half the obligation of a good mentor: he has provided a potentially worthwhile challenge but no support to help Peter learn from it. Peter may keep himself afloat by latching onto the life support of Harold's capacity for self-initiation, but borrowing, even hiring fourth order capacities is not the same as being helped to evolve them for oneself.

The requirement to be self-evaluating and self-correcting demands an internal standard. More than cross-categorical values, it requires a theory or a philosophy of what makes something valuable, a meta-leap beyond the third order. Our loyalty is transformed from adherence to a value to the process of originating or inventing what is valuable, a determination that heretofore has been made by the psychosocial surround.

Employers unwittingly demanding fourth order consciousness want nothing more than to stop being this kind of determining psychological surround for their employees. Writing as a school principal about the nervousness he observes in teachers whose classrooms he may visit, Roland Barth surmises

> that teachers live under a cloud of preoccupation with the discrepancy between performance and expectation, between "what I am doing" and "what they want and expect me to do . . . " As principal, one of my personal goals is to be able to walk through the school at any time, with any guest, enter any classroom largely unnoticed by children and teacher. I delight in being ignored, because the response suggests a busy, committed teacher, less concerned about what the outsider thinks than whether the activity is going well for as many children as possible. I value this response because it suggests that teachers know what they have planned, and why. They know it works most of the time for them and for the class—and that sometimes it doesn't. When it does not work, they know it is a problem between teacher and child, not between teacher and superior. I find that teachers who respond to visitors with friendly indifference are generally confident and competent. They have personal and professional authenticity. For these teachers the discrepancy that matters is not between "what I am doing" and "what they want me to do," but rather between "what I am doing" and "what I want to be able to do." Teachers who are intent on making professional behavior consistent with their beliefs about children and learning are seldom preoccupied with conformity to the expectations of others. Conversely the teacher who is unclear on important questions finds that somebody will happily impose external clarity. An instructional vacuum—an empty teacher—is quickly filled by other teachers, parents, principals, school committees, and superintendents.[14]

Barth, one of our more thoughtful writers on school leadership, has an abiding commitment to the professional development of teachers. But even as he (unwittingly) champions the teacher with fourth order consciousness, he cannot avoid a punishing and probably inaccurate depiction of the teacher who cannot yet meet this demand. Why is the teacher who is subject to a superior's expectations called "empty" and "inauthentic"? From whose perspective? Maybe this teacher is full of beliefs and commitments that his behavior, however nervous, is *authentically* expressing. Maybe teachers constructing the world with third order consciousness do so as authentically as anyone else. Maybe "what [they] want to be able to do" *is* "what [they] want me to do"! A principal wanting to hire the psychologically self-employed may find this disappointing, but it seems unlikely that we will find the way to its amelioration by trying to fill the teacher up or get his "true self" to emerge.

The management literature on "burnout" is implicitly tied to this expectation that workers be more self-initiating and self-evaluating; it is also unintentionally punishing of the third order.[15] Much of it is written from a fourth order perspective suggesting that all adults are similarly fourth order and that those who burn out are essentially the weaker-willed, who lack the courage or self-esteem to carry off a way of operating that already makes sense to them. According to Freudenberger, who I believe first coined the term, when burnout occurs it is "almost always an indication that the person's goals have been externally imposed. Somehow he embarked on his present course because it was expected of him . . . He was never the authentic source of his choices and consequently they afford little real satisfaction."[16] Maslach describes the "burnout prone individual" as

> someone who is weak and unassertive in dealing with people . . . is submissive, anxious . . . and has difficulty setting limits . . . is often unable to exert control over a situation and will passively yield to its demands rather than actively limiting them to his capacity to give . . . The burnout prone individual is someone who lacks self-confidence, has little ambition . . . neither a clearly defined set of goals nor the determination and self-assurance needed to achieve them. He or she acquiesces and adapts to the constraints of the situation, rather than confronting the challenges and being more forceful and enterprising. Faced with self-doubt, this person tries to establish a sense of self-worth by winning the approval and acceptance of other people.[17]

But from the perspective of the third order, where the ultimate goal is being in alignment with—being in good faith with—a value-creating surround, it is not at all self-evident or necessary that trying to "establish a sense of self-worth by winning the approval and acceptance of others" is caused by "self-doubt." Does such a person necessarily "lack ambition," "a clearly defined set of goals," "forcefulness" or "enterprisingness," or are these possibly being evinced on behalf of a different construction of what is most important in the world?

The punishing nature of the literature on burnout demonstrates how unintentionally cruel our culture-as-school can be to those who, through no lack of conscientious commitment, are nonetheless currently not the masters of the school's curriculum. It is a poor school whose favorite students are the ones it does not have to teach. It may indeed be true that coming to work with third order consciousness where fourth order consciousness is expected leaves one especially at risk for burnout. But the way this gets seen—as exclusively the problem of "the burnout prone individual"—puts me in mind of a similar mismatch between "real" students and a "real" school. Although I have not been able to find the precise source, someone provided this memorable image while giving testimony before Walter Mondale's Senate Committee on school children at risk in the 1960s. The speaker asked the committee to imagine the young children of migrant farm workers watching their parents at work in the fields—children who, like all children, grow best in the light of their parents' love, admiration, and delight. By the age of four the children begin to be able to understand something of the purpose and meaning of their parents' work in the field and are physically able to help, or do something that feels to them like help. They pick a few fruits or lug a basket a few feet and are paid with the glow in their parents' faces. Their parents' pride and enthusiasm toward their efforts confirms the rightness of what they are learning, the importance of quick, strong, physical movement. Their parents' faces shine at these displays of bodily energy and intelligence. After a few years of this education in the fields they are then enrolled in schools where they understandably continue the same ways of being—before the new adults they find there—that filled their parents' faces with pride and delight. How happy a match could these highly accomplished children (accomplished in the energetic and intelligent uses of their bodies) make with a school that wants them to sit still, perform in turn, and "gather" without using their hands? How utterly bewildering to them must the shadowy frowns and disapproving speech they receive be when they carry on in the Anglo classroom with the same energetic intelligence and conscientiousness that was so meaningful, that turned the lights on in their parents' faces back in the fields. The biggest risk these children face is that, like the "burnout prone individual," they will be seen only as lacking something, as unaccomplished and perhaps even "unambitious," that the expression of their very integrity will be taken as evidence of their maladjustment!

What is really being asked for by the next demand on the list, that we be guided by our own visions at work rather than be without a vision or be captive of the authority's agenda? The fourth order's systemic or ideological way of knowing is almost by definition "guided by its own vision," that is, by its own internal way of authorizing. The demand for a vision is really a demand for an ideological way of knowing. By "ideology" I do not refer to "rigid belief," "blind faith," or a surrender of self to orthodoxy or dogma. I use the term just as the sociologist Karl Mannheim did to refer to a system of explanation amounting to a theory of relationships. An ideological way of knowing may be explicitly about power and social order, as it is for Mr. J., the Taiwanese union organizer performing an on-the-spot political analysis of the coopting nature of Young Boss's "patriarchal" appeals to his workers. Or these dimensions may be more implicit, as they are in Lynn's understanding of her work situation. But in both cases, the way of thinking permits a reflection on relationships and a creating of distinctions within those relationships that reorders existing arrangements according to new values. The expectation upon us might thus be less about the need to have a vision (what former president George Bush called "the vision thing") than about the capacity to organize our knowing in a way that can originate value.

Lynn demonstrates this capacity both explicitly and implicitly in her story about work at Highland Junior High. Explicitly, she reveals an organizing vision when she talks about the school as a "learning place." In (1) her analysis of how the school handles faculty evaluation; (2) her critique of the process by which the school board prepared the faculty for the shift to school-based management; (3) her stand on Carolyn's right to support in her own learning about collaborative leadership; and (4) her negative evaluation of her own expectations for her employer, the idea of the school as a "learning place" is more than just a slogan; it is a quick way of referring to a whole conceptual system that can manage a wide array of novel phenomena in a consistent and coherent fashion.

Nor is this "whole system" a rarefied mental theory, consistent unto itself but disconnected from the stuff of real life, real people, and real demands. It is able to operate in a swirling field of socially constructed realities, agreed-on conventions or traditions, and interpersonal loyalties and expectations (including Lynn's own expectations). But instead of being shaped by these powerful forces the system reconstructs and regulates them according to its own way of determining value. The rest of the organization may operate as if the evaluation process makes sense, or the principal is incompetent, or the faculty briefing was adequate, but Lynn's system holds these ways of shaping reality to her internal standard and independently finds them wanting. She can even hold her own expectation—that Carolyn move to collaborative leadership more smoothly—to that standard and find it wanting.

We see evidence of the same systemic capacity more implicitly in Lynn's critique of Carolyn's response to a council member's proposal. Lynn says, "She didn't identify any merits in the proposal. She didn't even acknowledge the implicit problems the proposal was at least trying to address. She didn't present her problems with the proposal as just *her* problems, which could still leave open for discussion whether these needed to determine the *group's* actual decision. She didn't invite anyone to help her with her problems with the proposal. She just said, 'This is something we can't do.'" Lynn's words are much more than a statement about her system; they are a live demonstration of the system in action. Implicit in her words is a complicated and richly layered "vision," or theory, about giving negative feedback. Lynn's statement frames the situation in ways that create new distinctions and liberate phenomena from their received meanings. Implied in her words, for example, are the following views or beliefs:

1. A negative evaluation of a proposal by the CEO does not necessarily mean that the proposal itself is not valuable.
2. It is better to give negative feedback on a proposal in a way that furthers conversation and exploration, even if the proposal itself is of little value.
3. The manner in which the CEO publicly evaluates a proposal is itself appropriately subject to its own evaluation.
4. We need to distinguish between the validity of a proposal and the validity of its implications (specific problems exist that need a solution).
5. We need to distinguish between one person's objections to a proposal and the idea that the proposal itself is objectionable.
6. Just because one person has an objection to a proposal, it does not mean other people will necessarily have the same objection.
7. The CEO's objection to a proposal does not have to be an issue for her subordinates.
8. People need to take responsibility for their reactions to a proposal and not confuse them with the merits of the proposal itself.
9. People can ask their co-workers for help not only in refining a proposal, but in preserving any of the distinctions already listed, or in improving the process by which the proposal is publicly evaluated.
10. Unilaterally negative evaluations ("This is no good"; "We can't do

that") contribute little to an evaluation process unless they are explained and discussed.

Probably another twenty similar statements could also be listed. These are simply the first ten that occur to me. The point is not that these statements are necessarily wise or uncontroversial but that they are all values, convictions, generalizations, abstractions—cross-categorical structures—*generated* by Lynn's system. They are third order "views" generated by fourth order "vision." Her "theory" (of giving negative feedback) is like a value-generating machine. She is probably not even aware that she holds these ten beliefs, since she did not generate her theory by first learning them and then bundling them together into a system. Rather, the system or theory creates, invents, generates the values. Fourth order consciousness issues third order constructions. Most people with third order consciousness could memorize this list of ten convictions and recite it, but if we were to ask them how they got to these convictions, why they are so, and what makes them true, they would not be able to take us back into the internal value-generating system that Lynn uses to create them.

Several items on the list also intersect with the next general claim upon us at work: that we take responsibility for what happens to us internally and externally, rather than see our present internal circumstances or future external possibilities as caused by someone else. We have already seen that Peter takes on responsibilities that are not his. Now, in hearing about the concerns of his co-workers and in seeing more direct links between his actions and their feelings, he has come to feel responsible for their concerns, for changing the nature of his co-workers' experience. Their concerns, or his responsible relationship to their concerns, become additional balls he must juggle. (It is ironic that because he is not able to own his own work he becomes, inappropriately, the owner of other people's work.) But in addition to taking on responsibilities that are not his, he assigns to others responsibilities that are not theirs: It is Ted who is making him feel guilty, so he is angry at Ted for doing that. It is Anderson who is causing his uneasiness at no longer having a roadmap to Anderson's expectations, so he is put out with Anderson for "keeping him in the dark." If only these people would act differently his experience would be different. It is these people, and not Peter himself, who are making up his inner circumstances.

For Peter to stop making himself responsible for his co-workers' concerns he would have to stop being made up by *their* experience (which would let him see that their experience belongs to them), and he would have to stop seeing the *others* as made up by their experience (which would let him relate to Ted as the "haver" of his own unhappiness and worry, rather than only as unhappy and worried). For Peter to stop making his co-workers responsible for what is not theirs he would have to stop seeing them as made up by *his* experience (so that Anderson is under no compunction to do anything to relieve Peter), and he himself would have to stop being made up by *his own* experience (so he would look more within himself than outside himself for the causes of how he is feeling). But as we saw in Chapter 4, one cannot simply resolve to stop doing these kinds of things. They all require the fourth order capacity to *relate to* one's interpersonal relationships and intrapersonal states rather than *be made up by* them.

Here is a typical problem with a co-worker anyone might experience:

> My associate and I have an agreement that he will take over the office for me every Wednesday at 1:00 P.M. so I can make this licensing course I'm taking over at the university. It's probably the only commitment of his I feel firm about as far as time goes because the course is important to me and he knows that. He has some specific time things I help him out with, in turn, mostly related to his family commitments. Anyway, as I say, the course is important to me—I'm going for certification—and he knows it's important. So, the point is, in the past month he'd already been quite late twice, and this had become a sore point for us. Yesterday was Wednesday and again I had to wait for him until 1:45. I'm sitting there ready to go for 45 minutes; the class has already started. No phone call from him, and in he walks, all full of apology about being caught in a meeting he just couldn't get away from. This is the third time now in five weeks! I wanted to kill him!

Now we might imagine what the speaker might say in response to the sort of question we typically ask in our research interviews, "What about this experience was the *most* upsetting (or annoying) to you?" One person might reply:

> I just feel it's so inconsiderate. He knows how I feel about this and he does it anyway. I just get very upset when I'm late for something like this, and I go out of my way to make sure it doesn't happen, and then he puts me right into the situation I'm trying to avoid. I don't think he can be very respectful of me or my feelings if he does just the thing he

knows I hate the most. The message seems to be: "My involvements are more important than yours; when I can make it, I will, and when I can't that's just how it is!" I feel most upset because I don't feel he's taking me into account enough in all this.

Another person faced with precisely the same situation might say:

> He knows how important this is to me, and yet he keeps not coming through for me. Most upsetting? As I was sitting there at 1:45 all ready to go, I started to think, "Wait a minute, who's really the jerk?" He's already shown me that he's not too reliable in this deal, but I keep depending on him. Maybe I have an associate who can't come through for me on a thing like this, and he and I are both going to have to figure out what this means, and I'm going to have to figure out how important it is to me. But the main thing for now is that I get myself into situations that place my own well being in his hands. There must be a lot of other ways I could be handling this that wouldn't leave me helplessly waiting for him to come through.

The first speaker constructs his experience in terms of his disappointment and his anger over what his associate might be communicating to him by his behavior. If we continued the discussion further and found that this stance—being unhappily made up by his interpretation of his associate's construction of the situation—was apparently the only position the speaker could take, we might begin to wonder if we had not reached a kind of limit, embeddedness, or constraint in the way he is able to see it. We might feel that we have discovered both the realm of what he *knows* he doesn't know (what exactly his associate is communicating through this behavior) and the realm of what he does *not* know he doesn't know (that the situation itself is not a given presented by life, that he does not have to be made up by whatever construction his associate does intend, that he has other options than that of being the aggrieved victim because he himself has a hand in how this situation is being constructed). If he is unable to reflect on this bigger question, although we provide all kinds of opportunities for him to do so, then we might begin to speculate that this reflects not only his *preference* but his epistemological *capacity*.

The second speaker seems to consider the experience within a broader framework. He not only attends to the realm of what is being communicated in his associate's behavior (the workings *within* the interpersonal relationship) but is also able to take a position as a setter of the terms in the relationship. He takes responsibility for the way the situation is organized and directs himself to a different kind of exploration that is not captive of the situation. He clearly sees the very designing of the relationship and its agreements to accord with his own standard or vision as within his province. This speaker now is in a position to take action *outside his skin* to alter his relationship with his associate, but that action is likely to be more effective than the hurt or angry victim response because he has first taken action *inside his skin* to alter himself. He has gone beyond bravely receiving the world according to the other's stamp and then assigning blame to the other for the way he feels, and has rediscovered his own hand in the matter.

Lynn demonstrates this capacity for a broader perspective when she develops a relationship to her own state of impatience and resentment toward Carolyn's unilateral rejection of Alan's proposal. Initially she holds "Carolyn" (as a separate person uninvented by her) responsible for causing her angry and upset state of mind. But before long she sees that what she had been calling "Carolyn" was, in this instance, more properly her own uncomfortable feeling of being unable to live up to her espoused values, a feeling that she had placed onto Carolyn. By not just identifying the internal state of resentment (a third order capacity) but seeing how she created it (a fourth order capacity), she relates to her inner state and to her relationship to Carolyn, transforming both. Both are able to change not because Carolyn does something different (as Peter wants Anderson and Ted to do) but because Lynn herself does something different.

If the expectation upon us to be masters of our work (rather than apprentices or imitators) is more a claim on mind than a demand for the acquisition of particular skills, this has important implications for the field of career development, which has been far more attentive to the development of the *career* than the person having the career. It is one thing to chart the phases of increasing responsibility, range of motion, or institutional authority through which one might be expected to pass as one journeys from a junior to a more senior position at work. Like phase-oriented developmental psychology in general, such an approach lays out a curricular sequence of socially defined tasks. In Table 5.1, Wortley and Amatea summarize such sequences as they derive them from the phasic theories of Levinson, Neugarten, Brim, Gould, Sheehy, Erikson, and others.[18] In our twenties, for example, we are ex-

Table 5.1 A Phaselike Sequence of Work/Career-Related Tasks

Decade	Exterior Tasks	Interior Tasks
Twenties	Job exploration, training/education, and trial entry; establishing career orientation and initial goals; commitment to specific work, area or reevaluation and change or continued job transience	Establishing specific work identity (importance of models); commitment to generativity or productivity with push upward/ahead (importance of formulating a "dream," i.e., some vision of what one is building toward)
Thirties	Committing to set career pattern and striving for vertical movement or readjusting, undergoing training modification; women entering/reentering career arena; women leaving career arena to bear children	Readjusting career goals to realign with changing expectations both of self and of significant others (compromising the "dream"); seeking mastery, promotion, recognition, credentials, confidence ("making it"); crystallizing work identity
Forties	Entering period of peak work commitment, achievement, and recognition; taking on supervising, mentoring, and management functions; possible midlife career change to meet changing personal values and priorities, or to develop own business, or forced change due to age-related organizational displacement	Redefining work role/goals in light of changing values/priorities/possibilities
Fifties	Career culminating, acting as mentor/advisor, "putting in time"; ensuring retirement security; unskilled may face increasing age-related employment problems or forced termination	Beginning to disengage from work role in preparation for retirement or postponing and ignoring upcoming retirement; evaluating and reviewing work accomplishments resulting in feelings of satisfaction/integrity or disappointment

Table 5.1 (continued)

Decade	Exterior Tasks	Interior Tasks
Sixties	Preparing for and realizing retirement; detaching from formal work role with related changes in status, income, and life structure; exploring part-time or volunteer work; cultivating avocations and leisure orientation—doing what one "always wanted to do, but didn't"; fulfilling honorific positions and sage roles	Redirecting physical and emotional energy into other activities or settling into satisfied or dissatisfied inactivity

Source: D. Wortley and E. Amatea, "Mapping Adult Life Changes," *Personnel and Guidance Journal*, April 1982.

pected to formulate, internally, a "dream" or vision of what we are hoping for from work and, externally, to make a trial entry into a specific line of work. In our thirties we are expected to crystallize a work identity and make a commitment to a set career pattern through which we will strive for promotion. In our forties we face the curricular tasks of redefining our work goals in light of new priorities or possibilities and assuming supervisory, mentoring, and managing functions. And so on. These psychological and social tasks parallel the age-defined tasks in the other domains of adult life, and many in the private domain are reminiscent of the expectations I discussed earlier. A list of the overall tasks for the decade of the thirties, for example, would look like this:[19]

At work: seeking mastery, promotion, recognition, credentials, and confidence ("Making It"); crystallizing work identity; readjusting career goals to realign with changing expectations of self and significant others (compromising "the Dream").

At home: balancing, integrating, and prioritizing multiple roles, responsibilities, and commitments to work, mate, family, community; instituting a "family plan" and adjusting this vision to the demands of reality; negotiating relationships to in-laws and extended family; committing to the demands of reality; committing to the "family plan" and investing in the growth, development, and social integration of family members; redefining the primary intimate relationship to reflect familial changes and shifting life style demands, or breaking the primary relationship if a couple cannot resolve growth differences and adapt to changing personal needs (second marriages peak at thirty-five); developing a system of familial intimacy.

This list includes a complex and varied set of tasks, but it also reflects a single common theme, what Neugarten refers to as "the executive processes of personality: self awareness, selectivity, manipulation and control of the environment, mastery, competence, the wide array of cognitive strategies."[20] This *implicit* call for a new level of personal authority, self-possession, and critical thinking in order to meet the demands of these many tasks stands in direct contrast to the *explicit* formulation of phase theorists that the sequence they describe is developmental only in the temporal sense: they do not presume that later curricular demands are inherently more complex, nor do they consider whether increasing mental growth may enable or accompany the successful completion of these tasks.[21]

Although the life phase literature suggests that individuals' internal perspectives are a crucial constituent in the quality of their coping, it fails to provide an understanding of how individuals, even of the same age, may differ in their meaning-interpretive capacity to order and make sense of the tasks before them. Although it considers that the sequence of adult phases tells a story about maturity, it fails to consider that, as in every other story about maturity, both the maturing individual and the accompanying socially constructed expectations do not merely change but develop or grow by becoming more complex. Although the life phase literature recognizes that not all adults are equally successful in accomplishing these phase-specific tasks, it accounts for these differences in success in large part, as Levinson argues, by "personality, social structure, gender, social roles, major life events, [and] biology."[22] But Levinson's list leaves out what may be an even more important factor, namely, the *order of consciousness*, the complexity of the individual's way of knowing. Is the capacity to perform what Neugarten calls the "executive functions" a matter of personality traits or biology or major life events?

The call for mastery in one's work is really more like an external analogue to the call for an internal standard or personal vision. It is more like a call to move beyond the *epistemological* place of identification with the loyalties and values of one's psychological surround than it is a call to move beyond the *temporal* place of apprentice or subordinate. What allows one to exercise mastery over one's work is not merely time on the job or promotion to increasing responsibility but the psychological capacity to find (or, really, to invent) one's own way of "doing it." "One's own way" will certainly be built out of a history of associations, loyalties, and identifications with previous masters and mentors, but one will have converted these to materials and tools that serve one's own way.

We know we have become masters of our work when we have occasion to consider (with a smile or a twinge of apprehension) that if our mentor/supervisor/original boss/sponsor were to see the way we had just handled a given situation he or she might "roll over in his grave"/"wonder if she had created a monster"/"fail to recognize me quite as *his* protégé." We have not forgotten our old associations, our respect for old lessons, our fondness for those who taught them to us. But we no longer pattern ourselves exactly after any of them. Their "way," however much admired, is, finally, not our way, and our way is not quite theirs. We have become "masters" when the pattern we are seeking to follow resides inside not outside. And we might not arrive at this "place" in the development of a career—phase theorists and career-path charters notwithstanding—at forty, might not even arrive at fifty, in spite of our rank or salary. Alternatively, we might arrive before forty, although we still hold a junior position. Our arrival is not a place on a temporal continuum guaranteed by the passage of time. It is rather a place on an *evolutionary* continuum made possible by the emergence of a qualitatively new order of consciousness.

The last claim upon us for effectiveness at work is to be able to conceive of the organization as a whole, to see the "big picture," to look at the business from "the outside in" and not just from our partial, provincial perspective. A claim like this gives us the chance to check in on our own intuitive theories about what makes for this kind of perspective, since we all recognize when people have this ability and, whether we know it consciously or not, we all have some idea about why those who have it have it, and those who don't don't. Perhaps it is just a matter of intelligence. Some people are smarter than others so they "get" more of what's going on. But if we consider people we know who are very smart but strategically naive, we may wonder if what we are talking about is more a matter of sophistication versus innocence: some people have learned the way the real world works and some have not. Or perhaps some people are just born strategists: thinking this way is a talent they have, like being musical or mechanically inclined. Maybe it is a matter of family history: people born into big families, or families with lots of intrigue, or in the right birth order slot to take the role of group strategist have an advantage in this regard. Maybe it has more to do with the power of concentration: some people are less easily distracted by ceaseless trivia and can therefore see the forest for the trees. Maybe it is not intelligence but emotional sensitivity that makes some people better equipped to tune in carefully to what others are feeling and this enables them to see the bigger picture. Maybe it is not a psychological thing so much as a social, systemic thing: a person in a high enough position in an organization is lifted to a vantage point that affords a larger perspective.

The fact is, however, that while there seems to be something plausible in all these explanations, we can think of people and circumstances that defeat each of them. Peter, for example, occupies a loftier position in his organization than Lynn does in hers and yet she seems to take a larger view. In every corporation there is at least one secretary or administrative assistant who has a better grasp of how the parts fit together than many of the executives. If "sophistication" is the opposite of "provincialism" or "parochialism" and refers to having been exposed to a rich diversity of ways of living and believing, we all know widely travelled people who are nonetheless unable to see past their own angle of vision. Some people do tune in emotionally to others more regularly and accurately—Peter perhaps among them—but some of them are also overwhelmed by all they can take in of what others are feeling, and like Peter are left burdened and beset by their sensitivity rather than more comprehensively informed. Some people do have greater powers of concentration but what is to keep them from concentrating on the trees instead of the forest? Peter is concentrating on Ted and his declining bottom line, and Anderson urges him to consider *four hundred* Teds and the company's *overall* bottom line.

The expectation to see "the forest for the trees," "the big picture," how the parts relate to the whole, may be related to family history, power of concentration, political instinct, emotional sensitivity, or sophistication, but I doubt that any of these is the key component. Some of these may be more related to how and whether one would exercise the capacity if one had it. But the capacity itself seems much more like the political or organizational equivalent of the same capacity that enables one to establish ownership of one's work, build an internal standard, create an overall vision, or master one's job. The ability to see "how the parts relate to the whole" describes the capacity for systems thinking, and it is probably greatly aided by the capacity to construct the self as a whole—an organization or a system—regulative of its parts. When the self has become a kind of psychological administrator of an internal institution it is more able to identify with or take the perspective of work as an institution.

Lynn holds a belief in the school as a "learning place," an idea that, stated as simply as this, may be organized in a third or a fourth order way. Lynn is also genuinely put out by Carolyn's resistance to collaborative leadership. Were she to hold her belief in the school as a "learning place" in a third order way, it would be regulated by her own experience of being interpersonally violated by Carolyn. This is the "tree" in the forest she would be attending to here. But this is not what happens. Lynn exercises her idea about the school as a "learning place" so that *it* regulates (but is not regulated by) her own experience of being interpersonally violated. She does not pretend that she is not put out by Carolyn; she does not bury, deny, project, or forget it. But it is not the center of her attention. She is able to hold on to but subordinate the tree of her interpersonal experience to the forest of her systemic identification with the school as a whole. This leads her to conclude that the school must be a "learning place" for everybody, the boss included, a "big picture" *whole* that regulates the *parts*, including the "part" that is Lynn's own upsetting experience with her boss.

The "parts" this demand calls on us to relate to a "whole" are quite complex in themselves. They are not just "facts"—what the organization is really committed to, how X genuinely feels about Y when she is not being diplomatic, how much is too much to spend on that budget item. They are more comparable to Lynn's sense that Carolyn is violating her hope, trust, or expectation for their relationship. For us to see the ceaseless flow of our own on-line experience at work, not just what happens to us but how we care about it, as itself a part (albeit a valuable part) of the whole requires something different than political instinct, emotional sensitivity, mental concentration, or sophistication. It requires the capacity to de-identify with third order parts so we can subordinate them to a fourth order whole. We can call this a kind of "intelligence," but we must be clear that what we are calling intelligence by definition has to do with the relation of parts to wholes, what we take as object and what as subject. We must be clear that this kind of "intelligence" is not something like political instinct or musical talent, which we either have at birth or don't. No one has fourth order consciousness at birth. We must be clear that what we are calling "intelligence" is a capacity that evolves and that this evolution can be encouraged.

When we look into this collection of expectations for success at work we discover that each actually demands something more than a particular behavior or skill. Each is a claim on our minds for a way of knowing. Each amounts to a slightly different way of demanding or expecting a single capacity for psychological authority. This capacity, by now familiar, represents a qualitatively more complex system for organizing experience than the mental operations that create values, beliefs, convictions, generalizations, ideals, abstractions, interpersonal loyalty, and intrapersonal states of mind.

It is qualitatively more complex because it takes all of these as objects or elements of its system, rather than as the system itself; it does not identify with them but views them as parts of a new whole. This new whole is an ideology, an internal identity, a *self-authorship* that can coordinate, integrate, act upon, or invent values, beliefs, convictions, generalizations, ideals, abstractions, interpersonal loyalties, and intrapersonal states. It is no longer *authored by* them, it *authors them* and thereby achieves a personal authority. Despite the surface differences between the various work expectations, they require a common underlying capacity, a common order of consciousness.

It is by now familiar because the order of consciousness these public work expectations require is exactly the same as that required by the roles of adult private life. Whether we are looking at our culture's literature of expertise in the realms of partnering, parenting, or providing, we see what seems to be a single, common, unrecognized claim on the minds of most contemporary adults for the degree of psychological authority described by the fourth order. When we compare this curricular demand to the real-life capacities of most contemporary adults, we glimpse the distinctive shape of the mental burden of modern life.

As different as their public and private lives may be, the order of consciousness to which Peter and Lynn have recourse in their partnering or parenting is not unlike the way of knowing they employ in their work lives. Peter's greater reliance on third order consciousness actively shapes his private and his public realities in a fashion significantly different from Lynn's, who appears to have access to fourth order consciousness. Lynn's and Peter's central organizing principles at work create realities that have striking parallels to the realities they create at home. The difficulty Peter feels over being pulled in too many directions at once by his loyalty to spouse, children, and parents when he is planning a summer vacation may have the same source as the difficulty he feels over being pulled in too many directions by Anderson, Harold, and Ted when he is deciding how to preside over his company.

But Peter and Lynn are not real people, they are fictional devices. We might ask, is the parallel between their public and private realities representative of real people? Do the differing orders of mental complexity that Peter and Lynn demonstrate have a developmental relationship to each other, as I have implied? And, finally, if there is an empirically reliable means of assessing the actual orders of consciousness to which individuals have recourse during their lives, then where "are" adults in their development of consciousness? Just how well matched with a fourth order curriculum, in other words, is the consciousness complexity of contemporary adults?

These are the empirical questions researchers have begun to address in the years since I wrote *The Evolving Self*, and they are relevant not just to the realm of work but to the entire exploration of the hidden demands of modern life we have undertaken thus far. I raise and address them now because we have come to a natural "viewing spot" in a long climb. Having considered realms of private and public life, we have now come far enough to look back and see the breadth of adult terrain over which my line of argument spreads. The basic shape of that argument should now be clear, but before we press on I want briefly to consider whether the "scenic vista" I have laid out is a landscape of my own imagination or whether there is some reason to believe it has some correspondence to the real terrain.

Is the parallel we see between Lynn's and Peter's public and private realities representative of real people? The most systematic exploration of this question I know of was undertaken by Lisa Lahey, who conducted "subject-object interviews"[23] with men and women exploring their constructions of their "love life" and "work life."[24] Despite how differently people may say they "feel" about love conflicts and work conflicts, and despite the clinical literature's understanding of how much more "primitive," "undefended," "unbounded," or even "immature" we experience ourselves to be in our private, intimate relations, what she found was an extraordinary degree of epistemological consistency within subjects across these different domains.

Although it would not be terribly startling to find that a person's constructions of love and work experience were both "roughly third-orderish" or both "roughly fourth-orderish," Lahey's work submitted the "consistency hypothesis" to a much more rigorous test. (Those readers interested in the technical details may wish to consult the chapter notes.[25]) Using a finely gauged measure of the gradual evolution from one order of consciousness to another—each point in the evolution affording a slightly different way of organizing experience—she found that the people she interviewed tended to use these same ways of organizing across the two realms of experiencing. The parallel we notice in Lynn's and Peter's constructions of home and work may not be mere invention. (Those readers interested in further discussion of the "consistency hypothesis" may also wish to consult the chapter notes.[26])

Throughout the preceding chapters I have implied that the differing orders of mental complexity Peter and Lynn demonstrate not only tend to function across the different realms of their living, they are themselves in a developmental relationship to each other. That is, Lynn's fourth order mentality may not just be analyzably more complex or encompassing than Peter's, it may be "more grown." This means that people who construct the world according to a second order mentality, say, cannot just learn or be taught the complexity of the fourth order; they have to "outgrow" the second order and, even then, have to pass through the *third* order before they can organize the world in a *fourth* order way. This point, like the last, is also empirical. That is, in analyzing Lynn's and Peter's different meanings or the complexity inherent in a given cultural demand, even if I have clearly made the case that what we are seeing here are qualitatively different orders of mental complexity, analysis alone cannot sustain the argument that the different orders of complexity are developmental. But if the different orders *are* developmental then "mastering the fourth order" is more a matter of a gradual process of holistic mental growth or transformation—the evolution of consciousness—than of mastering new mental skills.

We can support the claim that the different orders of mental complexity are developmental only through longitudinal research—carefully following people, especially adults, over a period of several years, conducting and reconducting interviews, for example, and seeing whether and how people's structures change. The only study of this kind I know of is the one that Lisa Lahey, Emily Souvaine, Nancy Popp, Stephanie Beukema, and I have been conducting for the past nine years. In this study, twenty-two adults were reinterviewed annually for four years and then again five years after the last annual interview. Though we have not completed the analysis of this last round of interviews (nine years from inception), the results of the first four years are suggestive. As Table 5.2 indicates, the overwhelming impression from the data is that an increasingly complex way of constructing reality is gradually unfolding. With very few exceptions, if a person's order of consciousness changes from one year to the next, it changes in the direction of greater complexity. Without exception, if a person's order of consciousness changes from one year to the next it changes only very gradually (never more than two discriminations, that is "fifths" of the way from one order of consciousness to another). Given that the interviews were assessed without knowledge of assessments from prior years (and with high interrater agreement), these are quite remarkable findings. If the orders of consciousness assessed by the study are not developmental but susceptible to being taught or learned in and of themselves, why is there such overwhelming directionality to them over time? Why are the changes so extraordinarily gradual? Why is there no skipping from the third order, for example, to the fifth? It seems much more likely that what the data are chronicling is the gradual evolution or unfolding of a mental capacity.

And just what capacities, what orders of consciousness in particular do research studies suggest real adults possess? If the demand for fourth order consciousness now appears to be a pervasive, if unrecognized, claim upon contemporary adults across the many contexts of their lives—a *cultural* demand that saturates all of life as opposed to a parochial demand called for in a specific arena—and if people are fairly consistent in the order of consciousness they use across different contexts (see note 26), then it makes sense to ask: How well does the consciousness of contemporary adults match the complexity of the mental demands made of them? Just how common is the phenomenon of being "in over one's head"?

The answer, insofar as we can come to any preliminary conclusions, is that the experience of being in over one's head as an adult—even a relatively privileged, well-educated, middle-class adult—in contemporary culture is a widespread phenomenon. At any given moment, around

Table 5.2 Longitudinal Study of Adult Orders of Consciousness

Subject	No interview	3	3(4)	3/4	4/3	4(3)	4	4(5)
AA			Year 1, 2	Year 3	Year 4			
BB	Year 2			Year 1			Year 3, 4	
CC			Year 1	Year 2, 3	Year 4			
DD	Year 1, 4						Year 2, 3	
EE	Year 1						Year 2, 3, 4	
FF	Year 2				Year 3	Year 4	Year 1	
GG				Year 1	Year 2	Year 3, 4		
HH			Year 1		Year 3?	Year 3?	Year 2, 3?, 4	
II	Year 2	Year 1						
JJ		Year 1	Year 2	Year 3	Year 4	Year 2		
KK				Year 1?	Year 1?	Year 2, 3	Year 4	
LL			Year 1	Year 2	Year 3		Year 4	
MM					Year 3	Year 4	Year 1	Year 2
NN					Year 1	Year 3	Year 2, 4	
OO				Year 1	Year 2	Year 3	Year 4	

Table 5.2 (continued)

Subject	No interview	3	3(4)	3/4	4/3	4(3)	4	4(5)
PP	Year 3		Year 1?	Year 1?, 2?	Year 2? 4?	Year 4?		
QQ	Year 2		Year 1		Year 3, 4?	Year 4?		
RR	Year 3, 4	Year 1?	Year 1?, 2					
SS				Year 1	Year 2	Year 3	Year 4	
TT	Year 4				Year 1	Year 1	Year 2	
UU				Year 1, 2	Year 3		Year 4	
VV	Year 1				Year 4	Year 3	Year 2	Year 3

Information from research by R. Kegan, L. Lahey, E. Souvaine, N. Popp, and S. Beukema.

The Subject-Object Interview can make six reliable distinctions between any two orders of consciousness. Between the third and the fourth orders it distinguishes between a way of organizing in which (1) only the third order is in evidence (designated "3"); (2) the third order begins to be reflected on, but the fourth order is not yet constructed (designated "3(4)"); (3) both the third and fourth order principles are in evidence, but the third order predominates (designated "3/4"); (4) both the third and fourth order principles are in evidence, but the fourth order predominates (designated "4/3"); (5) the fourth order is the governing principle but it must work at not letting the third order intrude (designated "4(3)"; and (6) the fourth order is securely established (designated "4").

one-half to two-thirds of the adult population appear not to have fully reached the fourth order of consciousness.

I have arrived at this estimate after reviewing those studies of adults using subject-object interviews and random sampling procedures (Table 5.3[27] summarizes these studies). I have obviously excluded from this survey studies based on stratified samples, in which researchers pre-selected for comparison a like number of persons using different orders of consciousness. I have also excluded studies of exclusively "non-normal" populations, such as incarcerated adults or hospitalized psychiatric patients. (I am not assuming that the distribution of order of consciousness in hospitalized psychiatric patients is necessarily different from that of the population at large, but I wanted a composite sample that is as nonspecial and as representative of the general population as possible.) Even so, as we can see from the descriptions of the studies in Table 5.4, the resulting composite sample of 282 adults turns out to be a disproportionately favored group of Americans who are whiter, wealthier, and better educated than the general population. This makes it more difficult to make estimates about the general population, but the sample is nonetheless an excellent one to which to bring the question, How common is the phenomenon of being "in over one's head"? Since it is reasonable to assume that being less wealthy, less well-educated, and from a discriminated against racial group might provide fewer supports and opportunities for growth, it is likely that the incidence of being in over one's head would be *greater* for the general population than for this advantaged sample. In other words, if the phenomenon appears to be widespread in this advantaged sample, it is likely to be even more widespread throughout the general population. (Indeed, as Table 5.5 shows, in just those studies whose samples are more representative by social class and level of education a wider spread of orders of consciousness is represented.)

So what do the data tell us? A definite pattern of distribution is evident. Although we can always find something to quarrel with in the design of any one study that might raise doubts about how much credence we should give to its results, the benefit of so many studies is that when a recurring pattern emerges it is harder to discount it. When the findings of the dozen dissertation studies, each done with a relatively small sample, are taken compositely, the distribution of order of consciousness is quite similar to that of the single largest study, that by Bar-Yam.[28] By complete good fortune, the range of ages and the male-

Table 5.3 Distribution of Order of Consciousness from Random Sample Studies of Adults

Order of Consciousness	(1) Goodman (1983) N=24	(2) Jacobs (1984) N=40	(3) Alvarez (1985) N=30	(4) Lahey (1986) N=22/44	(5) Dixon (1986) N=24	(6) Allison (1988) N=19	(7) Beukema (1990) N=20
5	0	0	0	0	0	0	0
Between 4 and 5	2	3	4	3	0	0	2
4	8	15	14	13	0	12	12
Between 3 and 4	6	10	12	24	12	3	3
3	3	11	0	4	1	3	3
Between 2 and 3	1	0	0	0	10	1	0
2	4	1	0	0	1	0	0

Order of Consciousness	(8) Sonnenschein (1990) N=11	(9) Binner (1991) N=12	(10) Osgood (1991) N=19	(11) Greenwald (1991) N=27	(12) Roy (1993) N=12	Dissertation Composite (Studies 1–12) N=282 (100%)	(13) Bar-Yam (1991) N=60 (100%)
5	0	0	0	0	0	0 (0%)	0 (0%)
Between 4 and 5	0	1	2	0	0	17 (06%)	6 (10%)
4	5	3	7	6	2	97 (34%)	25 (42%)
Between 3 and 4	6	4	4	5	2	91 (32%)	22 (37%)
3	0	1	2	5	7	40 (14%)	7 (11%)
Between 2 and 3	0	1	2	6	1	22 (08%)	0 (0%)
2	0	2	2	5	0	15 (05%)	0 (0%)
						%F=67% %M=33%	%F=67% %M=33%

Table 5.4 Samples of Order of Consciousness Studies

Study	Sample
1	12M, 12W; parents of 11–13 y.o. sons; 1/2 clinic pop.; mean age=39.45
2	20M,20W; married couples, 28–55 y.o.; middle class
3	15M, 15W, 25–40 y.o., highly educated
4	11M, 11W (each interviewed twice), 30–40 y.o., professional, all w/graduate degrees
5	24W, 19–30 y.o., students at 2-yr. technical college
6	10M, 10W; married couples, 25–36 y.o., highly educated, most have graduate degrees
7	20W, 28–50 y.o., highly educated, 15 of 20 hold master's degrees
8	11W, 31–44 y.o., middle class, majority hold college degrees or more
9	6W, 6M; owner/founders of small businesses; 31–66 y.o., 11 of 13 college graduates
10	7M, 13W, parents of teens
11	27W, 40–49 y.o., randomly selected from a single town, widespread educations
12	6W, 6M; 35–48 y.o.; six middle-class married couples; 10 of 12 college graduates; 5 of 12 advanced degrees
13	40W, 20M; 25–55 y.o.; Americans in military service in Europe, their dependents, and civilians employed by military; all pursuing graduate degrees

Table 5.5 Four Samples for Comparison

Order of Consciousness	Original Dissertation Composite (Studies 1–12) N=282		"Full SES" Composite (Studies 1, 5, 11) N=75		"Professional Highly Educated" Composite (All but 1, 5, 11) N=207		Bar-Yam Study (a highly educated sample) N=60	
5	0	0%	0	0%	0	0%	0	0%
4–5	17	6%	2	3%	15	7%	6	10%
4	97	34%	14	18%	83	40%	25	42%
3–4	91	32%	23	31%	68	33%	22	37%
3	40	14%	9	12%	31	15%	7	11%
2–3	22	8%	17	23%	5	2.5%	0	0%
2	15	5%	10	13%	5	2.5%	0	0%

female composition of the Bar-Yam sample and the dissertation composite sample are nearly identical (two-thirds female; one-third male; ages twenty-five to fifty-five). The Bar-Yam sample, which consists entirely of adults who are pursuing graduate degrees, is only somewhat better educated than the composite sample (and interestingly it lacks the wider distributional spread), but the distributional pattern in the two samples is quite similar: about half the population in these relatively advantaged samples does not fully reach the fourth order of consciousness (59 percent in the composite sample; 48 percent in the Bar-Yam sample).

If we separate out the three studies (1, 5, and 11; N=75) whose samples are more representative of the fuller range of socioeconomic classes and which include adults who do not have college and graduate degrees, we then have a chance to consider the suggestion that the in-over-one's-head phenomenon will be greater in a more normally advantaged group and the suggestion that the phenomenon is nonetheless still widespread among a more consistently advantaged, highly educated professional group. Table 5.5 provides these comparisons and supports both suggestions. The "Full SES" Composite, based on the three studies with more representative samples, shows far fewer persons at the fourth order of consciousness or higher (21 percent, as compared to 41 percent in the original composite). But when a highly educated, highly professional composite is created out of the remaining eight studies, the phenomenon of being in over one's head remains widespread. Here, over half of the sample has not fully reached the fourth order of consciousness. (We might also note from Table 5.5 that the distribution in this newly created, highly educated sample is nearly identical to that of the completely distinct highly educated sample of about the same size from the Bar Yam study, a confirmation of the depiction of this population.)

While the more representative sample shows a greater incidence of meaning-making less complex than the third order, and a lesser incidence of meaning-making more complex than the fourth order, it is also interesting that the percentage of people embedded in the third order, or using a combination of the third and fourth orders, is nearly identical across all four samples (third order: 14 percent, 12 percent, 15 percent, 11 percent; between the third and fourth orders: 32 percent, 31 percent, 33 percent, 37 percent). If the fourth order of consciousness is demanded for success in contemporary adult life, more people in the general population may be in over their heads, but the phenomenon is not by any means primarily associated with the less favored, less educated, or less wealthy. It is not primarily associated with the "working class" or those who work at "jobs" rather than "careers." Even among those adults we generally see as the most affluent, most sophisticated, best educated, and most "professional," about half have not fully reached the fourth order.

The related research of William Torbert and his associates provides corroboration of these claims. Torbert's theoretical approach to the study of work and management makes explicit use of subject-object theory,[29] but he uses Loevinger's Sentence Completion Test as a measure for complexity of mind, with which rough approximations to the subject-object measure can be made. In separate studies, most with good-sized samples, of first line supervisors, nurses, junior and middle managers, senior managers, executives, and a group Torbert calls "entrepreneurial professionals," the most frequent consciousness position for every group but the last was equivalent to one between the third and fourth orders.[30] In most of the studies the majority of subjects did *not* reach the threshold of the fourth order. In fact, if the studies are taken together, in composite a sample of nearly five hundred professionals, 58 percent of the sample does not reach the fourth order.

The crucial questions for assessing any curriculum are these: What order of complexity does the curriculum demand of the student? What order of complexity is the student capable of? How good is the fit between curricular demand and student capacity? Our analyses of the expectations of private and public life suggest an unwitting but harmonious cultural chorus that points to a specific consciousness threshold, yet according to the empirical information, a goodly proportion of us have not reached this threshold. It is here, in the gap between demand and capacity, that we begin to get a clear idea of the mental burden of modern life.

6

Dealing with Difference: Communication between the Sexes/ Communication between the Theories

> Psychological problems are not so much caused by the unconscious as by deprivations of full consciousness. If we had paths to more valid consciousness all along through life, if we had more accurate terms in which to conceptualize what was happening, if we had more access to the emotions produced, and if we had ways of knowing our true options—we could make better programs for action. Lacking full consciousness, we create out of what is available.
> —Jean Baker Miller, *Toward a New Psychology of Women*

Lynn's and Peter's ways of knowing about work clearly differ, and their differing ways of knowing leave them with different chances to accomplish our culture's hidden curriculum for success at work. But the general idea of a "way of knowing" now appears in many psychological theories. Do the theories all refer to the same thing? What kind of "way of knowing" do we mean when we say that Lynn's and Peter's so clearly differ?

Subject-object theory brings together two powerful lines of intellectual discourse that have influenced not only the field of psychology but nearly every corner of intellectual life in the West in this century. These two lines of thought are *constructivism*, the idea that people or systems *constitute* or *construct* reality; and *developmentalism*, the idea that people or organic systems evolve through qualitatively different eras of increasing complexity according to regular principles of stability and change. Subject-object theory is a "constructive-developmental" approach to human experience. It looks at the growth or transformation of how we construct meaning.

The general idea of "ways of knowing" derives from the tradition of constructivism. It implies that we are active in our apprehension of reality. We do not just passively "copy" or "absorb" already organized reality; instead, we ourselves actively give shape and coherence to our experience. Constructivism implies that there is a consistency or holism to our meaning-making. Each apprehension on our part is not merely a response to a momentary stimulus. Instead, from moment to moment and across different spheres of living, our ways of knowing share the design of a common organizing principle or system.

Certainly subject-object principles share these constructivist features. We have seen that Peter's cross-categorical principle actively shapes reality in ways that differ significantly from how Lynn's systemic principle would shape the same reality. And we have seen how Lynn's and Peter's central organizing principles at work create realities that have striking parallels to the realities they create at home in their marriage and their parenting. Peter's feeling of being pulled in too many directions at once by his loyalties to spouse, children, and parents when he is planning a summer vacation may have the same source as his feeling of being pulled in too many directions by Anderson, Harold, and Ted when he is deciding how to preside over his company.

But what sort of way of knowing is this? Subject-object principles are certainly not the only candidates for active, consistent, holistic "ways of knowing." In the field of work and management training, Carl Jung's ideas about "personality types" have had an indirect but enormous influence through the use of the Myers-Briggs Type Indicator, an easily administered test that distinguishes sixteen different ways people approach experience. This widely used measure (according to its publisher, two million people took the test in 1990), invented by Katherine Briggs and her daughter, Isabel Briggs Myers, derives its types from four pairs of personality preferences. People identify whether they are more typically an "introvert" or an "extrovert," a "sensor" or "intuitive," a "thinker" or a "feeler," a "judger" or a "perceiver." These represent assessments, respectively, of how we "prefer to receive stimulation and energy, prefer to gather data, prefer to make decisions, and how structured or spontaneously we prefer to orient to our lives."[1] Since test-takers can only answer one way or the other on each pair, the test generates sixteen possible "types."

The Myers-Briggs type approach to "ways of knowing" has resulted in countless seminars and publications intended to help people understand the workings of their own personality type and those of their colleagues. In the world of work, Kraeger and Thuesen's *Typetalk at Work: How the Sixteen Personality Types Determine Your Success on the Job*[2] is a good example. It seeks to describe how each of the different types handles typical aspects of work—goal-setting, conflict resolution, team-building, and the like—and gives advice on how to deal with people who are a different type than you are. For example, the authors consulted with a work team of eight professionals who were not getting along with their new CEO:

> The new CEO was an opposite of the other eight's predominant group type. The predominant group type was Introvert/Intuitive/Thinking/Judging. The new CEO was an Extrovert/Sensor/Feeler/Perceiver. When this revelation came to light, a lot of things started to make sense. When both sides became aware of how naturally different they were, a lot of the anger began to dissipate. It became clear, for example, that the CEO's constant thinking out loud grated against the engineers' need to retreat to their drawing tables and calculators [an Extroversion vs. Introversion difference]. The CEO's call for detailed plans for everything was heard as nitpicking and riding herd, when engineers would rather be left to themselves. (After all, the engineers knew the system; they didn't need him to show them the ropes [an Intuitive vs. Sensing difference].) The CEO's willingness to hold decisions in favor of more information was seen as indecisiveness and lacking direction [a Thinking vs. Feeling difference]. And so it went . . . One of the most important benefits of all this was that the blame being heaped on the CEO could be better defined and understood, as could the CEO's frustration with his underlings. For example, the engineers began to understand that as an Extrovert, the CEO did hear what they said, but he tended to talk over them, making it appear that he wasn't listening. The Judging engineers wanted specific directions, but the Perceiving CEO tended quite naturally to offer more questions than answers. The more they talked, the more insights they got and the more they were willing to lay aside these things that were blocking their effectiveness. That allowed them to stop bickering at work.[3]

The "type" approach to "ways of knowing" shares with subject-object structures the two central constructivist features. First, it posits a way in which people actively design rather than "happen upon" their realities. For example, according to Kraeger and Thuesen,

> the information that Sensors take in deals more with the specifics of what has been said or has taken place. Precise words and events are key here and are subject to subsequent recall and scrutiny. For Intuitives, implications and meanings about what's transpired are far more important. This difference leads to a variety of "yes, buts," which sound something like this:
>
> *Sensor:* "Yes, but this is what you said . . ."
> *Intuitive:* "Yes, but this is what I meant . . ."
> *Sensor:* "Yes, but if that's what you meant, you should have said it."
> *Intuitive:* "Yes, but I shouldn't have to speak the obvious to intelligent people."[4]

And second, the "type" approach claims a holism and consistency across different life contexts. The Intuitive/Sensor/Thinker/Judger is presumed to approach a variety of work issues this way and to approach family life in a similar way.

But there are important differences between Myers-Briggs *types* and subject-object *principles* as ways of knowing. The first is that one's type is not presumed to change, while one's subject-object principle gradually may. One's Myers-Briggs type is presumed to be one's Myers-Briggs type for the rest of one's life, like blood-type or handedness. A second difference is that Myers-Briggs types are simply *preferences about* the way we know, rather than *competencies* or *capacities* in our knowing, as is the case with subject-object principles. The differences between types are non-normative differences of epistemological *style* not hierarchical differences of epistemological *capacity*.

The benefit of such non-normative distinctions is that, if properly applied, and if the distinctions really hold up empirically, the construct of types can help to remove an inappropriate judgmentalism: a "thinking" preference is not inherently better than a "feeling" preference.

The limitation of distinctions between ways of knowing that do not get at lesser and greater capacity is that, popular though they may be in management training circles, they may actually have little to do with worker competence. Since they do not suggest a journey of increasing epistemological vision, the only curricular purpose such stylistic distinctions imply is an enhanced ability to understand one's own and others' preferences and, perhaps, learning self-consciously to use a style to which one is not naturally drawn. Phillip Lewis and T. Owen Jacobs, who take a constructive-developmental perspective on this issue of leadership style and capacity, argue that, although greater awareness and flexibility of style may play a role in work effectiveness, epistemological capacity plays a much larger role.

> The lack of support for the direct effect of personality traits on leader effectiveness has not, however, deterred contemporary leadership theorists from trying to identify personality style differences which they feel are relevant to leader effectiveness. Driver, Brousseau and Hunsake describe . . . five basic decision making styles . . . Kirton has identified two other management styles . . . Interestingly, like most theorists who claim to have identified key leadership style differences, both Kirton and Driver et al. are careful to point out that no single style is better than any other style . . . Clearly, then, a close reading of these contemporary proponents of leadership styles approaches reveals them to be unwilling to assert that they have identified personal characteristics which distinguish between effective and ineffective leaders . . . Despite our gut level feeling that there are important stylistic differences between effective and ineffective leaders, differences in interpersonal style, decision making style, or other personal preferences may not be *directly* related to leader effectiveness. Approaches which focus on leadership style tend to ignore what is most fundamental about leadership. Leaders add value to their organizations by exercising discretion and making sound decisions. The style with which those decisions are made is not, ultimately, very important. What *is* important is the quality of these decisions . . . The critical individual difference variable in leader effectiveness is the conceptual competence to do the required work. Good leaders are, first and foremost, competent to undertake their leadership responsibilities. A leader's awareness of his or her preferred style and that of others may marginally improve communication, but it won't, ultimately, get the right decisions made.[5]

Ironically, the same quality that makes a "type" approach more user-friendly—its nonjudgmentalism—may in fact render its use only marginally valuable in facilitating effectiveness. Once we grant that one style is not necessarily any more effective than another, our defensiveness about having our style evaluated may be reduced, but so may our opportunity to learn what makes for greater effectiveness.

Theoretically, the difference between a "types" approach and a "subject-object" approach to ways of knowing is quite clear, but when the lenses focus on real phenomena it may be less clear whether something is better understood as a matter of epistemological style or capacity. The difference between "extroversion" and "introversion," for example, is unlikely to be confused with the difference between "cross-categorical" and "systemic" principles, but how about the difference between "thinking" and "feeling" styles? "Thinkers" are described as "think[ing] it's more important to be right than to be liked" and not "mind[ing] making difficult decisions," in contrast to "feelers" who "will over-extend [themselves] meeting other people's needs" and "prefer harmony over clarity."[6] Are these fourth order versus third order phenomena or are they stylistic differences? One implication of the difference between subject-object principles and the Myers-Briggs types or any of the other personality styles, such as Kolb's learning preferences,[7] is that if a person's style is in fact durable throughout that person's life, then the form or complexity of that style should alter throughout the person's lifespan. I might prefer an "extroverted" or "judging" style in both my twenties and my fifties, but if the order of my consciousness changes between twenty and fifty, as it does for many people, then the form of my "extroverting" or "judging" could also be expected to change. Perhaps some of the stylistic descriptions provided by the Myers-Briggs Type Indicator are unrecognizedly constructed from a particular order of consciousness, so that style and capacity are being confused.

The implication here—that we would do well to take a jointly stylistic and structural approach to our understanding of psychological phenomena—might be especially important when it comes to work on gender differences in our ways of knowing. By considering this work we can not only further this more complex bi-theoretical approach, we can also make clearer how subject-object principles differ from the styles of knowing current research links to gender. I am especially eager to do this, since my own lack of clarity about that distinction ten years ago is reflected in *The Evolving Self* and contributes, I believe, to a conflating of the two. Those who have read that book in the context of the work of Jean Baker Miller or Carol Gilligan,[8] particularly women, often pose a number of questions, usually with a certain edge to their voice: Isn't *cross-categorical* knowing a more typically *female* way of organizing experience (notwithstanding the fact that my example of cross-categorical knowing, Peter, is male)? Isn't the embeddedness in the psychological surround that characterizes cross-categorical knowing a female orientation? And isn't the capacity to stand apart from this surround a male orientation? Isn't the capacity to construct an overarching system, theory, or authorizing ideology a typically male orientation? The edge in the voice comes from the sense that stylistic differences, which are neither better nor more intrinsically valuable than each other, are being placed in a hierarchy in which women are arbitrarily disadvantaged. The tone of these questions asks its own good question: Aren't men's styles being privileged in this theory purporting to be a theory of consciousness? How do we know that the difference between the third and fourth orders of consciousness is not in fact a difference between a more and less complex evolution of mind, but a difference in styles, and a difference, Peter and Lynn notwithstanding, that typically divides women and men?

In this chapter I plan to arrive at answers to these questions through an appreciative analysis of what I consider the most promising feature of the gender styles approach: its capacity to enhance communication across non-normative differences by helping us to resist our tendencies to privilege what is familiar and judge critically what is different. This tendency exacts its cruelest price on the unpowerful and the excluded when the powerful and the included make right and true that which is merely familiar to them and make wrong and false that which is only strange to them. In order to clarify the meaning of a gender styles approach to "ways of knowing" I will explore the question of whether communication between women and men might be improved if it were looked at more as a cross-cultural event. In order to consider the complementarity of the gender styles approach to "ways of knowing" with the order of consciousness approach, I will explore the following two questions: Does the social movement to enhance respect for differences (such as gender differences) carry its own hidden mental demand? Are the underlying hopes and mission of a "gendered" approach to ways of knowing helped or hindered if we join that approach to an "order of consciousness" perspective?

Constructivism backlights the image of human beings shaping their own reality. There is power in this image of creative activity, but it is a power that cuts both ways. Shaping, selecting, and patterning reality in some fashion also means not designing it in some other fashion. The word *decide* refers to "cutting," and although cutting can imply shaping, it can also imply "cutting off." Being active in our seeing and hearing can mean being actively blind to what we do not see and deaf to what we do not hear.

Some years ago I was involved in a series of study group meetings that, in the fashion of typical academic self-importance, we thought to routinely tape-record. During one meeting in a colleague's office the phone on his desk rang, and as he answered it he assured us that he would only be a moment, that we should continue the conversation without him, and that we could catch him up when he jumped back in. He was and we did, but when we tried to catch him up there was some disagreement about what we had actually said while he was on the phone. Someone remembered that since the tape recorder had been running we could easily settle the argument. We happily rewound the tape to the ring of the phone but were dismayed to discover that it was nearly unintelligible. Why? The microphone was somewhere between us and the telephone, and the machine had recorded all its ambient sound, both the group's conversation and our colleague on the phone, and the simultaneous talk was too hard for us to unravel. And this is just the point. The tape recorder is an amazing machine, faithfully recording all the sound around it. But human beings are even more amazing, for we were doing something the machine could not: though sitting roughly in the same place as the microphone and subject to the same two conversations, none of us had had any trouble following the group conversation while our colleague talked on the phone. Our ears did not just pick up ambient sound; quite automatically and unconsciously we tuned in to the sound of our group's conversation and tuned out the sound of our colleague. And we did this not once but continuously, second after second, selecting for one sound and selecting out another.

This incident demonstrates not just our constructivism—our capacity to select, regulate, act upon, and make decisions about raw data—but the two-edged sword of our constructivism. We select in, but we also select out. We decide, but we also cut off. Having an active way of hearing also meant that we were deaf to other perfectly "good" sound in the room. We just didn't hear it. For us it wasn't happening. This is also constructivism.

But is this a feature of our constructivism with which we necessarily stay in touch? Having put our world together, are we awake to the fact that it is an *invented* reality, a *made* world? Do we regularly look for some quite different way the same experience could cohere and so render a whole different meaning? Or do we tend to take our construction of reality as Reality, as the fact of "how it is out there"? In 1757, the British passed a calendar reform stating that September 1 would become

September 12. Thousands of people protested passionately that the government was robbing them of twelve days of their lives. (I mentioned this recently to a friend and she chuckled, and then said, under her breath as she was leaving, "But you know, I'd kind of hate that too, since the fall is my favorite time of year and I'd hate to see the season shortened"!) More recently, the British changed their monetary system from pence to "new pence." Someone surveyed the populace about the switch and an elderly woman said, "It's very confusing and I think it's too confusing for the older people. Why couldn't they wait until all the old people were dead before they did it?" We look up into the heavens and we see the constellations. The Big Dipper hangs right up there every night, year after year. It's very easy to think that those seven stars actually do have some relation to each other that intrinsically has a greater integrity than any of dozens of other combinations that could be formed with neighboring stars. There is a recurring order in the heavens that we did not invent, but the chunking of one collection of stars into one constellation, the belief that the stars are actually a part of this whole we call a constellation, is obviously completely invented. But do we tend to look at it that way? Are we aware that it is we who are doing the constellating, not the stars or the heavens?

So we "make sense," but we do not always take responsibility for it as made. We are more likely to believe it is "the way the world is made" (and to leave out the agent of that passively constructed sentence). Some of our meaning-making is completely idiosyncratic and falls under no governance or regularity other than the regularity of our unique personalities. And some of our meaning-making may derive from our membership in various subgroups of the human family, such as social class, ethnicity, gender, and culture. These subgroups may endow us with their own meaning-regulative principles, ways we know or see that derive from our membership in these subgroups. The failure to take responsibility for the invented nature of our meaning-constructions when these constructions are regulated by culture is in fact the essence of ethnocentrism. We can approach the subject of "gender-centrism" more powerfully if we first pass through the analogous territory of culture as a constructivist influence.

We all know that to some extent each of us is a creature of the culture in which we were reared. We are imbued with our culture's ideas about everything—what can be eaten and what cannot, how we find a mate, earn a living, raise our children, care for the elderly, defend ourselves against enemies—in short, about how we shall live. The meaning-regulative principles of a culture that are passed on to its members may be what makes a culture a culture, what gives it its distinctive stamp. So long as we do all our living in the culture into which we were born and have nothing to do directly or indirectly with people of another culture, our only task as we grow up, relative to enculturation, is to learn the rules of our culture. We need only learn what it means to become a human being (or an adult, or an adult woman or man) in this particular culture. But since we have no contact with any other culture, this will amount to learning what it means to be an adult human being *period*. Even today, in a nation as diverse as modern America, it is nonetheless possible for Americans—living in a country so large they need not be constantly aware, like Europeans, of neighboring cultures and one so filled with pockets of regional, class, and ethnic homogeneity they need not face difference every day—to cling to the idea that all people are like Americans or something very close to it. Scratch beneath the merely surface difference, so this view goes, and everyone is really the same—meaning that nearly everyone is an American like Uncle Charlie in Cedar Rapids. Henry Kissinger has suggested that Americans took so quickly to Mikhail Gorbachev because they could find their Uncle Charlie in him, which confirmed their view that the differences be-tween Soviet and Western culture were really trivial. (Kissinger said he had an American friend who believed "British people don't really talk like that; they just do it to make Americans feel inferior. If you sneaked into a British person's bedroom at three in the morning and suddenly woke him from a sound sleep, he would momentarily forget himself and talk just like your Uncle Charlie from Cedar Rapids.")

This is a naiveté befitting a young country. Because it says, "We're really all the same," it is even a big, friendly naiveté befitting a *generous* young country. It is the friendly naiveté of unearned familiarity that many older cultures mock in amusement or disdain (the Asians call it "the 'Hi!' 'Bye' culture"). But however friendly its intent, its result can be ugly, because "we are really all the same" translates to "You are really all like me." The friendly naif becomes "the ugly American" who wants to know, as he holds up a shirt from a cart in the market square, what ten thousand lire come to "in real money." What is real to him is what is familiar to him. Everything is evaluated in terms of how closely it reproduces the standard with which we have identified truth, reality, how life *is*.

A friendly naiveté becomes ugly because if someone *is* includable, it is because his difference can be translated to what we take to be real, and if his difference cannot be so translated, he is not includable. In the movie *Little Big Man* we learn that the word *Cheyenne* means "human being." Where does that leave those who are not Cheyenne? The Cheyenne chief who knows the "other" as "the white man" defines all others in these terms. Asked if he is familiar with the African, he says, "Oh yes. The black white man." Jews call non-Jews "gentiles" and Mormons call non-Mormons "gentiles." The Jewish epithet for "gentiles" is *goyim*, which is simply Hebrew for "others" or "other nations." The best a friendly ethnocentrism can do is to include difference by discounting it and, where difference cannot be discounted, to know the other not on his own terms but only as "not us."

If indeed we could sustain a life in which we would only meet people from our own culture and never have a thing to do, directly or indirectly, with people from other cultures, we might need to learn only the rules of our own culture and adhere to them. But such a world is rapidly disappearing if it is not already gone. Diversity of cultural experience may once have been the province of the adventurous, the open-minded, and those too poor to live where they wished. Tomorrow it will be the province of all. Even now the American *workforce* is undergoing a transformation by which the majority—white men—is becoming a minority.

What happens if our inevitable encounters with difference are mediated by ethnocentrism? Edward T. Hall recounts how American diplomats stationed in Arab countries were briefed on the more overt cultural differences but not necessarily on the subtleties.[9] What, for example, is the "proper" distance two nonintimate conversers should stand from each other as they talk, let us say, in the hall of an embassy? The "rule" of American culture, of which few Americans had any reason to be aware, is apparently several inches farther apart than the Arab "rule," of which Arabs had little reason to be aware. According to Hall, the Arab diplomat may be most comfortable if he can feel the breath of his American counterpart on his face.

When I give this example in American lecture halls, it never fails to provoke in some listeners a reaction of disgust or discomfort at the thought of a stranger's breath continuously bathing one's face. This reaction in itself is worth considering. There is certainly no correct "natural" distance to stand from a conversational partner. A distance shorter than the one with which we are comfortable is not a violation of God or nature. It is a violation of an invented norm or value. Yet our reactions to such violations can take the form not merely of intellectual dissent or even emotional discomfort but of bodily revulsion! This is how attached we are to our constructions. This is how daunting the task of seeing them as constructions is, of being in relation to our constructions rather than embedded in them. If we experience a visceral disgust and sense of unnaturalness, we need only consider how our own "naturalness" might disgust others. We may be appalled at the practice of inserting rings inside one's lips, stretching them to three times their natural size for purely cosmetic reasons. But people of other cultures might be appalled at our practice of putting holes in one's ears or implants in one's breasts for purely cosmetic reasons. What to one culture is the mutilation of one's body might to another be the route to attractiveness and enhanced self-esteem.

But let us return to the Arab and American diplomats standing in the embassy and trying with words to conduct a civil conversation, while nonverbally each is negotiating for a space between their bodies that he finds comfortable. A bird's-eye view would see a comic dance down the hallway as the Arab advances to his proper distance and the American retreats to his. But there is more than comedy being played out here. It is highly likely that each is also making unpleasant attributions about the other on the basis of this nonverbal "conversation." "These Americans are certainly a standoffish, cold, distant lot," the Arab could well feel. "These Arabs," the American could easily feel in turn, "are certainly intrusive and smothering." Such attributions would be entirely understandable, entirely consistent with the constructed rules with which each is identified, but *entirely wrong*. However "far" or "near" each one stands, however unpleasant the other finds this, neither may have any intention to be aloof or smothering.

What happens if our inevitable encounters with cultural difference are mediated by ethnocentric identification with our own constructions? At the very least, we literally fail to understand even what the difference is! We end up constructing not only our cultural rules but the difference itself! It becomes the *attributions* we make about the other ("aloof," "smothering") out of our experience of difference, rather than being the difference between the other's rules and our own. The difference thus becomes all about our meaning and not about the intended meaning of the other.

One solution to this problem of misunderstanding would be for us to teach other cultures to "shape up"—to start having the same rules about how reality should be constructed as we do. At the least, if people are going to come and live in our culture, they should have the decency to learn not just our spoken language but our way of making meaning. We, in turn, would have the decency and generosity to include them. We would be "open." We would not exclude people just because they were different. We would change the face of our company, community, or country. This can actually feel like a generous, welcoming, and magnanimous stand. Unfortunately, it conveniently ignores the fact that "we" were probably not always "here" ourselves, and that each new culture to immigrate to America brought its own stamp to the existing cultural rules and often stamped on them. In truth, it is a position that says "You can be included, so long as you learn our cultural rules and at least act as if you are beholden to them. Black people, you can come in to our company as long as you act like whites. Women, you can come in too as long as you act like men."

This solution to the problem of misunderstanding places all the burden for solving the problem on those who are most vulnerable, the most newly arrived, the least powerful in the hierarchy of influence. It is inhumane, but it can also be attacked on purely self-interested grounds, as any biologist, psychologist, or sports enthusiast knows. This sort of psychological assimilation amounts to a process by which difference and diversity are systematically removed, which runs exactly contrary to what ensures the success and survivability of a species. Biologists tell us that the ongoing variability of the gene pool is a key to the health of any organism. When the range for natural selection is too greatly diminished, the future of the organism is imperiled. The more a family intermarries, for example, and succeeds at preserving the "purity" of its line, as has happened throughout history with several dynasties, the greater the likelihood of physical and mental debilities in its issue. Psychologists tell us that the single greatest source of growth and development is the experience of difference, discrepancy, anomaly. Systematic moves to enfeeble the capacity of difference to challenge the limitations of our existing ways of knowing may comfort the valuable and necessary conservative side of our mental processes, what Piaget referred to as assimilative activity and Freud as the pleasure principle; but it may also disturb a wholesome and natural balance with the equally valuable and necessary progressive side of the same mental processes, what Piaget called accommodative activity, and Freud the reality principle.

Any knowledgeable participant or fan of team sports knows that a team does not tolerate but actually depends on the coordination of a diversity of talents for its success. As spectacular as are the ball-handling skills of an NBA guard or the close-to-the-basket skills of an NBA front-court man, no NBA team would do well with a starting squad of five all-star guards or five all-star centers. The talents of the all-star guard and the all-star center are different, but they are equally valuable. Neither is welcomed to play on the other's team with the stipulation they *give up* their own conception of what to do with a basketball for team success. Each requires the other's difference for team success.

These images—of species survival, wholesome mental processes, team success—suggest an entirely different context in which to consider the subject of social diversity. They raise the possibility that diversity is best conceived not as a problem in need of a solution, but as an opportunity or a necessity, to be prized and preserved as a precious resource.

As America becomes an older, more sophisticated country it is gradually coming to understand that different cultures have their own ways of going. There is at least a somewhat greater tolerance, if not respect, for these differences. More people are able to say to themselves in the face of discomfiting difference, "Perhaps this isn't about right and wrong; maybe it's a cultural thing." American educators, for example, are being taught to consider the possible misattributions they may be making of an Asian child's tendency not to speak up in class. As the educational anthropologist Jaime Wurzel reports,

> When a job interviewer in this country says to a prospective employee, "Why should we hire you?" the young American knows how to respond . . . "Because I have the skills your organization needs." But for those raised in an Asian culture, such a reply is over bold, obnoxious. An Asian might say, "Because I need the job." We value the notion of individual initiative and aggressiveness. Even in elementary school, the more articulate you are, the better you do. But the Japanese have a saying, "The nail that sticks out should be hammered down." And yet we expect the Japanese and other Asian children in our schools to speak up.[10]

What happens, then, if we think of gender differences as more like cultural differences? What happens, for example, if we make use of recent research on gender styles to consider communication between men and women at work as something closer to a cross-cultural event? Let us consider a very basic, seldom-discussed question about communication at work: how should we talk in a task-oriented work group—a committee or staff meeting, a meeting of Lynn's Leadership Council, or a team meeting of Peter's salespeople? What is an acceptable form of discourse? As it turns out, when we look at how people would naturally speak in such groups, some are inclined to speak narratively, personalistically, and experientially, fashioning a web of linking stories and thoughts that gradually build toward a general idea ("What's the best way to handle this? Let me tell you what happened once at another place I worked where we tried something like this . . ."). Others naturally speak more abstractly and objectively, first creating an overarching idea or intellectual framework that establishes and bounds the context for joint exploration ("The best way to handle this? I think this is a situation where 'less is more.' There comes a point when people are oversold on a product, and they just start backing off").

What kind of difference is this? It is *not* a difference between "being emotional" versus "being cognitive." Cognitive and emotional elements are present in both, and either could predominate in each. It is *not* a difference between "irrational" and "rational." The content of either way of speaking could be characterized by either of these adjectives. It is certainly *not* a difference between "simple-minded" and "more sophisticated." Again, one's "story" or one's "general idea" might be either of these. The difference is stylistic, much like the difference in how far we stand from each other in conversation. There is no nonarbitrary basis for judging one style "better" than another. Each has its own integrity, its own genius. Unlike the space between speakers, which is a style closely related to *culture*, modern researchers suggest that in Western culture this stylistic difference is correlated with gender. Women more often prefer the personalized narrative style, it is claimed; men, the "objective" decontextualized style.

Our style preferences, I have suggested, are not usually the mild sort ("How spicy do you like your 'Bloody Mary'?"). More often they are of the sort that register dramatically within us when violated, like the revulsion some people experience in having their face bathed in a stranger's breath. If we bring no "cross-cultural" sophistication to a work group meeting and find people speaking in a style that is the opposite of our own, how might we react? I have found from my own inquiries into people's group experience that a common phenomenon emerges. Those who are most comfortable with a personalized narrative style listen to those who are speaking in an objective decontextualized style and they begin to make unfavorable attributions: "This person is just intellectualizing! He's talking a hundred miles up in the air! Why can't he get down to the business at hand?" The objective decontextualized speakers listen to the personalized narrative speakers and they begin to make unfavorable attributions: "What does she think this is, group therapy? I didn't come here for story hour! Why can't she get down to business?" Each comes to feel that the other is essentially violating the unspoken contract or agreement to take the work seriously and engage it directly. Each sees the other as in some way avoiding or too indirectly engaging the task at hand. These are fascinating but highly costly attributions, since they are so likely to be wrong and to lead to an ongoing succession of subtle and overtly unpleasant actions and reactions, resulting in a highly complex tangle of chronically impaired communication.

In addition to this reciprocal misattribution, another pernicious non-reciprocal element, which has its own expensive price tag for a work group, inevitably applies. Because it is seldom the case that a work context or preexisting culture is equally receptive to both styles or both ends of the continuum, one side is subtly but powerfully proclaimed the "right" (culturally sanctioned) way to speak. In the historically male-dominated work world it is the objective decontextualized style that "wins." In this situation, the personalized narratizers, keenly aware that how they are speaking is seen as "wrong" soon stop, or stop speaking in their own voice. This loss of voice, in turn, leads to a further set of destructive and erroneous attributions on the part of the "winning" sanctioned style, which sets in motion a complicated, ongoing series of dysfunctional actions and reactions. If the person who loses her voice is silent, the absence of information invites would-be listeners to fantasize about its cause. We typically see silent members of a group as bored, scared, angry, knowing nothing, not up to speed, or less "with it," all highly unfavorable attributions and each possibly quite wrong. Or, if the person who loses her voice does not remain silent but tries to speak in what she gathers is the proper mode, her attempt to speak a foreign language might be seen as calculating, constricted, or inauthentic.

Hence, in a number of studies and writings, not to mention popular lore and literature, the American man is depicted as a space-hog in group conversations.[11] In work groups and classrooms, males speak more frequently and for longer periods of time, commanding the floor when they do speak and surrendering it only when they choose.

Women, in contrast, tend to dart in and out around the edges of the conversation, interjecting brief remarks that have the effect of "asides" between masculine perorations, seldom taking over the conversation, and surrendering the stage when interrupted whether they are finished or not.

This portrayal of the man as a space-hog, interestingly enough, may not in itself be a stylistic difference but rather the consequence of establishing a particular style as "correct." Those who study male domination in work groups and classrooms, where decontextualized, objective styles have been historically favored and built into the disciplines and rituals of those cultures, should take a look at intimacy-oriented contexts, such as psychotherapy, where personalized narrative styles have been institutionalized. In a mixed-gender therapy group, for example, it is my experience that one will find the roles of "space-hog" and "marginal darter" reversed. Women speak most frequently and longest, authoritatively claim the floor when they speak, and defend their ownership from intrusion, while men make brief comments on the side (frequently satiric) and play a conversational role that suggests they see themselves as something closer to bystanders in the proceedings.

Stylistic issues become political issues, matters of power and influence, when one style is granted "home court advantage" and those who prefer a different style are seen, and come to see themselves, as "visitors." When those granted "home court" uncritically accept their unfair advantage, the subject of "interesting stylistic differences" must be recast as one of "subjugating gendercentrism." If the work place (or the academy) is one that advantages a particular style and that style is more closely associated with men, then women, no matter how vigorously recruited or warmly received, will remain visitors where they work. A work environment refashioned as a truly respectful "multicultural" environment would be one in which neither gender feels like a visitor. But to engage in the difficult process of getting from here to there will necessarily involve a period in which neither gender will feel perfectly at home.

Certainly the stylistic differences that seem to be associated with gender go far beyond "personalism" versus "objectivism," and their expression at work goes far beyond how to talk in a work group. Let us quickly consider a few equally fundamental questions about work conduct and elaborate the stylistic differences expressed through the answers. What does it mean, for example, to be well prepared for a meeting? What does it mean to lead well, even to lead a meeting well? What do we see as a crisis at work, as opposed to merely a problem? What aspect of organizational life do we first seek to repair when damage has been done?

Some people think that being "well prepared" means something like this: "I spend time in advance of the meeting getting a clear sense of what I think the most important issues are, what the salient questions are, and possibly begin to form some thoughts about the answers or solutions. I come well prepared to participate actively and thoughtfully in a collaborative exploration and construction of a solution, plan, or approach." Others may think that being "well prepared" means something more like this: "I spend time in advance of the meeting formulating my solution or plan. I come well prepared to participate by presenting, advancing, defending, and winning assent to my idea." These two different constructions of "prepared" suggest very different conceptions of the *purpose* of the meeting in the first place. Each might be extremely well prepared for the meeting each plans to attend. The problem, of course, is that each is often attending the *same* meeting! And although it is never discussed, their way of participating in that meeting may amount to a subtextual battle to define its very purpose.

What misattributions and probable dysfunctions could result from this kind of "conversation at cross-purposes"? The first person sees the second person as essentially campaigning for his solution and wonders, "Why does he even bother to have a meeting or invite me to it? He's all closed and decided before we've even begun! He must regard me and the meeting as a bothersome obstacle that needs to be endured en route to his destination!" The second person sees the first person initiating a discussion in order to arrive at an eventual solution and thinks, "Why didn't she prepare? I have my solution, where's hers? If she can't deliver the goods, why is she taking up our time with her questions? We did our work and she didn't do hers. Why should I do her work for her?"

What kind of difference is this? It is certainly not a difference between wimpy spinelessness and courageous conviction, since the second person's "stand" could amount to little more than apple-polishing advocacy for what he has divined is the CEO's preference, and the first person could be required to display considerable courage in speaking up against prematurely foreclosing the conversation. The difference is not normative or hierarchic. Neither approach can be said to be better than the other, though in some situations one or the other may be prefera-

ble. Nor do they represent differences on some continuum of better-
ment or increase, such as intelligence, complexity, mental health, or
organizational skillfulness. They are, again, just stylistic, not epistemological differences, here perhaps best characterized as "inductive" versus "deductive." The first preparer starts with the raw materials (problems, questions), and seeks a context to act collaboratively on these
materials so that the group process can collectively make something
whole from the parts. The movement is from the particular to the general. The second preparer starts with a product (the "cooked" solution
or plan) and seeks a context in which to test its capacity to handle any of
the concrete situations, particular objections, or personal concerns others may raise about it. The movement is from the general to the particular. Each sees differently. Neither sees more. But in a world that arbitrarily favors the deductive style (more commonly male), those who
prefer the inductive style are consistently at a disadvantage.

Some people think the way to lead a meeting well is to cultivate a
participative process that allows for the greatest number of voices, issues, and concerns, even if the leader doubts that all these problems can
be solved. The focus is on process, and the evaluation is of that process.
Others think that leading a meeting well involves helping the group
handle the work on the table efficiently. Discussing problems that cannot be solved is distracting, and thus discouraged by this good leader or
indulged only where unavoidable. The focus is on product, and the
evaluation is of that product. Again, we are seeing different styles. Although neither can lay any claim to absolute superiority, one will almost
always *feel* more syntonic with our own personal style, and predictable
misattributions leading to discomfort, annoyance, or resentment can
result from being led in a style that is dystonic with our own. Preferring
either style, when we run into a leader who prefers the other we can feel
that this leader is not helping the group to get anywhere but is instead
undermining the group's effectiveness in deference to some peculiar
and distracting personal need ("to hash everything out," "to get
through the agenda"). The point is not just that the differences produce
explainable discomfort but that the attributions we make about others
may be wrong. Neither kind of leader may be undermining the group's
purpose. Each may be unwaveringly holding the group on course for its
destination. The problem is that each view has a different notion of
what that destination is.

In the face of a crisis, organizational or personal, some people seem to move first to preserve, protect, repair, or reinstate their connections or relations to others. Once these are secured, they move to recover their own balance or position. Others move first to restore, protect, or repair their personal security, position, or balance. Once this is secured, they move to repair their connections to others. I have been told that when American POWs from the Vietnam era were first released, nearly all performed the same two first acts after being flown to Wiesbaden, Germany: they took showers and called loved ones. But the men were far more likely to shower first and then to call loved ones. The women were more likely to call loved ones first and then to shower. The difference is not necessarily that the men are more selfish and care more about their own bodily comfort than about their loved ones. The men could well have felt what was most important to them was to talk to their loved ones, but they couldn't do what they most wanted until they had cleansed, or psychologically restored, a self that could even be reconnected to their loved ones. The difference is not between "selfish" and "altruistic"—both groups may have been doing first what they needed to do to restore the self, and both, in that sense, could be said to be "selfish." The difference is in how the self is made whole. For some, the self is restored by itself and is not until then capable or fit for precious connection. For others, the self is restored in and through connection.

Once again I would repeat that this is not a normative or hierarchic difference. It is a difference in fundamental "orientation," or what I am here calling "style." And although it is often referred to (in Gilligan's work and that of her colleagues, for example[12]) as the distinction between a "separate" versus a "connected" style, it is important to see that this is not a matter of dichotomy or polarity, as if people favor either separateness or connection, but one of figure and ground. As I stated in *The Evolving Self*, we may all be in the thrall of both these two great human yearnings: "the yearning to be included, to be a part of, close to, joined with, to be held, admitted, accompanied" and "the yearning to be independent or autonomous, to experience one's distinctness, the self-chosenness of one's directions, one's individual integrity. David Bakan called this 'the duality of human experience,' the yearnings for 'communion' and 'agency.'"[13] The stylistic difference is not one of favoring one to the exclusion of the other, but one of figure and ground. Some of us may make the experience of connection the base from which we then move toward experiences of agency that may also be greatly important to us. Others may make the experience of independence the base from which we then move to experiences of connection that may also be precious to us or of paramount importance.

Having identified some of the features of a non-normative stylistic difference that may be strongly associated with gender (see Table 6.1), we can now return to the question of how this difference compares or relates to the subject-object differences that guide our inquiry here. What is the relationship of "voice" differences (as relational theory refers to the constructivist distinctions it makes) to "structural" differences (as subject-object theory refers to the constructivist distinctions it makes)? I believe our discussion has basically pointed us toward two kinds of answers to this question: (1) relational theory and subject-object theory are making completely different but complementary kinds of distinctions; and (2) people's capacity to make positive use of relational theory (or any style-oriented theory) for overcoming forms of "ethnocentricism" is itself an unrecognized epistemological demand implicating subject-object theory.

Is subject-object theory really a non-normative "style differences" theory purporting to be a theory of the development of consciousness? Worse yet, is subject-object theory essentially privileging a male style of knowing and disadvantaging a female style of knowing by calling the first a higher order of consciousness than the second? Isn't the

Table 6.1 Gender-Associated Differences in Preferred Ways of Knowing or "Voice"

"Feminine" style	"Masculine" style
Narratizing	Abstracting
Personalistic	Decontextualized
Experiential	Objective
Linking ideas in conversation to build out toward generality	Overarching idea or general principle frames context for conversation
Inductive	Deductive
Process-oriented	Product-oriented
From the ground of "connection" or "relation" moves to issues of "independence"	From the ground of "independence" moves to issues of "connection" or "relation"

embeddedness in the "psychological surround" that characterizes cross-categorical knowing a female style? And isn't the capacity to stand *apart* from this surround a male style? Isn't the capacity to construct an overarching system, theory, or authorizing ideology that is called a qualitatively higher order of consciousness a typically male style?

Actually, the answer to all these questions is no, but the confusion is understandable and is fueled by much past theoretical writing, including, I hasten to confess, my own. In the ten years since *The Evolving Self* was published (and, for that matter, Gilligan's *In a Different Voice*, published in the same year), it is possible to see a gradual move toward disentangling or unconfusing two different sets of distinctions that were originally conflated. This gradual process of differentiation, which enables a *relationship* between the parts that could not exist before, mirrors within an intellectual field the development of individual consciousness.

The confusion has a number of sources, but perhaps the most important are these two: (1) We have confused what relational theory calls "separateness" or "independence" with what subject-object theory calls "autonomy." The self-authorizing capacity to "decide for myself" does not also have to implicate the stylistic preference to "decide by myself." I can be self-authorizing in a relational way; and (2) we have confused what relational theory calls "relational" or "connected" with what subject-object theory refers to in general as "embeddedness" or "undifferentiation" or in particular as "embeddedness in the psychological surround." A relational preference, or a "connected" way of knowing, does not refer to an inability to differentiate from any epistemological principle, cross-categorical or any other; instead it names a preferred way of relating to that from which one is differentiated. In other words, if the two theories are making completely different kinds of distinctions, it should be possible to be both (stylistically) "separate" and (structurally) "embedded in the psychological surround" and to be both (stylistically) "relational" or "connected" and (structurally) "autonomous." It should be possible to construct experience according to the principle subject-object psychology calls the third order of consciousness (cross-categorical knowing) and be "relational" *or* "separate." It should be possible to construct experience at the fourth order of consciousness (systemic knowing) and be "relational" *or* "separate" (see Table 6.2). And this is exactly what a number of theorists have since suggested and what researchers have since found.[14]

I confused these ideas in *The Evolving Self*, for example, in writing

Table 6.2 "Voice" and "Order of Consciousness" as Independent Constructivisms

STRUCTURAL distinctions (from subject-object theory)		VOICE distinctions (from relational theory)	
		Connected	*Separate*
	3rd order consciousness (cross-categorical)	Relationally embedded in the psychological surround (e.g., Nora, during her "dollhood")	Separately embedded in the psychological surround (e.g., Torvald, Nora's husband)
	4th order consciousness (systemic)	Relationally self-authorizing (e.g., Virginia Woolf, having killed the "Angel in the House")	Separately self-authorizing (e.g., Anderson Wright, Peter's employer)

about the move from third order to fourth order knowing when I invoked a saying from the women's movement that "in order to get yourself together you have to get yourself apart," an association of the *structural* move toward personal authority with the *voice* orientation of separateness, exactly the confusion of "deciding for oneself" with "deciding by oneself." If one's important connections are unwilling to support our moves toward personal authority, then being faithful to the forward motion of our own lives may indeed involve the extraordinary cost of having to take our leave from these connections (precisely as Nora leaves husband, children, church, and community at the conclusion of *A Doll's House*). But there is no necessary *identity* between taking command of ourselves and taking leave of our connections. As Belenky et al. point out in *Women's Ways of Knowing*, it is entirely possible to find connections and contexts of support and recognition that will continue to hold us and literally *re-cognize* us as we grow from the third to the fourth order of consciousness (or, in the language of Belenky et al., from "received" knowing through "subjective" knowing—a transitional position, it seems to me, between the third and fourth order—to "procedural" knowing).[15]

Moreover, I confused *style* and *structure* throughout *The Evolving Self* by using an organizing metaphor or image I have since come to "repent" (literally, "to think again"). The image was that of a helix, suggesting a certain oscillation in development between orders of consciousness that could be characterized one way (the first and third) and those that could be characterized another (the second and fourth).[16] The principal way I defined this difference was with respect to what I called the two fundamental (and often contradictory) longings in human experience, the longing to be next to, a part of, included, connected, and the longing to be distinct, to experience one's agency and the self-chosenness of one's initiatives. Of course, I still believe in the usefulness of this distinction, but by fusing this distinction with the distinctions between orders of consciousness, I equated certain orders of consciousness (the first and third) with the style of *connection* and other orders of consciousness (the second and fourth) with the style of *separateness*. Unconfusing these sets of distinctions involves seeing that each order of consciousness can favor either of the two fundamental longings.

Gilligan promoted a similar kind of confusion of voice-oriented categories with structural categories in *In a Different Voice* when she wrote that "by changing the lens of developmental observation from individual achievement to relationships of care women depict ongoing attachment as the path that leads to maturity," in contrast to the traditional male-biased view that "independence" or "autonomy" or "increasing differentiation" (she uses all three terms interchangeably) is the path to maturity.[17] Here Gilligan seems to be making "ongoing attachment" and "individual achievement" mutually exclusive, a tough position to sustain, but what is more important, she defines "autonomy" or "increasing differentiation" as "*not* attachment."

Gilligan's major contribution has been to make it clear that the story of development or maturity when told as one of "going away" or "leaving home," of ever-unfolding separation from valued connections and relations, is not the story of everyone's development. It is not even the story of every man's development, but it is certainly not the story of every woman's development (or that of those from non-Western cultures). Yet I think a more helpful way to characterize this insight would be to say that the story of development as "increasing differentiation" or "increasing autonomy" is not a story that should be told in only one way. "Increasing differentiation" may indeed be part of the story of everyone's development, but "increasing differentiation" can itself be the story of staying connected in the new way, of continuing to hold onto one's precious connections and loyalties while refashioning one's relationship to them so that one *makes them up* rather than *gets made up* by them. "Increasing autonomy" does not have to be a story of increasing aloneness. "Deciding *for* myself" does not have to equal "deciding *by* myself." "Autonomous" means self-regulating, and that regulation might well be on behalf of preserving and protecting one's precious connections according to an internal compass or system. Sharon Parks invokes the images of both "home" and "pilgrimage," the activities of both abiding and journeying, as contexts for transformational development.[18] The problem with "increasing differentiation" as a characterization of everyone's development, men's and women's, is not that differentiation itself is a male conception of growth but that the traditional rendering or interpretation or "voice" of differentiation has been male-biased.

It is important to use the same care in cross-cultural comparisons as well. It seems true, for example, as many have argued, that North American culture promotes and expects individuation and separation, while many South American, African, and Asian cultures promote and expect the self-in-the-collective and the maintenance of attachments. But it may *not* be true that South Americans, Africans, or Asians partake any less than North Americans in processes of increasing psychological differentiation, self-regulation, or even autonomy. Rather, they may partake of such processes *in the context of the collective.* Anthropologist Robert LeVine argues, for example, that however much the concept of self is subordinated to the collective in African subsistence cultures, each member is even *more* autonomous, internally differentiated, and psychologically self-regulating in some spheres of life than the average North American.[19] Differentiation itself may be neither male nor Western, but its fusion with a male or Western "voice" will make it seem so.

It is differentiation, after all, that creates the possibility of a new relationship to that with which one was formerly fused. It is differentiation that Kaufman et al.[20] are championing when they name their essay "Distancing for Intimacy in Lesbian Relationships." The structural "distance" of epistemological distinction does not have to create the social or emotional "distance" of separateness. On the contrary, the capacity to take a more differentiated position can permit us to move closer to another. It is differentiation, after all, that Virginia Woolf is talking about when she says she had to kill the Angel in the House:

It was she who used to come between me and my paper when I was writing reviews. It was she who bothered me and wasted my time and so tormented me that at last I killed her. You who come of a younger and happier generation may not have heard of her—you may not know what I mean by the Angel in the House. I will describe her as shortly as I can. She was intensely sympathetic. She was immensely charming. She was utterly unselfish. She excelled in the difficult arts of family life. She sacrificed herself daily. If there was chicken, she took the leg; if there was a draft, she sat in it—in short she was so constituted that she never had a mind or a wish of her own, but preferred to sympathize always with the minds and wishes of others . . . I turned upon her and caught her by the throat. I did my best to kill her. My excuse, if I were to be had up in a court of law, would be that I acted in self-defense. Had I not killed her she would have killed me.[21]

These are not words about "voice" alone, nor is the change Woolf speaks of here about a change of "voice." In turning upon the Angel she had been—turning upon a part of herself, a way of knowing with which she had been identified—she saves the life of the self she is becoming. In making the Angel object rather than subject, she brings into being the self-authorizing capacity to have a way of knowing (even to have it "by the throat" when need be) rather than be *had* by it. "Turning upon" is differentiating, and differentiating is as much a part of women's development as it is of men's.

That all four combinations of voice and structure depicted in Table 6.2 are quite possible can readily be seen in our discussion of work. If we return to any of the expectations or demands for work effectiveness I discussed in Chapter 5, we quickly recreate the structural distinction between the third and fourth orders of consciousness. For example, over and over again in the management literature one finds a description of the employee who must look to the employer to lay out the objectives, provide routes to their accomplishment, and evaluate whether the work done is of value. This description is then contrasted with that of the employee who is mindful of the employer's views and takes them into account, but who also has his or her own contribution to make toward understanding the goals, planning for their accomplishment, and evaluating the outcome. Of course, the literature has a curricular preference for the second employee rather than the first, but my point is that the personal authority demonstrated by the second is not the result of personality traits, such as higher self-esteem or greater self-confidence, or of learned skills, such as greater assertiveness or better decision making; instead, it reflects an evolution in the gradual development of psychological complexity, namely, the fourth order of consciousness. Management's unrecognized preference is to hire the psychologically "self-employed." But the two employees, as described in the management literature, might easily be referred to as "dependent" and "independent," words that have a voice-oriented ring to them. If in fact the distinction between the two kinds of employee is best understood as a structural one, with no relation to "voice" orientation, then it should be possible for employees to fit either description in *either* voice (see Table 6.3).

The first sort of employees, the so-called "dependent" employees, will derive their sense of the questions, the priorities, and even the quality of their work from the psychological surround, but they may do so in different ways and for different reasons depending on their preferred voice. It is one thing to derive these definitions and identify with them as the *means* of creating, maintaining, and experiencing strong, harmonious relationships; it is another to do so in order to derive a personal agenda that one then sets out to accomplish. No matter how "independently" (unilaterally, self-interestedly, strategically) the latter carries out his mission, the source and regulation of that mission is not internal but is derived from the psychological surround.

The second sort of employees, the so-called "independent" employees, will exercise their own personal authority at work even in relation to their employers, but, again, they may do so in different ways or on behalf of different ends depending on voice. It is one thing to exercise personal authority at work on behalf of unilaterally advancing or enhancing one's own agenda, valuing or fostering relationships as a means of accomplishing one's ends, and quite another to exercise it on behalf of fostering, preserving, and enhancing relationships. No matter how "oriented to" or "identified with" relationships and connections the latter may be, this is quite different from "an embeddedness in the psychological surround." The self-authorizing "relational" employee may "make herself up" via her connections, just like a relational employee at the third order of consciousness, but since the self she is making up is a system that acts upon the psychological surround and authors its own values, it is made up by connections according to its own standards. On behalf of her own agenda, to give relationships and connections the priority she believes they deserve, the self-authorizing "relational" em-

Table 6.3 The "Dependent" and "Independent" Employee in Two Voices

		VOICE distinctions (from relational theory)	
		Connected	*Separate*
STRUCTURAL distinctions (from subject-object theory)	3rd order consciousness (the "Dependent" employee)	Takes on the employer's expectations, goals, and strategies as a means to creating, maintaining, experiencing, and exercising strong, harmonious connections; susceptible to having the quality or value of one's work ultimately determined by employer	On behalf of ends or goals derived from the employer directly or indirectly (e.g., via other employees) unilaterally advances, strategizes, argues, competes, negotiates, promotes own position; susceptible to having the quality or value of one's work ultimately determined by employer
	4th order consciousness (the "Independent" employee)	Exercises personal authority on behalf of inclusivity, keeping communication open for maximum participation and input, preserving connections and surfacing threats to colleagues' collaborative capacities; personally evaluates employer expectations and own performance relative to these kinds of priorities	Exercises personal authority on behalf of advancing or enhancing one's own position, status, advantage, agenda, mission, or profile; relates to others on behalf of furthering unilateral ends rather than deriving ends out of relationship; personally evaluates employer expectations and own performance relative to these kinds of priorities

ployee can stand up to the competing claims and expectations of others just as forcefully as the self-authorizing "independent" employee.

Distinguishing in this way between the *consciousness* dimension of our culture's expectations for work success and employees' *stylistic* preferences (the demand is not for a "connected" or "separate" employee but for a self-authorizing one) could help make the work world a more welcoming place for styles that are now less favored. If male employers, for example, understood that their demands for the psychologically self-employed (the fourth order) can be met as easily by "connected" as by "separate" employees, they might come to support a wider range of interpersonal styles at work.

Consider, for example, the subject of "leadership style."[22] As more women enter management positions we are hearing more about a new leadership style, one that is warmer, more personal, more inclusive, and less hierarchical. In comparing the merits of this style with the more traditional, more male, more formal, more "top down" style, the literature on work asks, "Is a more personal style less professional?" But what if the real issue of "professionalism," or management competence, has less to do with style than with whether style is joined to a self-authorizing order of consciousness? As Table 6.4 suggests, it is quite possible to be a self-authorizing leader using either style. And to the extent that what people mean by "professionalism" is the fourth order of consciousness, it is possible not only for the warm, personal style to be "unprofessional," but for the traditional, formal, hierarchic style to be unprofessional as well! The question for the personal management style is not whether a manager errs or is "too soft" if she provides a shoulder to cry on. The question is whether, having done so, she is able to be empathic toward her employee's pain but not identified with it. If, for example, she now comes to feel responsible for her employee's pain, she may not match well with the hidden curriculum's definition of "professionalism," but the cause of her mismatch has nothing to do with her style. Her behavior may be considered an error, or "too soft," but the same behavior is as easily replicated by a manager with the formal, hierarchic style who defensively personalizes criticism or makes his employees responsible for his own negative feelings at work.

As these considerations demonstrate, the distinctions that relational theory makes and the distinctions that subject-object theory makes are thus of a completely different kind, independent but complementary, yet it is easy to see how we have confused them. Relational theory's "independent" or "separate" (seeing the self first as a separate person who then "has relationships," rather than seeing the self first in *the context of* relation) is not the same as subject-object theory's "independent" or "autonomous" (having a personal authority, whether "relationally" or "separately"). Relational theory's "being made up by relation," which will be true for a relational person at any stage of development, includ-

Table 6.4 Management Style and Order of Consciousness as Independent Variables

	Warm, personal, inclusive management style	Formal, hierarchic, traditional management style
3rd order consciousness (embedded in the psychological "surround")	May be inclusive and collaborative, e.g., because in need of direction from others; not sure where I stand until I know what is wanted by others; the leader who can't say no May provide a warm "shoulder to cry on," but then feels identified with, responsible for, the other's pain	May have top-down, in-control, chain-of-command, or by-the-book leadership style, but authority and direction derived externally (from one's superiors, e.g., or the company's code or tradition) May have a formal, socially bounded interpersonal manner, but nonetheless may personalize criticism, take responsibility for what is actually the responsibility of others, project responsibility onto others for what is actually one's own
4th order consciousness (self-authorizing)	May be collaborative with and inclusive of others as self-governing persons, seen and respected as such (including seeing oneself as such); collaboration, inclusion, or non-hierarchic leadership is expressive of a personal philosophy or belief system *brought to one's work with others* May provide a warm "shoulder to cry on" but is able to be empathic with, and *in relation to*, the other's pain (versus identified with it and responsible for it)	May lead hierarchically and unilaterally but out of a vision that is internally generated, continuously sustained, independent of and prior to the expectations or directives of the environment May have a formal, socially bounded interpersonal manner, but respects others, as well as oneself, as psychologically responsible, self-governing persons; preserves psychological as well as social boundaries on behalf of neither assigning to others responsibilities which are not theirs, nor taking on responsibilities which are not one's own

ing the self-authorizing fourth order of consciousness, is not the same as subject-object theory's "being made up by one's psychological surround," which is the case at the third order of consciousness whether one's style is "relational" or "separate"; the "connected, dependent" kind of employee is "made up by" both his psychological surround *and* relation.

Both sets of distinctions are constructivist in the sense that they are about a way of organizing experience. They are both—as I have also said of the Myers-Briggs distinctions and would say of all constructivist distinctions—about "ways of knowing." The form of one's "way of knowing," the "size" of the perspective, is a question of its parts, what is an element of the perspective and what is the perspective itself, what is object and what is subject, the question subject-object theory addresses. How one prefers to relate to the elements (whatever they might be) is a stylistic question, a question addressed by categories like relational theory's "separate" and "connected," or in a different way, like Myers-Briggs's "judging" and "perceiving," or in yet another way, like Kolb's "converger" and "diverger."

The distinctions of "voice" or relational theory are different from the distinctions of "structure" or subject-object theory, but the foregoing discussion suggests that they can be profitably brought together. From my point of view, this is already beginning to happen among those researchers and theorists of women's psychology who implicitly or explicitly join a developmental perspective to their study of women's "relationalness." The work of Belenky, Clinchy, Goldberger, and Tarule on "women's ways of knowing," and of Surrey on women's development of a self-in-relation are two excellent examples.[23] While both explicitly attend to the stylistic dimension (Belenky et al. distinguish "connected" from "separate" knowing; Surrey looks at the way women construct a self in the context of relationship), subject-object principles implicitly undergird the developmental distinctions made by each. Belenky et al., for example, distinguish between a way of knowing that is subject to the psychological surround ("received knowing") and one that has its own internal procedures for declaring something to be knowledge ("procedural knowing"). Surrey writes about the development of a self that is increasingly differentiated *in* the relationship rather than *from* the relationship. Such increasing differentiation eventually enables an empowered self capable of "caring for the relationship" and sustaining a complex sense of difference from those to whom it is nonetheless closely related.

These works implicitly or explicitly point the way to a jointly structural and stylistic apprehension of the self and its development. They provide further illustrations, for example, of how one can be both relational and self-authorizing. They take us a step further than my earlier point that differentiation and directionality (and even, for that matter, developmental hierarchy) are not in and of themselves necessarily male orientations to the study of development. They themselves tell stories of differentiation, and distinguish one way of knowing or one construction of self-in-relation as more complex (even "more grown") than another (hence, their stories admit of hierarchy). But they tell us versions of that story that fit the experience of women in development.

Belenky et al., and Surrey, in other words, are really not just constructivists; they are constructive-developmentalists. There is a subject-object dimension to their theories. But they are understandably quiet about it, and I am not sure they would even agree with me (from personal conversation I know that Belenky, Clinchy, Goldberger, and Tarule don't even agree with each other on this issue!). There is good reason to highlight one's constructivism and downplay one's constructive-developmentalism. Stylistic distinctions by themselves are non-judgmental. They are merely different orientations or preferences; one is in no sense "better" than the other. Subject-object distinctions presume to tell a story of increase, of greater complexity. They are thus more provocative, discomforting, even dangerous, and appropriately evoke greater suspicion. Any time a theory is normative, and suggests that something is more grown, more mature, more developed than something else, we had all better check to see if the distinction rests on arbitrary grounds that consciously or unconsciously unfairly advantage some people (such as those who create the theory and people like them) whose own preferences are being depicted as superior. We had all better check whether what may even appear to be an "objective" theory is not in reality a tool or captive of a "ruling" group (such as white people, men, Westerners) who use the theory to preserve their advantaged position.

But should we experience an explicitly normative theory like subject-object theory as a kind of unwelcome spoiler, as an opponent of the humane spirit of stylistic theories? Such theories, including relational theories, nobly carry the promise and the mission of impeding our eth-nocentric (or gendercentric) tendency to make judgmental comparisons of the familiar and the strange when such judgments are not appropri-ate. Isn't a judgmental theory, like subject-object theory, antagonistic to this hope and project? Not only is the answer no, but what is more significant, the very distinctions subject-object theory makes are at the heart of whether stylistic theories will succeed in their mission to upend our ethno- or gendercentrism! Why do I say this?

Let us consider again the voice differences that appear to be strongly associated with gender. Actually, there is evidence from those who study the life course that one aspect of this gender difference tends to reverse itself for many at midlife, since women tend to become more comfortable with their aggressive, competitive side, and men with their nurturant, affiliative side. Or, as Ric Masten put it in a memorable little poem:

> I have noticed that somewhere around forty
> The man comes in from the field
> Wearily, he throws his hat on the hook and says,
> "You were right, Grace. It ain't out there!"
> And she, with children grown at last
> Pulling her coat down from the hook, says
> "The hell it ain't!"
> Coming and going they pass in the doorway.[24]

I have often read this poem to audiences, and there is always a burst of laughter after the penultimate line, "The hell it ain't," in sympathy or support, it seems to me, for Grace's liberation from her domestic cap-tivity. But the laughter stops after the final line and a saddened silence takes its place. The image of men and women in different worlds, meet-ing only briefly as they leave their own and cross into the other's at midlife, is dispiriting. The promise inherent in the explorations of sty-listic differences is the possibility that we can meet because we under-stand our differences rather than because we hope to eliminate them. A better understanding of the differences means seeing them in terms of their origin in different values, rules, or definitions (such as cultural val-ues, rules, and definitions) rather than in terms of the attributions we make when we view the other exclusively through our own rules and definitions. But what does it take to achieve this better understanding?

If I come to a work meeting prepared to propose and defend my solution and to listen to other well-prepared people propose and advance theirs, and instead see that my colleague, Dianne, is not going to advance a solution of her own but ask the rest of us to join with her to create a solution, I may inevitably have a negative reaction to Dianne. There may be no getting around the conclusion that she is not acting as I prefer to act or in accordance with how I believe a first-rate colleague should behave. But it is a very different thing to react to my own unpleasant experience by evaluating *Dianne* ("Dianne is not only poorly prepared, but she is now trying to make us pay the price for her incompetence by asking us to slow down the group's work and build the solution right here as she should have done on her own before she got here") and to react to my experience by evaluating *myself* ("My negative reaction to Dianne may be a clue to me that she has violated one of my cherished rules. From my point of view, she is behaving incompetently because for me, being prepared means having your own design to present. But I don't know if Dianne has the same definition of being prepared. Maybe she is not just violating my definition; maybe she has quite a different one of her own, and if I understood it I could at least see how she is behaving in terms of what she *is* doing rather than just in terms of what she *is not* doing").

But being able to think this way is not just a discrete skill, it is an active demonstration of a mind that can stand enough apart from its own opinions, values, rules, and definitions to avoid being completely identified with them. It is able to keep from feeling that the whole self has been violated when its opinions, values, rules, or definitions are challenged. While such differences may always be experienced as transgressions, it is the capacity to have our opinions, values, or definitions as *object* rather than as *subject* that makes the transgressions "preliminary" rather than "ultimate," and our reactions to the transgressions potentially "mediate" rather than "immediate." We can do something about or with our reactions only if we "have" them. When they have us there is no *there* there to overcome the ethnocentricity. Subject-object theory clarifies the distinction between cross-categorical embeddedness in the values, beliefs, and definition of the psychological surround, and the psychological authority to reflect upon values and beliefs (one's own and others'). And far from being an opponent of the humane spirit of stylistic theories, subject-object theory identifies what may be the major contributing factor to our capacity to use the insights of stylistic theories to upend our tendency to canonize the familiar. The biggest heart and the best intentions to be an "enlightened traveler" rather than an "ugly American" may still be undone if they are not joined to a mind with the capacity to transcend third order consciousness.

Our discussion of the difference between subject-object "ways of knowing" and stylistic "ways of knowing" has thus led us to yet another unrecognized claim on the minds of adults in the work place and, indeed, in public life in general. The demand that we "respect diversity" is sounded, as it should be, in every quarter of public life even as a backlash against it is heard in the call to "return to traditional values." When we make and enforce the claim to respect diversity through the force of law (by legislating against discrimination, sexual harassment, unequal access) we reduce it to one of behavior and seek, as we should, to inhibit and reduce the most egregious acts of misbehavior, but we do not address the real source of the capacity to "respect diversity." When we try to satisfy the claim through workplace training we run the risk of reducing it to one of needed skills. In the process, we leave open the possibility that what we are learning is to keep our unfavorable attributions and characterizations of the other out of our public conduct and decisions, not that our attributions and characterizations are in themselves a failure to "respect diversity." The kind of learning that would help us to see that the actual differences we experience are differences of attribution—differences we create by viewing the other according to the rightness of our own preferences—is what Gregory Bateson called "deutero learning," learning that reflects on itself.[25] This kind of learning cannot be accomplished through *in*formational training, the acquisition of skills, but only through *trans*formational education, a "leading out" from an established habit of mind.

This conclusion often strikes people as bad news because the goal of supporting gradual development, the evolution of consciousness, is obviously a slower and more ambitious undertaking than skills training. But I would caution against short-sighted discouragement. If one is interested in helping adults at work only to be effectively respectful of diversity, or only to be clearer about what is and is not their responsibility, or only to be guided by their own vision, it can be discouraging to hear that what one is hoping for is not a matter of skills but an order of psychological complexity. A bigger investment is called for if these helpers must be not simply trainers but developmental educators. But if we consider the fact that, remarkably, all the expectations, demands, and prescriptions for adults discussed throughout this book reflect a common fourth order claim on adult minds, the cost-benefit analysis looks somewhat different. Then, a single investment could pay multiple dividends. Were we to refashion our ideas about worker and management education around the single goal of helping more people reach what amounts to a consciousness threshold, what Jean Baker Miller called fuller consciousness, we might encourage greater effectiveness on all these fronts at once. The next two chapters, which explore the epistemological demands in adult pursuits of self-expansion—psychotherapy and adult learning—will give us the chance to look more closely at those very processes through which consciousness is indeed helped to develop.

7

Healing: The Undiscussed Demands of Psychotherapy

There are nearly as many adult Americans who are engaged in formal activities aimed at self-expansion, such as psychotherapy, support groups, and classroom learning, as there are Americans who work. This striking fact is testimony to the real work of the modern world. In the modern world, as in the traditional world, the person labors. But in the modern world labor is carried out largely on behalf of oneself (and one's private associations) rather than as an expression of one's membership in a communal or tribal whole. And because the modern world expects of each adult the capacity for personal autonomy and authority, the self is not only a laborer, it is an arena of labor (we "work on ourselves"). The self itself becomes a project.

Accordingly, the "work" of public life—and its attendant mental burdens—needs a bigger canvas than that of paid employment. "Self-expansion" is my term for the myriad organized endeavors to "work on" the self. These can include participation in religious and spiritual institutions, self-help groups of all sorts, and psycho-educational movements such as EST or the addictions recovery movement. But I have chosen to focus on two of its most common forms, therapy and classroom learning. "Therapy" refers to the work adults do as individuals, members of a couple or family, or in groups with all varieties of helping professionals, including psychiatrists, psychologists, social workers, marriage and family counselors, addictions counselors, and clergy and pastoral counselors. "Classroom learning" refers to the work adults do as learners in credit or noncredit courses, in degree or nondegree programs, in community colleges, universities, graduate programs, centers for adult education, continuing education programs, recertification courses and programs in the professions, and in-house corporate training. In this chapter I consider the hidden curriculum of therapy for adults, and in the next that of adult learning.

Although therapy can be seen as a kind of "work on the self," it may nonetheless seem strange that I refer to it as part of an adult's public life. After all, in therapy we often discuss the most intensely private aspects of our lives and therapists go to great lengths to preserve the privacy of a therapeutic session and the confidentiality of its contents. Before we inquire into the mental demands of modern psychotherapy, perhaps it would be worth taking a moment to be more explicit about the distinction I am making between the "private" and the "public."

By "private" I refer to adult relationships of love, family, and friendship governed principally by bonds of blood or affection. By "public" I refer to adult relationships regulated principally by the contexts of work, business, or hire. All public relationships are really "business relationships," whether they are professional relationships between colleagues, where neither is hiring the other; civic relationships between public servant and constituent, where the "hiring" is highly indirect; or customer relationships, where the hiring is quite direct. Of course, money may figure in many, if not most, private relationships (younger children are economically dependent upon their parents, nonemployed spouses on their employed spouses); but it is blood, love, or affection, not money, that is the governing principle or medium of exchange. And, conversely, affection and even love may develop in public relationships, but, again, it is not love or affection that is the governing principle; rather, it is the preexisting "terms" of, for example, a professional code of conduct or a contract-for-hire. Money for service is the principal medium of exchange in a public relationship, no matter how warm or loving that relationship has become.

I grant neither public nor private relationships superior virtue; each has its own integrity. But there is a very clear boundary between them. What corrupts the integrity of either is its becoming more like the other. A private relationship is corrupted when money is not merely an ingredient but a determining factor in its design. If a spouse remains in a marriage principally for its economic benefit, whether by choice or by necessity, the relationship has become more like a public than a private one. At the same time, a public relationship is equally in jeopardy of being corrupted when the exercises of affection or love become not just attendant to it but governing of it. Should the service provider not only feel the affection of the client but begin to expect or require it as a condition of the relationship, then the relationship has crossed the line and become more like a private than a public one. Should the service receiver remain in the relationship not principally to receive the service but to receive the love or affection of the provider, this too makes the relationship more like a private than a public one. Psychotherapy—however "private" an activity, and however personal, warm, or loving the relationship between patient and therapist—is properly a part of one's public life.

Creating and preserving this distinction between public and private life have often been identified as characteristic of modernity. But like so many descriptions of "the modern," cultural observers tell us about it as if it is something that has already happened, as if it is an accomplished cultural condition no more likely to disappear than any other "product" of the modern world. But from the perspective of subject-object psychology, the mental conditions of modernity are not static, already accomplished facts. They are an ongoing demand or burden upon individual, real-life adults. The mental "products" of modernity are not presumed to have been created once and for all back at the dawn of the modern era; they are continuously coming into creation, or failing to, as individual adults do or do not personally compose an order of mental complexity that can successfully respond to these demands. The distinction between the public and the private is not just a feature of modern life, it is an ongoing expectation or claim upon us as adults not to let "publicness" corrupt our private relationships or "privateness" corrupt our public relationships.

Therapists, for example, must keep their experiences in the often intense therapist-client relationship from governing the course or purpose of that relationship. They must bring these experiences—their longings and their fears, their attractions and their revulsions—under the regulation of a system of belief that will direct the relationship on behalf of its public purpose. The binding energies of affection, or even love, should these be present, can be used as fuel on behalf of the goals or purposes of the engine, but if we allow fuel to burn for its own sake, the situation becomes explosive. For the therapist, the distinction between the public and private is not "an established condition of modern life," it is an ongoing fourth order claim on the mind to regulate or direct interpersonal relations and intrapersonal states of affection.

In many public relationships, even those of unequal power, the responsibility of keeping a public relationship from becoming a private one falls upon all the parties involved. In a therapy relationship this responsibility clearly falls upon the therapist alone. We regard clients, even adult clients, as potentially being in so vulnerable a position that we also see their initiatives to turn a public relationship into a private one as the responsibility of the therapist to countervene. Thus we may make the fourth order claim upon therapists to preserve the distinction between the public and the private but exempt clients from this claim. If the adult client in a therapy relationship is exempted from a fourth order demand in this one respect, would we find that in therapy this is consistently so? What are the mental demands therapists and therapy make on adult clients?

Jamie is a never-married thirty-two-year-old, the older of her living parents' two daughters.[1] Her younger sister, her parents, and she have apartments only blocks apart in Queens. For several years Jamie was the assistant manager of her father's furniture store, the kind of place that might have carried Peter's BestRest mattresses. Her father sold the store about two years ago on his retirement at age seventy. Since then Jamie, in her own words, has been "just hanging out." She has not worked, is not actively looking for work, and is only "a little concerned" about her lack of interest in finding work. Nothing else seems to interest her much either. She socializes infrequently and superficially and has not been romantically involved with anyone since high school. On a typical day she might talk to her parents by phone or visit them, go to the gym to work out, watch television, shop for groceries, talk to her sister on the phone. By her own admission there is nothing much doing in her life, though she seems neither greatly concerned about her aimlessness nor to be deriving any pleasure from it. She presents herself as quiet, unassuming, pleasant but colorless in her appearance and speech, a little constricted physically, articulate, bright. Only occasionally a little half-smile or twinkle in her eye or wryness in her voice will creep into her brief, uninterested replies to the family therapist, who is trying to get a picture of her present-day living. Her replies are polite but unengaging, suggesting either that she feels there is nothing remarkable about a healthy thirty-two-year-old person with no plans or interests, or that if there is anything remarkable you will have to talk to someone else about it because she herself has no ideas on the matter. It is just how things are.

When she is told by the therapist that her parents and sister, who are sitting there beside her, are concerned about her, that they feel she is "depressed" and "stuck," or when she hears her mother say she "cannot possibly be happy doing nothing—no bright person can be happy doing nothing," she shrugs or curls her mouth up slightly into a little smile. She says she doesn't think she is very depressed.

Meanwhile, Jamie's parents are in something of a quandary about their own lives. Ann, Jamie's mother, says that James, who "can't stand the winters in New York any more," wants to spend his retirement in Florida. Ann, who has misgivings about moving, has agreed in principle that she would be willing to try an arrangement where they kept their New York apartment and lived most of the year in Florida, but she cannot see how she can put the plan into action "until the children are settled," which, upon examination, really means "until Jamie is happy with what she's doing."

Jamie's father appears to be an earnest, serious, slightly depressed man, not very comfortable with the language of how people feel or why they may feel as they do, a man who has worked hard and reliably provided for his family for forty years, who loves his daughters and wants the best for them, who believes he knows something of what it takes to succeed in this difficult world, and who feels alternately frustrated and saddened that his older daughter—"she has the credentials, and the brains, and makes a good appearance"—seems to lack the wherewithal to "jump into life" and "compete" and "try something, *anything.*" Though he speaks little in therapy and then largely in platitudes, his demeanor suggests that if he were to let everyone in the room know the real depth of his sadness and frustration about these things, he would be unprepared for and unmanned by the loss of his composure.

It is Ann who seems to do most of the talking and public feeling for the family. Hers appears to be a warm, wry, steady, and emotionally available presence in the family. She wants to know "what does everyone want to do and where does everyone want to live." She worries about everyone, about Jamie and James, especially, about Jamie's lack of involvement in anything, about her husband's colitis, about his hating the northern winters, about his upset about Jamie.

Anita, the younger sister, smartly dressed, attractively made up, a hardworking woman with a busy life, acknowledges that she, too, is worried about her sister, but thinks maybe everyone should just let up on her. "Maybe we're making too much of this. She's a little stuck, but eventually she will get herself into gear."

The therapist asks the parents to describe the families they grew up in. Ann explains that she was the youngest and only daughter with three older brothers, all of whom were troubled in some way. Ann, it appears, became an "assistant mother" in childhood and uncomplainingly assumed caretaking responsibilities. James was one of six children, had "a wonderful dad who took good care of us" and an "irresponsible, self-centered" mother who "abandoned us when we were little, ran off with a bum, left my father to raise us."

Thus does a family of four adults present itself to a therapist for help. For over two years the forward course of at least three family members' lives has been stalled—Jamie's move into establishing an adult life, and her parents' move into the retirement phase of theirs.

After consultation with her professional team, the therapist presents an intriguing formulation to the family as to the cause of their stuckness:

> We're impressed with what you [speaking to James] learned from your father about being a good father and how important that is. Our sense is that, for you, supplying a super mother for your family was probably the highest priority in your life, you know? We don't know how you managed to do that but you did. Because you [Ann] *are* a super mother, and I think you [James] had a lot to do with that. You did that in collaboration with her. The trouble with that, the problem, the dilemma, is that [turning to Ann] in order to be a super mother you've got to have kids. And the dilemma for you [Jamie] is that if you're going to help your father in his lifework you've got to remain a child. So it's a problem. And I guess it's not going to change until you [Ann] or your husband is convinced that you will not be abandoning the children if you get on with your own life together, that you don't have to keep proving to him that you're never going to abandon these children. So we're stuck. And this is where *you're* stuck [turning to Jamie]. How are you going to be a good daughter and grow up at the same time?

The therapist's formulation is complicated. She does not just make inferences or generalizations, such as, "It seems that others in the family see Father as fragile, but no one is being explicit about it," or "Jamie seems to have the role of keeping the family members in touch with each other," or "Between Jamie's *not* working and Mom and Dad's *not* retiring to Florida, there is a lot that is 'on-hold' for this family." What she presents instead—more than a collection of discrete inferences—is a single, more comprehensive, overarching *theory* or *system* which not only integrates the inferences but implies many more inferences which have not yet even been named. In the same way, more than focusing on family members' various relationships (how Jamie and her father relate, how the parents relate, how the sisters relate) the therapist's formulation focuses on the relationships between the relationships, the way the various relationships are all under the governance of a single principle of undiscussed family loyalty and devotion. Along the same lines, the formulation attends to more than the feelings family members have inside them, or, we might say, it attends to the family members themselves as something more than the suffering carriers of painful feelings of worry, discouragement, and frustration. Instead, it constructs the family members—each one of them—as active creators of their feelings. This formulation responds sympathetically to the painful *effects* of the family's stuckness, but it also suggests that each person is a *causer* of the family's stuckness.

The formulation retells the family's story from one of incapacity (Jamie can't work; the parents can't retire; Jamie's sister and parents can't do anything to help her) to one of ability and accomplishment: All four members of the family are not failing but succeeding in the exercise of their loyalties. Father is faithfully protecting his family from the impermissible abandonment of a family's mother that he experienced. Mother is faithfully carrying out the role ordained for her so that Father's lifework might be fulfilled. Jamie is successfully preserving her mother's opportunity to perform this role, which frees Anita to pursue a reasonably independent course, while presumably monitoring the situation closely enough that she can step in and provide a need for her mother to mother should Jamie leave the job of needy child. While the family, to varying degrees, feels that Jamie is failing at life, the therapist explicitly calls Jamie a success at keeping the family stable, at being a good, devoted daughter, at staying a child who needs a mother's close attention. In the face of any danger that her mother might relent and agree to move to Florida, thereby disturbing the whole system, Jamie, the therapist suggests, would at once effectively and competently take action to save the family: "You'd dig in your heels, and complain a lot, and get more depressed and make sure that you give her good reason to stay here."

After the interpretation, the father suggests that "in due time this will all be ironed out actually" and Jamie will get mobilized, as if the family is experiencing a problem which might be healed by time. The therapist refutes the idea that this is a problem in need of healing: "I don't think so," she says. "What makes you think that?" James asks in surprise at being so directly contradicted by the therapist. "Because," she says, quite confidently, "the way it is, is the way it has to be. I don't think, if you're hanging around waiting for Jamie to take care of everything and make the change that will free you, supposedly—that's a pipe dream. That's never going to happen."

In sum, since the focus of the therapist's formulation is not inferences but the system that organizes or creates inferences, since its focus is not relationships but the relationship between the relationships, what governs the relationships, and since its focus is not on people as the repositories of their feelings but as active creators of their feelings, the formulation is at a fourth order of mental complexity. It "goes meta" on third order constructions (inferences, relations, inner states), subordinating them to a higher order of complexity. Now one last observation: *Not one member of the family understands the formulation at this level!*

When the therapist says she would be worried about the father, James, if Jamie were to get unstuck, they all assume she means she would *not* be worried, or that then *he* would no longer be worried. They find unfathomable the suggestion that the father who is so distraught by his daughter's immobility could be in difficulty were she to mobilize herself. But even after the therapist explains again why she would be worried, not one member of the family ever utters a sentence that suggests he or she understands the wider implications of the therapist's suggestion—namely that they are the agents, the creators, not just the victims of the situation, that they are all responsible for the way things are, not in the sense of being blameworthy but in the sense of purposefully, if unawarely, making them be exactly as they are.

Ann, the loyal wife and nearly lifetime mother, does not give us the impression that she has chosen to devote herself to her husband's preeminent value—that his family not be like the one in which he grew up. She does not, for example, appear to be making a distinction between "his agenda" and "my agenda," or to be deciding, as an expression of her commitment to her own authority, to lend herself to his agenda. James and his namesake daughter conscientiously, even heroically, seem made up by the values derived from their respective parent generations, rather than themselves being the makers of their values.

So perhaps it is true that no member of the family can understand the therapist's interpretation in its fourth order fullness. So what? Does it really matter if the formulation is over the heads of its clients? Family systems therapists may think not. Many of the theories that guide family therapy express skepticism of the whole concept of the individual mind, let alone the concept of its development. These theories regard the concept of the individual mind with its own integrity, apart from the social system or context that is making it up, as a fiction—perhaps a useful fiction at times, but a fiction nonetheless (a position, I might mention, with which I am not wholly unsympathetic, and which I address in Part Four on postmodern claims on the mind). Family therapists who are guided by these theories are thus less drawn to attending to changes in an individual's personal psychology and more interested in engaging and "unsticking" the "group mind," believing that any individual change that does not alter the nature of the group mind will be essentially meaningless.

I agree. Individual change that does not alter the nature of the group mind may be meaningless. But I *also* believe in the power of individuals' ways of constructing reality and think that changes made by the family that do not arise out of a transformation in a family member's mind may be meaningless. For example, if the mother, Ann, stops carrying out her duty to be a "super mom" as her husband defines it and takes up the duty of "even more effective super mom" as she understands the therapist to define it, then she may agree ("I'll do anything it takes to make Jamie happier") to move to Florida (which is in fact what happened with this family), and Jamie may be less depressed (which is also in fact what happened), feeling that she is now free to take up other activities. But their predicament, being captive to their own loyalties to the family, will not necessarily have been altered, because neither Ann's move nor that of her daughter involves a changed *relation to* the group mind. Jamie's need, after all, is not just to live more geographically separate from her family, or even to be more economically independent of them. Indeed, either of these might be accomplished without a *psychological* separation or *psychological* independence from the family's agenda. Although the altered *terms* of that agenda may now make it possible for her to be less depressed or to take up associations of work and love outside the family—a not inconsiderable accomplishment—what is to prevent these new associations from themselves being characterized by Jamie's captivity to the loyalties, agendas, or group minds into which she will now be inducted? What is to prevent her, now that she is somewhat free of her family, from taking up this same role in the *next* family of which she may be a part, as it appears her mother did? Is being free of psychological service to her parents enough if it leaves her no less likely to be swept into service to another set of persons, authorities, or loyalties? Although the terms of the family mind might have changed, if there is no change in the structure of at least one family member's mind, it seems doubtful that anyone's relation to "the family mind" will be different.

This is why I suggest that it *does* matter that no one in the family yet understands the therapist's interpretation at its full fourth order level. It matters because if they cannot understand it, they cannot themselves be constructing the world at a fourth order level, and if no one is constructing the world at a fourth order level, then no one is in a position to alter his or her captive relationship to the group mind. We can share the family therapist's goal to facilitate change in the group mind, but what does such a goal really amount to? If the change is to endure after the therapist withdraws, if it is to have some source *inside* the family, then the goal of facilitating such a change makes a demand or a claim on the mind of someone in the family to construct reality at the fourth order. The therapist can neither ignore individual minds nor presume (as she may have unwittingly presumed in presenting her complicated formulation) that individual minds can already understand reality constructed at the fourth order. The therapist must help someone in the family to make the move. Who will it be? Where the family members are all adults, as in the present situation, this is a claim that could be taken up by any one of them. If it is the children, Jamie or Anita, who take it up, then each is presented with the special difficulty of having to establish adulthood not only by leaving her parents' home but also by leaving her parents' *mind*, departing *epistemologically*, yet still somehow experiencing herself as loving them well and maintaining her closeness to them. If it is a parent, James or Ann, who takes it up, then the generative, "launching" dimension of parenting may extend to supporting a launching *from* rather than *within* the family mind.

In any case, the attention paid to the group mind in the family therapy may unwittingly amount to a simultaneous fourth order claim on the individual minds of adult family members. Far from continuing the fourth order exemption from the responsibility to keep a public relationship public, which I suggested adult clients are given in therapy, here the fourth order claim upon adult clients is reinstated. And as different as various therapy approaches may be, most unknowingly share this important commonality. All manner of therapies, including family therapy, have the potential to be of vital assistance to adults in facilitating this very movement from the third to the fourth order, but in many instances, therapeutic practices are as guilty as the rest of the culture for providing a challenging curriculum without the necessary support to master it. Therapy can be one of the most important sources of support for facilitating the capacity for modernity, yet many of its practices presume that such a capacity already exists.

The famous film series *Three Approaches to Psychotherapy*[2] is a striking example of the pervasiveness of the therapist's expectation of fourth order complexity in adult clients. Everett Shostrom arranged this admirable series in order to demonstrate a variety of quite different ways of doing individual therapy. Carl Rogers, Fritz Perls, and Albert Ellis each conducted an initial interview with a woman in her thirties called "Gloria," a generous and courageous person talking about her real-life concerns, not an actress delivering scripted lines. The therapists' respective approaches—client-centered therapy, gestalt therapy, and rational-emotive therapy—each of which has been enormously influential, directly and indirectly, on contemporary therapeutic practice, led them to dramatically different encounters with the client. Yet as different as the sessions are in many respects, each one makes fourth order demands on the client, who has barely begun the long transition from the third to the fourth order.

Carl Rogers's "client-centered" or "nondirective" therapy has had an enormous influence on the training and practice of three generations of counselors and therapists.[3] His passionate commitment to "joining," "receiving," "welcoming," or "accompanying" clients' own gradual processes of discovering and claiming their meanings lead to a clinical operationalizing of existential psychology and philosophy. But, in light of our exploration of the hidden curriculum of modern life, it is interesting to ask whether Rogers didn't really have a *particular* constellation of meaning he was most especially eager to "welcome," and whether, in this respect, his method was really as nondirective as he supposed.

Rogers is probably famous for—or caricatured by—his refusal to answer his clients' questions directly. Faced with a question, he was most likely to "join" the client in her experience of having such a question, rather than let himself be the source of the answer. "Are my eyes all red?" a client asked him once at the end of an especially tearful session as she was pulling herself together and getting ready to leave.[4] Rogers's response was something like, "You're wondering, are you, what you might look like to the world that's waiting for you outside this office?" An exasperated student of Rogers, listening to this exchange on a tape in a seminar, could not contain himself: "My goodness! What's the harm in answering a simple thing like *that?* Can't you just give the lady the information she's looking for?" "Of course I can," Rogers is said to have replied. "And so can a mirror," the implication being that he was committed, every moment she was with him, to giving her something she could *not* get from a mirror, the experience of another human being alongside her at the level of her internal feeling and experiencing.

But to what end did Rogers provide this empathy? His own ways of generalizing the goals of therapy suggest that among the variety of constellations of meaning subject-object psychology depicts, Rogers had an unwitting favorite. The client, Rogers hoped, would come "to perceive his standards as being based upon his own experience, rather than upon the attitudes or desires of others . . . to perceive himself as the evaluator of experience, rather than regarding himself as existing in a world where the values are inherent in and attached to the object of his perception . . . to place the basis of standards within himself, recognizing that the 'goodness' or 'badness' of any experience or perceptual object is not something inherent in that object, but is a value placed on it by himself."[5]

Of the many "meanings" a person may be creating, it is most apparent, in looking at Rogers' actual work samples, that it was the meaning of the fourth order he especially hoped would appear. In his therapy sessions with "Gloria," after carefully avoiding her many attempts to get him to answer questions he would rather she discover by looking to herself (that is, her fourth order "self"), he hears the following:

Gloria: (After a pause) I do feel like you have been saying to me—you are not giving me advice, but I do feel like you are saying, 'You know what pattern you want to follow, Gloria, and go ahead and follow it.' I sort of feel a backing up from you.

To which he responds:

Rogers: I guess the way I sense it, you've been telling me that you know what *you* want to do and yes, I do believe in backing up people in what *they* want to do. It's a little different slant than the way it seems to you.

At this, Gloria's face goes cloudy. Brought up short by Rogers's uncharacteristic nonconfirmation of her feelings, and at a time of great puzzlement, she gets out just four halting words before Rogers—again quite uncharacteristically—interrupts her to try to make better the point it has now apparently become urgent for him to drive home:

Gloria: Are . . . you . . . telling . . . me—
Rogers: You see, one thing that concerns me is it's no damn good to do something that you haven't really *chosen* to do. That is why I am trying to help you find out what your own inner choices are.

Rogers may call his approach "nondirective," but about one thing, at least, he is willing to be quite directive: "Thou shalt not see me as supporting you in your efforts to live inside my authority or to establish value-directing bonds of connection and loyalty to me. That's not what I'm doing. And if that's what you're doing, it's 'no damn good.'" Rogers is not happy with Gloria's construction that he is supplying her with the guidance she needs, so he rearranges her architecture. Instead of taking up the position she assigns him in her meaning-making, that of a source *before* her she can come to and draw from, he seeks to escape and move around to a place *behind* her, looking over her shoulder, where he can see out with her and, as he says, "back [her] up in what [she] wants to do." But the worry here is that in this very moment of declaring his intention to support her meaning-making he may indeed be refusing to support her meaning-making by refusing the role she assigns him. He may really be saying, "I'm here to back up your fourth order meaning-making." He says that his way of understanding what they are doing is just "a little different slant than the way it seems to you." But what if this "little difference" is not so little? What if it amounts to a qualitatively different order of consciousness?

Fritz Perls's "gestalt therapy" also represents the thoughtful and influential operation of a constructivist philosophy, the *gestalt* school of the 1930s, oriented to the holism of people's perceptual meaning systems.[6] In personal manner and clinical practice, Perls could not have presented a greater contrast to the gentle, nonintrusive, patient, White-Anglo-Saxon-Protestant Dr. Rogers. A provocative, intense, hairy, and

German-Jewish ethnic, Perls saw himself as something of a drama coach or sculptor, passionately coaxing, urging, even goading his student or his artistic material to shape itself into a new, more "actualized" form. Different as their spoken philosophies and manner of practice were, however, when we consider the particular *kind* of dramatic performance or sculptural form Perls hoped to bring into being, it is remarkable how similar to Rogers's his unwitting epistemological goal was.

"My aim," Perls said, is that "the patient should transform his energies from manipulating the environment for support into developing greater and greater self support, [coming to] rely on his own resources. This process is called maturation. Once the patient has learned to stand on his own feet emotionally, intellectually, economically, his need for therapy will collapse."[7] If we stay with it a moment, this is a remarkable statement. Deriving "support" from an identification with the cultural surround, the essence of the third order of consciousness, is here framed as "manipulating the environment." Constructing the self as a source of support is not just growth but "maturation," a kind of end-state of development apparently, since one would not need therapy any longer. How might one fare in such therapy if one is largely identified with the third order? One will need, for certain, to be cured of one's manipulativeness.

Accused essentially of being manipulative or "phony" in her session with Perls one too many times for her liking, Gloria finally lashes back. She tells him she is angry with him and accuses him of not respecting her. Of course this exhibition of forthrightness on Gloria's part is applauded by Perls, and we are again faced with an irony. On behalf of eliminating "manipulation" has Perls manipulated Gloria into the kind of behavior of which he most approves? In response to Gloria's claim that he does not respect her, he adopts his gentlest tone:

Perls: I respect you so much as a human being that I refuse to accept the phony part of yourself and I address myself to the genuine part. Right now, the last few minutes, you were wonderfully genuine. You weren't playing anymore. I could see you really were hurting.

Gloria: Well, I don't feel I've got a right, when I don't like somebody or I disagree with what somebody's doing. If I should respect them, if they're above me, if they're superior to me, I don't feel I've got a right to really, really tell you how mad I am.

Perls: (Lifting his hand in front of her face as if to tell her to shut up, and then waving his hand dismissively) That's rubbish. You're just yackety-yackety now. You're getting back into your safe corner. Yack-yack-yackety.

Gloria: Well, that's the way it feels. That's the way the safe corner feels to me.

Perls: Good, go back to your safe corner. Because we have to part very soon. You were in your safe corner. You came out for a moment. You nearly met me. You could get a little bit angry with me. Now go back to your safety.

Gloria: (Angrily) I feel like you're telling me the only way you respect me as a human being is if I'm aggressive and forceful and strong. I feel like you couldn't even accept my—I'd be scared to death to cry in front of you. I feel like you'd laugh at me and call me a phony. I feel you don't accept my weak side, only when I'm yelling back at you or hollering at you . . .

Like Rogers, Perls wants to foster a particular way of making meaning, but his therapeutic choices often end up assuming that the fourth order capacity is already there, that it is only in need of encouragement, rather than actually helping it to come into existence. That a third order way of knowing is "phony" and a fourth order way of knowing is "genuine" appears only to be Perls's view of the matter, not Gloria's.

Albert Ellis's "rational-emotive therapy" or "RET" is yet another powerful influence in the training and practice of contemporary therapists.[8] His work contributed to the burgeoning of the field of cognitive-behavioralism. Here the category of "behavior" to which social scientists could direct their attention was extended "inside" to include the person's internal mental behaviors as well as her external observable actions and reactions. Ellis's therapy focuses on the internal behavior of sending defeating, catastrophizing, antagonistic, and irrational communications to oneself. He is interested in helping people "talk" to themselves differently in order to come to feel and act more wholesomely. His work also reflects the constructivist theme that people are actively in the process of creating much of the pain they are currently experiencing. Their pain is not primarily due to the unfortunate things that happen to them or the fortunate things that fail to happen to them but to the hopeless or personally hostile meanings they make of these events. Such hopeless and hostile constructions may have their origins in the person's past, but, what is more important, they are being constructed by the individual right now, today, "because he is still re-indoctrinating himself with the same philosophies of life, the same values, he imbibed and taught himself in youth."[9] Neither the warm, polite "receiver" nor the ill-mannered provocateur, Ellis's persona is that of the cool but concerned rational scientist who will help a person solve his problem. Lacking the organismic or developmental foundations characteristic of the intellectual heritage of Rogers and Perls, Ellis is promoting not so much a new stage of development as the acquisition of specific kinds of learning that would allow a person to extinguish certain dysfunctional behavior. He wants to "get the individual to learn, and learn for the rest of his life, to challenge and question his own basic value systems, his own thinking, so that he really thinks for himself."[10] But as his goals suggest, different though he may be from Rogers or Perls in manner or approach, he is unwittingly trying to get his client's mind into the same fourth order shape. Since the behaviorist tradition rejects the notion of a self holistically or coherently directing our behavior, it is understandable that Ellis would confuse the mental behavior of the fourth order capacity with the structure of mind that gives rise to that behavior. Seeking the latter, he ends up teaching the former. Unfortunately, it is hard to talk people into a new order of consciousness.

But Ellis tries. After Gloria talks about her displeasure with her own shyness and self-consciousness around men, he urges her to be more self-accepting:

> *Ellis:* You're giving a very good illustration of why other-directedness doesn't pay. Because if you really are defining yourself in terms of others' estimation of you then even when you're ahead of the game and you're winning them, you have to be saying to yourself, "Will I win them today? Will I win them tomorrow? Will I keep winning them?" You're always focussed on, "Am I doing the things that please *him?*," and you never are yourself. You never have a self. While if you're saying, "What do *I* want to do in life? There must be *some* human beings who would like me as I am. Let's see if this is one of those human beings," then that's the only way, isn't it, that you can be yourself, you see?

The irony here is that if she could really "see" what he's saying in the actual form in which he is saying it—if she could truly understand the kind of "self" he is talking about "having"—she would probably not need the lecture he is earnestly giving her. "What have you got to lose?" he asks her about letting a man know she'd like to see him. "The worst he can do is reject you, and *you* don't have to reject you, and that leaves *you* intact. It just leaves you unfortunately not, for the moment, getting what you want." Who could "hear" this message and understand what "*you* don't have to reject you, and that leaves *you* intact" really means? What if the person who could hear it is one who already has the capacity to stop "reindoctrinating" herself, the capacity to look at her values and beliefs? What if, to the person who does *not* yet construct the world at the fourth order—the person for whom Ellis's curriculum (and Rogers's, and Perls's) is best suited—the lecture is over her head?

As different as these three approaches are, their basic commonality (besides the fact that they all make fourth-order claims) is that they are all focused on the present life of the client. They differ from the more psychodynamically influenced approaches, which place great importance on the client's past, the interpretation of and insight into the client's psychological biography. Do these approaches also make fourth order claims on their clients?

In the memorable movie *Moonstruck*, the lead character, Loretta (played by Cher), reluctantly fulfills a promise to her fiancé, visiting his estranged brother to invite him to their wedding. At our first meeting with this younger brother in his bakery, we, along with Loretta, see at once that he is an intense, tormented soul, and that he is missing one of his hands. Though he will at first have nothing to do with her, when he learns that Loretta intends to marry his hated brother, he eventually agrees to let her cook a meal for him in his sparely furnished apartment above the bakery. Here Loretta learns the source of the estrangement. He was once a happier man, he tells Loretta, in love himself with a woman he planned to marry. But then, one fateful day, his brother entered the bakery, distracting him while he was working and causing him to slice off his hand in the breadslicer. He lost his hand, his woman, his appetite for life!—and all because of his brother.

Sitting across from him at the kitchen table, Loretta converts the setting to one more akin to a psychotherapy office and proceeds, without solicitation, to reframe the story of the tormented brother's life. "What happened to you has nothing to do with your brother," she tells him. "That woman you were with was the wrong woman. You were trapped, like a wolf whose foot is caught in a trap. And like a wolf who wants to live, you tore off your paw so you could live. You tore off your paw to get out of the trap."

With this, the brother, first silent and stunned, rises from his chair, throws over the table, and sweeps Loretta into his arms and off to bed where, reunited by her words with his passion and vitality, they make wild, life-changing love. It makes for good movie-watching, but any therapist might be forgiven for asking, "Why don't my 're-frames' ever have quite the same transforming effect?"

In fact, the contrary is often true. The variety of efforts in individual therapy to convert a client's stance toward the past or present story of his life from one of helpless victim to creative agent not only fails on many occasions to release people from their psychological captivity but can cause them to feel unhappier still. The implicit message in such reconstructions, sometimes conveyed more explicitly, is that "you are responsible for your life." It is true that if I am your client and I already construct the world at the fourth order I am more likely to hear this as a confirmation of my personal authority, a reminder that while the things that others do to me or that happen to me may not be in my control, the meaning I make of them can be, a reminder that while I cannot change the wind, I can change my sails. I may hear the message then as a confirmation of my own power. But if my construction of reality is under the influence of the third order, I am likely to hear the same message as a declaration of my blameworthiness. "You are responsible for your own life" is then less an inspiring rallying call to self-authorship than a humiliating and dispiriting judgment that I have only myself to blame for the fix I am in.

In a similar vein, Maria Broderick suggests that there may be an unwitting fourth order demand in the way psycho-educators in behavioral medicine tend to appropriate the findings that cancer patients who display "fighting spirit" live longer and better.[11] Research shows that adult patients who feel they can do something about their illness, who eschew a victim's role, who get involved in their treatment, who challenge their doctors, apparently do better. But, as Broderick points out, there may be something misguided about then trying to teach patients the behavior associated with "fighting spirit" when it may be the form of the mind giving rise to the behavior that is the more important source of their "doing better." In other words, patients who construct meaning at the fourth order may experience encouragement to challenge their doctors as a recognition that they, the patients, can continue to be in charge of their lives in sickness as well as in health. But patients at the third order may experience the very same encouragement as a frightening undermining of the powers of modern medicine in which they wish to place their faith.

"Empathic breaks" between therapist and client owing to the therapist's unwarranted and unwitting expectation of a fourth order capacity in the client are likely and can sometimes be very subtle if no less abandoning.[12] A client who has uncritically internalized the family's value to be happy at all times, for example, who suffers under this injunction but never complains about it, will eventually provoke a therapist into reflecting, or inviting the client to reflect, on how difficult it must be to have to live by this rule, or how unfair or unrealistic such a rule is. As a therapist I have been trained to attend to and respect the feelings that arise in me during a therapy session as possible clues to what may be going on with my client, an idea that, as a subject-object psychologist, I consider useful but dangerous if taken too literally. It makes sense that anyone—in the presence of someone who is speaking uncomplainingly about experiences we think should be accompanied by anger—would wish to supply the missing ingredient and correct "what's wrong with this picture." An untrained person might correct the picture by getting angry himself, not quite realizing why. A therapist would, ideally, first recognize the feeling and identify it as "belonging to the story" although not necessarily to him. It is common for therapists to invite the anger to come from the person who is telling the story: "I wonder if some small part of you doesn't feel furious that it is never okay to be miserable." This would welcome the client's acknowledgment of her anger without asking her to take complete leave of the stance she has already presented. "You're a complicated person," the therapist's inquiry implies, "and you feel just as you've said you feel. That may even be how you mostly feel. But I wonder if, to even a tiny extent, there isn't also this other way you feel, too."

The problem here is that, while the therapist demonstrates the fourth order capacity to reflect on rather than be driven by the feeling that shows up in him, he may be forgetting that it was he, after all, who created the feeling of anger, and that unless his client is also constructing experience in a fourth order way there is no guarantee that any part of her feels angry as he does. Attending to the feelings that arise in me, the therapist, as clues to the feelings of my client is fine, so long as I do not assume that my way of putting the client's experience together, leading to whatever feelings this leads to, is necessarily the client's way. That the client does not express the feelings I would feel is not necessarily denial. The idea that the client can just zap her unexpressed feelings into me at the same order of complexity in which she constructs experience—which then makes it legitimate for me to assume that my client constructs her experience in keeping with the order of complexity of the feelings that show up for me during therapy—strikes me as paying a bit too much "respect" to my feelings in therapy! My suggestion to her to own the feeling—that a rule to be happy all the time might be too difficult, unfair, or unrealistic, or one she does not really feel she wants to live by—may miss the possibility that from her third order perspective the feelings she is having do not concern how the self relates to the rule (which would involve taking the family value as an object to critique) but how guilty or self-disapproving she feels when she violates, or even contemplates violating, the rule (a loyalty with which she is still identified, to which she is still *subject*).

A mainstay of most therapeutic approaches that attend to adults' psychological history, in individual or couples therapy, is that of promoting insight into the connections between present experience and past events. The abstracting capacities of the third order make it possible for those who think in this way to discover themes and patterns to their life history, to make connections between present and past experiencing, and to "have insight" into why they act and feel as they do. But the actual demands insight-oriented therapies make of their clients in relation to insight involve something more than this, and the "something more" outstrips third order capacities. Insight-oriented therapists may be unaware that they are requiring the fourth order of mental complexity, but they are very much aware of the difference between clients who just "have insight" and those who "make productive use" of it. Consider this exchange between two therapy clients sitting in a waiting room:

> "So, are you learning anything in your therapy?"
> "Oh, absolutely! Each week I learn more and more about why I'm such a mess."

If such a result falls a bit short of the kind of progress therapists are hoping for, the important question may be whether therapists look to their "recalcitrant" clients or to themselves for the cause. Unless therapists consider that their own disappointed hopes reflect an expectation for something more than the capacity to make thematic or causative connections between past and present, they are likely to adopt the self-comforting stance of the teacher who laments that his students learn so little of what he teaches so well. What is it they are really asking for?

We might recall the case of William in Chapter 4. William learns in therapy that his painfully upset feelings in reaction to his wife's poor health are related to the fright and anger he experienced as a child over his oft-hospitalized mother. His third order consciousness allows him to tie present experience to generalizable motives and biographical themes. He grasps the insight. He "learns more each week about why he is such a mess." But in order for these insights to have a transformational effect, in order for him to stop holding his wife responsible for causing the unpleasant feelings that show up inside him, his relation to these insights would have to change. He would need to relate to the insights generated in therapy not simply as sources for better understanding why, in the audience of his experiencing, he reacts as powerfully as he does to what he sees on stage. Rather, he would need to use these insights to better understand why, as the author of his own experiencing, he writes the play the way he does. Fourth order conscious-

Drawing by R. Chast; © 1990 The New Yorker Magazine, Inc.

ness would not guarantee that he would do this, but without fourth order consciousness he could not do it.

Surely contemporary adult psychotherapy hopes to be a place to heal the wounds and strengthen the hearts of those who are buffeted by the forces of modern life. It would be a cruel irony if we were to decide that sometimes psychotherapy is less a support in meeting the demands of modernity than itself another source of these demands. Its escape from such judgment may depend on the extent to which it can join its clients in the actual processes by which they form and transform their way of knowing.

Rita is a patient in therapy who has a difficult time confronting anyone at work.[13] She makes it very clear that other people's approval and their opinion of her determine how she feels about herself from day to day. When she considers making her views known, she worries about upsetting people, and she worries about this in a way that suggests that their reaction will automatically reconstitute her own sense of self-acceptability.

If Rita is currently constructing the world at the third order of consciousness, as seems likely, then any of the perfectly reasonable therapeutic approaches we have just explored, which unwittingly demand fourth order consciousness, would be over her head. These include attending to Rita's own creation of her painful feelings of apprehension about others' opinions of her; expecting her not merely to understand how her psychological history inclines or directs her but to free herself from its grip; expecting her, in Carl Rogers's words, to construct "her standards as being based upon her own experience, rather than upon the attitudes and desires of others, to perceive herself as the evaluator of experience, rather than regarding herself as existing in a world where the values are inherent in and attached to the objects of her perception"; expecting her, in Fritz Perls's words, to "transform her energies from manipulating the environment for support into developing greater and greater self-support"; expecting Rita, in Albert Ellis's terms, to stop sending herself hostile and hopeless messages that come from her "re-indoctrinating herself with the same philosophies of life, the same values, she imbibed and taught herself" when young.

All of these expectations are over her head. They essentially fail to make therapy a place where a bridge to fourth order consciousness might be collaboratively built. But if we can err, as therapists, by imag-

ining that such a bridge already exists, we can also err by never thinking
to build one. In these instances the potential mutability of an
individual's order of consciousness is ignored, and therapy ends up taking the form of helping that individual to cope or gain nontransforma-
tive insight. Rita, for example, says she has learned in therapy that she
is too influenced by others' potentially negative opinions, and she has
developed three strategies for alleviating the pressure of this kind of
concern: First, she is gradually developing "more confidence that people really do think well of me." Second, she is learning that "when people think ill of you they generally forget about it before long, so it's not
eternally damaging." And third, in regard to those who are not covered
by the first or second strategy, she is learning that some people's opinions should count and other people's opinions should not, and bad
opinions of her from people who don't count don't matter. Of course,
all these strategies are as third order as the original construction of who
decides one's ultimate worth, which necessitates the strategies in the
first place! We might notice, for example, how different it is to develop
greater self-assuredness by becoming more confident that others really
do think well of us than by becoming more confident in the validity of
our own definition of approvability and meeting it irrespective of
whether others think well of us. "Coping" amounts to directing one's
energies to live better in the world as one constructs it, rather than directing one's energies to reconstructing it.

Rita has also learned in therapy why it is so hard for her to get mad at
anyone or even to contemplate that she might ruffle other people's
feathers. From the time she was a small child and during all her growing
up years, she and her mother (there were just the two of them) had to
live with relatives. Here she got the very strong message that she was
never to misbehave, make noise, or upset anyone in the household because she and her mother, "who were very lucky to have any roof over
our heads," would be put out onto the streets. This constitutes an insight for her, a connection between past and present she had never
made before, and one that seems compelling to her. But her way of
telling it, at least at present, is one of "now I know why I got this way."
To the extent that she is still being written by her history (however
much more conscious of it she may be), rather than writing a new future, she is a better informed audience, not a transforming author.

We can imagine how the path of Rita's development might have transformed a social situation into a psychological one: she might have taken on, urgently and fearfully, the control of her impulses in a way that reflected how her mother controlled her. At a time when other youngsters her age were moving with increasing autonomy and independence into the world of childhood and exuberant self-expression, Rita might have been using the same capacities to control herself and others on behalf of concrete, self-preserving goals related to not being put out into the cold. And we can imagine this circumstance continuing on in a new form during adolescence, when her third order, cross-categorical capacities might lead her to be loyal to and protect her mother, now not just concretely and self-interestedly but psychologically—protecting her, for example, from the psychological annihilation of being unable to protect her own child, or identifying now not only with her mother's outer activities but with her inner beliefs. Whatever the actual particulars in Rita's case are (which therapist and client could together discover in therapy) the point is that the purpose of learning these particulars is not merely so that Rita can learn how it is she "came to be this way." What from some psychotherapeutic approaches is the Promised Land in the therapeutic journey—the place where connection is made between the events of the past and the quandaries of the present—might be better constituted as an important stop along the way. Since there may be more possibilities for Rita than to learn those coping strategies that essentially preserve, while making more bearable, the third order epistemology causing these coping strategies to be necessary in the first place, so there may be more for her than simply accumulating an increasingly insightful understanding of the historical sources of her present difficulty.

But what are the therapeutic possibilities for Rita besides approaches that, on the one hand, aim too high in being over her head, and, on the other, aim too low in amounting only to nontransforming insight or better coping?

If Rita is not at a time in her life when she is ready to transform the very distinction she makes between subject and object, and if she is not to be left feeling merely that she understands "how I got to be this way," then therapy can still offer her the opportunity to change the character of her third order construction into a more generous or less constricting one. The work of such change would need to go on in the context of Rita's third order way of organizing her knowing and not require her to abandon the sense of herself she derives from her loyalty to, and membership in, co-constructed relationships of shared values, beliefs, and ideals.

One possible way of accomplishing this change is by providing Rita with the opportunity to consider how the "character-shaping people" in her life (for example, her mother) may have been experiencing their own lives back at the time of the social events that were critical in Rita's later-formed psychology. Making use of her third order capacity for empathic identification to consider the mother she had back then, Rita may come to the idea that her mother might really have wanted to stand for values in support of Rita's independent initiative, self-assertion, and, when necessary, outspoken opposition. Rita might come to feel that in expressing these values she would not necessarily be abandoning her mother or violating the tenets of her implicit "faith." This change would allow Rita to preserve her identity "within the faith" while altering the toll her membership currently takes on her.

Another approach that would support Rita's reworking of the way she holds a third order capacity together without leaving the order itself is that of using the therapy itself as a new context for loyalty to, and membership in, co-constructed relationships of shared values and beliefs. In this case, the therapist provides a new voice and a new loyalty. Rita's internal orientation to it permits her a more expansive and generous way of treating herself. Rita would become no less "faithful," but the object of her faith would change.

But if, as is often the case, Rita is ready to begin transforming the very structure of the way she knows, a whole different set of possibilities exists for working with her. Especially when the transformation is the one most common in adulthood—the move from the third to the fourth order—such a development can help an individual handle not only the curriculum of modern life outside the therapist's office, but the hidden curriculum inside the office as well. Although the move to the fourth order does not by itself actually ameliorate the most visible and gripping circumstance joining therapist and client—the client's psychological pain—it creates in the client qualitatively new mental tools that can be put to use on behalf of therapy's mission to remove or reduce the client's psychological suffering.

To an extent that we may not sufficiently realize, the circumstances surrounding the need to move from the third order may cause a variety of long-standing psychological vulnerabilities that do not appear earlier to surface. Jamie's and Rita's cases provide examples. In Jamie's case, a long-running dysfunctional family alignment is losing its serviceability to her. Her role of providing herself as a child in order to vitalize the other roles people in the family need to play now leaves her increasingly devitalized in the face of current adult demands to establish an independent life. Although such an arrangement is dysfunctional the moment it begins, it does not necessarily show up as problematic while Jamie can still be thought of as an adolescent. But now that the newer claims and expectations of adulthood are joined to the long-standing family rules that she be enough of a child to need mothering, Jamie is stuck. Yet it is not just the conflicting set of family rules that has caused her to be stuck. Her third order captivity by those rules is a crucial contributor to her stuckness. The third order is not itself the pathology or dysfunction, but it throws the dysfunction into high relief.

Rita's case demonstrates another common version of how the constraints of the third order can cause long-standing vulnerabilities to surface in adulthood. Resourceful, well-functioning, resilient people like Rita often deal with the most painful features of their early life experience by using their increasing power to control their lives to shape a personal world that banishes those situations most likely to reevoke such painful feelings. Through this unconscious plan an unrecognized definition of a "successful" life emerges: a life that can be lived with fullness but need never again go near those painful feelings. The trouble here is that, when we are least expecting it, while pursuing the expansion of our present-day life without a thought to the past or our vow never to revisit its darkest side, we find that something we are moving toward in our love life or work life, perhaps, brings us perilously close to exactly the place we told ourselves we would never again visit. At this moment, if we do not turn toward that darkest region instead of away from it, we will block our forward motion on our life path. Once again, the third order is not itself the pain; and the transformation to the fourth order will not guarantee that the person will turn to and heal the pain. But the third order contributes to the block because the pain cannot be turned to, or turned on, until the self has become separate from its story, until the story has become object, until the self is no longer subject to the third order.

Thus, if it is inappropriate for therapists to assume the preexistence of the fourth order in their clients, it may be highly appropriate for them to value therapy as a context for collaboratively building the bridge to the fourth order. It is an appropriate goal even if they consider that the purpose of therapy is not to expand the mind or better equip their clients to handle the mental demands of modern life but to relieve them of their long-standing, life-historical psychological suffering. The lack of a fourth order capacity is not the source of such suffering, but it is often implicated in suffering's present intractable expression. The evolution of a fourth order capacity does not suffice to heal such suffering, but it can be an important ally in that healing.

Whatever means therapists employ to aid and encourage the evolution of our structures of consciousness, any successful approach will have to be both "cognitive" and "psychodynamic." That is, it must be aware of the actual contours of a client's way of knowing and match it closely. At the same time, it must honor the violations of faithfulness, loyalty, orthodoxy, and precious connection that a client inevitably experiences in changing her mind. As a therapist and a consultant to others' therapy work, I have found that a special use of metaphor can be productive in this endeavor.

The images, "frames," malleable maps, or metaphors that therapists of whatever theoretical inclination offer their clients have a number of salutary features, especially when they are introduced tentatively, with an ear to the client's own use of images and a readiness to abandon the offered metaphor if the client does not incorporate it into her own discourse. Metaphorical language offers the benefit of engaging the left and the right side of the brain simultaneously, combining the linear and the figurative, the descriptive and the participative, the concrete and the abstract. A metaphor is interpretive, but it is an interpretation made in soft clay rather than cold analysis. It invites the client to put his hands on it and reshape it into something more fitting to him. Especially when the therapist's metaphor addresses the internal circumstances of being a maker of meaning-structures, the client may find that, drawn to put his hands to reshaping it, he is engaged in reshaping the very way he knows.

The following examples are taken from actual therapeutic sessions:[14]

The client might be twenty or forty, man or woman, college junior or office manager. The "problem" is an inability to work, rarely because things have gotten too difficult, more commonly because "I just don't seem to be doing it." The client reports no precipitating event, no specific anxiety. The client is as bewildered as you are. He has lost his ability to focus, he says. Maybe she is just a lazy person, she suggests, who has finally let the truth come out. The client and therapist spend time together, declaring and witnessing to how costly this condition is becoming, how terrible it will be if it is not reversed, how powerless it feels not being able to get back into the swing. Eventually, after the therapist says something like, "You just can't get yourself to do the work . . .?" and the client agrees that this is so. "It's almost as if some part of you has gone on strike . . .?" the therapist suggests. The client again agrees, a little less glibly this time. Then the therapist says, "I wonder what the worker's demands might be . . ." For the first time, another side of the client begins to speak.

Another client, at a little different place in her development, is newly available to the variety of her own internal views and desires. She finds herself troubled to be drawn to such a multiplicity of possibilities, especially since many of them seem to be self-contradictory. She is not sure which she feels worse about: the presence of ideas and feelings she had not formerly considered could be a part of her, or her uncertainty about which of these ideas and feelings she should give her allegiance to. At some point in their consideration of her experience the therapist finds himself saying, "Perhaps we are all doomed to live our inner lives, ah, in committee?" Some weeks later, the client returns to the metaphor on her own and leads the therapist through an introduction of the various characters sitting around "my inner table," each insisting on "putting in its two cents—or five dollars." "We may be doomed to live our inner lives in committee," the client says, "but the real question is, 'Who's gonna be Chairman of the Board?'"

Still another client, again a little further along in his development, continues his discussion of how painful it is to continue to be in the grip of a lifetime family injunction never to let himself be overly enthusiastic about anything. Whenever he feels himself developing a passion or zest for anyone or anything, he is now able to identify the source of his inevitable tendency to undercut or deflate his own attraction. "Passion was for zealots and True Believers, my family taught me. Circumspection, bordering on cynicism, was what was respected in my family. You demonstrated you were intelligent enough and discerning enough to belong to my people by your capacity to bring a critical eye to any prospect for passion." The client had the insight into why his life was so much paler than he wanted it to be, but he continued (and was aware it was *he* who was doing it) to drain the color out of his living whenever it became inflamed. One day he talked with his therapist about the latest chapter in this story, a collaborative business venture that had been exciting him for several weeks and which he could see he was now unwarrantedly devaluing, and on the verge of dismissing. "Maybe that's your dog," the therapist said, unsure himself exactly what he meant, though the thought had probably suggested itself from the client's earlier casual reference to being "dogged" by these old family rules. "Suppose you have a dog," the therapist said, trying to answer his client's quizzical look. "A big-hearted, high-energy dog who begins to bark, and won't shut up, every time someone approaches your door. Now one day your dog starts into howling something fierce. He sounds a terrible alarm. You look out the window and it's just your friendly neighborhood mailman. So what do you do? You aren't going to shoot your dog dead. He's a pain but you wouldn't think of it. Your dog loves you. He barks to warn you when *anyone* approaches. He wants nothing bad to happen to you. That's just how he is. Problem is, he's completely indiscriminate. He thinks everyone's a danger, barks at anyone who approaches. That's just how he is, too. You wouldn't want to shoot such a loving dog, but you're also not going to start shooting out the front window every time your dog sends up his terrible alarm. *You're going to have a look for yourself.* In this case, you're going to see it's the mailman. You're going to bend over and stroke your dog. 'Down boy,' you say. 'It's just the postman. No harm here, silly guy,' you say, patting and stroking your big-hearted, high-energy, indiscriminately watchful watchdog."

We can consider the purpose these metaphors serve in the context of Martha Robbins's *Midlife Women and the Death of Mother*.[15] Robbins takes a simultaneously constructive-developmental and psychodynamic approach to the evolution of meaning, naming a series of phenomenological steps in the transformation from the third to the fourth order of consciousness. Each move involves a different relationship to inner conflict. In her particular study the conflict is between adult women and their psychological constructions of their mothers, but the conflicts to which she refers might be with anyone or anything, and underlying them all is the inner experience of a changing relationship to one's third order principle of knowing.

In Robbins's first position, the individual has no conscious awareness of inner conflict but something is clearly not right. He or she may feel diffusely depressed with no speakable object or origin, exhausted, devitalized, befuddled, scattered, in a haze. This seems a fair description of Jamie, elder daughter of the family that "cannot move." There is no conflict here at all from Jamie's point of view. She can feel irritated by her father's hectoring to "get a life," but no enduring inner or outer conflict figures in her presentation of herself. And this describes the clients suggested in the first vignette as well. They may deprecate themselves, call themselves lazy, but no one on the inside is fighting back. "There's no conflict here," they seem to say. They just "don't work," in the passive sense of that construction, like a clock that now inexplicably "doesn't work."

The therapist's metaphor (Kiyo Morimoto's) in the first vignette invites the client to consider a more active construction for "I don't work," something that is *happening by me* rather than something that has *happened to me*. But the therapist's words do not require the client to make as big a leap from passivity to activity as, say, *Moonstruck*'s amateur therapist, Loretta, who asks for a change all at once from a victimized amputee to a heroic, life-preserving wolf tearing his paw from the trap. This therapist is much closer to the earliest moves of a gradual transformation. He is just trying to get the very beginnings of an internal conflict to emerge. After listening, perhaps for weeks, to a misery that speaks only from the side of the self that cannot work, he is trying, without any wish to banish this side, to get an additional side to speak up in the office, the side of the self that will not work. He is inviting—if the client is ready—a psychological mitosis, a making of this monolithic self into two. "You just can't get yourself to do the work?" he asks innocently enough, an easy colloquial expression that welcomes two different "yous" into the room. "Like some part of you has gone on strike?" continues this invitation ("you are not just one actor here"), but we might notice how empathically close it stays to the prevailing, victimized, "done-to" side, resonating to its sense of powerlessness and futility at having had this shutting down thing happen to it. Perhaps this assurance that the "happened to" side is fully seen makes it possible to follow the metaphor's movement to the other side of the self, the "on strike" side that has its reasons for shutting down. When the picket signs can be read, the third order of consciousness has begun its move from subject to object.

This takes us to Robbins's next position, where, in loosening our identification with our former loyalties we at once seek to preserve this distance and are frightened by it. Our conflict is noticeable to us now and useful in preserving an emerging differentiation. But since we are still more identified with our third order construction than the emerging fourth order construction, we also experience the conflict from the point of view of the third order. We see ourselves abandoning our psychological duty or sacred oath. We may feel guilty about those who may not be safe or able to survive without us. We may be fearful for them, or for ourselves now bereft of the protections afforded by our faith. Most of all, we may feel a basic sense of wrongness or disorientation at having become so "plural," entertaining, albeit fearfully or guiltily, so many new possibilities.

William Perry's metaphor of the "internal committee" in the second vignette seems to speak to and support this effort to preserve the differentiation of the self from its loyalties where before no such distinction existed. The image of the internal committee makes an acceptable place for all these voices at the table and establishes a way of acknowledging that our inner experience has become more complex without becoming a hopeless cacophony. Each voice can have its seat and its say. The characters who speak in these voices can be evaluated in turn. There may be many voices but one table. Finally, the metaphor does more than support the new differentiation. Its dramaturgy invites the self's shift to a greater identification with the fourth order side: a structure that will coordinate or regulate the voices and shape them into a single team, that will exercise authority over the table. "The real question," the client begins to think, "is, 'Who will be Chairman of the Board?'" This metaphor not only makes more room for the transformation under way, but by drawing the client's hands to its wet clay it invites reshaping—of the metaphor and one's own relationship to the interior third order voices.

The metaphor does not by itself effect transformation. The idea is not that all is suddenly different because the therapist has pronounced some magic words. Metaphor is not the silver bullet of therapy. What these vignettes are about are subtle moments in therapy in which a new kind of conversational field opens up. When such metaphors are helpful, they may enable the client to talk about his experience in a new way. Raising the question "Who's in charge here, anyway?" may *begin* something by redirecting the flow of self-exploration, but not in itself accomplish it.

A further move in this evolution of consciousness, according to Robbins's study, is the self's gradually greater identification with the emerging fourth order structure. Now the conflict, no longer seen so much through third order knowing, is less likely to evoke guilt or fear and more likely to evoke anger. We repudiate the old loyalties. They are more emphatically *not me*. But in railing against them we have not yet found a new place for them. They still exercise power, however un-welcome. The fourth order has not yet established a new equilibrium of consciousness. We are still in a place of conflict and disequilibrium.

The fellow inveighing against the family rule of circumspection in the third vignette is angry about its costs to his passion. The rule is no longer his rule, and he expresses a disdain for it, but he is still stuck with it. Unlike the person in the second vignette, he has decided that it is he who will be chairman of the board, but, having decided so, it is not that easy to get everyone around the inner table to agree. Those who have power do not easily give it up. The conflict now is colored not by guilt or fear but by angry battling over authority.

The therapist's metaphor (this one from my own work) would proba-bly not have been helpful without many weeks of supportive attention to the client's tally of the costs of his family rule, his angry case against his former loyalty, and his frustration with its hold upon him even still. Once all this was seen and reseen in their shared space, he was perhaps ready to see something *more* (not something *else*). The metaphor of the barking dog, which became an ongoing reference in the therapeutic dis-course, stays with the feeling of being plagued and interrupted by a powerful and alarming inner voice warning one away from life's callers, from that which calls one. But the dramaturgy of loyal, loving dog and discerning master invites just that reconstitution of the roles for which the client may be ready in his epistemological evolution.

A number of therapeutic suggestions are embedded in the metaphor: "The parental voice of warning or criticism, with which you are in such battle, may not be all bad." "That voice itself may intend your good, however annoying it may be." "Not only may it be impossible to re-move it completely from your inner psychology, but you may actually not want to." "That voice may be your family's way of telling you how dear you are to them, how much you are loved. If you eliminate the voice entirely you might lose the annoying text, but you'd also lose the loving subtext." "But you may know all this deep down, and that in fact is why you are in such a protracted conflict: You don't want to follow the dictates of the voice, but you also don't want to turn your back on it. You can't live with it and you can't live without it." The metaphor of-fers a way out of this conflict, a way to turn toward the voice, not away from it, a way to turn toward the voice without capitulating to it. The metaphor makes no party in the conflict into the bad guy. The critical, demanding voice is nonetheless a loving, companionable voice that means well. The prospective controller, evaluator, and often, even dis-counter of the voice is nonetheless a loving and appreciative master. The metaphor stays close to the structural agenda—the claiming of fourth order authority—but "consults," as it were, that emerging capac-ity, reminding it that there is still a place for its third order affections, that it must include its past in order to assume a future that is neither brittle nor hollow.

The early voyagers, from their perspective, risked their very lives when they sailed near to what they regarded as the edge of the universe. Nei-ther the world as they knew it *nor their very way of knowing it* would be the same after the voyage as before it. Likewise, a change in our order of consciousness is not just a change in the figures of our attention, it is a change in the very ground from which we attend. The extraordinary voyage that sets out to discover a new part of the world ends up being a voyage to a new way of understanding what the world is. The therapist's effort to provide good company for a client's travels in therapy needs a way—when those travels include the travels of consciousness—to un-derstand the inner experience of a voyage that can seem to put at risk one's very life.

The themes of dangerous voyage or travel, of course, suggest them-selves as broadly operative metaphors for the inner experience of the evolution of consciousness. Especially when travel is elaborated into the metaphor of emigration, it captures qualities of leaving home, leaving precious affections behind, even abandonment or disloyalty. But the metaphor I have found most helpful in my own efforts to be a good companion in therapy, and the one to which I have already made im-plicit reference throughout this chapter, is that of *family religion*.[16]

The transformation from the third to the fourth order of conscious-ness is akin to leaving the family's faith. I have found this to be a close approximation to the burdens such change may place on our abiding loyalties and precious connections. Thinking about it this way not only keeps one attending to the other's inner experience, but—where the client herself finds the analogy fitting—it can be an endless source of fresh metaphors. By *faith* or *religion*, I do not, of course, mean the po-lite, contained, once-a-week affair that is a largely undetectable feature in the public life of a modern person in a pluralistic world. I mean the kind of orthodox, traditional faith that is as public as private, a constant minute-to-minute foundation and guide to the purpose of life and the means of realizing that purpose. Who, you might say, grows up with such an orthodox faith these days, aside from rare exceptions like the Amish of Pennsylvania or the Hasidim of Brooklyn, whose way of living is seen as so special and remarkable it has taken on a museum quality? My answer is that *every one of us grows up with such an orthodox faith*, and that, in fact, the third order of consciousness amounts to that time in our lives when we move from being "brought up in the faith" to becoming ourselves spiritual adherents *to* that faith. A man and woman of modernist mind do not mate and give birth to a modernist baby. The ordeal of modernity is that each person—and not until adulthood—must suffer the loss of the traditionalist mind. It is the traditionalist mind that is faithful to the family religion.

The religion to which I refer is not the denominational affiliation of the parents that is passed down to their children by attendance at a particular house of worship and nourished in the ritual and custom of a publicly identifiable institutionalized faith. Some families have such religions and some do not. The religion to which I refer is one that every family has, one that operates powerfully and mysteriously in every family, is passed down to children by their attendance at the house they grow up in, and is nourished in the private rituals and customs that enact and enforce the family's deepest idiosyncratic beliefs of what life is really about.

The arrival of a child transforms a one-generational couple and marriage into a two-generational family, a pair into a group, a relational plane into a three-dimensional space. This transformation is animated by the parents' posture toward life's powers, toward its dangers and its possibilities. This is the spirit that fills the three-dimensional world the child is born into and (especially a first child) brings into being. Every family is a naturally and unselfconsciously religious place because every family is a place where day after day, year after year, a coherent and often undeviating disposition toward ultimate reality is being expressed. The beliefs, rules, values, ideals, prejudices, passions, promises, betrayals, terrors, demons, and angels that every family passes before and onto its children declare, finally, where we who belong to this family stand in relation to the awesome powers of the universe. How generous or unforgiving, gentle or terrible, just or capricious is the Life Force? What is required of us to be in good faith with our Maker? How dangerous or how exhilarating is it to be alive?

The "introjects" or "scripts" of early life in the family do far more than influence our "self-esteem" or "object relations." They do far more than lay down repeating patterns of interaction that can be studied by social science. They do far more than shape the expression of desires driven only by our bodies or biology. These myriad reflections of an underlying creed or holy order induct us into a community of faith. They enroll us in a group or collective to which we feel bound (the very word *religion* is about such "binding"). They enroll us in a group or collective that lets us know how we matter and insists to us that the primary business of this group is our attention to the gods, the Biggest Powers with whom we contend, the Terms of our mattering by which we are kept from perishing. The family religion is emphatically not the neat, civilized, weekend activity of well-dressed, well-behaved Judeo-Christians. It is more like the messy-faced, heart-thumping, life-defining natural folk religion of idol and offering, demon and desire, sacrifice and salvation.

When we view our psychological history or inheritance as an induction into a family religion, it reminds us that much of what we get from our families, as vulnerable, innocent, choiceless inductees into the faith, is nonetheless life-giving, spiritually nourishing, and necessary for a sense of the significance of being alive. The idea of family religion is thus in part a saving influence that counters the tendency of many psychological perspectives to demean, belittle, undervalue, indict, or pathologize every aspect of our inheritance. It bids us to take a respectful and appreciative inventory of the life-sustaining, significance-bearing elements of our upbringing, however much other aspects of our early experience may also have been present.

But the idea of the family religion is not a romantic, rose-colored one. It makes equal room for our consideration of the potentially unwholesome dimensions of our psychological inheritance. Religions can deepen and nourish our connections to life. But we all know they can also distort and narrow our connection to life. (In fact, readers who find themselves at this moment leery or disdainful of this unwelcome appearance of the language of religion may be among those whose primary or only association with religion is negative for the very good reason that they found their personal experience with institutionalized religion to be distortive and injurious to their connection to themselves and to others.) Religion can induce guilt, fear, dependency, hatred toward those who do not know our god, and hatred toward ourselves when we violate our faith. So the concept of the family religion provides us a context in which we can be open to both the life-giving and life-stealing dimensions of our personal histories.

Viewing our personal histories in light of a "family religion" also requires us to attend both to the inevitably hierarchical nature of psychological history and to the ultimate nature of the context in which this hierarchy is played out. Religions have gods and priests at the top and servant suppliants at the bottom. We are always the little one in the psychological drama we inherit. And parents are not just bigger physically, they are bigger spiritually: life comes from them and can be taken by them. The prospect of losing a parent's care casts a chill shadow that beckons us toward the void. Every child of a disappointing, pain-delivering, or abusive parent has to choose between this god or no god, and every child makes the same choice. Every child thus learns how to love its parent, however costly such learning might be, because its life depends on learning how to give love to, and receive love from, this life source, an ultimate matter, a matter of life and death, precisely the relation of a primal suppliant to his or her god.

The idea of a family religion holds onto the key psychoanalytic recognition that the essence of our family drama from early childhood is a story about love, but it offers a new context in which to consider what this loving might be about. In contrast to both the classic and modern psychoanalytic languages of *drive satisfaction, romantic rivalry,* or *relational potential,* a more three-dimensional context, a more spiritually ultimate context for loving is evoked in the language of *devotion, surrender, atonement, cosmic protection.* The child's love is about something more than biological drives or romantic hope. It may be about the spirit's hunger to be whole, feel ontologically safe, entrust itself completely to the powers of the universe, be connected to the significance-bearing dimensions of life. The child's love may not only be about forestalling bio-energetic frustration or even psychological aloneness, but about forestalling spiritual exile or the death of the soul. Loving of this sort creates bonds not fully described as *libidinal* or *relational;* rather they are devotional bonds from which it would be difficult or impossible to separate without having to contend with the ontological guilt of disappointing our Maker, or the ontological dread of standing alone in the universe without the protection of the Light.

It may not be enough to subject the terms of our faithfulness to the puny light of rational analysis (à la Albert Ellis), or even the soft clay of metaphors, which suggest that we can so easily replace the chair of our inner committees or keep our barking dog in check. There may be very good reasons, reasons connected to extraordinary powers, why Jamie cannot take a job outside the family store, or Rita get angry. Such moves might feel not just wrong but heretical—tempting fate, disturbing the universe.

But as soon as they are seen as such, something different may have already happened. What might become of our sense of ourselves were we to consider deeply that our lifelong tendencies to diminish ourselves or constrict our experience may be a function not of our limits and incapacity but our astonishingly competent exercise of faithfulness and devotion to the terms of our family religion as we learned them in the house of worship where we grew up? Such a reconstruction creates the possibility of reunion with one's own power and of redirecting such competent faithfulness to worthier objects. And what might become of us were we newly to regard the inevitable parts of ourselves that have run *counter* to the family religion, that we have had to disown to continue in the fold or hold onto at the price of feeling a secret sinner? With the proper supports, these abandoned parts of ourselves, brought into view, might move, in the fashion Robbins suggests, from being painful evidence of our sinful unworthiness to frightening agents of our spiritual undoing to the very vehicles by which we transform the terms of our loyalty and acceptability.

The idea that leaving the third order of consciousness is akin to leaving the family religion does not mean that the move to modernity of necessity requires us to leave the family or the religion. What it requires is that we construct a new relationship to the family or the religion. Like all such metaphors sent in to aid the remaking of mind, the new spaces it can create are not necessarily separations between people but distinctions within a person, differentiations within a relationship or a faith. The prospect of leaving the family religion can foster a host of such distinctions: the distinction between "having a religion" and "being had by one's religion"; between "believing as my parents believed" and "believing as I believe"; between "believing as my parents believed *because it is how my parents believed*" and "believing some of what my parents believed because I have come to find it is also what I believe"; between "finding *my own way* of practicing what is still a form of the family religion" and "leaving the faith altogether"; between "leaving behind some of what my parents believed" and "leaving behind my precious sense of connection to them." The creation of such distinctions builds a trembling bridge from the third to the fourth order of consciousness.

8

Learning: "The Teacher Wants Us to Be Self-Directing"

In *The Evolving Self* I told the story of a mother getting breakfast ready for her son on a school day. Hearing nothing indicating that he was up and getting dressed, she went to his room, only to find him in bed. "Are you okay?" she asked. "I'm okay," he replied, "but I'm not going to school today!" Being a modern mother, she decided to engage him in conversation. "Well, then," she demanded, "you give me three good reasons why you aren't going to school." "Okay," said her son. "I don't like school. The teachers don't like me. And I'm afraid of the kids." "Okay," said his mother, "now I'm going to give you three good reasons why you *are* going to school. Number one, I'm your mother and I say school is important. Number two, you're forty-five years old. And number three, you're the principal of the school!"

It may be hard to leave home at any age, but the truth is that, in spite of the difficulty, there are a lot more adults going off to school than just those who are employed there. Though we may associate school and classroom learning with children and adolescents, adults in America now go to school in extraordinary numbers. According to the College Board's Office of Adult Learning Services, those twenty-five and older constitute the largest and most rapidly growing education sector in the nation. By the fast-approaching turn of the century, over half of all available jobs will require a college education and over half of those studying for undergraduate degrees will be twenty-five or older.[1] The great majority of students attending our country's community colleges—one of the last great democratizing institutions in America—are

271

adults, and the majority of graduate students are over twenty-five. To stretch one's mind, to better adjust to new demands in one's private life, to advance in one's job or career, to change jobs or reenter the workforce after one's children are grown or one's marriage has ended, adults go to school. And when they do, many find that, like the reluctant school principal, they are asked to "leave home." They are asked to leave the mental homes they have furnished and made familiar. Whether those who design their schools and teach in their classrooms fully understand it or not, what they are asking these adult students to do is to go out of their minds.

Increasingly, adults fill seats in higher education classrooms that were traditionally occupied by the eighteen- to twenty-two-year-old "late adolescent." Those who lead these institutions may be enthusiastic about replacing a shrinking customer pool (late adolescents) with a growing one (adults), but their enthusiasm may be outstripped by their lack of preparation for the different life circumstances of older students. Late adolescents, for example, often enter higher education as part of a process by which they gain greater distance from the families that made them. Adults, in contrast, often enter higher education surrounded by the families they themselves have made. The powerful subtext of why they are there, where they are going, and where they are coming from is different. Their teachers, too, facing a student who is in many respects different from the one they are used to teaching or had thought to teach when they prepared for a career in higher education, often find themselves with mixed feelings. For every teacher who warms to a description of the classroom benefits of the "greater life experience" adult students bring, there is another who speaks with frustration about the way the lessons adult students feel they have already learned make learning new lessons difficult. For every teacher who values the "motivation" of adult students whose learning goals are tied to real-life concerns, it is not hard to find another who bemoans their overweening "practicality" and lack of patience for reflective attention to the bigger philosophical questions.

The truth, however, is that we may not yet be ready for all these adult students, but this should not be surprising or embarrassing. Their dominance is, after all, a very new thing on the education scene. In the early 1980s, when I became the education chair of Harvard's Institute for the Management of Lifelong Education, a program serving leaders in adult education throughout North America, educators serving the "older returning student" occupied marginal roles on their campuses. Their constituents were guests at someone else's party. Just ten years later their constituents, increasingly, are why there is a party at all. And the "adult educators" who ten years ago might have had titles such as "Assistant Dean for Nontraditional Students" and reported to vice presidents they could only hope would get the right message across to their presidents might now be deans or vice presidents themselves reporting directly to their presidents. It is one thing to let new people into an ongoing party; the newcomer is the one who must struggle to fit in. It is another thing to *change the party;* now it is the educator and the institution that must struggle to fit in. What exactly is the philosophical mission of adult education? We might consider the goals that anchor our education of the young: The fundamental growth of the mind, transformational learning, qualitative changes in *how* the student knows, not just *what* the student knows. But do we understand what these goals would really mean when applied to adults? Do these goals even make sense for adults who are, after all, "grown up?," who come to school to better meet the practical demands and responsibilities of real adult life but do not necessarily have the luxury of "finding themselves," "learning for learning's sake," or pondering great abstract questions divorced from real-life concerns?

In some quarters adult education as a field of practice is paralyzed by what it perceives as a choice it does not want to make: Shall it support its traditional noble mission—the liberation of the mind and the growth of the student—at the risk of losing a large portion of its adult clientele, who will feel that what it has to offer is irrelevant to and neglectful of their practical adult needs? Or shall it respond to what it perceives as its adult clients' demands for practical training, expedient credentialing, increased skills, and a greater fund of knowledge at the risk of demoralizing or losing its best teachers, who are dismayed to find their professional and career identities being refashioned according to those of vocational education?

While higher education administrators may worry about its relevance or attractiveness to practical-minded adults, some sense of a central intellectual mission for adult education, personified by the image of "the self-directed learner," is beginning to crystallize in the literature of the field. Surely anyone who reviews the literature on adult education with an eye to discovering what is being demanded of students will be struck by this particular convergence of curricular aspirations.[2]

From my point of view, these aspirations constitute yet another intriguing series of demands upon the minds of adults. Gerald Grow summarizes these well. Self-directed learners, he says, are able to

> examine themselves, their culture, and their milieu in order to understand how to separate what they feel from what they should feel, what they value from what they should value, and what they want from what they should want. They develop critical thinking, individual initiative, and a sense of themselves as co-creators of the culture that shapes them . . . Self-directed learners set their own goals and standards, with or without help from experts. They use experts, institutions, and other resources to pursue these goals . . . [They] are both able and willing to take responsibility for their learning, direction, and productivity. They exercise skills in time management, project management, goal-setting, self-evaluation, peer critique, information-gathering, and use of educational resources.[3]

The literature also reflects a goodly amount of frustration, disappointment, surprise, and even, at times, disdain toward the large numbers of adult students who have difficulty achieving or who do not achieve these goals.

When we view these demands on the adult learner in the context of our consideration of the fuller set of mental burdens in modern life, an interesting relationship emerges between the goals for adult education and the crisis it faces. After all, what *is* this demand for "self-directed learning"? Does it consist in a set of trainable skills or does it, yet again, reflect something more like a qualitative order of mental complexity that would in turn permit such skills? The goal of "self-directed learning" may represent a far greater convergence than that composed by several scholars in the single field of adult education. It may reflect a culturewide convergence, a culturewide curriculum calling across every frequented arena of adult life for the fourth order of mental complexity. If the goal of "self-direction" is reconceived as the goal of fostering the order of consciousness that *enables* self-direction, then adult educators may not only gain a greater measure of patience and greater sense of possibility in their work, they may also find a way around the forced choice between a "practical" and a "mind-liberating" curriculum for those adults who want to cope better with the demands of real life. After all, our analysis of the private and public burdens we face at home and at work suggests that they may not best be seen solely in terms of a need for particular skills or techniques, or the mastery of new information.

Adults who enter learning settings with an understandable need to meet practical, real-life demands for greater success in their work or family lives may actually need, for that very success, just that transformation of mind their instructors, as liberal educators, are dedicated to encouraging. If adult educators would seek not so much to train for self-directed learning but to *educate* for the order of mental complexity that enables it, this might well constitute the most effective way to address the very "practical" aspirations of adult learners.

When the adult education experts tell us they want students to "understand how to separate what they feel from what they should feel, what they value from what they should value, and what they want from what they should want," they may not be taking seriously enough the possibility that when the third order dominates our meaning-making, what we *should* feel is what we *do* feel, what we *should* value is what we *do* value, and what we *should* want is what we *do* want. Their goal therefore may not be a matter of getting students merely to identify and value a distinction between two parts that already exist, but a matter of fostering a qualitative evolution of mind that actually creates the distinction. Their goal may involve something more than the cognitive act of "distinction," a bloodless word that fails to capture the human wrenching of the self from its cultural surround. Although this goal is perfectly suited to assisting adults in meeting the bigger culturewide "curriculum" of the modern world, educators may need a better understanding of how ambitious their aspiration is and how costly the project may seem to their students.

Educators seeking "self-direction" from their adult students are not merely asking them to take on new skills, modify their learning style, or increase their self-confidence. They are asking many of them to change the whole way they understand themselves, their world, and the relation between the two. They are asking many of them to put at risk the loyalties and devotions that have made up the very foundation of their lives. We acquire "personal authority," after all, only by relativizing—that is, only by fundamentally altering—our relationship to public authority. This is a long, often painful voyage, and one that, for much of the time, may feel more like mutiny than a merely exhilarating (and less self-conflicted) expedition to discover new lands.

Where one's "natural religion" has a publicly recognizable "congregation" (social class, institutionalized religion, or ethnicity, for example), we may be tempted to depict the peril of adult-education-as-heresy as a problem "those people" face. Adult educators in Boston have asked me how they can be more helpful to groups they find have the greatest difficulty—say, the working-class Irish from South Boston who, they can see, feel as if they are being forced to choose between their loyalty to the people in their neighborhood and success in a professional, middle-class world that leaves them alienated from that neighborhood, "even if I choose to keep living there." The question is an important and poignant one, but is it really a question about social class?

I have heard the same question, the same concern, the same misgivings about what one is up to, from educators in Salt Lake City and Anchorage, who notice that Mormon students or Alaskan natives feel they are in danger of becoming strangers to the church or tribe that has nourished and sustained them. In one locale it may seem that it is social class that makes one especially vulnerable to the effects of adult education; in another it may be religious preference; in another, ethnic identification.

But these are really local instances of a single thing, and in many respects its name is legion, intimately if unawarely shared by the white, single mother in Sauk Centre, Minnesota, who may have learned to please others and follow their lead, or the civil engineer in Great Falls, Montana, whose alcoholic family taught him not to rock the boat. These two people belong to no identifiable minority and would say they have little in common with a working-class Irishman from South Boston whose people have lived in the same neighborhood for three generations, or an Alaskan native from the bush who hunts for subsistence and, even in his thirties, understands that he should be silent and listen when his elders speak. "You don't have to be Jewish to be guilt-inducing," an aunt of mine once said, "but it does help." You don't have to belong to a "great public religion" like religious fundamentalism, the ethnic working class, or a chief-led tribe to suffer the burdens of adult education. In some cases it may help. But ultimately, these burdens are not the private possession of social class, religious preference, or ethnic identification, nor does such membership guarantee that one will be particularly burdened. It may be important for us to know that we are all in this together. We all have some kind of natural religion. We all experience modernity's demand that we change our relationship to this religion. The tighter the hold of the natural religion, the more difficult it will be. The greater the unwillingness or the inability of the natural religion to reinclude and recognize our new relations to our precious family the more difficult it will be. But class and church and tribe do not have a monopoly on the circumstances that can make the growth of the mind difficult. The woman in Sauk Centre or the man in Great Falls may suffer no less acutely for doing so in relation to a unique and private family religion rather than to the great public "religions" of class, church, or ethnicity. The labor is shared among us and across all the diversity that so commonly divides us. Its origin cannot be found in social class or religious denomination or ethnicity. Its origin is in the demand upon consciousness to enter (for better or for worse) the modern world.

We can see the kind of work involved for adults in meeting the mental demand to be a "self-directed learner" if we look at such seemingly elementary activities as reading and writing at school. There, the demand to understand the difference between what we value and what we should value, to "set [our] own goals and standards," to have "a sense of [ourselves] as co-creators of the culture that shapes [us]" quite readily appears as requiring nothing less than the reconstitution of the self.

The developmental theorist and educator William Perry created a course at Harvard to help students—initially adult students—with the burden of reading the volume of material assigned in a higher education curriculum.[4] So beleaguered were they by their discovery that higher education meant falling behind in the reading at the beginning of a semester and never catching up, and certain that their inability to keep up reflected unfavorably on their intelligence, the students staggered into Perry's course hoping, as he said, to learn to hold the printed page up to the light and read both sides simultaneously. The experience of the course, which I was privileged to teach under Perry's supervision, reveals how fundamental and how frightening is the demand for "self-directed learning," as well as some clues about how to help people meet the demand by fostering the complexity of mind that would enable it.

The class began each day with the room going dark and a screen descending. A printed page was projected on the screen, the words on the page nearly all in shadow except for an illuminated fragment of a printed line. In tachistoscopic fashion the light moved across the page, setting the pace at which the students would read, effectively taking their eyeballs "by the hand." This was followed by a test of comprehension. The students were informed that each class would begin this way, the speed of the tachistoscope and the width of the illumination increasing each day, and the students trying to keep their comprehension at a high level.

Although, as Perry knew, such an eyeball-training exercise can in fact permit only the most modest increases in reading rate, the opening exercise has the virtue of making sense to the conscientious student who believes that his lack of skill—it certainly cannot be his effort or interest in meeting the expectations of his teachers—accounts for his difficulty. He engages the exercise in hopes of training his eyeballs to move so rapidly they are practically steaming in their sockets, and he hopes that if he can read a given assignment more quickly he will be less likely to succumb to his greatest failing: the ubiquitously cited "lack of concentration." (We are all familiar with this "lack of concentration." It is the thing that leads us to awaken to a little pool of saliva on the printed page, in spite of our sincerest intent to "sit down and not get up until I've done the reading.")

In fact, Perry's opening exercise is an intuitive demonstration of Kierkegaard's good instructional advice almost a hundred and fifty years ago. "If real success is to attend the effort to bring a person to a definite position," Kierkegaard wrote in his *Journals*, "one must first of all take pains to find him where he is and begin there. This is the secret of helping others . . . In order to help another effectively I must understand what he understands. If I do not know that, my greater understanding will be of no help to him . . . Instruction begins when you put yourself in his place so that you may understand what he understands and in the way he understands it."[5]

It is not enough for us to know what our students understand, Kierkegaard reminds us, like a good constructive-developmentalist. We must also know "the way he understands it." Subject-object psychology was created expressly to respond to Kierkegaard's conviction. If our students' meaning-making is under the influence of the third order, there would be little benefit in sermonizing about the need for self-direction or in making our students in some way "wrong" for caring as much as they do. Perry understood that if developmental education is a matter of collaboratively building a "consciousness bridge," then the bridge builder must have an equal respect for both ends, creating a firm foundation on both sides of the chasm students will traverse. Firmly anchoring the bridge on one end by welcoming rather than disdaining "the way they understand," as Kierkegaard put it, Perry then invited his students to join him in constructing what they would only gradually come to see was a bridge they could choose to walk out on.

Perry next distributed a brief text and told his students not to bother reading it. He wanted them to do something else instead. Since "reading" to most of his students meant reading the first word first and the next word next, as God intended, he knew that most of the things he would ask his students to do would bear little resemblance to "reading." What he did instead was to pose a question to his students—"Why did Balboa set out on his expedition," for example—suggesting that they might find the answer or answers somewhere in the text and challenging them to skim through the text as quickly as they could until they'd found it, like an embedded figures exercise. It would be a kind of race against themselves, Perry suggested, with him jotting the time elapsed on the blackboard and them trying to better their speed with successive texts each day. The students were game if unsure about what the exercise had to do with better "reading."

Later, Perry distributed a brief text and again asked the students not to bother "reading" the material. This time they were to skim briefly until they had some idea what the text might be about. Perry suggested that they might do this best by skimming the end material first, since this is where many writers finally come to the point or sum up the essence of what they have to say. Having in brief order determined what the text might be about, the students were then to generate a question themselves to take to the text in the same way they had used Perry's question in the earlier exercise. That is, they were not supposed to actually "read" the material, just ferret through it gathering material on behalf of their question.

We can see where this is heading. Like our constructive-developmental therapists of the last chapter, Perry is working not so much on the particular issue at hand—better reading—but on how the students' own dissatisfaction with the results of their reading can be a vehicle for the transformation of "the way they understand," as Kierkegaard put it, a transformation that may affect the way they understand everything, including even what "better reading" amounts to. Starting out with an exercise to train his students' eyes, Perry anchored the bridge at the other end by inviting students to consider the questioning mind that directs the eyes. The much bemoaned "lack of concentration" is revealed for what it is: the impossibility of passively receiving material for any length of time with no place to put it. The mind does not mysteriously wander when we are reading for a specific purpose we continue to care about. On the other hand, if we have no purpose and notice our mind wandering, what exactly do we call the mind back to?

Perry's bridge is completed on the fateful day he invites his students to bring in the actual reading they are being assigned in their "real" (that is, graded) courses, and to start "reading" this material in the active, questioning way they have learned. Their work together has completed the bridge. It is now clear that the course does not aim to improve their reading as they had defined it but to suggest a whole different idea of what reading is. And just because the bridge has been made, it does not mean that anyone actually wants to walk on it! Some students get angry at this point in the course and see it as a kind of fraud, which failed to deliver on what it promised. Others, forced to admit that the course does deliver—at least for those who do cross the bridge and now find themselves able to handle four and five times as much reading in the same space of time as before—are morally offended. "Maybe this is a way to read faster," they say, "but it's actually a trick, like cheating. I'm not going to cheat. Maybe I won't do as well in my courses as those who use it, but at least I'll know I came by my grade honestly."

But what most of the students feel at this point is fear, the understandable terror at having to leave a familiar home. "Directing the purpose of my reading does totally change the way I read, what I retain, what I can do with what I read. But tell me this: How do I know that my questions will be my professor's questions? How do I know that my purposes will be her purposes?" Having built the bridge, the students understandably ask, "How do I know it will hold up? How do I know I won't go plummeting to my death at the bottom of this deep chasm?" Invited to place their own questions behind the wheel of their learning, the students make their first tentative moves onto the bridge by reconsidering, Perry says, what the challenge to "read better" actually consists of. They had thought that good reading was a challenge to their intelligence. Rather than change things by helping them to be "more intelligent" (whatever that means), Perry's course changes things by changing the challenge. "They come to see 'better reading' is *not* a challenge to their intelligence," Perry says, "but a challenge to their courage." It *will* be scary—there is no question about it—to trust their own questions in this way. And Perry will be there, when they are ready to make the leap of faith onto the bridge, to accompany them in their fear and courage. It is a harrowing walk, especially the first time. But it is a walk away from more than dutiful reading. It is a walk away from being subject to someone else's questions, a walk away from the third order as the very principle by which they make sense of the world.

And what of those, it might be asked, who are not ready yet to take even the first step onto the bridge? The goal here might be only that the person be able to stand poised before the bridge rather than run from it. The goal here might be that the person be helped to find a way to at least stay in the learning environment and not feel that the very place is unholy and heretical. This goal can only be accomplished if students come to feel that they are not required to leave their old loyalties at the door of the school but can bring them in and have them respected. Laurent Daloz, another constructive-developmental educator who writes about mentoring the adult learner, offers a graceful demonstration of this good hospitality in a different kind of story about a student and her reading:

> I am sitting in my office with some loose time on my hands since one of my students can't make her appointment. Comes a knock on the door, and in walks Martha, a sixtyish, handsome woman, dressed for the late 19th century. Something about the expression on her face says that *she* would never do anything wrong. Although her reputation as a firm believer in Biblical Christianity precedes her, I have never met her, and I must say, I am curious.
>
> She tells me she is about to finish her Associate's Degree, and wants to go on for a degree in Education. She has to have the qualifications to help her get a job in the local Bible school. "There's a teacher there who plays favorites, and I don't think that's good," she told me. "I want to learn how not to play favorites."
>
> I explain to her that she won't have to be certified to teach in a private school, and go on to tell her what she will need to do. She seems satisfied. But then, as I think she is leaving, she reaches down into her purse and takes out a book. "There's one other thing I want to ask you about," she says, suddenly stern. The book in her hand is a standard health text. She opens it at a marker and slides the book across the desk toward me, her finger on a paragraph. "Just read that. Don't say anything. You don't have to say anything."
>
> It turns out to be some pretty explicit material about sexual behavior. I say nothing, and she then points to a picture on another page of two men holding hands. Beneath it is a discussion of homosexuality.

She is shocked by it, she tells me. It is pure pornography. The whole book is a scandal. Useless. She tells me, scolding, that when she saw that she wanted to drop out of the course immediately. And then she begins to cry. Right there in my office! And I have never even met her before!

I wait for the tears to slow down and then ask her if she has spoken to her teacher or to the community college staff about it. She replies that they just don't understand. It wouldn't do any good, she goes on. Then, at a forty-five degree angle, she asks, "Will your school be like this? Will I have to read this sort of trash in your program?"

I assure her that she won't need to if she doesn't want, and that I can understand how deeply disturbing it is to her. I make a special effort to sympathize with her feelings about it and tell her again that she will not be forced to read what she feels is "trash."

We talk on for some time about it and she vents about how disturbed she is. Finally, I say, "I do want to answer your question a little better about whether our school would be like this." And I say, "Our school will be the way you need it to be, Mrs. Findlay. But I have faith that as you get more schooling, you'll be less easily shocked by this sort of thing. I hope that you'll be more able to take it in stride. You don't have to believe it's right, but I would hope that you can gain more distance from it so that it won't cause you so much turmoil."

She sits there and nods. She seems to be listening, though I feel a little as if I am giving her a lecture. As it happens, I spent part of the morning working with a student who was writing a paper comparing Frost's "The Hired Man" with the parable of "The Prodigal Son." So I am providentially able to quote chapter and verse from *The Bible*.

"Remember," I say to her, "that one of the remarkable things about Jesus is that he was able to go and speak to the publicans and the Pharisees right where they lived. He wasn't afraid to descend among them and witness to them; he went and spoke to the sinners and the wicked and the despised in the world. And he was able to love them, no matter how wicked."

She is definitely listening now. I feel a little hypocritical about this, but it's true. Jesus was amazing that way. I go on.

"Respectable people in the community were shocked by this," I tell her, "but not Jesus. He was able to see through their eyes. It wasn't a matter of whether he disapproved or not. He was just able to see as they saw and still love them. That's probably why he *did* love them. That was what was so amazing about him, Martha. He didn't have to agree with their homosexuality to find it in himself to love and forgive them."

She sits there for a moment. I can see she is still listening. All at once she straightens up, puts her Kleenex back in her handbag, and declares with surprising genuineness, "Well, yes. I guess I'm not perfect." We both laugh. We chat a little more after that, and I suggest that she go and talk with her Health teacher some more before she decides to drop out. Then, with a formal nod, morality back in place, she leaves the office. I'm left wondering what's happened.[6]

Again, like the constructive-developmental therapists when they work with someone not yet ready to change her relation to the family religion, Daloz neither disdains nor departs. He does not require Martha to leave her religion at the gates of the university. He seeks rather to extend the gates to include her religion and in so doing allows Martha— not at her direction but that of Jesus—to stay in school, to understand how school might be meaningful according to the terms with which she is still identified. Whether Martha will ever distinguish Jesus' authority from her own only Martha can decide. In the meantime, should she find it agreeable, "higher education" of this sort can continue to offer her the opportunity to reflect on the terms of the authority to which she does feel bound. But make no mistake. Despite what the adult education experts might suggest, Martha is no less a "self-directed" learner than those who can meet the experts' expectations. It is just a different self she is directing. It turns out that the experts' expectation is really not for just *any* "self-directed learning," it is for learning directed by a self organized at the fourth order.

> We ask our adult students to write a paper. We tell them we want them to think for themselves and not just parrot the party line, the professor's view or that of their reading. After all, we want them to be "self-directing." They write the paper and we don't think much of it. We give it a C (or, on many campuses, the C of the 1990s, a B+). The student comes to see us and she's not too happy. "I don't get it. You told us to think for ourselves and I took you at your word. The paper is filled with my honest opinions. What are you telling me, I have B+ sincerity?"
>
> Something has gone wrong here, we tell ourselves, but what? And come to think of it, this is not the only student with whom we experience a "communication problem" over the papers. We begin to feel as if our criticisms, no matter how tactfully or supportively rendered, are far too devastating to many of our students. We don't want to be ignored, but our voice seems to carry much *more* weight or consequence

than we intend. Or maybe it is just that the whole interaction seems to be about a lot more than the paper. For that matter, we're also feeling a little uneasy that it is so exciting and such cause for celebration when we *like* a paper. And what about the many students who seem to write so *dutifully*, who ask how many pages we want, as if they plan to sit in front of fifteen empty sheets of paper and figure out a way to fill them up? And then, we think, there are the ones who are so paralyzed they cannot write at all. What about them?

These may all be failures at a certain kind of "self-direction" but what if, given what Kierkegaard called "the way they understand," no other options are currently possible? If students are subject to third order structures, their writing is primarily addressed to us on behalf of their loyalty or devotion to the bonds that join us. They know we consider it a good thing that they are aware their writing will be read by someone else, but we would also like them to be writing to parts of themselves, conducting an inner conversation. That would be more "self-direct-ing," they know, but might it not also require them to take up a position outside their sense of what we expect of them, to stand outside their loyalty to our bond? If their writing is primarily to us on behalf of their loyalty or devotion to the bonds that join us, then isn't it understand-able that our not liking their paper is a disappointing event of major proportion? After all, they have done their best to meet our expectation, and our negative evaluation of their paper means not only that they have failed to do so, but that the perpetuation of our very bond may be in jeopardy. They know we would prefer that our evaluation not essen-tially complete the act of writing, not be itself immediately a part of the creative invention. We would prefer to be positioned not in front of supplicant students offering their gift for our approval but over the shoulder of a fellow inventor ready to comment upon their independent invention, on what *they* are making, not what we are finishing (or finish-ing off) by our evaluation. We would like them to feel their work exists independent of our evaluation. They know that would be more "self-directing." We would like them to listen to and consider our evaluation, to be sure, but not to be *determined* by it. But this would require an internal system for self-evaluation, a system that itself creates value, a fourth order request. If they are subject to the third order we cannot fault them for feeling whole when we like their work, incomplete when we do not, paralyzed by the prospect of having to watch their perfor-mance through our eyes, running every word they ever think to write through our mind as they reckon our mind to be. (And we should not be surprised at how alert they are to any possibility of learning more about what we do think.) We would like them to understand that when we told them to think for themselves, we did not really mean "be sincere, use your own opinions," but that's what it means to them. We want them to hear "think for yourself" as something more like "take charge of the concepts of the course and independently bring them to an issue of your own choosing." They suppose that, too, would be more what we call "self-directed." But as far as they are concerned, *every* single thing they are doing that we would prefer they do otherwise is highly selfdirected! It is just that the "self" they are directing is not the one we want!

Thus the experts' expectation that adults be "self-directed" learners may really be a claim on mind for a specific *kind* of self and a specific *kind* of direction, namely that of the fourth order. Nor is this the only claim adult students face. In fact, we can see the fourth order structure of the claim for self-direction mirrored in a second, equally pervasive claim upon higher education students to engage their learning materials with a qualitatively greater measure of cognitive sophistication. Though intellectual complexity or sophistication and intellectual independence ("self-direction") are two quite different subjects, when we look into what higher education is calling for specifically, the fourth order nature of the desired complexity is as evident as we have already seen the desired independence to be. Nothing in the higher education literature suggests any recognition that the capacity of mind that permits a measure of personal authority in one's learning is the same capacity that would permit a learner the cognitive sophistication to master the knowledge-generating and knowledge-validating processes of an intellectual field or discipline.

But we need only return to our paper writer who hears "think for yourself" as "be sincere, use your own original opinions and views," rather than "take charge of the concepts or theories of the course and bring them to an issue of your own choosing." This construal implicates more than the inability to "develop critical thinking, individual initiative, or a sense of [oneself] as co-creator of the culture that shapes [one]." It may reflect an inability to relate to an intellectual discipline as itself a system for generating knowledge, treating inferences, evaluating "opinions." The triumph of the third order is its capacity to construct the abstracted forms of generalization, hypothesis, value, ideal. Concrete *data* can be brought under the organization of inference. But inference itself cannot be acted upon because the order of consciousness is no more complex than *inference*. Sharon Parks makes this third order–fourth order distinction when she talks about the difference between "reflective consciousness" and "critical consciousness."[7] So do Mary Belenkey and her colleagues when they distinguish "subjective knowing" from "procedural knowing."[8] The third order can reflect upon the world and honor its own subjectivity. But it cannot evaluate or relate to its reflections or its subjectivity. It has no internal procedure for subjecting its inferences to systematic evaluation or critique, nor can it organize its inferences into a more complex whole (a *formulation*) or create a complex whole that will itself generate inferences.

Intellectual disciplines or fields of study are neither repositories of discovered facts nor families of related opinions. They are each—be they in the sciences, social sciences, or humanities—systematic procedures for generating and evaluating ideas, hypotheses, and "sincere opinions." They are public procedures for relating to third order constructions. Taking charge of a discipline, as higher education asks its students to do, requires of them more than just the "personal" sophistication of "self-direction." It requires the cognitive sophistication to construct complex systems, the structure of the fourth order.

If an adult is currently a part of that half or more of the population that does not yet fully construct the fourth order, then how different is the actual experience of "meeting a discipline" from that expected and possibly imagined by higher education instructors? When the two-dimensional figure in *Flatland* meets the three-dimensional sphere, it neither sees a sphere nor has any sense that there is more than what it sees—namely, a two-dimensional circle, that piece of a sphere its plane runs through. If students meet a fourth order discipline with third order consciousness they will recognize in it its third order structures— values, opinions, hypotheses, inferences, generalizations. And "engaging the discipline" will be a matter of learning these and perhaps, encouraged to use their own minds and be original, bringing their own values, opinions, and inferences, into conversation with those they meet. They will not—for failing to see that the discipline is itself a method, procedure, or system of interpretation for reflecting on hypotheses, evaluating values, validating knowledge—feel that they have missed anything. Not, that is, until we give them a C–.

Higher education, like psychotherapy, can richly assist adults in creating the order of consciousness the modern world demands. Here is a mission for adult education that will not lack for people to serve. Or, less optimistically, these and other contexts for self-expansion may merely be additional arenas in which many adults will find themselves faced with yet more versions of a single mental claim that is over their heads. The fourth order claims inherent in much of higher education are perfectly suited to the demands of the hidden curriculum modern adults face in their public and private lives. But it would be the cruelest of ironies for a school, of all places, to assume the mastery of its curriculum at the outset rather than to teach toward its gradual accomplishment over time. If the wider culture-as-school gets higher marks for the rigor of its curriculum than for the coaching sympathy it provides its adult "students," it is only appropriate that we look to the expectable institutions of support, such as the schools, to set a model in providing this support for the wider culture rather than fall into step with its indifference.

Higher education will disappoint the real learning needs of many modern adults if it assumes that the hidden curriculum, inside and outside school, is already mastered; if it tries to train adults to master that curriculum (by focusing too exclusively on the skills and behaviors associated with mastery) rather than to *educate* adults to the order of consciousness that enables those skills and behaviors; if it aims too low by joining, without disturbing, third order capacities; or if it aims too high by unwittingly making a claim on capacities beyond the fourth order. I am suggesting that the principal mission of adult education should be support to modernity's order of consciousness.

Aiming too low and aiming too high, the last two forms of abandoning that mission, ironically have their origins in the same intellectual movement, namely, "social constructivism." Kenneth Bruffee's thoughtful work is a provocative example of this nondevelopmental constructivism applied to the conversation about the undergraduate curriculum, and by extension, adult education.[9] Bruffee suggests that what is really going on in college teaching and learning is a process of inducting students into the rules of discourse in a particular intellectual region or domain of like-minded folk. Thus education, Bruffee contends, is really a process of socialization, not anything so obscure as the facilitation of increasingly complex mental structures. In a refreshingly direct contradiction to some of the fundamental assumptions guiding my argument here, Bruffee states, "There is no such thing as a structure of thought; only an agreement, a consensus arrived at for the time being by a community of knowledgeable peers."[10] If we want students of history or physics to be respected by historians or physicists, he continues, we should then abjure the needlessly roundabout and ineffective method of "expanding the mind" of our students and go to work teaching them to talk in ways historians and physicists respect. Teaching should involve "focusing people's attention so that their conversation increasingly occurs in the language of the community they want to join."[11]

Such an argument has an interesting parallel in the family therapists' claims about the fictional nature of the individual mind. And as was the case with that argument, there are elements of Bruffee's position I not only agree with but think are important. I will come to these shortly. But one element I obviously do not agree with is ignoring the reality-constituting (and constraining) powers of the individual mind. It is not necessary to pretend our students do not come to us with their own ways of constructing reality, including the constructing of what and how we teach, in order to champion effectively the power of social context to constitute reality. Our students' ways of knowing both engage and are engaged by social context, but it seems to me a big mistake to ignore the long history of their engagement, which has led to current habits of mind that will not yield so easily to present social influences.

The habit of mind I call the third order of consciousness establishes the person as a citizen, one capable of joining a community as a fellow participant rather than as a ward who must be watched over for his own good and the good of those around him. The third order, the culmination of adolescence, makes one both capable of, and vulnerable to, socialization. It is just this order of mind that would indeed allow one to be socialized into a "discourse community." Thus socialized, the student may now indeed be able to speak the language that historians or physicists respect, but does this necessarily constitute an education? The third order of mind is both capable of, and subject to, socialization. It is not able to reflect critically on that into which it is being socialized. It is responsive to socialization not responsible for it. Perhaps it is Bruffee's view that it is the teacher's job to be *responsible for* the community into which the student is socialized. Maybe so, but it is also a teacher's job to put herself out of business by preparing her student to do for himself what she currently does for him. How does socialization into a discourse community hasten the day the teacher is put out of the business of assuming responsibility for the student?

Social constructivists admirably remind us of the value, power, and virtue of social participation and community. Like the authors of *Habits of the Heart*,[12] they raise, as they should, an important alarm against canonizing the modernist virtues of psychological self-control and self-authorship. They reject, as do I, the vision of personal authority and psychological independence as the peak of maturity and warn us against its dangers—isolation and the myopic aggrandizement of the powers of personal control. But on behalf of a value they see disrespected and underappreciated, they may romanticize "the community" and inadequately attend to the hazards, the dangers, and even the horrors potentially attendant to processes of socialization from which one cannot stand apart. Education as socialization into a discourse community may be fitting to the student's third order capacities, but it may also leave the student with no greater capacity to resist induction in the future into communities of discourse less benign than the ones social constructivists imagine—totalitarian "discourse communities," for example. It may amount to an education for inauthenticity, since one learns the right moves and the right words but accomplishes no "inside out" mastery of the locality's discipline. As a civil polity the majority of the adult population is already socialized in just this manner into the language of the constitutional "discourse community," for studies regularly show that more than half of the population, while supporting the language of the Bill of Rights, would nonetheless, when queried about the merits of its actual concepts, deny the majority of those "guaranteed" rights to themselves and their fellow citizens. What Bruffee's suggestion may amount to is an education for a new conformity, if one is just reinducted into a new set of values and "made up by" a new set of loyalties, essentially a lateral move in the evolution of consciousness.

Socialization into a discourse community might be the fanciest version yet of substituting *training* for *education* and changes in *learning* for changes in *knowing*. With no intention to do so, social constructivists may be prescribing a mode of teaching that "aims too low," that exploits third order capacities for socialization but sells short the student's restless, creative capacity to remake "the way he understands," as Kierkegaard put it. If a given epistemological way of understanding is as robust and long-lived as my own research would suggest, then altering this kind of knowing cannot be as easy as teaching people to speak a foreign language. It inevitably involves separations from the self. It is more akin to teaching people to unspeak their native tongue, the language whose very rhythms and timbre carry with them powerful feelings of loyalty and identification.

But if the social constructivists aim too low, in another sense they aim too high. By failing to consider that their students and they themselves may come to school with a consciousness agenda, they are in no position to consider whether these agendas may be different. I deeply respect what to me seem the twin passions motivating the social constructivists who have entered the discussion about higher education. The first of these I have already described as a thoroughgoing suspicion of psychological independence as a preeminent value and a commitment to revalue the virtue of connection in and through the community. The second of these is a recognition of the relative nature of the intellectual disciplines: they do not possess or generate The Truth but are more or less internally consistent systems or procedures for declaring something as knowledge, just as I said when I was discussing what it meant to "control a discipline." The social constructivists have moved to a different position in relation to a discipline's capacity to treat, regard, and generate inferences. They are not just taking charge of the internal logic of their respective disciplines; they are standing outside these systems, taking them as object and seeing them for what they are. They see that the logical power a system has on its own terms is flawed and incomplete when viewed from outside or in relation to other logics. They see that each system—each "way of knowing"—is inevitably "decisive" in the literal sense of cutting some things off and including others, that each way of knowing is a way of not knowing, that each discipline is itself an ideology offering the power of explanation but at the price of inevitably advantaging someone or something and disadvantaging someone or something else.

But what they may not see is that their own illuminating critique is itself an expression of their consciousness agenda. Their recognition of the limited and potentially isolating power of personal control and self-authorship, and of the ideological nature of the disciplines may have a wisdom, but a wisdom born of what order of consciousness? (See Table 8.1.)

Many social constructivists attending to higher education advocate that teachers make clear to their students the partial, ideological, "privileging" nature of the disciplines they teach. What sense should we

Table 8.1 Orders of Curricular Complexity (Using History as an Example)

Curricular form	Appropriate audience	Cognitive operation	Claim on mind
The Story of History The *concrete facts* and the *narrative line* (e.g., the "story" of "settling the West" or "how the world went to war")	*School Children* Grades 1–3 (a stretch), grades 4–6 (elaborating an emerging capacity)	Data	2nd order of consciousness (durable categories)
Elementary Historiography *How* history is written; its dependence on the perspective of the historian; the themes and values expressed in "a history" of given events	*Adolescents* Junior high students (a stretch), high school students (elaborating an emerging capacity)	Inference	3rd order of consciousness (cross-categorical structures)
Historical Theory The discipline's system or systems for creating historical knowledge, generating, regarding, evaluating, and relating inferences	*Adults* Any higher education setting (a stretch for many)	Formulation	4th order of consciousness (complex systems)
Critical Theory Critical reflection on the discipline itself; subjecting its prevailing theories to analysis not just from the perspective of another contending theory but from a perspective "outside ideology"	*Adults* Any higher education setting (a stretch for most); graduate programs in history and within the history profession itself (a stretch for many)	Reflection upon Formulation	5th order of consciousness (trans-system structures)

imagine their students will make of this generous, teacherly impulse to share the truth as they know it? For just a moment, we might attend to the principal population these advocates have in mind, that shrinking pool of "traditional" undergraduates, eighteen- to twenty-one-year-old youth. Since our research suggests that almost no one this age has fully constructed the fourth order of consciousness, how comprehending of a message that arises from transcending the fourth order of consciousness should we expect these students to be? The academic social constructivists would be delivering a message about the limitations of ideology and systemic procedure at the very time the receivers of this message are taken up with the hard work of gradually developing a capacity to conceive ideology and systemic procedure! The social constructivists want to share their hard-won discovery of the partiality of systems of explanation (which organize particular values into a coherent whole) at the very time their students are making their first efforts at exercising a discipline's (or a self's) capacity to bring surrounding values (or expectations) before an only half-created internal standard.

But what is clearly a form of communication that aims too high, abandoning youthful undergraduates, is only somewhat less so when addressed to a general population of adults, more than half of whom may also be unlikely to fully construct the fourth order. In suggesting that the primary agenda for adult education should be support for the move toward personal psychological authority, the order of consciousness modernity demands, I do not mean to endorse the ultimate value of self-authorship and self-control as the hallmark or end point of mental maturity. But notes sounded by the social constructivists as to the limited power of self-authorship and the ideological nature of academic disciplines may be pitched to a range that is out of the hearing of most of their students. What if the teachers' message is reflective not of their students' curriculum but of their own?

For a majority of the adult population, social constructivists who would heed Kierkegaard's principle may be called upon to support a move to just the order of consciousness they themselves are currently happy to be leaving behind. If the differentiation from the fourth order is fairly recent, this may be an especially unappealing assignment, since there is no order of consciousness that holds less charm for us than the one we have only recently moved beyond. Perhaps the questions that arise here make up the preeminent challenge to our teacherly capacities for generativity: Are we willing to support people's moves to places we ourselves have already been? Are we able to be good company on the path to fresh discoveries no longer fresh to us?

Only a fraction of the adults entering school programs do so with the hope or intention of personally growing from being in school. Most have what they (and we?) would consider far more *practical* goals, such as getting ahead in their work lives. Yet school experience in adulthood places one, as Charles Seashore puts it, "in grave danger of growing."[13] And, ironically, the kind of growth that is most likely to occur—from the third to the fourth order of consciousness—may be the very height of practicality in a modernist culture. "The decision to return to school did not seem to signal major change," wrote one adult returning to school. "As I envisioned it, having a degree would enable me to do better what I had been doing all along. It wasn't until much later that I realized the undercurrents of my need for change were already eddying beneath what appeared to be a placid surface. I did not anticipate that within five years my life would completely transform."[14]

We have only to take another look at the longitudinal study reported in Chapter 5. The people in the study were all returning students in a graduate program. Table 5.7 shows that over 70 percent of them (men and women from their midtwenties to their midfifties) had not reached the fourth order threshold of consciousness when they entered their program at Year 1—they had scores less complex than 4(3). But by the time most of the students were getting ready to graduate from the program, at Year 4, 70 percent of them *had* reached this threshold—they had scores at least as complex as 4(3)! Although we don't have a comparison sample of similarly situated adults who did not attend school over the same four years, since we do have a great many single-time studies of such adults at various ages and we never find such a large percentage of those at or beyond the fourth order, it does seem likely that the schooling has had something to do with the developmental result. What enabled this development?

What may have happened for most of these people was their own version of the two central experiences that seem to run through accounts of adult transformations in school. The first is taking on the role of student outside the school as well as in it, a role that is organized around their interests, their goals, their learning, their accomplishments. This significantly alters the nature of preexisting but still-continuing relationships (especially for the largest group of adult students, women who are returning to school after a period of not being in school). The second is that, in school itself, a combination of support (being taken seriously, acknowledged, attended to, and treated as a responsible, self-governing adult) and challenge (being asked to make decisions, design your own program, formulate, act, resolve, negotiate relationships, master a discipline, and contend with competing values, theories, and advice) facilitates growth.

The first of these experiences, which is often overlooked, can be as powerful as the second. What makes "school" transformative for adults is that it creates a "bridging" environment, but it does so not only in the intentionally fabricated, temporary, and "rented" world of school itself; it also reaches into the preexisting, ongoing, real-life world of the student's relational field and seeks to make it a part of the bridging environment. Students are shaken up by going to school but so are their family members, friends, and even work associates. All of these people are eventually required to see the student differently, and in so doing, they knowingly, or more often unknowingly, become adjunctive members of the bridging environment. In fact, these people are so important to the student's chances of growing that if they will *not* become adjunctive members of the student's "school," the student is often unable to continue, let alone to grow. Friends and family members who are immediately and easily able to reconstruct their relationship with the student in recognition of the inner and outer demands of her schooling (a rare phenomenon) are of course supporting her development. But even if friends or family members initially object to the changes brought about by the student's schooling, these conditions too can be positive, if they are alterable. This is because they require the student to take a new perspective on herself and on her relationships, to redefine and reorganize them, all of which is productive grist for the transformation from the third to the fourth order. In this way, as a source of either support or challenge, the response of the student's real-life relational field can facilitate growth.

Kathleen Taylor's careful study of adults returning to school[15] provides rich examples of the role the student's nonschool relations play in school as a transformative environment. Some were immediately supportive:

> *Bea:* [My husband] was all for it [her return to school]. When I went to [the first meeting]—I think I mentioned it the day I was there—he

said, "Well, I guess this is 'goodbye' for a year or so." [Laughter] 'Do what you have to do.' He was behind it 100% once he knew what the program was about.[16]

Cindy: [He let] me know that I was really very brilliant. [Sometimes] it would be something as minor as, he would make a flip comment and I would come back at him real fast, and he would say "a stupid person can't come back like that" [laughter] . . . He was always reinforcing how smart [I was] . . . and really minimized the intimidating factors of getting through school.[17]

Some were not:

Maura: For one of the very first times in my life I decided I'm putting myself first, ahead of everyone else and, yes, there's plenty of reaction, you betcha . . . He didn't think it was the right time for me to do it. He cited my health as possibly a problem, that he was worried that I would run myself into the ground trying to do all these things. But it was that I was going to do what I want to do rather than what everybody else wants done. What I sensed was a lot of anger at me for changing the rules in the relationship. His wants, needs, and desires [were] not going to be first any longer. His goals and his growth process wasn't the focal point.[18]

Penny: "You think you're better than us," was coming from my mother, at one point [laughs] . . . She said something like that. That's the way I perceived that. I don't remember word for word. "High and mighty." [Laughs.] . . . I was trying to work full time, still be the Room Mother, and still drive the kids to school, and be there on time, and feed the dog, and make sure that dinner was on the table at five o'clock . . . The kids called me by my first name, I remember that. That was a big joke in the house . . . Because they said they didn't see me anymore . . . There was a lot of complaining that there had to be baby sitting done and I wasn't earning money at it—at what I was making him babysit for . . . Yet when I would cry and break down and go "why aren't you supporting me?" [he'd say] "oh yes, I still love you, yes" and "I will" and "I'm sorry" . . . Yeah, all of a sudden I wasn't giving him all the attention that he needed and that he required.[19]

But of relationships that were not initially supportive, some were eventually reconstructable, and it was evident that in these cases the student's successful redefinition of the relationship was itself transformative:

Betty took a three month break and discovered that when she wasn't actively a student "everybody just reverted right back to depending on me in ways that I didn't even realize they were . . . 'Mom could do this,' 'Betty can do that' . . . It was just automatic, sort of. I was the one that recognized it and said, 'hey [laughter], this is not gonna work for me.' And they said 'Okay.'" ["But how did they react when you said that?"] "They realized that that was true. They'd all been so relieved that I wasn't in school that quarter and now I could—it could be like it was. Then they realized it's not ever going to be like it was." ["It's not ever?"] "No. Not *ever* going to be like it was."[20]

Taylor's study, which looks explicitly at the experience of adult learners from an order of consciousness perspective, also provides examples of the way school activities themselves, through both their support and their challenge, can foster development from the third to the fourth order. In *Effective Teaching and Mentoring*, where he draws on a number of constructive-developmental theories, Laurent Daloz also emphasizes this theme of support and challenge in his consideration of the transformative potential of adult learning. As he demonstrated in his work with Martha, he places a premium on "moving to confirm the student's sense of worth and helping her to see she is both OK where she is and capable of moving ahead when she chooses."[21] Taylor's informants spoke to how important they found such support:

Jackie: You know, we all look for validation. We say we don't but we all do. When you're young, you get it from your parents all the time, but you think, "Well, they['re] my parents, they're my family, so they gotta say that kind of stuff." When you get it from the outside world, "It's ok you did this. It's ok what you did"—[getting] that [in this program] was real important for me.[22]

Cindy: [You] understood my neurotic love-dance and didn't let me shuffle off to Buffalo. [Laughter] It was like, as I was heading for the door, Sandy and you slammed it shut, stood there with your arms locked and said, [laughter] "You're not leaving." ["I don't remember this incident."] Emotionally, emotionally, that's [the message] I got. It [was] like, "You made an agreement to do this and you're gonna do it. And I know you can. And it's ok to be scared, and to do whatever it is you're doing, but you also made an agreement to do this and I'm going to make sure that you're going to have the support *you* need and what *you* recognize as support to get through it."[23]

Paired with this support, the student who grows at school has also experienced a kind of challenge ideally suited to crossing the bridge from the third to the fourth order. In another instance of the ubiquitous nature of the demand for "self-direction" in the literature of adult learning, Taylor identifies the challenge exactly this way. And she refers to Alverno College, a leader in the explicit use of constructive-developmental theories to shape the learning environment. Alverno College sees its program as providing "a content sequence in which our diverse learners progress toward self-direction . . . [as they encounter] three basic issues: (1) that learning is a change in the self; (2) that newly learned (or newly recognized) abilities can be adapted to varying situations . . . ; and (3) that one can take charge of the learning process integrating and to some extent directing the changes in one's self and one's world."[24]

> *Charlotte:* It's not just learning material about computer science, which I happen to be in. That's not it. It's a lot more than that. . . . It's the [practice] you get in taking the lead and directing things for yourself in what you need to accomplish.[25]

> *Burdette:* As I tried to chart out the [degree plan] I had to keep telling myself: "Don't listen to these words, these voices, these people in the back of your mind. They don't know what you want. They just keep telling you what you can't do and can do." Pretty soon as I started looking into what I wanted to be, and . . . [when I] was able to start thinking of what I wanted to do, it started coming out: what it was that *I* wanted.[26]

> *Maura:* I know [these changes] would not have happened if I was going to another kind of institution because [here] you have to keep turning back to yourself . . . I don't see how anyone can do [this without] . . . finding out who the hell they are . . . [Because] every time you sit down to write a learning agreement you have to say "what do I want to learn out of this? What's valid? What is it that *I* need to know so I can do the work I want to do?"[27]

> *Janet:* This school has been the vehicle for me to say, "Yeah, I can acknowledge my own responsibility to my own life." I may have been given all these—it's kind of like that quiltmaker—you get all these pieces in life and those are the ones you get. And what you can afford you get, and what you're given is what you get. But it's how you put it together that makes the difference. That emphasis on how *I* put it to-

gether, not on what I get . . . I'm responsible for how much meaning I get out of it. It's just so different to assume the responsibility.[28]

A school's demand for self-direction, along with support inside and outside the school for the transformation of mind required to meet that demand, may be one major reason why studies like our own and Taylor's report so much development to the fourth order. It has been my experience from teaching in professional schools that another potential source of growth is the use of the same supports to meet an altogether different demand, one which seems to be much less recognized. This is a demand that harkens back to our considerations of intimacy, the demand to give up a romanticized or idealized relationship to the beloved. In this case, however, the objects of our affection are our professional field, our graduate training program, and/or our very conception of ourselves as practitioners of the profession.

Adults in training to be psychologists, for example, inevitably discover during their course of study and internship how limited and in doubt is their own capacity to relieve another person's suffering or promote necessary change, how partial and contradictory is the state of existing knowledge in their field, how flawed and beset with the usual share of inadequacies is their faculty and training program. Like the academic version of a well-known cold remedy, these differing disappointments and shocks act like tiny time capsules, activating themselves at different points throughout the entire program to ensure that the student will have the benefit of their effect. Disillusionment with one's own capacity to heal another—what Baird Brightman refers to as "the narcissistic injury of the training experience"[29]—is more likely to be activated early in training, during the first practicum or internship. It may only be toward the end of the training experience that one can see one's program and faculty in the clear light of day, when the earlier glare, created by one's own anxious enthusiasm and need for one's choice of schools to be a good one, has receded.

Whenever they occur, these kinds of experiences can unsettle the third order need for an external authority worthy of one's faith. But on the other side of this sense of loss they can also promote the process by which one puts together one's own psychology, one's own program, even one's own way of being a psychologist, relieved of the need to live up to some perfect standard (since even the "perfect standards" are seen not to live up to the standard).

For some fifteen years, the fourth year class at the Massachusetts School of Professional Psychology has invited me to address them on the subject of their imminent departure. The only part of my remarks that seems to be memorable, judging from conversations years later, is my ever-accumulating list of good reasons why they should reconsider their plan to graduate and remain students forever. Here are a few samples from the list:

So long as your program was not complete you could always quell your feelings of being inadequately prepared with the comforting thought that you have more time to learn these things before you graduate. The message behind the comforting thought was that graduate education is an enormously long undertaking, but at least when you have completed it, if you were conscientious and well-disciplined, you will be a completely trained, completely educated psychologist. Well, now here you are, about to conclude a long period of study and training in which you certainly have been reasonably conscientious and reasonably well disciplined. And you know as well as I do that you may not exactly feel like a completely trained, completely prepared psychologist. You know that you still don't know anything much about this, or really how to do that. And you thought you would. So I have the solution: Don't graduate!

If you let yourself finish and graduate, you are surrendering forever the refuges of provisionalness, of apprenticehood, of being embarked on an easily explained journey to a respectable destination. You will have to stop journeying and arrive. You will have to be not just training to be a doctor, but the doctor him or herself; not just promising, but someone who delivers. All the perfectly good reasons not to be a grown-up, a status that graduate education has been an ingeniously acceptable way of forestalling, will now reappear more clearly than ever. Who wants the responsibility? For that matter, who wants to leave behind one's parents, neither of whom perhaps was a professional? one's social class? one's siblings? one's spouse? There is one good solution to all this: Don't do it! Stay in the program!

In order to graduate you're going to have to say your thesis is complete. Saying your thesis is complete means that you must now face the inevitable gap between the thesis you imagined you would write and the one you really wrote, between the thesis you hoped to write and thought you would really write when you proposed it, and the thesis you in fact did write. Every limitation you've spotted up to now that you told yourself would be gone or fixed before it was done must now be faced for what it is, a limitation that will *not* be fixed or gone. But then that's only if it is done. If you don't graduate, your thesis never has to be done.

If you really let yourself finish the program you are going to have to deal with the fact that your marriage, your relationship with your children, your sex life, or your backhand—all those things whose disrepair you have been attributing to the stresses of being back in school—may actually *not* get any better now that school is over . . .

This might seem a bizarre or even unfriendly way to speak to people, but from the sounds in the room (other than my own voice) while I am saying these kinds of things, they seem for some strange reason welcome, even pleasurable things to hear at the end of a long process of schooling. The sounds are mostly laughter—knowing, self-accepting laughter, with a smattering of other sounds of relieved surrendering thrown in (a sudden burst of air, or the appreciative, if pained, groan a person makes when the masseuse is working on a tightened knot). Of course, the last thing a near-to-graduating student wants to hear is an invitation, let alone a suggestion, to reenroll in school. The idea itself is as welcome as the suggestion to a pregnant woman to carry the baby for another nine months.

Students close to graduating have "had it." Whether they loved the school or hated it they want out. But "out" means facing things like those I refer to in my list, and one can only do that, one can only counter the absurdity of my suggestion and preserve one's enthusiasm for leaving by accepting that "out" also means leaving behind (or reducing one's allegiance to) the third order idealizations that fuel the list. The list pretends to champion and validate the idealizations, and the students' responses of self-recognition may acknowledge that such idealizations (or some of them) were indeed a part of how they made meaning. But their responses may also involve their recognition or acknowledgment that they are no longer as identified with this way of making meaning, that to some extent they can construct these same matters in a sufficiently de-idealizing or self-authoring way to make these new burdens acceptable or even welcome. "No, maybe I will not satisfy all these expectations I took on," something in the student may say amid the laughter, "but perhaps what I have done is acceptable to my own standard."

Indeed, school can be a most fertile context for the transformation of consciousness in adulthood. But as our own study shows, as Taylor and Daloz describe, as Brightman and Alverno College and Knowles and the other champions of self-direction we have discussed in this chapter imply, the principal transformation we are talking about is the move from the third to the fourth order.[30]

Jackie, from Taylor's study, describes the way her schooling has led her to feel that she no longer has to live up to someone else's ideal:

> Because I know who I am now . . . There's no need for me to keep trying to change [to fit someone else's ideal]. That's one thing I would have done before: "OK, maybe if I were thinner, or if I looked like *this*, or [wore] my hair like *that* maybe then—" But now this is who I am . . . I don't feel the need to put down who I am, and a lot of times [in the past] I would—you know, how bright I was, or how metaphysical that I am. I would shut a lot of that down. I tore myself down in order to make them feel comfortable.[31]

The transformation is one of self-authorship, of becoming the definer of one's acceptability. And, as Taylor points out about the women in her study, the move toward the fourth order does not have to be a move away from the orientation to connection: "Despite their new-found ability to establish boundaries, these women do not appear to have lost what Gilligan suggests is women's fundamental orientation toward connection; what has changed is their relationship to it. Burdette, for example, still emphasizes her family responsibilities; but she no longer disappears into that role. Jackie definitely wants to find a successful relationship with a man; but not if it means she has to pretend to be other than who she is. Betty will never go back to being the way she was; but her daughters' development is still a major concern for her."[32]

I do not mean to suggest that there is no appropriate audience for claims, like those of the social constructivists, beyond the fourth order. There is, in fact, a large one. For the portion of the population that may fully construct the fourth order, the social constructivists make a claim that is within reach, a claim that calls upon us to loosen our identification with form, system, ideology, and with our personal authority and self-control. Indeed the secondary mission of adult education ought to be precisely that: providing support for those who are ready to make this move beyond the fourth order.

After such a thorough exposé (throughout the last six chapters) of the hidden curricular demand to achieve the fourth order (summarized in Table 8.2) I would forgive anyone for now asking, about the move beyond the fourth order, "Is this next trip really necessary? Isn't it enough

Table 8.2 The Mental Demands of Modern Life: Claims for Fourth Order
              Consciousness

As parents

Take charge of the family; establish rules and roles
Institute a vision and induct family members into it
Support the development of the young within and away from the family
Manage boundaries between the generations
Set limits on children, ourselves, and those outside the family

As intimate partners

Be psychologically independent of our partners
Have a well-differentiated and clearly defined sense of self
Transcend an idealized, romanticized approach to love and closeness
Set limits on children, selves, extrafamily involvements to preserve couple
Support our partner's development
Listen empathically and nondefensively
Communicate feelings directly and responsibly
Have an awareness of how our psychological history inclines or directs us

At work

Be the inventor or owner of our work (rather than see it as owned and created by
   the employer); distinguish our work from our job
Be self-initiating, self-correcting, self-evaluating (rather than dependent on others
   to frame the problems, initiate adjustments, or determine whether things are
   going acceptably well)
Be guided by our own visions at work (rather than be without a vision or captive
   of the authority's agenda
Take responsibility for what happens to us at work externally and internally
   (rather than see our present internal circumstances and future external possibilities as caused by someone else)
Be accomplished masters of our particular work roles, jobs, or careers (rather than
   have an apprenticing or imitating relationship to what we do)
Conceive of the organization from the "outside in," as a whole; see our relation to
   the whole; see the relation of the parts to the whole (rather than see the rest of
   the organization and its parts only from the perspective of our own part, from
   the "inside out")

As citizens of a diverse society

Resist our tendencies to make "right" or "true" that which is merely familiar, and
   "wrong" or "false" that which is only strange (contravene our tendencies toward
   ethnocentrism, gendercentrism)
Be able to *look at* and evaluate the values and beliefs of our psychological and cultural inheritance rather than be captive of those values and beliefs
Be able to recognize our *styles* (how we prefer to receive stimulation and energy,
   prefer to gather data, prefer to make decisions, and how spontaneously or structured we prefer to orient to our lives; our orientation to separateness or connection) *as preferences* (rather than as superior apprehensions)

Table 8.2 (continued)

In psychotherapy

Perceive our standards as based on our own experience (rather than upon the attitudes or desires of others)

Perceive ourselves as the evaluators of experience (rather than regard ourselves as existing in a world where the values are inherent in and attached to the object of our perception)

Place the basis of standards within ourselves, recognizing that the goodness or badness of any experience or perceptual object is not something inherent in that object, but is a value placed on it by ourselves

Transform our energies from manipulating the environment for support into developing greater and greater self-support

Learn to stand on our own feet emotionally, intellectually, economically

Learn to stop reindoctrinating ourselves with the unwholesome philosophies of life, or values, we imbibed and taught ourselves in youth

Learn to challenge and question our own basic values, our own thinking, so that we really think for ourselves

Take responsibility for our lives

Learn the psychological myths or scripts that govern our behavior *and reauthor them* (rather than just use insight for better understanding of why the script is as it is)

In school

Exercise critical thinking

Examine ourselves, our culture, and our milieu in order to understand how to separate what we feel from what we should feel, what we value from what we should value, and what we want from what we should want

Be a self-directed learner (take initiative; set our own goals and standards; use experts, institutions, and other resources to pursue these goals; take responsibility for our direction and productivity in learning)

See ourselves as the co-creators of the culture (rather than only shaped by culture)

Read actively (rather than only receptively) with our own purpose in mind

Write to ourselves and bring our teachers into our self-reflection (rather than write mainly to our teachers and for our teachers)

Take charge of the concepts and theories of a course or discipline, marshalling on behalf of our independently chosen topic its internal procedures for formulating and validating knowledge

---

to accomplish the fourth order?" If contemporary culture consisted only in a modern mentality the answer would be yes. But in fact, the distinguishing feature of contemporary culture is that for the first time in human history, *three* mentalities exist side by side in the adult population, even in the postindustrial, so-called "developed" or "First

World" societies—the traditional, the modern, and the postmodern. As we shall see in Part Four, the claims of the social constructivists are but one instance of the claims of postmodernity, claims that reach into our private lives and our public lives, claims that burden even those who construct the fourth order of consciousness, claims that, for nearly *all* of us, are over our heads.

IV

The Mental Demand of Postmodern Life

9

Conflict, Leadership, and Knowledge Creation

Happy families," Tolstoy said, "are all alike." But I'm not so sure. Consider two happy marriages, that of the Ables and that of the Bakers. Both couples have been married twenty-five years. All four spouses are about fifty. Let us look at the way these two couples experience and construct difference and conflict.

If the Ables spoke in a single voice, here is what they might say:

Twenty-five years? Sometimes we can hardly believe it ourselves. Where did all those years go? We wouldn't kid you and say it's been nonstop wine and roses, but the truth is we both feel enormously grateful for our relationship and for each other. If you asked us, we'd say we have a very good marriage. Of course, it hasn't always been the *same* marriage. But at this point we'd give it very high marks, and we'd say we deserve them, because we've worked hard at it.

So you wanted to know about conflict and differences, and on that subject we could tell you a lot. That certainly has been a part of our hard work. It took us years even to learn how to fight. It's a funny thing. You marry someone because you feel you've found a soul mate, someone whose way of thinking and feeling about things is so much like your own. So you get married, and what do you start to notice? All the *differences!* Where you want to live, how to raise the children, what's a fun vacation, how much mayonnaise to mix into the tuna fish. The truth is we really are very different people. When we are tired at the end of the day and need a recharge, one of us wants to exercise and the other one wants a nap. One of us takes a much more political view of how the world is organized and how we'd like it to change, the other looks at things more aesthetically. One of us is contemplative, the other more active. One is stricter with the kids but looser with the money, and the other is more laissez-faire with the kids but is always saying we need to make a budget. What a riot! In many respects we are like night and day.

This is something we can talk about, even laugh about, *now*. Earlier in our marriage our differences were less discussable, more threatening, more disguised. We were both probably acutely aware of the situations or topics likely to highlight important differences too starkly. We mostly avoided those situations and topics, usually without even being aware we were doing so. Today we would say that our differences are one of the great strengths of our marriage. We won't deny we still get on each other's nerves occasionally, but for the most part we have developed a lot of respect for each other's way of looking at and relating to the world. And, to tell the truth, we've probably each developed a lot of respect for our *own* way of looking at and relating to the world as well. We are both a lot clearer that we each have a way it took us fifty years of living to create, that it's who we are and we're comfortable with it. We're probably more comfortable with each other because we're a lot more comfortable with ourselves.

Anyway, we've become a good team. We find that our differences are often complementary. One picks up what the other one misses. Yes, we still fight sometimes. We don't always listen or consider that there might actually be a whole different take on a matter besides our own that also makes sense. Or we don't always, in truth, have an easy time finding the sense in the other's view. We can get stubborn and dig in behind our own positions. But more often the fights lead to a better result. They make one or both of us come over and take a look from the other one's point of view, and we see that there's a good reason why it looks different to the other one. We are a good problem-solving team. Neither of us feels we have to do it our way all the time. We compromise. We take turns. And sometimes we even find a way to create a solution that includes a lot of both of our views. We stopped trying to get the other person to change a long time ago. We are who we are. At this point, we're not so sure we'd even *want* the other one to change. Our differences are an asset for the most part.

Not every problem has a solution, either, and sometimes you just have to live with that. That goes with the territory of two strong people with minds of their own. And once in a while we've noticed an odd thing. All the strife and struggle can go out of an issue we've been fighting about without our ever having solved it at all. We feel back together, feel like everything's fine again, and actually nothing's been decided or changed regarding the problem but somehow it doesn't seem like much of a problem anymore. We both find that odd. It's a little irrational, but it does happen once in a while.

Now let's hear from the Bakers:

Twenty-five years? Sometimes we can hardly believe it ourselves. Where did all those years go? We wouldn't kid you and say it's been nonstop wine and roses, but the truth is we both feel enormously grateful for our relationship and for each other. If you asked us, we'd say we have a very good marriage. Of course, it hasn't always been the *same* marriage. But at this point we'd give it very high marks, and we'd say we deserve them, because we've worked hard at it.

Now you wanted to know about conflict and difference, and on that subject we could tell you a lot. Certainly that's been a part of our hard work. First we had to learn how to fight, to figure out what we really thought, apart from what the other one thought, and trust we would not scare ourselves or the other one too much in the process. But that was early on. For better or worse, neither of us has much problem telling you where we stand on anything now. In fact, these days, it is the way we've been able to let up a little on how proud we are of our stands that has been the most difficult and the most rewarding thing about how we currently handle conflict.

If you asked our children or our friends or, to be honest, if you asked us, you'd hear this very clear description and distinction between the two of us. One of us would be described as athletic, the exerciser, the other as sedentary. One looks at the world like a politician, tends to see things in terms of power, the other looks at the world like a visual artist, tends to see things in terms of balance and form. The one who is tough on the kids is carefree about the money, and vice versa. These are the ways we're known and have known ourselves for years. When we're at our very best, though—and this is definitely only in the last few years of our relationship—we are able to stop pretending that these differences and opposites can only be found in the *other* person, or that the battles we get into are only with the other person. We realize that this polarizing or dichotomizing serves a purpose for each of us, and we are less enamored with that purpose. We see it's not the whole truth.

When we are at our best, we get a good glimpse at the fact that the activist, for example, also has a contemplative living inside him. The one who is strict with the kids has a part of herself that has a whole other, looser way of feeling about them. And on and on. It isn't easy, and it doesn't happen all the time, but our favorite fights are the ones in which we don't try to solve the conflicts but let the conflicts "solve us," you could say. We mean by that that if a conflict doesn't go away after a while we've found it's a good bet that one of us, or both of us, has gotten drawn back into being too identified with our more comfortable position. Like the end we're holding onto so passionately is our whole story, our whole truth in the matter. When we can get out of the grip of our more familiar side then the fight doesn't feel as if the other one is trying to make us give up anything. The fight becomes a way for us to recover our own complexity, so to speak, to leave off making the other into our opposite and face up to our own oppositeness.

Working out our conflicts this way generates a different kind of intimacy than we've ever known. We've laughed and said there's still a lot of kicking and screaming in our fighting, but it's more a matter of the way our relationship is now dragging us out of the fiction that we're so "day and night," that one of us is all "this way" and the other all "that way." More and more we're refusing to act out the other's opposite, to be the "stand-in" for the other's own oppositeness. This makes each of us get connected to the quieter, less comfortable side of ourselves. And as we do that, we are connected to each other in a different way too. We would say that we have always felt a lot of intimacy in our relationship, but this is definitely a different kind of intimacy than we've experienced in the past.

If the epistemological underpinning of modernism is actually the fourth order of consciousness, then it is clearly a modern marriage that the Ables depict in their account of how they experience conflict and difference. Theirs is a story of surviving the disillusionment of an earlier romantic truth, in which their bond was based on their sharing a common identity. But the loss of this truth does not leave them like lonely statues, standing near but coldly, with no interest in or possibility of connecting, like some caricature of postromantic "modernism." Giving up the romantic truth does not mean giving up their hopes for closeness. It means discovering a new form of closeness. The Ables have created a different but deep connection. It seems to be rooted in a mutual appreciation of the other's capacity to enter relation as a distinct and whole human being. They each seem to recognize and respect both the other and themselves as complicated persons who bring something important and different, but often complementary, to the relationship.

As self-possessed persons who share a commitment to sustaining a relationship they treasure, they do not seem surprised by the appearance of differences, nor do they take them as a suspension of their connection, nor expect that the differences will be resolved if one of them simply molds herself or himself to the preferences of the other. Not only does the relationship continue in the face of the difference, but they seem to find their successful, collaborative handling of the differences to be an especially satisfying aspect of the relationship. Both their closeness as a couple and their evaluation of the quality of their decisions are enhanced, rather than troubled, by their difference. Difficult though it may be, they ultimately value the experience of being forced by the other, or by their commitment to the relationship, to take seriously the integrity of the different world view from which the differing preference, opinion, or plan of action arises. Like respectful and enlightened anthropologists, they regularly visit, and deeply appreciate, the other's "culture of mind." At their best, they suspend the tendency to evaluate the other's "culture" through the lens of their own, and seek rather to discover the terms by which the other is shaping meaning or creating value. Not only does each seem to benefit from frequent "travel" to the other's "culture," but the one who is "being visited" also seems to appreciate the experience of having the other come in with a nonimperial stance to see how reality is being constructed.

Of course we could imagine many couples with these same fourth order capacities for self-authorship and personal authority who would not have the generosity, personal comfort, freedom from self-absorption, or interest in intimacy to fashion such a rich connection. The point is not that everyone who constructs the world at the fourth order would necessarily sustain such bonds, but that there is nothing about the fourth order or about modernism that necessarily prevents a highly satisfying, mutually nourishing, deep form of intimacy.

However intimate the fourth order might be, it is clear that the Bakers' account reflects a qualitatively different way of constructing conflict and difference. Theirs is *also* a story of surviving disillusionment, but the truth they have been seeing as an illusion is not the truth of romance, it is the truth of modernism. Long ago, they say, they set aside the truth that the source of their closeness lay in their sharing the same identity. The truth they are now in the process of setting aside is that the source of their closeness lies in the respectful cooperation of psychologically whole and distinct selves.

Unlike the Ables, the Bakers are prouder of the way they suspect rather than honor their sense of their own and each other's wholeness and distinctness. At least they are suspicious of any sense of wholeness or distinction that is limited to an identification of the self with its favorite way of constructing itself. They are suspicious of their own tendency to feel wholly identified with one side of any opposite and to identify the other with the other side of that opposite.

When they take this suspicion to their experience of conflict or difference in their relationship, a quite different picture emerges from that sketched by the Ables. The Ables consider themselves at their best when, in the face of difference, they do not disdain the other but seek to discover how the other's point of view arises out of a "culture of mind" with its own coherence and integrity. But what is never open to question is that the respectful anthropologist is visiting a foreign culture. In contrast, the Bakers consider themselves at their best when, in the face of difference, they stop to see if they haven't, in fact, made the error of identifying themselves wholly with the culture of mind that gives rise to their position (which now shows up as a kind of ideology or orthodoxy) and identifying their partner wholly with a foreign culture of mind that gives rise to their partner's position (which now shows up as an opposing ideology or heterodoxy). Mr. Able comes over to discover the world of Mrs. Able, but in all his respectful discovering he never questions his premise that this is not his world. When Mr. Baker comes over to try on the perspective he has identified with Mrs. Baker, however, he is vulnerable to discovering another world within himself.

The Ables value conflict as a confirmation of the good working of the self and a satisfying recognition on the part of the other of how that self works. So do the Bakers. The difference is that the Ables are constructing *fourth* order selves, so for them the good working of the self and its recognition by the other begin with the shared premise that each brings a distinct and whole self *to* the relationship. The relationship is a context for the sharing and interacting of two whole, distinct, self-possessed, self-authoring selves. Two distinct selves will inevitably have conflicts. This is a part of their interacting, and it has its origins in their very wholeness and distinctness. If they were not whole and distinct, but romantically shared a common identity, as they might have done when they were constructing third order selves, they would be less likely to have conflict.

The Bakers, in contrast, are constructing fifth order selves (or, more precisely, are somewhere in the transformation from the fourth to the fifth order). As depicted in Figure 9.1, the fifth order moves form or system from subject to object, and brings into being a new "trans-system" or "cross-form" way of organizing reality. For the Bakers, the good working of the self and its recognition by the other begins with a refusal to see oneself or the other as a single system or form. The relationship is a context for a sharing and an interacting in which both are helped to experience their "multipleness," in which the *many* forms or systems that *each self is* are helped to emerge. While the Ables begin with the premise of their own completeness and see conflict as an inevitable by-product of the interaction of two psychologically whole selves, the Bakers begin with the premise of their own tendency to *pretend to* completeness (while actually being incomplete) and see conflict as the inevitable, but controvertible, by-product of the pretension to completeness.

Both the Ables and the Bakers satisfy the demands of the modernist curriculum to construct the self as a system or form. At the heart of the difference between their constructions of conflict are these two related questions about that self: (1) Do we see the self-as-system as complete and whole or do we regard the self-as-system as incomplete, only a partial construction of all that the self is? (2) Do we identify with the self-as-form (which self then *interacts with* other selves-as-forms) or do we identify with the process of form creation (which brings forms into being and subtends their relationship)? Another way of putting this second question is: Do we take as prior the *elements of* a relationship (which then enter into relationship) or *the relationship itself* (which creates its elements)?

The idea that a relationship can be prior to its parts may sound strange, but when we start to think about it, the idea that things exist first and then enter into relationship can come to sound just as strange.[1] An example I have often used is this: Imagine a glass cylinder or tube that is open at each end lying on its side. Inside the cylinder is a marble. We are going to push the cylinder so that it is rolling, and we wonder out of which of the cylinder's two ends the marble will escape. As we discuss this, it is perfectly natural for us to distinguish between the two ends or openings of the cylinder (if we are standing on the same side of the cylinder, we might refer to them as the "right opening" and the "left opening"). If we began to pay a lot of attention to these two openings (perhaps they are not identically shaped and we think one end is a more likely exit for the marble) we could conclude that what the cylinder really is, is two openings connected by a glass tube. We could see the glass tube as the connector or relater of the two ends. Although this is an unfortunately static, reified image of a relationship, the tube is, in a sense, the bond or link between the parts, the two ends. The parts "have

	SUBJECT	OBJECT	UNDERLYING STRUCTURE	LINES OF DEVELOPMENT
			Single Point/Immediate/Atomistic	**K** COGNITIVE
				E INTERPERSONAL
				Y INTRAPERSONAL
1	PERCEPTIONS *Fantasy*	Movement		
	SOCIAL PERCEPTIONS			
	IMPULSES	Sensation	●	
2	CONCRETE *Actuality* Data, Cause-and-Effect	Perceptions	Durable Category	
	POINT OF VIEW **Role-Concept** **Simple Reciprocity (tit-for-tat)**	Social Perceptions		
	ENDURING DISPOSITIONS Needs, Preferences Self Concept	Impulses		
3	ABSTRACTIONS *Ideality* Inference, Generalization Hypothesis, Proposition Ideals, Values	Concrete	Cross-Categorical Trans-Categorical	
	MUTUALITY/INTERPERSONALISM **Role Consciousness** **Mutual Reciprocity**	Point of View		
	INNER STATES Subjectivity, Self-Consciousness	Enduring Dispositions Needs, Preferences		

TRADITIONALISM

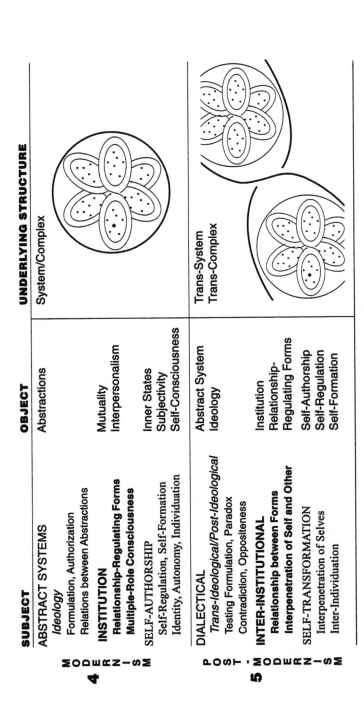

SUBJECT	OBJECT	UNDERLYING STRUCTURE
4 — **M O D E R N I S M** **ABSTRACT SYSTEMS** *Ideology* Formulation, Authorization Relations between Abstractions **INSTITUTION** Relationship-Regulating Forms Multiple-Role Consciousness **SELF-AUTHORSHIP** Self-Regulation, Self-Formation Identity, Autonomy, Individuation	Abstractions Mutuality Interpersonalism Inner States Subjectivity Self-Consciousness	System/Complex
5 — **P O S T - M O D E R N I S M** **DIALECTICAL** *Trans-Ideological/Post-Ideological* Testing Formulation, Paradox Contradiction, Oppositeness **INTER-INSTITUTIONAL** Relationship between Forms Interpenetration of Self and Other **SELF-TRANSFORMATION** Interpenetration of Selves Inter-Individuation	Abstract System Ideology Institution Relationship- Regulating Forms Self-Authorship Self-Regulation Self-Formation	Trans-System Trans-Complex

Figure 9.1 The Five Orders of Consciousness

a relationship" to each other and the tube defines it. But it would make just as much sense to say, "Wait a minute! The cylinder does not *connect* the two openings. There wouldn't be any openings without the cylinder. It *creates* the openings. All there really is, is one thing, a cylinder. The cylinder has the openings, not the other way around. The relationship has the parts. The parts do not have a relationship."

These kinds of questions—about the completeness or priority of the self-as-a-form—are actually hiding behind all manner of contemporary analyses of adult experience. Whether it is marriage psychologists or labor mediators thinking about conflict, educational theorists or family therapy theorists thinking about the very usefulness of a concept like the self, critical theorists thinking about the ideological nature of our intellectual disciplines, political scientists thinking about leadership and followership, or a host of others, questions like these underlie the distinctions these theorists are making between two different ways of understanding. These kinds of questions—about the completeness or priority of the self-as-form—are in fact epistemological questions about the difference between the fourth and fifth orders of consciousness. The question "Do we take as prior the self-as-form or the process of form creation?" could as easily read "Do we take *as subject* the self-as-form (the fourth order) or do we take the self-as-form *as object* (the fifth order)?" And these same kinds of questions, it is also true, go directly to the distinction between modernism and postmodernism. What "postmodernism" even is, is still up for grabs and will continue to be so until we stop calling it "postmodernism" and are able to name what it is rather than only what it is not.

In these last two chapters I am going to state what I think postmodernism is. I am going to suggest that at the frontiers of our various noncommunicating disciplines, which implicitly or explicitly say what we must do to be successful in our private and public lives, there is, in fact, a collection of mental demands that are different from those calling for personal authority. Like the demands of modernism, these can also be analyzed in terms of their epistemological complexity. By considering the postmodern curriculum in three exemplary areas— the meaning of conflict or difference, good leadership, and knowledge creation—I hope to demonstrate what these curricular demands all have in common: they all require an order of consciousness that is able to subordinate or relativize *systemic knowing* (the fourth order); they all require that we move systemic knowing from *subject* to *object*. In other words, they are all "beyond" the fourth order.

How the curricular demands differ is that some represent an earlier, and some a later, moment in the transformation from the fourth to the fifth order of consciousness. In other words, I am going to suggest that what we call "postmodernism" is not just a *different* way of thinking, it is identifiable on the continuum of the evolution of consciousness; that the different "strands" or "faces" of postmodernism others have identified correspond to slightly different places on this continuum; that what postmodernism is "post" to is the fourth order of consciousness. Such an analysis will lead us naturally to a set of perplexing implications and questions: If a given threshold of consciousness must be reached in order to comprehend the implicit demands of postmodernism, what does it mean that, although we are told we are living in "a postmodern age," the best empirical evidence shows that very few of us have actually reached this threshold and even then never before midlife? Thinking of the "students" of this curriculum, how will postmodern demands be experienced when understood according to a traditional or modernist consciousness? Thinking of the "teachers" of this curriculum, if the growing edge for most adults is not the move to postmodernism but to modernism, then even if their long-range goal is that more people master the *post*modern curriculum, won't they need to have far greater sympathy and respect for the process of mastering modernism?

What are the unrecognized demands of this newer curriculum? We might return for a bit to the subject of conflict not as it applies to the private realm of intimate relations but as it applies to the public realm of social controversy and protracted dispute. Developments in the field of conflict resolution among representatives of antagonistic positions, groups, or states mirror the distinction between the marriages of the Ables and the Bakers.

Since the 1960s, a group of social scientists has endeavored to develop a theory and practice for creating productive contexts in which disputing parties can break the patterns of stalemate or escalation of their conflict.[2] Though the various action-research projects differ somewhat among themselves, they all share features of the Ables' mutually respectful, enlightened, and modernist approach to conflict. Coming largely from the field of social psychology rather than international diplomacy or labor negotiation, these ground-breaking pioneers suggest that when conflicting parties can recognize each other's needs, views, and fears, and consider solutions which reassure the other that their most precious interests will be respected, a new dynamic for unsticking their conflictual relationship can replace the traditional dynamics of threat, deterrence, and force. These traditional dynamics arise from unilateral strategic analyses of advantage and vulnerability and essentially assume that the only changes that will occur in protracted conflicts are changes in behavior, not changes in attitude.

In contrast, the social psychologists, like the Ables, who try to avoid simply finding ways to get the other to mold to their preference, seek ways to change the actual thinking and feeling of each party. It should also be noted that, like the Ables, the social psychologists assume the wholeness and distinctness of the conflicting parties. That is, the kind of learning they promote is about the willingness and ability of each party to understand and respect the position of the other. Although in their writings they often refer to their goal of "transforming" the relationship, what they are actually transforming are the attitudes each party has about the other's capacity to respect their position, not the positions themselves. The changes in thinking and feeling they effect involve improved understanding of the other's and one's own position, altered attitudes about the other's capacity and willingness to understand one's own position, and new thinking about the possibility of developing solutions that preserve the most precious features of each other's positions. In situations of protracted conflict, especially in the international arena, such changes could be of historic and life-saving proportion.

But these changes also differ from those the Bakers attempt in their disputes and those that are implicitly sought by newer contributors to the field of public dispute. It is one thing to seek a process for resolution in which each side respectfully visits the preconstructed constraints and genius of the other's way of seeing the world, and each transforms its attitude about the possibility of solutions that preserve the integrity of both (the so-called "win-win" solution). It is quite another to seek a process that uses the conflict to transform one's identification with one's own "side," one's sense of its inevitability or intractable integrity, one's need to have that side "win" even if the other side also wins. It is one thing to provide mutual assurance of respect for the *integrity* of the other's position. It is another thing to mutually suspect that what passes for integrity (one's own and the other's) is also *ideology*, necessarily partial, and an unworthy prize, finally, over which to risk one's entire treasure.

This second, postmodern approach to conflict and its resolution does not assume the wholeness, distinctness, or priority of the competing parties. It does not begin the story with, "Once upon a time there was Position X, and it lived and existed happily enough until one day it ran into Position Not-X, and then there was a conflict." Even the most enlightened, nonstrategic, nonpower-based approaches to conflict implicitly start the story this way and confirm, in their practice designs, the disputants' perceptions of the logical priority of their distinct existences. Though much is made of the distinction between the win-lose and win-win processes of conflict resolution—and the distinction *is* an important one—a postmodern conception suggests that both positions (win-win and win-lose) share an axiomatic faith in the prior distinctness of the disputing parties.

Thus, whether the conflictual process is marked by domination, a willingness to meet in the middle, or even a commitment to mutually preserving win-win results, any of the outcomes of these processes is guaranteed to keep hidden from view, and thus untransformed, the assumption-taken-as-truth: that each side has no need of the other for its existence and that their relationship is an after-the-fact inconvenience with which they must contend. Even from the most enlightened of these perspectives, the designs for dispute resolution will confirm each party's quite natural feeling that "my life, or my people's life, would be so much better if the other side would just disappear, but since the protracted nature of our conflict suggests they will not, we have to find the best resolution possible."

The postmodern view suggests a quite different conception, something more like this: "The protracted nature of our conflict suggests not just that the other side will not go away, but that it probably *should* not. The conflict is a likely consequence of one or both of us making prior, true, distinct, and whole our partial position. The conflict is potentially a reminder of our tendency to pretend to completeness when we are in fact incomplete. We may have this conflict because we need it to recover our truer complexity."

From the postmodern view, the relationship Palestinians and Israelis, pro-choice and pro-life proponents, environmentalists and land developers, rich and poor, black and white, men and women all find them-selves in is emphatically *not* an after-the-fact matter in which each side just happens to be in a conflict because, in addition to the existence of its own take on the world, there just happens, inconveniently enough, to be a contrary take that it runs into. The "left opening" of the hollow cylinder does not just "happen to" have a relationship with the right opening; the "left opening" has its very existence *because of* the "rela-tionship," because of the cylinder. From the postmodern view, the conflictual relationship creates the parties; the parties do not create the relationship.

To this the modernist replies, "Wait a minute. If the conflictual rela-tionship exists prior to the parts, how come many disputants not only experience their independence and self-sufficiency from their opponent once the conflict is joined, but also experience a long history of happily existing before they ever knew of or ever experienced themselves as in a conflictual relationship with their opponent? How can my conflictual relationship with a poor person, a black person, or a woman, be prior to my existence as rich or white or male, when I've been rich or white or male for a long time without any experience of being in a conflictual relationship with these others?"

To this the postmodernist replies, "The fact that you haven't experi-enced a conflictual relationship before now certainly doesn't mean it hasn't existed before now. If you are in the more powerful position in this relationship, you might not have experienced any pain that would cause you to even be aware of the existence of the relationship, and if you are in the less powerful position, you may have had a need *not* to experience your pain in terms of a relationship to someone or some-thing to whom you would then have to see yourself as opposed."

In essence, the postmodern view bids disputants to do several things: (1) consider that your protracted conflict is a signal that you and your opponent have probably become identified with the poles of the conflict; (2) consider that the relationship in which you find yourself is not the inconvenient result of the existence of an opposing view but the expression of your own incompleteness taken as completeness; (3) value the relationship, miserable though it might feel, as an opportunity to live out your own multiplicity; and thus, (4) focus on ways to let the conflictual relationship transform the parties rather than on the parties resolving the conflict. Postmodernism suggests a kind of "conflict resolution" in which the Palestinian discovers her own Israeli-ness, the rich man discovers his poverty, the woman discovers the man inside her.[3]

Though they don't spell it out quite this overtly, this approach to conflict resolution is implicit in the work of those who come to the field from family therapy theory[4] and the Chris Argyris wing of organizational theory.[5] Except for William Torbert, who explicitly incorporates a constructive-developmental perspective, none of the psychological approaches to conflict resolution—not the efforts of pioneering social psychologists, nor the more recent work of the family therapists or the organization developmentalists—attend to the individual's development of consciousness. As a result, none of these theorist-practitioners is in a position to consider the demands their respective curricula make on mental capacity or to assess a person's readiness to engage their designs.

Argyris, however, has been candid in reporting that even highly advantaged, graduate-educated, organizationally high-ranking adults have a great deal of difficulty mastering—or simply cannot master—what it is he is teaching.[6] But this should be no surprise, because what he and the other postmodern conflict resolutionists are asking people to do is to organize experience at a level of complexity beyond the fourth order of consciousness, something few people are yet able to do.[7] Refusing to see oneself or the other as a single system or form, regarding the premise of completeness as a tempting pretense, constructing the process of interacting as *prior* to the existence of the form or system, facing protracted conflict as a likely sign of one's own identification with false assumptions of wholeness, distinctness, completeness, or priority—all of these ways of constructing reality require that the epistemological organization of system, form, or theory be relativized, moved from subject in one's knowing to object in one's knowing.[8] They all require a "trans-systemic," "multiform," or "cross-theoretical" epistemological organization. In other words, they all require the fifth order of consciousness.

In an illuminating essay, Ronald Heifetz and Riley Sinder review the various conceptions of leadership and criteria for leadership success that exist in their field.[9] They note a remarkable convergence of expectations among contributors to the topic irrespective of their political, ideological, or scholarly differences. The successful leader, these thinkers agree, must combine two talents: an ability to craft and communicate a coherent vision, mission, or purpose; and an ability to recruit people to take out membership in, ownership of, or identification with that vision, mission, or purpose. The first requires powers of conception and communication; the second tests interpersonal skills and capacities. We can imagine people who might be especially talented in one of these abilities, but who would still fail as leaders because they lacked the other.

Although these expectations might be directed to different aspects of personal competence, together they form a single demand on consciousness. In somewhat different terms they are an echo of the fourth order expectation upon parents as leaders of the family to shape a value-generating vision or theory by which the family will be led, and to induct their followers, the younger generation, into this vision. Heifetz and Sinder's review amounts to yet another identification of the pervasive modernist demand for fourth order consciousness in yet another domain, this time that of public leadership.

But Heifetz and Sinder's purpose in their essay is to propose an alternative to the highly agreed-upon vision. Here, in what amounts to quite a different but equally unacknowledged mental claim, they begin to lay out the postmodern "honors curriculum" for reconceiving the successful leader. However benign, admirable, or "inclusive" the leader's vision happens to be, it is still a unilaterally constructed one that comes into existence prior to its contact with prospective followers. From the view of established wisdom—the modernist view—this preconstructed vision is the leader's "gift," it is the "goods" she has to deliver, the way she shows she's got the right stuff to be taken seriously as a leader.

In contrast, Heifetz and Sinder call for an exercise of leadership on behalf of *providing a context* in which all interested parties, the leader included, can *together* create a vision, mission, or purpose they can collectively uphold. Heifetz and Sinder are aware, as Lahey and I have discussed,[10] that this kind of leadership practice will have to contend with the dismay of those followers who have a different construction of what a leader should be and do. "What kind of a leader are you?!" some people will certainly think. "You say you want to lead us to a better place, but when we say, 'We're ready to follow you, show us the way, show us your plan,' you say, 'We need to figure that out together.' So what you're saying is you haven't *got* a plan! If you've got nothing to stand up for, how can you lead us? And if you can't lead us, don't stand up and say you can!"

In reply, whether she says it only to herself or to those who are challenging her, the kind of leader Heifetz and Sinder are proposing might think something like this: "I agree with you that I don't have a whole cut-and-dried plan for how we can get to where we want to go. I have my ideas to add, of course, but so do you. And I even agree that a person has no business posing as a leader if he doesn't have something to stand up for. But that's exactly why I think I *am* a leader, why I think I'm actually *being* a leader right now in refusing to treat my ideas and plans as whole and complete, however internally consistent and comprehensive they may be in their own terms. I *am* standing up for something right now, for the importance of our suffering through this inevitably frustrating and awkward process of cobbling together a collectively created plan for getting where we want to go. And once we have the plan, you know what? I'll want to lead by continuing to stand up for the likelihood of *its* incompleteness, and for our need to keep seeking the contradictions by which it will be nourished and grow."

The leader Heifetz and Sinder describe in their essay not only transcends an identification with the internally consistent system, form, or theory. She goes beyond the discovery we identified in our consideration of conflict that the form is neither prior to its relationship nor complete. Having created a disjunction between herself and fourth order structures (form, system), having dislodged it from the place of "subject" in her epistemology, she has come to a place beyond merely disdaining or deconstructing the claim of any internally consistent theory or form to objective truth. She is doing something more than determining that any self-consistent theory is inevitably "ideological" either in the Mannheimian sense of being a system of explanation or in the Foucaultian sense of being necessarily partial and power-delineating, covertly privileging some interests and disadvantaging others.[11]

In other words, it would be possible to recognize the fact that the established view of the good leader falsely presumes the completeness and priority of the leader's vision and nonetheless have quite a different kind of reply to the claim of the dismayed follower. This reply could be something more like this: "You're right that I have no plan, at least none I would think to offer you as being right for more than me. And maybe you're right that I'm not much of a leader either. Maybe I'm the leader who has come to put an end to leaders. Any plan I would give you, any plan anyone else you'd like to lead you will give you, any plan any of you might come up with, and, for that matter, *any plan we might collaboratively come up with*, is still going to be a plan. It is going to make decisions. It is going to say yes to something and no to something else. It is going to establish what is 'in' and what is 'out.' It is going to create difference, normativeness, hierarchy. It is going to say what is true, what is important, what counts now, and what is not and does not. Thus, any plan is going to be inevitably saturated with ideology and unworthy of your identification with it. Identifying yourself with any plan essentially brings you back to a position of reification and reunion with the assumptions of distinctness, priority, and completeness you have already rejected."

Both of these leaders are "postmodern." Both challenge the unacknowledged epistemological assumptions behind modernist conceptions of the unilateral leader. But while the first finally does have a place to stand and lead from, it is more questionable whether the second one does. Even if it were to be suggested that the second leader *is* leading on behalf of the position that it is important to remain skeptically disengaged from any plan or system for arriving at plans, it can be asked, "But is this not also a position? And if so, by the speaker's own logic, why should it be credited with any authority or granted any legitimacy?" But the second leader has a question, in turn, for the first leader: "Since you *do* have a place to stand and you *do* hold out the hope of a plan, or a system for arriving at plans, with which you would advocate our identification, how is this not a backsliding reification—a reauthorizing or relegitimizing of that which we both know to be false?"

The distinction between these two kinds of postmodern leaders illustrates a lively division of thinking that runs throughout postmodern writing in general, especially recent considerations of knowledge creation. I refer to this division as the distinction between *deconstructive* postmodernism and *reconstructive* postmodernism, but I am certainly not the first to have noticed it. In a wonderfully clarifying essay on the implications of postmodernism for the goals and practice of education, Nicholas Burbules and Suzanne Rice make essentially the same distinction between what they call an "anti-modern" brand of postmodernism (what I call "deconstructive") and a brand of postmodernism that seeks to reelaborate and reappropriate modernist categories (such as reason, freedom, equity, rights, self-determination) on less absolutistic grounds (what I call "reconstructive" postmodernism).[12]

Burbules and Rice begin by identifying three features they say are common to *all* postmodern writing (and in the process they give us a sense of how certain postmodern theorists talk):

> First is the rejection of absolutes. Postmodernists usually insist that there can be no single rationality, no single morality, and no ruling theoretical framework for the analysis of social and political events. The conventional language here, deriving from Jean-François Lyotard, is that there are no "metanarratives" that are not themselves the partial expressions of a particular point of view. As Zygmunt Bauman[13] puts it:
>
> > The philosophers' search for the ultimate system, for the complete order, for the extirpation of everything unknown and unruly, stems from the dream of having a firm soil and a secure home, and leads to closing down the obstinately infinite human potential. Such search for the universal cannot but degenerate into a ruthless clamp-down on human possibilities.
>
> Second is the perceived saturation of all social and political discourses with power or dominance. Any metanarrative is taken to be synonymous with the hegemony of a social and political order. [As Lather puts it:]
>
> > To learn to see not only what we do but also what structures what we do, to deconstruct how ideological and institutional power play in our own practices, to recognize the partiality and open-endedness of our own efforts, all of this is to examine the discourses within which we are caught up. Imploding canons and foregrounding the power/knowledge nexus by deconstructing "natural" hierarchies demonstrate that what had seemed transparent and unquestionable is neither. All of this is to participate in the radical unsettling that is postmodernism in ways that have profound implications for pedagogy and curriculum . . . In this context of ferment, educational inquiry is increasingly viewed as no more outside the power/knowledge nexus than any other human enterprise.[14]
>
> A third idea that recurs in the Postmodern literature is the celebration of "difference." Rather than attempting to judge or prioritize the explanatory or political significance of given elements in a social situation, the Postmodern trend is to argue that, because all signifiers are mere constructions, there is no clear reason to grant any one special significance or value over others. [Bauman again:]
>
> > What the inherently polysemous and controversial idea of *postmodernity* most often refers to . . . is first and foremost an acceptance of the ineradicable plurality of the world—not a temporary state on the road to the not-yet-attained perfection, sooner or later to

be left behind, but the constitutive quality of existence. By the same token, postmodernity means a resolute emancipation from the characteristically modern urge to overcome difference and promote sameness . . . In the plural and pluralistic world of postmodernity, every form of life is *permitted on principle;* or, rather, no agreed principles are evident which may render any form of life impermissible.[15]

All three of these ways of thinking reflect the disjoining of fourth order "system" from its ultimacy as epistemological *subject*. Each way of thinking relativizes the attributions of wholeness, distinctness, and priority. But, having thus relativized the truth of the form or system—that is, having discovered its subjectivity—what now becomes the nature of one's knowing?

One pattern is forever repeated in the evolution of our structures of knowing, whether we are looking at mental development in infancy or the highly elaborated order of consciousness that underlies postmodernism. That pattern can be described like this: *differentiation always precedes integration*. How could it be otherwise? Before we can reconnect to, internalize, or integrate something with which we were originally fused, we must first distinguish ourselves from it. The two-year-old's "No" is literally its first *objection*, a declaration that it is *making into object* the people and things with which it had formerly identified itself. What can feel to the parents like a contrariness directed at *them* is as much directed at the child's old organization of self, the expression of a need to maintain a hard-won and still tenuous differentiation. When the disjunction comes to feel secure, and closeness to the parents no longer threatens reabsorption into the old organization, the negativism subsides and the child can reconnect with the parents on new terms. Differentiation precedes integration, that is, it simply precedes it in time; I do not intend to imply any *philosophical* priority.

This same pattern is observable in all the qualitative evolutions of mind subject-object psychology studies. In our longitudinal study of adult development, in which a majority of the subjects are gradually navigating the evolution from the third to the fourth order, one continually sees that a critique of one's identification with the values and loyalties of one's cultural or psychosocial surround precedes the construction of a fourth order system that can act upon those values, set them aside, or modify and reappropriate them to a new place within a more encompassing organization. Differentiation precedes integration. Conflict precedes *re-solution*. This does not mean that actual social or personal distance must precede relational reconnection, as in Shakespeare's *Macbeth:* "In order to make Society the sweeter welcome / we will keep ourselves till suppertime alone." The differentiation that must precede integration is epistemological. Whether or not it is also accompanied by separation from real persons and social arrangements depends on the support those persons and social arrangements are able to extend to the processes of evolution.

Likewise, the three "common" features of postmodernist thinking that Burbules and Rice identify all reflect the fact that no matter what else has happened to one's way of knowing, one has differentiated from the fourth order system. But what about the next question: Is postmodern thinking also about a new kind of integration? For the kind of postmodern thinking Burbules and Rice call "antimodernism" it is not:

> The antimodernist position is characterized by a strong antipathy to the language, issues, and values of modernism . . . it defines itself in opposition to modernism, not as a position growing out of and moving beyond modernist concerns. Hence it is not concerned with recapturing and reformulating modern values, such as reason or equality, but with deconstructing them. Not surprisingly, this tradition in particular has been more convincing in pointing out the limitations and contradictions of modernism than in reformulating positive alternatives.[16]

Antimodernism is clearly the position of differentiation before integration, a position whose energy is necessarily devoted to maintaining a valuable disjunction and whose gift it is to make clear the good reasons for doing so. The prospect of reconnection with what one is working hard to differentiate from can only be known at this position in the unacceptable terms of reabsorption into a former discredited organization. The problem with this position is that, although it makes very clear where one should not stand, it has no place where it can stand, indeed, no place where it can stand in order to promote the values implied in its differentiation. Although Burbules and Rice tell us that postmodern thinking does "not attempt to judge or prioritize the explanatory significance" of various differences, the most valuable part of their essay, to my mind, finds them judging and prioritizing the difference between this antimodern brand of postmodernism and another, more integrating brand of postmodernism:

> We do not question for a moment the relations of dominance, or histories of conflict and hostility, or gulfs of non-understanding or mis-

understanding across differences, that undercut conventional educational aims and practices. Indeed, identifying and criticizing these is the necessary starting point for any new thinking on the problems of education. But unless one conceives freedom only negatively (as the mere avoidance or removal of such impediments), it is not clear what follows from this critique for educational or political practice. Antimodernism lacks a clear conception of a "positive freedom" that identifies social conditions in which freer thought and action are possible; lacking this, antimodernism has not been able to articulate a clear and defensible educational theory . . . The view we have termed antimodernism has been largely content with emphasizing points of critique. The educational practices that are generated from the antimodern perspective seem largely dependent upon the preferences of those who advance them. This is not necessarily to denigrate such practices, but merely to stress, again, that antimodernism cannot justify them by reference to generalizable values. As a result, value assumptions that actually do underlie these practices are frequently left implicit and unexamined . . . On the one hand, post-modernism provides strong reasons for valuing diversity, for not assuming homogeneity when it does not exist, and for avoiding modes of discursive and non-discursive practice that implicitly or explicitly exclude subjects who do not participate in dominant modes of thought, speech, and action. This position might even be pushed a step further, to insist that, given occasions of conflict and misunderstanding, we ought to err on the side of respecting the self-identification and worldview of others, especially for members of groups who have been traditionally *told* who they are, what is true, and what is good for them.

However, at some points in the literature, this position lapses over into claims that are much more problematic. Specifically, the celebration of difference becomes a presumption of incommensurability, a denial of the possibility of inter-subjective understanding, and an exaggerated critique that *any* attempt to establish reasonable and consensual discourse across difference inevitably involves the imposition of dominant groups' values, beliefs, and modes of discourse upon others. These views are antimodern in their rejection of such goals as dialogue, reasonableness, and fair treatment of alternative points of view; such legacies of the modernist tradition are not only regarded as difficult and sometimes impossible to attain—which they are—but as actually undesirable ends.

In our view, this antimodernist position is unsustainable either intellectually or practically. It derives from a deep misunderstanding of the nature of difference and has counter-educational implications for pedagogy. The literature that espouses this view is often internally contradictory, suggesting that such a severe critique is difficult to sustain consistently; many authors who advocate strong antimodern critiques later find themselves reversing direction when the time comes to offer positive recommendations.[17]

In contrast to "antimodernism," and without acknowledging that they are violating a supposed postmodern proscription against judging and prioritizing among differences, Burbules and Rice clearly prefer what I call a "reconstructive postmodernism," one that seeks not only a differentiation from the forms of modernism but their reintegration into a new way of knowing that abjures the absolutism of the forms, that does not take the forms as complete, distinct, or prior.

> There is no reason to assume that dialogue across differences [necessarily] involves either eliminating those differences or imposing one group's views on others; dialogue that leads to understanding, cooperation, and accommodation can sustain differences within a broader compact of toleration and respect. Thus what we need is not an antimodern denial of community, but a postmodern grounding of community on more flexible and less homogeneous assumptions . . .
>
> As Nancy Harstock has pointed out, it is exceedingly ironic that at the very time that traditionally disadvantaged groups are beginning to find their voice, an epistemological view has gained currency that legitimates relativizing their claims to credibility and respect.[18]

The distinction between deconstructive and reconstructive postmodernism introduces the possibility that not every "theory," "stand," or "way" is necessarily absolutistic or ideological. Not every "differencing," normatizing, or hierarchizing is necessarily a hidden and arbitrary privileging of a special interest. Not every kind of judging or prioritizing is impermissible modernist domination. To return to the imagined dialogue between the two postmodern leaders, the possibility of a reconstructive postmodernism suggests that one could in fact advocate identification with a theory, a stand, or a way, and that such advocacy need not necessarily be a backsliding reification of one kind of modernist authority or another. An example would be a theory that was really a theory about theory-making, a theory that was mindful of the tendency of any intellectual system to reify itself, to identify internal consistency with validity, to call its fourth order brand of subjectivity "objectivity." The expression of such a theory's "maturity" would not be the modernist capacity to defend itself against all challenges, to demonstrate how all data gathered to it can find a place within it, but to assume its incompleteness and seek out contradiction by which to nourish the ongoing process of its reconstruction.[19]

This distinction between a deconstructive and a reconstructive relation to theory suggests two dramatically different postmodern relationships to the intellectual disciplines. Like the two postmodern leaders I have described, one uses the limits of a given discipline, theory, or scholarly approach to demonstrate its unacknowledged ideological partiality and therefore its unacceptability. This is the stance of the deconstructive university professor, who has essentially come to teach that any of our disciplines, theories, or scholarly approaches is ultimately unworthy of our commitment to it, and, by implication, that ultimately the only intellectual activity that is worthy is deconstruction. By this definition, the well-educated person would be the one who has discovered the separate bases for deconstructing the widest range of intellectual disciplines.

In contrast, the reconstructive approach would have an equal interest in bringing the limits of the disciplines and its theories to center stage in our learning, but for the purpose of nourishing the very process of reconstructing the disciplines and their theories. We could argue that the purpose of this reconstructing—this creating of better and better theory—is to arrive eventually at the Complete Theory, but a truly reconstructive view would actually be more likely to associate such a "victory" with death. As long as life goes on, the process will need to go on. We nourish reconstruction not as a means to the end of the Complete Theory but as an end in itself. When we teach the disciplines or their theories in this fashion, they become more than procedures for authorizing and validating knowledge. They become procedures about the reconstruction of their procedures. The disciplines become generative. They become truer to life.[20]

A theory that is also a theory about theory-making and a stand-taking that is also about the *way* we take a stand will by necessity make judgments about and deprioritize those procedures, theories, and stands that are not self-conscious about their own tendency toward absolutism. Although they are judgmental and hierarchizing in this fashion, they themselves are not necessarily being absolutistic. Thus, the fact that a theory or system does indeed "privilege" or "valorize" something (two favorite postmodern words) is *not* sufficient evidence that it is modern, absolutistic, partial, or ideological.

In the same way we need to reconsider equating generalization and universality with impermissible modernist absolutism. Not every generalization or proposed group universal is necessarily a forcing of the excluded or marginalized into terms or categories that fit only the dominant group. Universals or generalizations—about the processes of meaning-making, for example (that differentiation precedes integration or that negentropic processes of greater complexity, increased organization, and more highly concentrated energy characterize all living systems) or about the forms of meaning-making (that they can be analyzed with respect to the question of what they can look at, or take as object, and what they are embedded in, or take as subject)—are not necessarily, ipso facto, absolutistic (whereas the assumption that they are or must be *is* absolutistic!).

Reconstructive postmodernism thus reopens the possibility that some kinds of normativeness, hierarchizing, privileging, generalizing, and universalizing are not only compatible with a postideological view of the world, they are necessary for sustaining it. Once these possibilities have been reopened, it is only a quantitative, not a qualitative leap for postmodernists to consider the outlandish and heretical idea that a theory such as the one I have outlined in this book—in spite of the judgments, generalizations, and claims to universality it makes and in spite of its unabashed privileging of "complexity"—is at least potentially an ally, not an enemy of postmodernism.

Indeed, subject-object theory might be much more than that. It may actually be a sympathetic guide to the long and arduous labor of gradually creating a postmodern view of the world. For the self may indeed be multiple, not unitary, as postmodernists are fond of arguing, but *not* right away. Multiselved postmodern parents do not mate and give birth to multiselved postmodern babies. Half a lifetime, if not more, precedes these discoveries. And good company is required every step of the way.

And good company—sympathetic support—is required even after one has left the modern world behind. Burbules and Rice at times sound downright put out with the antimodernists. They call the antimodernist position "unsustainable," "deriving from a deep misunderstanding," "countereducational," "exaggerating," "unnecessarily prejudicial," "counterproductive," and "oversimplifying." How would they help these wrong-headed folk to give up the error of their ways? Are they hoping to argue the antimodernists out of their view by the sheer force of their presentation of the alternative? Do they expect a deconstructive modernist to read their essay and slap himself on the forehead exclaiming, "But of course! Why didn't I see this all along? My deconstructionist thinking is flawed. I'm switching to reconstructivism!"? I doubt it. But what happens if they take seriously the possibility that the antimodernist position actually "derives" less from any "deep misunderstanding" than from the fact that it represents an earlier stage of complexity in the gradual evolution from the fourth to the fifth order of consciousness?

The first thing Burbules and Rice might reconsider is their claim that the position is "unsustainable." Anyone making this claim should read through our years of subject-object interview transcripts. ("Do you think Senator Humphrey's position on the war is untenable?" Eugene McCarthy was asked by an interviewer during a presidential primary season. "Well, I don't think we can say it's *untenable*," the former Jesuit and Latin-literate McCarthy responded, "because he's been *holding* to it for quite a while now.") The antimodern position may be unsustainable from the standard of fifth order logic, but from its own position (just enough beyond the fourth order to critique its limits but not yet able to create a new order) it is completely sustainable—and the self is sustained in creating the world in this way. The antimodernist cannot move from a deconstructive to a reconstructive position without disturbing the self.

The next thing Burbules and Rice might do is to stop characterizing the antimodern position as "oversimplifying." This term suggests that the antimodernist not only expresses a simpler order of mental complexity but could alter it as if it were an "error" he could "correct" without cost. If Burbules and Rice tried on a developmental formulation of the distinction between the two positions, they would see that characterizations like "overly simple" and "counterproductive" are egocentric on their part; that is, they view the situation only from their own vantage point, not from that of the antimodernists, whose position is anything but simple to them and is at the same time completely "productive" of the mind's integrity as the mind is currently constituted.

Finally, if they were to conduct their own "dialogue across differences" (the title of their essay) in this constructive-developmental way, it would promote the possibility of dwelling for a time in the home of the other and developing an empathy for the coherence of the other's position and the costs that leaving it might entail. This kind of dialogue across difference might help in fashioning a bridge that is more respectfully anchored on both sides of the chasm, instead of assuming that such a bridge already exists and wondering why the other has not long ago walked over it.

I do not say all this to chastise Burbules and Rice, whose essay I obviously admire. Their annoyance with antimodernism I can readily identify in myself, since I have spent twenty years developing a theory that turns to dust in antimodernist hands; yet I notice that my own sense of annoyance is transformed to one of connection when I take seriously the developmental possibility. Their preference for reconstructive postmodernism is one I share. My intention is to resolve the unrecognized contradictions of their essay by showing how it is possible for us to enter a judging, prioritizing, generalizing, and universalizing theory like subject-object psychology *on behalf of* the postmodern project.

Let me conclude this chapter by summing up some of the specific ways subject-object theory might in fact be helpful. First, it demonstrates that privileging consciousness complexity (which subject-object psychology certainly does) need not necessarily entail absolutism. On the contrary, it can be a saving tool for avoiding absolutism. And it can help us preserve the distinction between the rejection of absolutes on the one hand, and the rejection of the possibility of any nonabsolutist ground on the other.

Second, subject-object theory makes explicit the conditions under which a judging and status-conferring relationship to difference (such as Burbules and Rice construct) is in fact consistent with postmodernism. For example, antimodernist positions are prized ahead of modernist positions and reconstructive postmodern positions are prized ahead of antimodernist positions, but not because the advantaged position is closer to some dominating, ideological absolute. Rather, each is preferred because it is closer to a position that in fact protects us from dominating, ideological absolutes. Constructions beyond the complexity of the fourth order of consciousness are prized above those embedded in the fourth order, and fifth order constructions are prized above those that are just a little beyond the fourth order, but not because complexity itself is a virtue. They assume an advantaged position because with each, the next way of constructing reality provides even more protection from the captivation and dominance of other reality constructions.

Finally, subject-object theory makes operational the criteria for determining whether one position is actually more complex than the other or merely fancies itself so. A status-conferring or judging relationship to difference is still a relationship: it does not have to create a discounting of what is less advantaged; it creates instead a connection to it. If one position is actually more complex than the other, it should be able to understand the other's position *on the other's own terms,* to extend empathy for the costs involved in altering that position, and to provide support for, rather than dismissal of, the prior position. If the positions are of equal complexity, each may be able to understand the other, but neither can build the bridge between orders of consciousness its false claim to superiority would imply. If one position is actually less complex than the other, it should not even be able to understand the other on terms that allow the other to feel that its being is adequately understood.

10

On Being Good Company for the Wrong Journey

At the leading edge of many intellectual fields and scholarly discourses—as I suggested in our consideration of conflict and difference, leadership, and the creation of knowledge in the last chapter—we can find yet another collection of expectations and demands on the minds of contemporary adults. What these diverse claims have in common is this: they all require a degree of complexity that goes *beyond* the fourth order of consciousness. Never mind that all of us will spend some portion of our adult lives overmatched by the demands of modernism, the compulsory "major" in our culture's curriculum. Never mind that at any given moment, probably one-half to two-thirds of us do not really understand that curriculum. It now appears that the experience of being both grown-up and in over our heads is not limited to that period when our way of organizing reality is less complicated than the fourth order. Even if we do construct reality at the fourth order, an additional set of assignments awaits! Nearly *all* of us are out of our depth when it comes to the "honors track" in the culture's curriculum: the mental burden of postmodernism.

As this newer set of expectations begins to find expression in an increasing number of public and private arenas of adult life, some among the culture's "faculty"—its intellectual authorities, experts, and discourse shapers—seem to be pushing for a compulsory "double major" or for the honors track to replace the regular course of study entirely. Modernism is "out," postmodernism is "in." With little understanding of how difficult even the regular course of study is for the majority of us, many of those who are pushing the new "curriculum" look down their noses at the epistemological premises of modernism. They are like those nettlesome teachers who, when they were students themselves, were gifted but incompletely socialized know-it-alls, oblivious hand-wavers, who even today might abandon their more supportive roles as teachers when their enthusiasm for some newly discovered aspect of their subject draws their attention from their students' struggles to their own passions. This is not to suggest that their enthusiasm for postmodernism is unwarranted, or their curriculum unmeritable. It is to raise the question of whose curriculum it really is, their students' or their own? It is to suggest that there is an important difference between a teacher who is brilliant and a brilliant teacher.

After all, if a great many of us are working with dignity and difficulty at the gradual transformation from the third to the fourth order, how can we be expected to appreciate or understand a critique of the limits of modernism? Despite the claims of professional postmodern enthusiasts, this curriculum actually engages the real-life struggles of far fewer people than the enthusiasts would have us believe. Misattributing the

"*Just go home and change, Worthington, and spare me any more talk about postmodernism.*"

Drawing by C. Barsotti; © 1990 The New Yorker Magazine, Inc.

nature of people's mental challenges jeopardizes our capacity to receive the actual people we would hope to support. Misattributing the nature of the real mental transformations people are seeking makes us good company for the wrong journey. As I am about to argue, preparations for the advent of the postmodern world are for most of us premature. To paraphrase Elvin Semrad, a renowned trainer of therapists, much of the enthusiasm for postmodernism is "a bright red apple in the wrong orchard."

If the consciousness complexity of postmodern discourse is over our heads, how will it affect us? Some of us will pass through its materials undisturbed. Some of us will be offended by its perceived disregard for the loyalties to which we are still attached or its perceived contempt for the form of personal authority and internal ideology we are just beginning to consolidate. But the most interesting and easily misunderstood relationship to postmodern discourse is this: some of us who are laboring along in our transformation from the third to the fourth order of consciousness—especially those of us who may not be white or male or heterosexual or Christian or middle-class or able-bodied, those of us who are likely to make the perfectly natural and dignifiable move of using our marginalized status as the axis around which we will organize our personal authority—we may very well make use of the materials, rhythms, and critiques of postmodernism not to transcend a fourth order but to *construct* one!

There is a big difference between the challenges to culturally dominant ideologies brought by a postmodern critique of the absolutism of *any* ideology, and those brought by yet another contending ideology. The postmodern analyses of knowledge creation, after all, got their start as much from a restiveness with the absolutism of Marxist ideologies as with that of dominant statism or capitalism. Genuinely postmodern, fifth order analyses should be as disruptive to left-leaning feminist, Afrocentric, or any other liberation ideology as they are to status quo ideologies of the right. But something confusing happens when the rhetoric of postmodernism is used to establish an ideological beachhead on the shores of the status quo. Now traditional theories or social arrangements are called "privileging," "valorizing," "hierarchizing," "advantaging," "normatizing," or "generalizing" not to indicate their identification with ideology in and of itself but to indicate that they are the captives of a particular, repudiated ideology. Now a language that was created originally to proclaim the withering of the authority of absolutism is being used to advance contending brands of absolutism.

Let us consider, for example, one of the most lively "reknowledging" projects in psychology, that of creating nonsexist theories of human development. Nancy Chodorow's *The Reproduction of Mothering*, for example, offers a brilliant and highly influential reconstruction of Freudian theory's account of gender differences.[1] We might watch what happens in her hands to Freud's account of the differing meanings of a little boy's and a little girl's first love relationships.

According to Freud, the little boy's close association with his mother inevitably leads him to desire her for his own, a romance that is blocked by the child's conception of the retaliatory father. Freud recognized that young children take interested note of the genital differences between boys and girls, and his work led him to conclude that little boys fantasize that angry fathers cut off their children's penises. This "decisive" fear, according to Freud, leads the little boy to literally rethink his designs upon his mother. Rather than pursue his actual mother, he "identifies with the aggressor," taking inside himself important aspects of his father. He can be *like* his father and in that way have someone *like* his mother. By internalizing the potentially punishing father he also develops an internal "conscience" or impulse-controller, which will eventually enable him to defer gratification and exercise discipline on behalf of his goals. Freud thus depicts the little boy's repression of his longings for his mother as an important psychological accomplishment that strengthens the self and eventually equips him for the responsibilities of work and authority.

The little girl, in contrast, is another matter. She has a strong relationship with her mother in her first years, but her discovery of genital differences leaves her feeling she has been short-changed, a situation for which Freud believed she tends to hold her mother responsible. While the discovery of genital differences leads to a decisive end of the Oedipal romance for little boys, the same discovery in effect initiates it for little girls, who turn now from their mothers to their fathers. What, then, does Freud presume ends this relationship for little girls? The answer is that there is no answer. Since girls do not have as powerful a motive to end the relationship, it lingers on. The result, according to Freud, is that women have weaker ego boundaries and less capacity for self-control and personal discipline, compromised aptitudes for the world of work and personal authority. A woman's tragic deprivation, according to Freud, is her lack of the experience of repression and the benefits that flow from it.

Chodorow's "post-Freudian" account in no way represents a departure from the Freudian universe but rather a reentering of it to tell, with all the same materials, a different pair of stories. She accepts the central premises concerning the "castration complex" and its role in either ending the Oedipal romance for little boys or initiating it for little girls. Her focus, however, is not so much on the costs of what the little girl does not do but on the costs of what the little boy does do. The little boy must repress or bury his long-lived connection to his mother begun in infancy. The little girl never has to repress her early relationship of depending, attaching, joining to a loved other. She merely adds a connection to the father. But the little boy must *deny* all this as the price of his individuation. It is the little girl, not the little boy, who emerges from the early years with a "strengthened" self:

> Girls emerge from this period with a basis for "empathy" built into their primary definition of self in a way that boys do not. Girls emerge with a stronger basis for experiencing another's needs or feelings as one's own . . . Girls come to experience themselves as less differentiated than boys, as more continuous with and related to the external object-world and as differently oriented to their inner object-world as well. Their experience of self contains more flexible or permeable ego boundaries. Boys come to define themselves as more separate and distinct, with a greater sense of rigid ego boundaries and differentiation. The basic feminine sense of self is connected to the world, the basic masculine sense of self is separate.[2]

Now what exactly has happened here? We are certainly in the presence of a challenge to the Freudian status quo, but of what sort? Like the Pentagon's neutron bomb, which is able to kill the enemy but leave all the buildings completely unharmed, Chodorow has taken an almost reverential stance toward Freudian premises while dramatically altering their meaning. The Freudian edifices (and Oedipuses) are still standing. But Chodorow has made a place for women to walk around in them with heads held high. The story is no longer one of female inadequacy but of female triumph.

To any knowledge community that subscribes to Freudian premises (an academic course or department, a branch of the psychology profession, a mental health clinic), Chodorow's theory offers a way to make room for a huge, devalued subgroup of the human family to be included without paying the price of their dignity and self-respect. The status quo is challenged by this offer. But what sort of challenge is it? Is it a challenge to the status quo to move beyond its absolutism or is it a challenge to include a more diverse humanity within it?

As Chodorow's theory is commonly appropriated, it may tend even to disqualify men from a place of dignity at the same time that it qualifies women. The way her theory is used, and perhaps even the way it is constructed, it certainly does not represent a challenge to ideology in and of itself. It is as generalizing and universalizing as Freud's theory on behalf of both similar and different universals and generalities. And, what is most contrary to postmodern principles, it is as arbitrarily normatizing and privileging. The theories differ only with respect to what is on top in their hierarchies. Freud's ideology, valorizing repression, is a story of male triumph and female inadequacy. Chodorow's theory, or at least the way it is used, valorizing attachment and connection, becomes a story of female triumph and male inadequacy. Both are modernist, absolutist theories.

But still dwelling within the Freudian premises, it is possible to tell the story a completely different third way. What happens if we consider not only that there is no nonarbitrary way of granting superiority to either "connection" or "separateness," but that these very differences, thought to be differences "between men and women," are not absolutely so. What happens, that is, if we consider that both men and women have powerful yearnings to experience themselves as well connected (the yearning to be next to, included, with, a part of) *and* well differentiated (the yearning to be distinct, whole, to experience the self-chosenness of their own initiatives)? What happens if we consider that men and women differ less in their constitutional identification with one of these yearnings than in their historic experience of satisfactorily realizing each of them? From these more fifth order premises, we might tell the story another way.

Let us suppose that a man's early experience, as Freud and Chodorow describe it, actually predisposes him to be more preoccupied with or sensitive to "connection" and that a woman's early experience predisposes her to be more preoccupied with or sensitive to "independence." Or, put another way, these may become the more vulnerable, less realized sides of a duality each shares. A man's worst fear might be to be abandoned or forced to leave, an experience he has endured twice over from early life. He loses his mother once in infancy during the earliest process of separation and individuation (there is reason to believe that mothers, feeling somehow that their sons must be or should be more separate from them than their daughters, let go more emphatically). Then he loses her again in the decisive resolution of the Oedipal relationship. Is it not possible that experiences of, and hopes for, connection place him in jeopardy, an arena of maximum vulnerability, and so he resists dependency and intimacy because he deeply suspects they will go badly again? Similarly, is it not possible that a woman's least comfortable psychological position, again consulting Freud and Chodorow's account of her history, is one in which she makes bids for individuation and autonomy, inasmuch as these have tended to end in her reincorporation, which might be her greatest fear? Neither her efforts at individuation in infancy nor at becoming disentangled from the Oedipal situation have gone completely successfully, and she may most resist venturing into the area of her truest vulnerability, the recreating of thwarted efforts for autonomy. Men, most fearful of unsuccessful connection (that they cannot sustain it, that they will be abandoned), might then overesteem their independence, in part as a consolation prize for the unmet half of their duality. Women, most fearful of unsuccessful separateness (that they cannot sustain it, that they will be thwarted or overheld), might then overesteem closeness and inclusion, in part as a consolation prize for their unmet half of the same duality.

According to this account men are not unconflictedly and happily "separate," nor are women unconflictedly and happily "connected." Each has perforce become a genuis of one half of the human duality. But because they have not successfully integrated both halves, each is ripe for relationships marked by projection and, at the fourth order of consciousness, the open conflict that signals their need to discover their overidentification with their favored half. By failing to integrate both halves, each position is to some extent a depressive one. The "separate" man and the "connected" woman might each wear masks behind which lie issues of compromised self-esteem or unacknowledged rage.

Now, which of these accounts—Freud's, Chodorow's, or this third, postmodern one—strikes the most passionately responsive chord among women who experience themselves as disenfranchised? (A little hint: it isn't Freud's and it isn't the third one.) From the point of view of a person who has been marginalized or devalued within the human family, for anyone who has suffered the disadvantages of being arbitrarily consigned to a less powerful position, the curriculum of postmodernism can quite rightly seem to be the irrelevant privilege or plaything of those who have been provided with support for the mastering of modernism. "Honors" curriculum indeed! For those who have been excluded, postmodernism looks more like extracurricular activities for those who do not have to work after school.

It is no criticism to suggest that the "diversity movement" does not necessarily signal the beginning of postmodernism. The "diversity movement" is a heroic effort to establish support for the disenfranchised to master the same curriculum the rest of the population is seeking to master (and receiving more support in doing so). Its challenges to the status quo are not about the limits of modernism. They are about the disgracefully uneven and systematically rationed supply of support given to adults to master modernism. They are about providing more people, across a more diverse collection of human subcommunities, opportunities for developing their own authentic brand of personal authority.

The development of postsexist, postracist, or posthomophobic knowledges may *not* be postmodern. But they may help us meet the need for fitting support to more people in the transformation from the third to the fourth order of consciousness. The "diversity movement" is a challenge to the culture to create a "school" where *all* students, including adult students, can thrive regardless of gender, race, or sexual orientation. It is a challenge to make a place where all can grow.

Any "community of ideology," whether it is a culturally embedded community, and thus less visible (such as the induction of those favored by the culture into the professions), or a community of counterdominant ideology and thus necessarily visible (such as induction into feminism or Afrocentrism), can serve as a support or a holding environment for evolving the fourth order of consciousness. At their best, such communities provide their members with more than the externally generated values and loyalties with which they become identified. They actually call upon their members to construct a theory of their own oppression and an internalized system or procedure for subjecting all their values and loyalties to reanalysis. In this way, communities of ideology, especially liberation ideologies providing a voice for those who have lived silently on the margins, constitute yet another source of fourth order demands upon contemporary adults. In order to become not just female but feminist, not just black but Afrocentric, not just a victim of a dysfunctional family but an Adult Child of an Alcoholic, one must disjoin from an identification with one's cultural surround and re-fashion these materials into the critical elements of a personal identity or authority, a reinterpretive ideology for authorizing reality.

But for those who are not members of a given counterdominant "community of ideology" but are interested in supporting adult develop-ment—their own and that of others—how might the diversity move-ment be a resource? Whether teachers, managers, leaders, or policy-makers open their doors to the diversity movement, find their doors kicked in by the diversity movement, or experience some confusing combination of the two, the inevitable conflict and challenge the move-ment carries with it can be a source of support to everyone's growth if those who are challenged also see it as an opportunity for them to grow.

How can it be a resource for the growth of those who are challenged? "I don't find *my* experience represented in this course/theory/program of study!" "I don't see enough of my people represented in your of-fice/leadership team/cabinet!" Few teachers, managers, leaders, or pol-icymakers will be able to escape such criticisms of exclusiveness, bias, or political incorrectness of one stripe or another at one time or another. The increasing demand upon us to respond to such challenges "inclu-sively," "nondefensively," or at least respectfully is itself yet another modernist claim on the mind of every person in a position of any au-thority who can be identified with the dominant culture (and this in-cludes nearly everyone in any position of authority, because those who are marginalized in one respect—they are black, for example, or les-bian—are likely to be of the ruling class in another—they are black but heterosexual, or lesbian but white). The fourth order is a necessary if not sufficient condition for meeting these demands.

Mr. and Mrs. Able are able to use their fourth order consciousness to keep from feeling severely wounded by the experience of their differ-ences, to keep from feeling that their relationship is severed by such difference. They see each other and themselves as whole persons, they do not expect that they will share identical "cultures of mind," and they work toward appreciating the distinct contributions each brings to their relationship. But when they run into differences, this is not always easy. They struggle. They are probably not, at every moment, "non-defensive," an overrated phenomenon when it comes to engaging and managing differences. Yet the Ables are not quick to damn each other with characterizations of defensiveness at its first sign, because they have come to trust that such reactions are followed by genuine efforts to solve their differences in ways that leave standing the wholeness, integrity, distinctness, and dignity of each person's "culture of mind."

Constructing the world at the fourth order does not guarantee that we will do this but that we can. There is no reason why the third or more of the adult population that can do this does not use the challenges of the diversity movement to practice doing this. That is, it is important for people in positions of authority, who do construct the world at the fourth order, to see that what is being asked of them by the diversity movement, for the most part, is not over their heads. These are not fifth order claims to surrender their own sense of the wholeness and integrity of their position; they are only claims to recognize the wholeness and distinctness of other people's ways of organizing the same materials. This the fourth order *can* do.

How? It would not be surprising if our first (and probably private) reaction to claims like "My experience is not included" or "My people are not included," or to complaints about our "political incorrectness" was "These complaints are so *ideological!*" Yet the only fair answer to ourselves, if we construct the world at the fourth order, is "But then my way of understanding is *also* ideological. My way differs not because it is any less ideological, but because it is more accepted, legitimated, or familiar." What happens if we view these differences as emanating from a different "culture of mind," a culture which, however strange it may be to us, is nonetheless worthy of our respect? We don't have to "go native" and pretend this is how we make sense. But we also cannot pretend that we are all from the same culture and making sense in exactly the same way. And we cannot pretend that the others are just "visiting" and will soon return "home." They *are* home. If this classroom/office/government/country is their home, too, then we are going to have to find ways to learn the curriculum/get our work done/solve civic problems/live together that leave each culture's distinctness, integrity, wholeness, and dignity still standing.

Developmentally speaking, given where we adults are in our consciousness development, I believe this is a much more realistic way of framing the challenges and possibilities of the diversity movement than to associate it with the admirable but currently out of reach curriculum of postmodernism. This view of the diversity movement expects all contending parties to understand and act like the Ables, not like the Bakers. It does *not* expect contending parties to extend their mutual suspicion of the other to a self-suspicion of their own incompleteness. It does not expect the contending parties to take their contention as a signal that one or both have become overidentified with their single system or ideology. It expects them to "solve their problems," not let their problems solve them. It expects them to fashion a relationship that lets all cultures be respectfully included. It does not expect all to discover the fictive, constructed nature of their distinctness prior to their relationship. If that were to happen, fine; for those who can, fine. But this should not be the expectation.

This view does not mean that the challengers are coopted into the status quo. It means that the old status quo is replaced by a new status quo. It does not mean that blacks can come into the office only if they act white. It does not mean that women's experience is included in the curriculum simply by changing pronouns and making a "Michael" example into a "Mary" example. It means that formerly marginalized people will come into the office, and they will have their own distinctive way of seeing things, setting the agenda, getting the goals accomplished; and it means that these ways will be recognized, acknowledged, and respected, provided that some common ground can be found where all contending "cultures" in their wholeness and distinctness can stand. This common ground becomes, in effect, a new status quo and a new ideology, but a much more wholesome one.

After the 1992 election, when President-elect Bill Clinton was being pressured to live up to his promise to appoint a cabinet that "looks like America," no one was pressuring him to represent the diversity of ideologies and philosophies that exist in America. Even the staunchest advocates of diversity fully expected him to appoint people with whom he could find common ground about how and where to lead the country. What diversity advocates wanted was a group of people with whom such common ground could be found who also represented the country's various genders, races, and ethnicities. They wanted Clinton to expect, recognize, and welcome the different integrities and ways of seeing that these people would bring. But if the president were unable to find common ground with a particular person, would anyone think of advocating that he or she should still be appointed? I doubt that the sort of diversity challengers were advocating was the sort that would be committed to the continuous *disturbing* of a favored ideology. I doubt that it was the sort of diversity that would look at its own differences as opportunities to falsify its assumptions of wholeness or completeness. Perhaps Clinton's cabinet *is* exactly of this sort; I don't know. My point is that what the diversity movement is advocating in business and government is not this kind of postmodern approach to difference. It does not expect employers to hire people with whom they cannot reach common ground. It simply wants more of these people to be nonwhite, nonmale, nonheterosexual, or nonable-bodied. This is a completely realistic, if challenging demand, as are all the fourth order demands of modernism. It is not a postmodern demand, nor would such be realistic at this time.

Similarly, within our universities, those who construct reality at the fourth order ultimately have nothing to fear from diversity challenges because, appearances and claims to the contrary by postmodern enthusiasts notwithstanding, they do not represent fifth order, postmodern demands. A history course on "American History from World War II to the Present" (or a literature course on "The Twentieth-Century American Novel" or a psychology course on "Adolescent Development") that turns out to be the history (or literature or psychology) of only white, male Americans (or white male authors or white male adolescents) *is* exclusive. But how exactly do offended students understand this violation, and how is it repaired?

For many students, it is repaired by representing the excluded identity sufficiently in the readings, lectures, and discussions of the course. For these students, the manner in which history, literature, or psychology are "knowledged"—how we study history, critique literature, tell the story of psychological development—is not the object of criticism. The course becomes acceptably inclusive by subjecting previously excluded experiences and materials to the same legitimizing attention given the original material. But for other students this is not sufficient to repair the violation. The methods and premises, the very ways of "doing history" or "writing the story of human development" are what the students see as exclusive, the possession of the favored class. But even here it is almost never the case that what offended students are asking for is a history or psychology course that will serve as a context for overturning any system of interpretation's claim to integrity or wholeness. Rather, what these students are looking for is the inclusion of more distinct systems of interpretation (a feminist system, an Afrocentric system) to which equivalent respect is paid. We are back to the admirable and wholly modernist "Mr. and Mrs. Able" approach to conflict, here making the challenging but attainable fourth order demand for an attitude of "cross-cultural" respect for differing systems of interpretation.

This demand will require that a faculty member consider the acceptability of a variety of ways of "doing" a field. At the same time, it will require that all contending parties once again establish the common ground of the course, a place where a variety of ideologies can stand (this place-making also colludes in the modernist conviction that such ideologies have a distinctness, integrity, and priority of their own).

If I were offering a psychology course on child development, I might confirm with my students that their election of the course creates as a common ground the learning of those concepts, ideas, and central premises the field regards as its knowledge on the subject. If this knowledge included those premises shared by Freud and Chodorow on the differing course of early attachments for boys and girls, it would be perfectly reasonable for me to expect my students to understand them. They do not have to agree with them, but they do have to understand them. Conversely, it would be perfectly reasonable for my students, once they had grasped these premises, to subject them to interpretations as diverse as those of Freud and Chodorow. Again, I do not have to find any one *interpretation* as compelling as the next, but I do have to find a good *understanding of the premises* treated from one fourth order system of interpretation to be as acceptable as a good understanding of the same premises treated from another. It is the good understanding of the premises, and the capacity to make use of them as elements of a formulation or interpretation, that is our common ground, not their use on behalf of any particular formulation or interpretation.

Of course, the majority of students who challenge the exclusiveness of a curriculum—themselves no different in the complexity of their consciousness than any other group—will not yet organize reality at the fourth order. More commonly, they will be gradually working through the transformation from the third to the fourth order. In these circumstances, teachers can use the very issue of diversity to enhance the context of the class and make it an even more fertile environment for supporting development to the fourth order. But, again, teachers will be helped in this endeavor if they understand that the transformation they are involving themselves in is not a move *out* of modernism but a move *into* it.

Faculty (and parents), for example, may find themselves being used by their students (and young adult children) as stand-ins for the cultural surround their students (and children) are in the process of repudiating. These internal epistemological disjunctions can be painful when we are cast into their external enactments, but they have always been part of the territory of teaching (and parenting) in one way or another. Although it may be more pleasant to be a participant in our students' idealizations than in their counteridealizations, we might consider (while we are licking our wounds) that we do not deserve their adulatory identification when it suits them to use us in that fashion any more than we deserve their vilification. At the same time, as teachers seek to be responsive to and respectful of the diversity challenges to their courses, they can also be of help to their students' development by inviting them to move beyond their identification with externally generated values, "politically correct" formulas, or slogan-thinking in order to construct for themselves an authentic, personal ideology that can ground and generate their own estimable beliefs and challenges. In response to their students' challenge, teachers should not assume that because they can construct the challenge in a fourth order fashion their students necessarily can, too.

Within our national borders the diversity movement, properly misunderstood, is the favorite evidence for heralding the coming of the postmodern age. But postmodern enthusiasts have riveting *international* evidence to submit as well. All across the globe historic transformations of the status quo seem to signal the beginning of a new world order. Old geopolitical and national arrangements are being reconstructed. Old authorities are being toppled. And, as in the case of the diversity movement, something real, transforming, and of extraordinary importance and value for the progress of human development is certainly happening. But what is it? (The sales pitch of a San Diego real estate agent takes advantage of the moment: "Well here we are entering a new decade and quite a new world as well. Our planet has been undergoing quite a change. Demands for freedom becoming reality in many different countries. Global economy becoming more intertwined everyday. Peace between the super powers replacing the cold war. And through all these changes one thing remains a constant: *Southern California Real Estate!*"[3])

To a very small group of highly privileged people, people with wildly disproportionate access to the shaping of our public discourse, these extraordinary international developments look like a transcendence of fourth order consciousness. They look like the withering not only of particular ideologies, authorities, and absolutes, but the end of ideology, statist authority, and absolutism itself. Vaclav Havel, for example, the former president of the former Czechoslovakia, an artist and an intellectual, speaking at the World Economic Forum in Switzerland, had this to say when he was still the president of what was still Czechoslovakia:

> In its deepest sense, the end of Communism has brought an end not just to the 19th and 20th centuries, but to the modern age as a whole. The modern era has been dominated by the culminating belief, expressed in different forms, that the world—and Being as such—is a wholly knowable system governed by a finite number of universal laws that man can grasp and rationally direct for his own benefit . . . This, in turn, gave rise to the proud belief that man, as the pinnacle of everything that exists, was capable of objectively describing, explaining, and controlling everything that exists . . . It was an era in which there was a cult of depersonalized objectivity . . . an era of ideologies, doctrines, interpretations of reality . . . The fall of Communism can be regarded as a sign that modern thought—based on the premise that the world is objectively knowable, and that the knowledge so obtained can be absolutely generalized—has come to a final crisis.[4]

The fall of communism can be regarded this way, and I have no doubt this is exactly how it strikes Vaclav Havel. But I do doubt that this is what it means to the millions of disenfranchised people for whom the fall of a totalitarian ideology may permit a greater measure of support for the development of their own distinctive voice and authority and the formulation of new "ideologies, doctrines, and interpretations of reality."

The fall of the old authorities has been accompanied by the rise of old ethnic, racial, and nationalistic hatreds in the former Soviet Union, Europe, and Africa, and by the rise in each of these areas of new nationalisms. These are worrying but not surprising developments. In some instances they may indicate that the modernism Havel thinks has come to an end has never actually begun for people whose animosities reflect their enduring loyalty to the ethnic subcommunities with which they have never ceased identifying themselves. For others these developments are signs of repudiation of and disjunction from traditional, third order loyalties, signs that more people are moving toward modernist personal authority and that counterdominant "ideology communities" are taking shape to support those moves. These are fragile, dangerous, but potentially triumphant moves for human evolution. But they are not helped by our imagining that they are moves beyond modernism. I would not expect Bosnians or Azerbaijanis to be terribly available to reflect on the limits of their own absolutist claim to nationalistic self-determination.

For all but a privileged few, the fall of communism and other forms of totalitarianism does not signal the end of modernism. It may in fact come to signal the greater realization of modernism. It may signal a loosening of the grip of traditionalism on the minds of more adults. It may signal the inspiring insistence on the part of more people for full participation in the modernist world of personal and collective empowerment, dignifying one's own and one's people's voice and having a hand on the levers and dials of one's own destiny.

But it may yet be true that the dawn of the twenty-first century will indeed mark the beginning of the postmodern era, if only in the way that the dawn of the twentieth century was the beginning of modernism. I doubt that fourth order consciousness was more evident in the 1890s than fifth order consciousness is today. For the third or more of the adult population that organizes reality according to the fourth order, the postmodern curriculum is appropriately challenging, and as a forward-looking "school" our culture must pay more attention to providing supports for its students to meet that challenge. But "postmodern era" or no, "late twentieth century" or no, the central curricular focus for the majority of contemporary adults is still that of mastering the *fourth* order of consciousness, the mental burden of *modern* life.

Throughout this book I have argued that there is an unrecognized cultural demand upon the minds of contemporary adults for a common order of mental complexity. Because the experts who study the different arenas of adult living do so from intellectual fields that seldom refer to each other, we do not even consider the curriculum of adult life as a single whole. But when we subject its parts to epistemological analysis we discover an extraordinary commonality in the complexity of mind our culture calls for. It is as if the "school" that is contemporary culture is a highly fractionated one, a school in which the academic departments—each vigorously engaged in its separate mission—have nothing to do with each other. According to this metaphor, perhaps I am acting here something like the culture's academic dean, urging a collective analysis of what the departments are actually doing to our beleaguered student (who becomes the sole point of convergence for these non-interacting departmental missions).

Perhaps I should send a memo. I should frame it in questions, aware, like any dean, of how little direct influence a dean really has:

> Dear Departments at our School of Contemporary Adulthood,
>
> Of course, what you each want students to understand is important and different. That's why we have departments. But what if *how* you want them to understand is astonishingly similar? And what if most of them, when you receive them (the moment they become adults, the moment they take on committed responsibilities at work, as intimate partners, as parents, as citizens) do *not* understand in the way you want them to? Then isn't it true that your mission must not only be to teach them *what* you want them to understand but *how* you want them to understand? And doesn't this mean, then, that to a very large extent, you all share a *common* mission? And wouldn't you all be more successful in pursuit of your separate missions if you worked much more collaboratively to fashion a single, richer context of support for your common mission than each of you can possibly fashion on your own? And, finally, since most of your students do not arrive ready to understand in even this most basic way, whom exactly do you serve by gearing up to teach an even more complex way of understanding? Is this more complex way at *their* growing edge or at *yours?*

Whatever the virtues of the fifth order, no one should assign us the postmodern curriculum until we are ready for it. Nor does anyone do us a service by assuming that we understand it when we do not or are engaged in it when we are not. Those who understandably champion its merits, and who disdain the limits of modernism, might consider that before people can question the assumptions of wholeness, completeness, and the priority of the self, they must first construct a whole, complete, and prior self. More people can be appropriately challenged by the postmodern curriculum when there are more people who have mastered the mental demands of modernism.

Those who long for more fifth order consciousness—for the recognition of our multiple selves, for the capacity to see conflict as a signal of our overidentification with a single system, for the sense of our relationships and connections as prior to and constitutive of the individual self, for an identification with the transformative process of our being rather than the formative products of our becoming—let them take heart. The aspiration for more fifth order consciousness has one extraordinarily robust asset on its side, though oddly enough, it is hardly ever remarked upon.

A hundred years ago the average American lived to an age we today call "midlife," the middle forties. Today the average American lives more than twenty years longer, an entire generation longer for each individual life. What might the individual generate given an additional generation to live? My candidate: a qualitatively new order of consciousness. I suggest that we are gradually seeing more adults working on a qualitatively different order of consciousness than did adults one hundred years ago because we live twenty or more years longer than we used to.

In our longitudinal study it is rare to see people moving beyond the fourth order, but when they do, it is never before their forties, the very age when life ended for most people at the turn of the last century. Highly evolved people do not mate and create highly evolved children. The evolution of human consciousness requires long preparation. We may gradually become ever more ready to engage the curriculum of the fifth order because we have found ways to increase the number of years we live. And why *are* we increasing the number of years we live? Are we living longer as a species precisely so that we might evolve to the fifth order? Who knows?

Epilogue _____

O ne last look in on Peter and Lynn. "Some things your children do and care about make perfect sense to you," Lynn muses, "and some make none at all." Their eight-year-old, Rosie, routinely returns from school, heads into the driveway, and, hour after hour, alone or with friends, happily hurls a tennis ball against the door of the garage.

Peter and Lynn might comfort themselves with the thought that perhaps this is how Chris Evert or Roger Clemens began. Perhaps Rosie does have fantasies of athletic heroics. Perhaps these solitary sessions will eventually give way to organized team sport and the development of skills under a succession of coaches who know what to do with a child's love for throwing a ball.

But what if the child has no interest in sports, or whatever interest she does have has little to do with why she likes to spend hours bouncing the ball off the garage door? Perhaps she has no idea herself why she does it. Maybe she just loves being inside the rhythm of it, or experiencing her certain connection to this flying object, however much it looks as if it is off on its own. Maybe she is fascinated by the different directions and speeds and arcs she can create after the bounce, depending on the initial spin she puts on the ball when she throws it.

Any of these ways of being intrigued can of course be captured by the most well-intentioned parent or coach and put to use in a variety of sports. And when they are, Peter and Lynn may rightly feel that something productive has finally come of all those hours they listened to the repetitive thumping resonating from the garage into the house. It is a wonderful thing to see a child's interests develop into rewarding discipline, socially satisfying recreation, or productive pursuits. Something is surely gained when these rudimentary loves find a fertile soil where they can grow.

But something is lost, too, if it is predetermined how they should grow. Better perhaps that something come from the love of bouncing a ball than nothing at all, but in our own need for our child's activity to have a point or lead somewhere we could be turning away from what is most precious and creative about the activity, namely, that it is passionate. Passion is its own purpose. Passion can be a bit disdainful of reasonableness and productivity. And passion is among the most sacred and fragile gifts the gods bestow on us. It is fragile before our devastating embarrassment and impatience. And it is sacred because it promises the possibility of new life.

If Rosie's love of bouncing a ball is channeled into some coachable sport, she may find considerable satisfaction and increase as she gains the progressively complex set of skills acquired by hundreds of thousands before her. This is the flowering of her interests according to a basic design constructed long before she and her interest ever came along. She might even be a very talented player. Then she will realize this plan that others created faster and with greater skill than most.

But none of this has anything to do with her passion or with creativity or with new life. In fact, the most gifted of those who play a sport, the few that come along in each generation, are probably those who find a way to sustain their passion in the midst of someone else's design. These are the ones who just love to play the game. And while everyone else is totaling statistics, or salaries, or championships won, they are attending to something else—not, like the fans, to what this game means for the season or, like the experts, to their extraordinary mastery of this or that subtlety of the game, but to something else—to a ball they are bouncing against the door of the garage. The greatest victory of a Kirby Puckett or a Monica Seles may never be in a championship game at all but in the triumph of their passion over the orderly, prefabricated home to which it was brought. And isn't this too much to ask of passion—that it only be allowed to ripen into its unique expression if it quiets our need to understand its point by holding, in the meantime, a respectable nine-to-five job?

If we could imagine all the possibilities a child might realize from her passion for bouncing balls, or setting suns, or the modulations of the human voice, it would be like saying that nothing new can happen in the world. All of life, we would be saying, has already happened, and minding children might be something like seeing to it that mail carriers meet their appointed rounds.

The Jewish mystics say that God makes human beings because God loves stories. This is quite a modest stance to give an all-powerful, all-loving God. Even God, the mystics are saying, does not know how we are going to come out, so why should we wish for greater control or need it? Better perhaps for us to emulate this kind of God, whose pleasure in us comes not from our obedience to God's laws and regularities, however subject we may be to them, but from God's sheer fascination with how we will live.

For a God like this one, we ourselves are the objects of passionate engagement, endlessly let go of and recovered for a purpose God himself (or God herself) may not yet know. We ourselves are endlessly let go of and recovered as we, all the while, reverberate against the garage door and throughout the whole House.

Notes _____

Prologue

1. Robert Kegan, *The Sweeter Welcome* (Boston: Humanitas Press, 1977).
2. Robert Kegan, *The Evolving Self* (Cambridge: Harvard University Press, 1982).
3. David Elkind, *The Hurried Child: Growing Up Too Fast Too Soon* (Reading, Mass.: Addison-Wesley, 1981).
4. Philippe Ariès, *Centuries of Childhood: A Social History of Family Life* (New York: Random House, 1962).
5. L. Lahey, E. Souvaine, R. Kegan, R. Goodman, and S. Felix, *A Guide to the Subject-Object Interview: Its Administration and Interpretation* (Cambridge: The Subject-Object Workshop, 1988).

1. The Hidden Curriculum of Youth

1. See J. Piaget, *The Construction of Reality in the Child* (New York: Basic Books, 1954, originally published in 1937); *The Psychology of the Child* (New York: Harper Torchbooks, 1966); "Piaget's Theory," in P. Mussen, ed., *Carmichael's Manual of Child Psychology* (New York: Wiley, 1970); see also D. Elkind, "Editor's Introduction," in J. Piaget, *Six Psychological Studies* (New York: Vintage, 1968); R. Kegan, "The Unrecognized Genius of Jean Piaget," in *The Evolving Self* (Cambridge: Harvard University Press, 1982).
2. See R. Selman, "The Development of Social-Cognitive Understanding," in T. Lickona, ed., *Moral Development and Behavior* (New York: Holt, Rinehart and Winston, 1976); *The Growth of Interpersonal Understanding* (New York: Academic Press, 1980); L. Kohlberg, "Stage and Sequence: The Cognitive-Developmental Approach to Socialization," in D. Goslin, ed., *Handbook of Socialization* (New York: Rand McNally, 1969); L. Kohlberg, *The Psychology of Moral Development* (New York: Harper and

Row, 1984); R. Kegan, "The Evolution of Moral Meaning-Making," in *The Evolving Self,* pp. 46–72.

3. See R. Kegan, "The Loss of Pete's Dragon: Transformation in the Development of the Self in the Years Five to Seven," in R. L. Leahy, ed., *The Development of the Self* (New York: Academic Press, 1985); R. Kegan, G. Noam, and L. Rogers, "The Psychologic of Emotions," in D. Cicchetti and P. Pogge-Hesse, eds., *Emotional Development* (San Francisco: Jossey-Bass, 1982); S. White, "Some General Outlines of the Matrix of Developmental Changes between Five and Seven Years," *Bulletin of the Orton Society,* 20 (1970): 41–57; and B. Carroll, "Subject and Object: Changes in Structure between the Ages of Five and Seven" doctoral diss., Harvard Graduate School of Education, 1986). For an excellent review of "cognitive development" from a constructive-developmental point of view, see T. Yates, "Theories of Cognitive Development," in M. Lewis, ed., *Child and Adolescent Psychiatry: A Comprehensive Textbook* (Baltimore: Williams and Williams, 1991).

4. This new principle includes the still-existing categories of persons as containing their properties, wants, or preferences, but it subordinates and links these categories to a cross-categorical construction that brings a whole new phenomenon into being, the person as superordinately relational. It is not just that the self can be related to the other in a new way, but that both self and other have *become* something different via their cross-categorical construction. "I used to worry that I would mess up," a newly cross-categorical adolescent once told us, "and that others would make me pay for it. Now I worry that if I mess up, others will worry." Both the "I" and the "others" have moved from categorical phenomena (defined by their own properties of intention and need) to cross-categorical phenomena (defined by the link between the categories).

5. What, for example, is abstract thought? Consider these three instances: (a) When this syllogistic question is posed to children: "All purple snakes have four legs; I am hiding a purple snake; how many legs does it have?," concrete thinkers object to the notion of four-leggedness or purpleness in snakes. Abstract thinkers, for the sake of argument, accept the facts, place them in the logic of the syllogism, and answer that the snake must have four legs. (b) When told that each of four teachers teaches the same four classes, each in a different sequence, given a few facts (such as "Teacher A teaches Group 1 at the beginning of his day"), and asked to figure out each teacher's instructional sequence, concrete thinkers quickly discover that the facts they have been given are insufficient to do so for even one teacher and give up. But abstract thinkers create a four-by-four, sixteen-box grid into which they put the few facts they have and then fill in the missing information. (c) When presented with four beakers of clear liquid and a

fifth empty beaker and told to find out which combinations of liquids make a yellow-colored liquid, concrete thinkers randomly try out various combinations, uncertain whether they will solve the problem and governed by no method but hope. Abstract thinkers have no doubt that they will solve the problem; they intend to try each two-beaker, each three-beaker, and the one four-beaker combination until the problem is, necessarily, solved.

What the abstract thinkers are demonstrating in each instance—in the forms commonly referred to as *propositional, inductive,* and *combinatorial* thinking, respectively—is the single ability to organize experience in the "trans-categorical" fashion. Rather than orient to the snake primarily in terms of its property-bearing character (color, number of legs) or being stopped by the apparent *violations* to the membership rules implied in the durable category known as "snake" ("who ever heard of purple snakes or four-legged snakes?"), the abstract thinkers *subordinate* the categoriness of snakes to the logic of the syllogism. The syllogism itself is an instance of a trans-categorical form: it holds two categories together and establishes a relationship between them (in this case, a "sufficiency relationship," that is, if x then y must follow), which subtends the categories. It is not possible to "get" the answer without being able to hold onto the two categories simultaneously. Holding onto the two categories simultaneously in this way actually creates in the world an entirely new phenomenon, invents the world in a qualitatively new way. A "something" exists that did not exist before for this mind's apprehension of reality; that something we call an abstraction.

When the abstract thinker creates the "grid" to solve the second kind of problem, she is again demonstrating cross-categorical consciousness. The "grid" consists of empty cells, placeholders for facts or concrete categories that are not yet known. The few facts given take their places in the appropriate cells (Instructional Group 1, for example, goes into Teacher A's first box), but most of the cells are empty. The grid subordinates the categories to the relationships between them: all four groups must be taught by each teacher, for example, and no one group can be taught by more than one teacher at the same time, so the single fact or concretion that Instructional Group 1 is taught by Teacher A in his first period has implications for all of Teacher A's remaining boxes (Group 1 cannot be in these boxes) and for the first period boxes of Teachers B, C, and D (Group 1 cannot be in these boxes). The grid is a visible depiction of cross-categorical consciousness at work because it literally creates the phenomenon of the "something" that is philosophically prior to the concrete. The grid is a fact-creating "machine." It creates spaces for facts "about to happen"—and this "something" is again what we call abstractness.

Finally, the certainty of solution the abstract solvers of the yellow liquid problem express, which is based in their recognition that there are only so many possible ways four liquids can be combined, is yet another demonstration of cross-categorical consciousness. Unlike the "plunge in and hope" approach of the concrete thinkers, for whom the reality of each liquid is confined to itself, this approach grasps a qualitatively different reality—the liquids' relationships to each other. In this new reality, the liquid's *thingness* participates in but is not the essence of its existence. Its essence is, for now, tied to the limited number of ways it can be different in relation to the other liquids. The earlier conception of essence is what we mean by *concreteness;* the new essence is what we mean by *abstractness.*

What we call "abstract thinking," in other words, is the ability to create a "category of categories" or a "class of classes" in which the properties of membership are not merely the aspects of a category but categories themselves. Concrete phenomena become instances of "metaphenomena," which we call abstractions, a whole new way of ordering and living in the world. The underlying *form* of abstraction is what I call the cross-categorical or trans-categorical order of mind.

6. We might compare these two different ways people answered our question, "How would you describe yourself?"

> Brownish, I mean blondish brown hair. Blue eyes. I'm medium in height. My favorite computer game is Atari. I have a little sister. I'm mad at her. I'm smart. I'm *very* smart and I color neat. I like BLT sandwiches. I like everybody who likes me. Especially my best friend Robbi. She's super nice to me.

> I'm becoming like much more confident. I used to be just super insecure and stuff, very self-conscious, and now I like myself much better and I think other people, like, are more comfortable with me, and like me better too, y'know what I mean?

Perhaps one is struck first by the contrast between what one might call a more *external* and a more *internal* way of referring to the self. The first speaker seems to describe the self more from the outside in, looking at an observably behaving self, while the second speaker seems to describe the self more from the inside out, naming not behaviors that are externally observable, like "coloring neat," but internal psychological behaviors, like becoming more self-confident. There certainly seems to be something to this way of putting the distinction, but does it really handle all the "data"? What are we to do with the first speaker's report that she is "mad" and "smart" (corrected to "*very* smart")? These are not exactly external phenomena.

I think we are truer to the full reach of the data if we grant that there may be a distinction along the lines of "external" and "internal" to be made here, but not in the dichotomous sense that the first is all one and the other all the other. Perhaps we could say that they differ *in the way* they are internal and external. To me it makes more sense to consider that a speaker like the first, who happens to be a spunky eight-year-old girl, is demonstrating the ability to hold together the durable category of the self (as opposed to a continuously changing flow of kaleidoscopically new arrangements of perception and sensation), a durable category containing a set of nameable characteristics that are ongoing members of the set that is the self. (This ability demonstrates at least a categorical order of consciousness.) Some of these characteristics are "external" (like physical features), and some of them are "internal" (like smartness or being mad). What seems to most distinguish this kind of speech from that of the second speaker, a young woman ten years older than the first, is that, whether it is naming external *or* internal characteristics of "the set," it is confined to the self as a single set. The characteristics the second speaker names ("becoming more confident," "super insecure," "self-conscious") are not just "internal"; they demonstrate a self that is not confined to a single "set" or category.

Feelings like "self-conscious" or "insecure" suggest "feelings *about* feelings," a self as a category having a feeling *and* the self as able to subordinate this category to some bigger context that regulates or reflects on it. Out of this bigger context, with which the self is now identified, appear feelings, which are experienced as *inner states* or *inner subjectivity*. The *form* of this new context is necessarily cross-categorical.

People give evidence of experiencing this more complex internal psychological life when they speak, for example, of feeling "conflicted," "guilty," "depressed," "insecure." These are all psychological *states* experienced *as states*. They all convey a self-reflexive, self as in between kind of quality. When I experience the state of feeling "conflicted," I implicate a "self" that is both the category "I want to do (or feel or am) X" *and* the category "I want to do (or feel or am) Y." But the feeling "conflicted" involves the holding of these two categories together. *The self's experiencing derives not from either of these categories but from their relationship.* Similarly, "guilty" implies a cross-categorical context in which the category of a self that "wants to do X" is being subordinated and integrated into a more complex context that regulates its relation to another category of a self for which it is "bad or wrong to do X." *The self and its experiencing are thus no longer either of these categories but their relationship.* "Depressed" involves the self's identification with its relation to the more simple internal psychological experience, "I am sad." "Insecure" implies a form larger than the set of a self "unable to do something" and the experience of the self *in relation to this set*, rather than the set itself.

7. *Values, beliefs,* and *ideals* are also the newly born issue of trans-categorical knowing, and these, too, are really abstractions. What makes the abstract abstract is *not* its separation from the concrete particulars or the committed involvements of the self. What makes something abstract is the cross-categorical *form* these treatments of the actual, these renderings of our beliefs take. The ability to create "the grid" (bringing into being the construct of "empty facts" or "unfilled sets" or "concretes that have not yet happened") can be brought to the realm of our mental construction of the world and how it could be better as easily as to the realm of solving math puzzles. "Ideals" always involve making imaginatively real the not-yet real and bringing the filled categories of "current actuality" into relation with these unfilled categories of "real possibility."

8. See R. D. Seymour, "Constructing a Personal Future Time Perspective" (doctoral diss., Harvard Graduate School of Education, 1991); E. Villegas-Reimers, "Judgments of Responsibility: Their Relationship with Self and Moral Reasoning in Venezuelan Adolescents" (doctoral diss., Harvard Graduate School of Education, 1988); and S. T. Hauser, S. I. Powers, and G. G. Noam, *Adolescents and Their Families: Paths of Ego Development* (New York: Free Press, 1991).

9. A. Fleck-Henderson and R. Kegan, "Learning, Knowing, and the Self," in K. Field, B. Cohler, and G. Wool, eds., *Motive and Meaning: Psychoanalytic Perspectives on Learning and Education* (New York: International Universities Press, 1989).

10. This combination of the *developmental* in nature with the *epistemological* in nature is what Piaget meant when he called his approach to the study of organisms a "genetic epistemological" approach.

11. Although I am often asked by Westerners if my theory isn't an especially Western theory, I have been struck by the fact that I am rarely asked this by Easterners (such as the many Asian students from Japan, China, Singapore, Korea, and the Philippines I have been privileged to teach over the years) or by Westerners who are Buddhist meditators. The central conception of growth as overcoming a kind of attachment ("subjectivity"), which enables one to reflect on, or make substantial ("take as object") that which otherwise recedes to forgetfulness, is quite consistent with Eastern conceptions. Experienced Buddhist meditators have told me on several occasions that *The Evolving Self* is a close approximation to "a Buddhist psychology" if Buddhism had any interest in articulating one (their frequent suggestion is that the book be retitled *The Evolving Non-Self!*). For those who are interested in the explicit conversation between Buddhist and subject-object perspectives, see Mara Sanadi Wagner, "The Evolution of the Deconstructed Self" (doctoral diss., Massachusetts School of Professional Psychology, 1985). For those interested in an integration of Eastern phi-

losophy with a constructive-developmental perspective more generally, see the work of Ken Wilber: *The Atman Project* (Wheaton, Ill.: Theosophical Publishing House, 1980); *Up from Eden* (Boston: Shambala, 1981); and especially, "The Spectrum of Development," in K. Wilber, J. Engler, and D. P. Brown, eds., *Transformations of Consciousness* (Boston: Shambhala, 1986).

12. Readers of *The Evolving Self* will note that this chart, and in fact much of this chapter, addresses a frequent and justifiable question directed at my theory as I presented it in the 1982 book, which is this: "You say that a given subject-object relationship organizes cognitive and affective and interpersonal and intrapersonal experiencing, and that a common subject-object relationship is implicated in each of these domains at any one time. But aside from being listed in the same subject-object relationship, what exactly do such elements have in common? In other words, how are 'impulse' and 'perception' really epistemologically similar? How are 'abstractness,' 'mutuality,' and 'inner subjective states' epistemologically similar? How are 'concreteness' and 'point of view' similar? You have not proposed what is *generally* common to a given epistemology that is shared by each of these elements from different domains (cognitive, affective, interpersonal, intrapersonal)." That is true, I had not. Here I do. I suggest the "general underlying principle" (the durable category, the cross-categorical, and so on), which similarly organizes the different phenomena (cognitive, affective, and so on) of the same order of consciousness.

2. Coaching the Curriculum

1. For a more thoroughgoing treatment of my perspective on sociopathy, see R. Kegan, "The Child behind the Mask: Sociopathy as Developmental Delay," in W. H. Reid, J. W. Bonner III, D. Dorr, and J. I. Walker, eds., *Unmasking the Psychopath* (New York: Norton, 1986). For an empirical test of my perspective, see P. B. Walsh, "Kegan's Structural-Developmental Theory of Sociopathy and Some Actualities of Sociopathic Cognition" (doctoral diss., University of Pittsburgh, 1989; University Microfilms International, no. 89-21423). For other constructive-developmental perspectives on delinquency and problematic conduct, see C. Blakeney and R. Blakeney, "Understanding and Reforming Moral Misbehavior among Behaviorally Disordered Adolescents," *Behavior Disorders*, 16: 120–126; C. Blakeney and R. Blakeney, "Reforming Moral Misbehavior," *Journal of Moral Education*, 19 (xxxx): 101–113; J. Hickey and P. Scharf, *Toward a Just Correctional System* (San Francisco: Jossey-Bass, 1980); and R. Selman, L. Schultz, M. Nakkula, D. Barr, C. Watts, and J. B. Richmond, "Helping

Children and Adolescents Improve Their Social Conduct: A Developmental Approach to the Study of Risk and Prevention of Violence," *Development and Psychopathology*, in press.

2. H. Cleckley, *Mask of Sanity* (St. Louis: C. V. Mosby, 1941).

3. R. Blakeney and C. Blakeney, "Knowing Better: Delinquent Girls and the 2–3 Transition" (unpublished paper, Harvard University, 1977).

4. E. H. Erikson, *Childhood and Society* (New York: Norton, 1963).

5. H. S. Sullivan, *The Interpersonal Theory of Psychiatry* (New York: Norton, 1953).

6. See Hickey and Scharf, *Toward a Just Correctional System.*

7. R. Kegan, *The Evolving Self*, p. 182. For more on explicitly constructive-developmental approaches to job training programs for adolescents, see R. Kegan, M. Broderick, and N. Popp, "A Developmental Framework for Assessing Youth in Programmatic Interventions" (unpublished background paper prepared for report to U.S. Department of Labor, Public/Private Ventures, Philadelphia, 1992); C. Blakeney and R. Blakeney, "A Developmental Approach to Job Training with 'At Risk' Youth" (unpublished background paper prepared for report to U.S. Department of Labor, Public/Private Ventures, Philadelphia, 1992); and M. A. Gambone, *Strengthening Programs for Youth: Promoting Adolescent Development in the JTPA (Job Training Partnership Act) System* (Philadelphia: Public/Private Ventures, 1993).

8. P. Graham, "Wit and Character" (speech delivered to the National Forum of the College Board, Dallas, Tex., October, 1983).

9. "Today, 72 percent of all high school seniors (and 40 percent of the ninth-graders) have had sex, according to a 1990 survey released Friday by the Federal Centers for Disease Control . . . The birth rate among girls age 15 to 17 rose by 19 percent between 1986 and 1989 . . . Recent research is clear about what doesn't work. Two studies, published in 1990 . . . found that teenagers didn't change their sexual behavior when exposed solely to moralistic programs (such as Sex Respect . . . and Teen Aid) that urged them to abstain from sex before marriage . . . Neither program prompted the participants to delay intercourse or reduce the frequency of intercourse, the studies found" (*Boston Globe*, January 6, 1992, story by Alison Bass). "Premarital sexual activity among adolescent women has accelerated during the last two decades—with a sharp jump since 1985—despite an increase in sex education and AIDS prevention programs, Federal health officials reported Friday . . . 51.5 percent of women ages 15 to 19 said they had engaged in premarital sex by their late teens—nearly double the 28.6 percent reported in 1970 . . . The largest relative increase occurred among those 15 years of age" (*Los Angeles Times*, May 16, 1992, story by Marlene Cimons). "My 15-year-old patient with pelvic pain lay

quietly on the gurney, as I asked her the standard questions. 'Are you sexually active?' 'Yes.' 'Are you using any form of birth control?' 'No.' Her answers didn't surprise me . . . Condoms are not being used. Many studies confirm this, including one survey among college women—a group we might presume to be as well-informed as any on the risks of herpes, genital warts, cervical cancer, and AIDS. In 1989, only 41 percent insisted on condom use during sexual intercourse! If educated women cannot remember to use condoms, how can we expect teenagers or the uninformed to do so?" (*Boston Globe*, July 18, 1993; from a public health column by Dr. Steven J. Sainsbury originally appearing in the *Los Angeles Times*).

10. Anthropologists tell us that adolescents were successfully inducted into a practice permitting orgasm by both partners but scrupulously abstaining from genital penetration among the Kikuyu in Kenya, East Africa, and several other Bantu societies, particularly in East and South Africa. The advent of Western educational practices and Christianity in the early part of the twentieth century led to the loss of the community's training adolescents in the practice, called *ngweko*, and it disappeared. See C. M. Worthman, and J. W. M. Whiting, "Social Change in Adolescent Sexual Behavior, Mate Selection, and Premarital Pregnancy Rates in a Kikuyu Community," *Ethos*, 15 (June 1987): 145–165.

3. Parenting

1. All these transformations, in other words, express the *same single capacity* to subordinate the durable category (whether concrete thinking, enduring disposition, or one's own singular point of view) to a qualitatively more complex organizational principle that takes the durable category as element or object. The organizing of our thinking can now be abstract, our feeling self-reflexive, our social-relating inductable into a commonweal or mutual relationship. This single mental capacity is what I call third order consciousness. Its organizational principle I call "cross-categorical."

2. Carla Osgood, explicitly incorporating a subject-object perspective, reviewed a number of prominent parent education programs, and concluded that they tended to regard all parents as essentially constructing experience in the same way. See C. Osgood, "Readiness for Parenting Teenagers: A Structural-Developmental Approach" (doctoral diss., University of Massachusetts, 1991). Reviewing "Toughlove," "Parent Effectiveness Training" (PET), "Systematic Training for Effective Parenting" (STEP), and the like, Osgood concluded that the designers of such programs expected parents of teenagers to be able to perform a number of complicated psychological tasks, such as setting limits, tolerating a diversity of ideas,

and taking a perspective on the way they parent. Osgood hypothesized that parents would be at different orders of consciousness, would therefore differently understand these expectations, and from some subject-object positions would have a hard time meeting them. When she conducted subject-object interviews with a random group of parents, she found her hypothesis supported. She then proposed ways that such parent training programs could take better account of the varied ways in which parents would engage the material. For other approaches to parenting incorporating a constructive-developmental perspective, see R. Goodman, "A Developmental and Systems Analysis of Marital and Family Communication in Clinic and Non-Clinic Families" (doctoral diss., Harvard Graduate School of Education, 1983); and P. Perry, "Mothers and Fathers—Different Perspectives: A Structural-Developmental Study of Parents" (doctoral diss., Massachusetts School of Professional Psychology, 1984).

3. Quoting Levy in S. Allison, "Meaning-Making in Marriage: An Exploratory Study" (doctoral diss., Massachusetts School of Professional Psychology, 1988).

4. Quoting Framo in Allison, "Meaning-Making in Marriage."

5. Quoting Rappaport in Allison, "Meaning-Making in Marriage."

6. P. A. Kaufman, E. Harrison, and M. L. Hyde, "Distancing for Intimacy in Lesbian Relationships," *American Journal of Psychiatry*, 14 (1984): 529–533.

7. Rainer Maria Rilke, *Letters to a Young Poet* (New York: Norton, 1963).

8. For approaches to partnering incorporating a constructive-developmental perspective, see Goodman, "A Developmental and Systems Analysis of Marital and Family Communication in Clinic and Non-Clinic Families"; S. Allison, "Meaning-Making in Marriage"; R. O'C. Higgins, "Psychological Resilience and the Capacity for Intimacy" (doctoral diss., Harvard Graduate School of Education, 1985); J. Jacobs, "Holding Environment and Developmental Stages: A Study of Marriage" (doctoral diss., Harvard Graduate School of Education, 1984).

9. I have taken this vignette from a paper by Katherine S. Kaufmann. See Kaufmann, "Parental Discipline and Constructive-Developmental Psychology" (unpublished paper, Harvard Graduate School of Education, 1985).

10. Ibid.

11. A. Miller, *The Drama of the Gifted Child*, trans. Ruth Ward (New York: Basic Books, 1981).

12. H. Bruch, *The Golden Cage* (Cambridge: Harvard University Press, 1978).

13. Miller, *Drama of the Gifted Child*, p. 4.

14. This distinction also reflects a controversy *within* the constructive-developmental paradigm. See L. Rogers and R. Kegan, "Mental Growth and

Mental Health as Distinct Concepts in the Study of Developmental Psychopathology," in H. Rosen and D. Keating, eds., *Constructivist Approaches to Psychopathology* (Hillsdale, N.J.: Lawrence Erlbaum Associates, 1990); M. Basseches, "Toward a Constructive-Developmental Understanding of the Dialectics of Individuality and Irrationality," in D. A. Kramer and M. J. Bopp, eds., *Transformation in Clinical and Developmental Psychology* (New York: Springer-Verlag, 1989); G. G. Noam, "The Constructivist Theory of Developmental Psychopathology and Clinical-Developmental Psychology," in E. Nannis and P. Cowan, eds., *Developmental Psychopathology and Its Treatment* (San Francisco: Jossey-Bass, 1988); and G. G. Noam and R. Kegan, "On Boundaries and Externalization: Clinical Developmental Perspectives," *Psychoanalytic Inquiry*, 9 (1989).

15. Miller, *Drama of the Gifted Child*.

4. Partnering

1. H. Ibsen, *A Doll's House* (New York: Dutton, 1958).
2. Mary Stewart Hammond, "Making Breakfast," *New Yorker*, April 23, 1990, p. 40.
3. D. Tannen, *You Just Don't Understand* (New York: Morrow, 1990); L. Rubin, *Intimate Strangers* (New York: Harper and Row, 1983).
4. R. Kegan, "Making Meaning: The Constructive-Developmental Approach to Persons and Practice," *Journal of Personnel and Guidance*, 58 (1980). I conducted the research reported in this paper with Laura Rogers.

5. Working

1. W. C. Byham, *The Lightning of Empowerment* (New York: Harmony Books, 1988).
2. P. Block, *The Empowered Manager* (San Francisco: Jossey-Bass, 1989).
3. R. Kelley and J. Caplan, "How Bell Labs Creates Star Performers," *Harvard Business Review*, July–August 1993, p. 131.
4. See S. Eaton, "Union Leadership Development in the 1990s and Beyond: A Report with Recommendations" (CSIA discussion paper no. 92-05, Kennedy School of Government, Harvard University, 1992); and S. Eaton, "Reflections on Adult Development and Union Leadership Development Work" (unpublished paper, Harvard Graduate School of Education, 1993).
5. Lin-Ching Hsia, "Learning in Conflicts" (doctoral diss., Harvard Graduate School of Education, 1992).
6. Ibid., pp. 66–67.

7. Ibid., p. 67.

8. Jean Watson, "The Moral Failure of the Patriarchy," *Nursing Outlook*, 38 (1990): 62–66.

9. Joyce Roberts, "Uncovering Hidden Caring," *Nursing Outlook*, 38 (1990): 67–79. See also A. H. Jones, ed., *Images of Nurses* (Philadelphia: University of Pennsylvania Press, 1987); and Sheila Norton, "Conflicts and Paradox in Nursing Education" (unpublished paper, Harvard Graduate School of Education). Sheila's work was a valuable reeducation about nursing.

10. Block, *Empowered Manager*, p. 39.

11. Ibid., p. 73.

12. Ibid., p. 25.

13. Wilfred Drath, of the Center for Creative Leadership, taking an explicitly subject-object perspective to the study of managers, suggests that many managers genuinely seek to empower their employees but are undermined in their efforts by their inability to construct experience in a fashion *more* complex than the fourth order. See Drath, "Managerial Strengths and Weaknesses as Functions of the Development of Personal Meaning," *Journal of Applied Behavioral Science*, 26 (1990): 483–499. For other research on work incorporating a subject-object perspective, see I. Penn, "The Restructuring of Work as a Context for Development in Adulthood" (doctoral diss., Massachusetts School of Professional Psychology, 1990); A. Smirnova, "The Meaning of Career Change for Women in Midlife in Relation to Their Psychological Growth" (doctoral diss., Massachusetts School of Professional Psychology, 1993); S. Levine, *Promoting Adult Growth in the Schools* (New York: Allyn and Bacon, 1988); E. Souvaine, "Creating Contexts for Effective Action and the Development of Meaning-Making" (unpublished qualifying paper, Harvard Graduate School of Education, 1985); K. W. Kuhnert and C. J. Russell, "Using Constructive-Developmental Theory and Biodata to Bridge the Gap between Personnel Selection and Leadership," *Journal of Management*, 16 (1990); K. W. Kuhnert and P. Lewis, "Transactional and Transformational Leadership: A Constructive-Developmental Analysis," *Academy of Management Review*, 12 (1987); M. Basseches, "Cognitive-Structural Development and the Conditions of Employment," *Human Development*, (1986); W. Hodgetts, "Coming of Age at Midlife: How Male and Female Managers Transform Relationships with Authority" (doctoral diss., Harvard Graduate School of Education, 1994); and P. Lewis, and T. O. Jacobs, "Individual Differences in Strategic Leadership Capacity: A Constructive- Developmental View," in J. G. Hunt and R. L. Phillips, eds., *Strategic Leadership: A Multi-Organizational Perspective* (New York: Quorum Books, 1993).

14. R. Barth, *Run School Run* (Cambridge: Harvard University Press, 1980), pp. 146–147.

15. See Katherine Crowley, "Burnout" (unpublished paper, Harvard Graduate School of Education, 1990). Crowley's work gave me background on the "burnout" literature.

16. H. J. Freudenberger, *Burnout: The High Cost of Achievement* (Garden City, N.Y.: Anchor Press, 1980), pp. 19–20.

17. C. Maslach, *Burnout: The Cost of Caring* (Englewood Cliffs, N.J.: Anchor Press, 1982), pp. 62–63.

18. D. Wortley and E. Amatea, "Mapping Adult Life Changes," *Personnel and Guidance Journal*, April 1982; O. Brim, "Socialization through the Life Cycle," in O. Brim and H. Wheeler, eds., *Socialization after Childhood: Two Essays* (Boston: Wiley, 1966); E. H. Erikson, *Childhood and Society*, 2nd ed. (New York: Norton, 1963); R. Gould, *Transformations: Growth and Change in Adult Life* (New York: Simon and Schuster, 1978); R. Havighurst, *Human Development and Education* (New York: Longman, 1953); D. Levinson, *The Seasons of a Man's Life* (New York: Knopf, 1978); B. L. Neugarten, *Middle Age and Aging* (Chicago: Chicago University Press, 1968); G. Sheehy, *Passages: Predictable Crises of Adult Life* (New York: Dutton, 1976); G. E. Vaillant, *Adaptation to Life* (Boston: Little, Brown, 1977).

19. Wortley and Amatea, "Mapping Adult Life Changes."

20. Neugarten, *Middle Age and Aging*, p. 256.

21. M. Basseches also addresses the issue of phase theory's problematic relationship to complexity; see Basseches, *Dialectical Thinking and Adult Development* (Norwood, N.J.: Ablex, 1984).

22. Levinson, *Seasons of a Man's Life*, p. 43.

23. The Subject-Object Interview is an approximately hour-long interview procedure used to assess the unselfconscious "epistemology" or "principles of meaning-coherence" to which an individual has recourse. My colleagues and I at the Harvard Graduate School of Education designed the procedures for administering and assessing the interview to access the natural epistemological structures I first wrote about in *The Evolving Self.* The formal research procedure for generating and analyzing the data of the interview is described in detail in Lisa Lahey, Emily Souvaine, Robert Kegan, Robert Goodman, and Sally Felix, *A Guide to the Subject-Object Interview: Its Administration and Analysis* (Cambridge: Subject-Object Research Group).

The interview procedure is in the tradition of the Piagetian semiclinical interview in which the experimenter asks questions to determine how an interviewee construes a given "content" (such as the same quantity of water in two differently shaped glasses). The chief innovations of the Subject-Object Interview are that the contents are generated from the real-life experience of the interviewee and involve emotional as well as cognitive and intrapersonal as well as interpersonal aspects of psychological organization. In order to understand how the interviewee organizes interpersonal and intrapersonal experiencing, real-life situations are elicited by a series of ten uniform probes (such as "Can you tell me of a recent experience of being quite angry about something?"), which the interviewer then explores at the level of discerning its underlying epistemology.

Interviews are transcribed, and those sections in which structure is clarified are the units of analysis. A typical interview may have from eight to fifteen such units. Each unit is scored independently and an overall score is arrived at through a uniform process. Interviews are usually scored by two raters to determine interrater reliability, at least one of the raters having previously demonstrated reliability. The psychological theory distinguishes five increasingly complicated epistemological equilibria believed to evolve in sequence, each successive epistemology containing the last. But the assessment procedure is able to distinguish five gradations between each equilibrated epistemology, so that over twenty distinctions, each a slightly different principle for meaning-organization than the last, can be made.

The first doctoral dissertation using the measure was completed in 1983. A bibliography of the many dissertations and research projects that have since used the measure is included in the *Guide to the Subject-Object Interview*, as is an appendix on the reliability and validity of the measure. Interrater reliability across studies has ranged from .75 to .90. One study reports a test-retest reliability of .83. Several report expectably high correlations with like measures, and high degrees of consistency among alternate forms of the measure, different domains of experiencing, and different "test items." But the single best gauge of its construct validity is the longitudinal study reported in this chapter, suggesting the measure's general capacity to capture gradual changes in subject-object development within persons in the expected direction over time.

24. L. L. Lahey, "Males' and Females' Construction of Conflict in Work and Love" (doctoral diss., Harvard Graduate School of Education, 1986).

25. Technically speaking, Lahey conducted forty-four subject-object interviews with twenty-two adults (eleven men, eleven women). Each person was interviewed twice, several days apart, on real-life conflicts from, in one interview, their love life, and in another, their work life. The subject-object interview is able to make *six* reliable distinctions between any two orders of consciousness. Between the third and fourth orders, for example, it distinguishes between 1) a system in which only the third order is in evidence (designated "3"); 2) a system in which the person has begun to separate from the third order ("3(4)"); 3) a system in which both the third and fourth orders are in evidence and either the third predominates ("3/4"); or 4) the fourth predominates ("4/3"); 5) a system in which the

fourth order is now the governing structure but it must work at not letting the third order intrude ("4(3)"); and finally, 6) a system in which the fourth order is securely established. I trouble readers with this degree of detail so they may better understand the meaning of Lahey's results. As I say, it would not be terribly impressive to suggest that a person's constructions of the realms of love and work were "both roughly third-orderish" or "both roughly fourth-orderish." But the scoring system for subject-object interviews puts the "consistency hypothesis" to a much more rigorous test. The degree of consistency Lahey found among real people's constructions of the realms of intimacy and work was this: subjects were no more than *one* discrimination apart in their two interviews ("one-fifth of the way," so to speak, in the journey from one order of consciousness to another) in eighteen of twenty-two cases (and in three of the other four cases they were only two discriminations apart).

26. A frequent and sensible set of questions that often come up when people consider my ideas about these epistemological structures go something like this: "Do you really think people tend to use the same epistemology [or 'order of consciousness'] across all the different domains of their living, or even in the same domain all the time? I mean, isn't it possible, or even likely, that I use one structure in my work life and another with my children? Isn't it possible that while I usually use the 'fourth order,' say, with my children, that once in a while, on a bad day, I may revert to a simpler order of consciousness? Might not people, under stress, use a simpler order of consciousness? When we evolve to a higher order principle of meaning organization, isn't it possible that some aspects of our experiencing do not 'go along' with the transformation, but get 'split off' or dissociated from the whole and go on being organized according to earlier principles?"

My answer to these questions—drawn from my vantage point as a clinician, researcher, and incurable observer of myself, my family, and my friends and associates—is "Yes, I think all these things are possible, *but this variation and dissociation is not without cost.*" In other words, I hold to a "consistency assumption" but not a simple-minded one. I do believe that the self seeks coherence in its organizing according to its most complex principle of organization, but it does not always succeed. Even when it does *not* succeed, however, I believe that forms of consistency are still in evidence. How can this be?

Perhaps a few examples will clarify what I mean. We might take a commonly posited form of inconsistency, the idea of *temporary regression* in response to stress or a disconfirming context, for example. We travel to our parents' home for the holidays. As the airplane touches down we say to ourselves, "This time it's going to be different. This time I will not feel as if I am regressing after three days with my parent(s)." But, alas, it is to no avail, and we do indeed find ourselves feeling like a child or just "not ourselves." In either case, the main internal experience is negative, and we do not like to feel this way. Or perhaps as adults we go back to school and find ourselves in a context in which we have less control over our work lives and less authority. Instead of people coming to us for consultation, we are seeking out hard-to-find faculty. This experience may also seem quite regressive, and we may feel "juvenilized." Now it may be that aspects of our thinking or feeling in this context are in fact younger or simpler than we now know ourselves normally to be. And here, again, we do not like the way we feel. If we are organizing our experiencing in these examples according to less complex principles, how can I say that a form of structural consistency is also present?

Although it may be true that we are organizing aspects of our experiencing according to a principle that is not consistent with our current, more complex capacity, it is also true that we do not like the way we feel. The way we are thinking does not feel to us acceptable or syntonic; we do not feel "like ourselves." But who or what is doing this evaluating? We do not feel unhappy in our juvenilized state because we were unhappy when we were juveniles. We feel unhappy because our *current*, more complex adult way of organizing is *still* at work evaluating the whole experience, finding it dystonic, and even lamenting that we are not able to "put into play" our fullest selves. If regression refers to an actual process of "devolution," of *losing* a more complex order for another simpler one, then these are not experiences of regression, because the more complex structure is still present and at work, however confined it may be at the moment. To the extent that we are unable to be fully consistent in such situations, it costs us something; we don't like it. But even in such situations of inconsistency a form of consistency continues to exist. The overall way we feel about, think about, or evaluate the situation is expressive of, and consistent with, our most complex principle of organization.

Let us consider further the phenomenon of "losing it." When I say modernism makes a mental demand on us for fourth order consciousness, I am not suggesting that parents who ordinarily structure experience at a fourth order level are in over their heads because they occasionally "lose it" with their children and fail to perform fourth order tasks, such as not being made up by the other's experience. We are in over our heads when we do *not* construct such lapses as "losing it," when we do *not* experience ourselves as having lost anything because it does not seem like a lapse at all. The very term "losing it" is evidence that, however inconsistent we may temporarily be with our more complex way of organizing, we are so identified with this way that when we deviate from it we actually construct the phenomenon *as a deviation*. The construction "losing it" is thus expressive of, and consistent with, that more complex principle of organization.

Finally, let us consider the more chronic phenomenon of "split off," encapsulated, or dissociated aspects of our experiencing, which fail to be transformed by the new, more complex principle of organization and continue to be organized according to earlier, simpler principles. The fact that such situations always take a toll on psychic life (cognitively, they can cause distortions; affectively, they can generate painful symptoms; biologically, they drain off energy that goes into keeping the parts separate) demonstrates that the self seeks consistency even if it cannot always achieve it. But even in situations like these, a form of consistency is being demonstrated.

Once again, if we look at the totality of the self's organizing—at the whole system rather than just the dissociated parts—what we see is a self that not only organizes different domains according to different organizational principles (an expression of inconsistency), it also "keeps out" or "holds back" certain aspects of the self's organizing from coming under the influence of the more complex organizational principle. Who or what is doing this "keeping out" or "holding back"? What principle of organizing is expressed in the defenses that sustain this lack of integration within the self? On logical grounds alone it would be counterintuitive to conclude that defenses that sustain this relationship could be *less* complicated than our most complex way of organizing. But I believe we also see it clinically demonstrated that the defensive structures that maintain the dissociation bear the mark of (that is, are consistent with) the self's most complex way of organizing. This is really another way of speaking to the two-sided nature of increasing psychological complexity. Development creates a potential resource for enhanced self-observation, but increased complexity can also be put to the purpose of creating ever more elaborate ways of holding off unintegrated parts of the self's meaning-making.

In sum, it would be too simple to suggest that one's most complex epistemological principle is the only way one organizes experience all the time, across all domains. But it may also be too simple to suggest that phenomena like "regression," "losing it," or even chronic "encapsulations" necessarily contradict the consistency hypothesis. In all such phenomena the expression of one's most complex epistemological principle can still be seen.

27. The thirteen studies Table 5.3 references are drawn from the following sources: (1) R. Goodman, "A Developmental and Systems Analysis of Marital and Family Communication in Clinic and Non-Clinic Families" (doctoral diss., Harvard University, 1983); (2) J. Jacobs, "Holding Environment and Developmental Stages: A Study of Marriage" (doctoral diss., Harvard University, 1984); (3) M. Alvarez, "The Construing of Friend-

ship in Adulthood: A Structural-Developmental Approach" (doctoral diss., Massachusetts School of Professional Psychology, 1985); (4) L. Lahey, "Males' and Females' Construction of Conflict in Work and Love" (doctoral diss., Harvard University, 1986); (5) J. W. Dixon, "The Relation of Social Perspective Stages to Kegan's Stages of Ego Development" (doctoral diss., University of Toledo, 1986); (6) S. Allison, "Meaning-Making in Marriage: An Exploratory Study" (doctoral diss., Massachusetts School of Professional Psychology, 1988); (7) S. Beukema, "Women's Best Friendships: Their Meaning and Meaningfulness" (doctoral diss., Harvard Graduate School of Education, 1990); (8) P. C. Sonnenschein, "The Development of Mutually Satisfying Relationships between Adult Daughters and Their Mothers" (doctoral diss., Harvard Graduate School of Education, 1990); (9) V. F. Binner, "A Study of Minnesota Entrepreneurship: Balancing Personal, Business, and Community Demands" (doctoral diss., Graduate School of the Union Institute, 1991); (10) C. N. Osgood, "Readiness for Parenting Teenagers: A Structural Developmental Approach" (doctoral diss., University of Massachusetts, 1991); (11) J. M. Greenwald, "Environmental Attitudes: A Structural Developmental Model" (doctoral diss., University of Massachusetts, 1991); (12) N. S. Roy, "Toward an Understanding of Family Functioning: An Analysis of the Relationship between Family and Individual Organizing Principles" (doctoral diss., Harvard Graduate School of Education, 1993); (13) M. Bar-Yam, "Do Women and Men Speak in Different Voices? A Comparative Study of Self-Evolvement," *International Journal of Aging and Human Development*, 32 (1991): 247–259.

28. Bar-Yam, "Do Women and Men Speak in Different Voices?"

29. See W. Torbert, *Managing the Corporate Dream* (Homewood, Ill.: Dow-Jones Irwin, 1987); W. Torbert, *The Power of Balance* (Newbury Park, Calif.: Sage, 1991).

30. See Torbert, *Managing the Corporate Dream*, p. 43. The studies are as follows: S. Smith, "Ego Development and the Power of Agreement in Organizations" (doctoral diss., George Washington School of Business and Public Administration, 1980); J. Davidson, "The Effects of Organizational Culture on the Development of Nurses" (doctoral diss., Boston College School of Education, 1984); W. Torbert, "Identifying and Cultivating Professional Effectiveness: 'Bureaucratic Action' at One Professional School" (paper presented at the annual meeting of the American Society for Public Administration, New York, 1983); A. Gratch, "Managers' Prescriptions of Decision-Making Processes as a Function of Ego Development and of the Situation" (unpublished paper, Columbia University Teachers College, 1985); R. Quinn and W. Torbert, "Who Is an Effective, Transforming Leader?" (unpublished paper, University of Michigan

School of Business, Ann Arbor, 1987); J. Hirsch, "Toward a Cognitive-Developmental Theory of Strategy Formulation among Practicing Physicians" (Ann Arbor: University Microfilms International, 1988).

6. Dealing with Difference

1. O. Kraeger and J. M. Thuesen, *Type Talk at Work* (New York: Delacorte Press, 1992), p. 94; see also I. B. Myers and P. B. Myers, *Gifts Differing* (Palo Alto: Consulting Psychologists Press, 1980).
2. Kraeger and Thuesen, *Type Talk at Work.*
3. Ibid., pp. 144–147.
4. Ibid., p. 136.
5. P. Lewis and T. O. Jacobs, "Individual Differences in Strategic Leadership Capacity: A Constructive-Developmental View," in J. G. Hunt and R. L. Phillips, eds., *Strategic Leadership: A Multi-Organizational Perspective* (New York: Quorum Books, 1993), pp. 4–12.
6. Kraeger and Thuesen, *Type Talk at Work*, pp. 21–22.
7. D. A. Kolb, *The Adaptive Style Inventory* (Cleveland: David Kolb, 1980).
8. J. B. Miller, *Toward a New Psychology of Women* (Boston: Beacon Press, 1976); C. Gilligan, *In a Different Voice* (Cambridge: Harvard University Press, 1982).
9. See E. T. Hall, *An Anthropology of Everyday Life* (New York: Doubleday, 1992); *The Hidden Dimension* (Garden City, N.Y.: Doubleday, 1966); *The Silent Language* (Garden City, N.Y.: Doubleday, 1959).
10. *The Link* (Boston University) 3 (April 1987): 1.
11. E. Aries, "Interaction Patterns and Themes of Male, Female, and Mixed Groups," *Small Group Behavior*, 7 (1976): 7–18; E. Aries, "Gender and Communication," in P. Shaver and C. Hendrick, eds., *Sex and Gender* (Newbury Park, Calif.: Sage, 1987); B. W. Eakins and R. G. Eakins, *Sex Differences in Communication* (Boston: Houghton Mifflin, 1978); M. Sadker and D. Sadker, "Sexism in the Schoolroom of the '80s," *Psychology Today*, March 1985, pp. 54–57; Sadker and Sadker, "Sexism in the Classroom: From Grade School to Graduate School," *Phi Delta Kappan*, 67, no. 7 (1986); K. Krupnick, "Women and Men in the Classroom: Inequality and Its Remedies," *On Teaching and Learning: Journal of the Harvard-Danforth Center*, May 1985; Krupnick, "On Learning Gender Roles," in K. Winston and M. J. Bane, eds., *Gender and Public Policy* (Boulder: Westview Press, 1992).
12. See C. Gilligan's *In a Different Voice*; L. Brown and C. Gilligan, *Meeting at the Crossroads*; M. F. Belenky, B. M. Clinchy, N. R. Goldberger, and J. M. Tarule, *Women's Ways of Knowing* (New York: Basic Books, 1986); N.

Lyons, "Two Perspectives on Self, Relationships and Morality," *Harvard Educational Review*, 53 (1983).

13. Kegan, *The Evolving Self*, p. 107.

14. See L. L. Lahey, "Differences: Must They Challenge Similarities in Males' and Females' Moral Development?" (unpublished qualifying paper, Harvard Graduate School of Education, 1984); S. Beukema, "Women's Best Friendships: Their Meaning and Meaningfulness" (doctoral diss., Harvard Graduate School of Education, 1990); M. Alvarez, "The Construing of Friendship in Adulthood: A Constructive-Developmental Approach" (doctoral diss., Massachusetts School of Professional Psychology, 1985); N. Popp, "The Concept and Phenomenon of Psychological Boundaries from a Dialectical Perspective: An Empirical Exploration" (doctoral diss., Harvard Graduate School of Education, 1993).

15. Belenky et al., *Women's Ways of Knowing*.

16. I still think there *might* be some merit to this idea in a very abstract sense in terms of the way the structures of the first and third orders share a certain "opening out" quality and the structures of the second and fourth orders share a certain "self-contained" quality. But each "quality" can be expressed in either a "separate" or "connected" way.

17. Gilligan, *In a Different Voice*.

18. S. D. Parks, "Home and Pilgrimage: Companion Metaphors for Personal and Social Transformation," *Soundings*, 72 (1989).

19. R. A. LeVine, "Infant Environments in Psychoanalysis: A Cross-Cultural View," in J. W. Stigler, R. A. Schweder, and G. Herdt, eds., *Essays on Comparative Human Development* (New York: Cambridge University Press, 1990).

20. P. A. Kaufman, E. Harrison, M. L. Hyde, "Distancing for Intimacy in Lesbian Relationships," *American Journal of Psychiatry*, 14 (1984): 529–533.

21. V. Woolf, "Professions for Women," in *The Death of the Moth and Other Essays* (New York: Harcourt, Brace and Jovanovich, 1942), pp. 236–238.

22. Judy B. Rosener, "Ways Women Lead," *Harvard Business Review*, Nov.–Dec. 1990, pp. 119–125.

23. Belenky et al., *Women's Ways*; J. Surrey, "The Theory of the Self-in-Relation," *Stone Center Work in Progress Papers*, no. 13 (Wellesley: Wellesley College, 1985).

24. R. Masten, *Speaking Poems* (Boston: Beacon Press, 1977).

25. See G. Bateson, *Steps to an Ecology of Mind* (New York: Ballantine Books, 1972); *A Sacred Unity: Further Steps to an Ecology of Mind* (New York: Harper Collins, 1991).

7. Healing

1. This case is taken from the work of the family therapist Olga Silverstein, as depicted in the film *Who's Depressed?* (New York: Ackerman Institute for Family Therapy, 1985).
2. E. Shostrom (producer and director), *Three Approaches to Psychotherapy* (film and video series) (Corona del Mar, Calif.: Psychological and Educational Films, 1965).
3. See: C. R. Rogers and R. F. Dymond, eds., *Psychotherapy and Personality Change: Coordinated Research Studies in the Client-Centered Approach* (Chicago: University of Chicago Press, 1954); Rogers, *On Becoming a Person: A Therapist's View of Psychotherapy* (Boston: Houghton Mifflin, 1961); Rogers, *Client-Centered Therapy* (Boston: Houghton Mifflin, 1951); W. U. Snyder, *Casebook of Non-Directive Counseling* (Boston: Houghton Mifflin, 1947); Rogers, *Carl Rogers on Personal Power* (New York: Delacorte Press, 1977); Rogers, *Carl Rogers on Encounter Groups* (New York: Harper and Row, 1970); Rogers, *Becoming Partners: Marriage and Its Alternatives* (New York: Delacorte Press, 1972).
4. Personal communication, 1977.
5. Rogers, *Client-Centered Therapy*, pp. 138–139.
6. See: F. S. Perls, *Gestalt Therapy Verbatim* (Lafayette, Calif.: Real People Press, 1969); *Gestalt Therapy: Excitement and Growth in the Human Personality* (New York: Delta Books, 1951); *The Gestalt Approach and Eyewitness to History* (New York: Bantam Books, 1976); *Ego, Hunger, and Aggression: The Beginning of Gestalt Therapy* (New York: Random House, 1969).
7. Shostrom, *Three Approaches to Psychotherapy*.
8. See: A. Ellis and R. M. Grieger, *Handbook of Rational-Emotive Therapy* (New York: Springer, 1977); Ellis, *How to Stubbornly Refuse to Make Yourself Miserable About Anything—Yes, Anything!* (Secaucus, N.J.: L. Stuart, 1988); M. E. Bernard and R. DiGiuseppe, eds., *Inside Rational-Emotive Therapy: A Critical Appraisal of the Theory and Therapy of Albert Ellis* (San Diego: Academic Press, 1988); Ellis, *Overcoming Resistance: Rational-Emotive Therapy with Difficult Clients* (New York: Springer, 1985); Ellis, *The Essential Albert Ellis: Seminal Writings on Psychotherapy*, ed. W. Dryden (New York: Springer, 1990).
9. Shostrom, *Three Approaches to Psychotherapy*.
10. Ibid.
11. M. Broderick, "Self, Cancer and Transformation: A Developmental Critique of the Cancer-Prone Personality Literatures," unpublished qualifying paper, Harvard Graduate School of Education, 1990.
12. This portion of the chapter (pp. 252–260) is drawn largely from L. Rogers

and R. Kegan, "Mental Growth and Mental Health as Distinct Concepts in the Study of Developmental Psychopathology," in D. Keating and H. Rosen, eds., *Constructivist Approaches to Psychopathology* (Hillsdale, N.J.: Laurence Erlbaum Associates, 1990). For other constructive-developmental approaches to aspects of clinical work see: L. Rogers, "Developmental Psychopathology: Studies in Adolescent and Adult Experiences of Psychological Dysfunction" (doctoral diss., Harvard Graduate School of Education, 1987); G. Noam, "Self, Morality and Biography: Studies in Clinical-Developmental Psychology" (doctoral diss., 1984); Noam, "Borderline Personality Disorders and the Theory of Biography and Transformation," *McLean Hospital Journal*, 11 (1986): 19–43; Noam, "The Constructivist Theory of Developmental Psychopathology and Clinical-Developmental Psychology," in E. Nannis and P. Cowan, eds., *Developmental Psychopathology and Its Treatment* (San Francisco: Jossey-Bass, 1988); G. Noam and R. Kegan, "On Boundaries and Externalization: Toward a Clinical-Developmental Interpretation," in W. Edelstein and M. Keller, *Soziale Kognition* (Frankfurt: Suhrkamp, 1982); G. Noam, "Marking Time in the Midst of the Hardest Moment: Adolescent Borderline Disorders in Lifespan Perspective," in K. Field, B. Cohler, and G. Wool, eds., *Motive and Meaning: Psychoanalytic Perspectives on Learning and Education* (New York: International Universities Press, 1984); R. Kegan, L. Rogers, and D. Quinlan, "Constructive-Developmental Organizations of Depression" (paper presented to American Psychological Association Symposium, "New Approaches to Depression," Los Angeles, 1981); R. Kegan, "Ego and Truth: Personality and the Piaget Paradigm" (doctoral diss., Harvard Graduate School of Education, 1977); Kegan, *The Evolving Self* (Cambridge: Harvard University Press, 1982); Kegan, "A Neo-Piagetian Approach to Object Relations," in B. Lee and G. Noam, eds., *Developmental Approaches to the Self* (New York: Plenum Press, 1985); Kegan, "Kohlberg and the Psychology of Ego Development," in S. Modgil and C. Modgil, eds., *Lawrence Kohlberg: Consensus and Controversy* (Sussex, Eng.: Falmer Press, 1986); Kegan, "The Child behind the Mask," in W. H. Reid, J. W. Bonner III, D. Dorr, and J. I. Walker, eds., *Unmasking the Psychopath* (New York: Norton, 1986); R. Goodman, "A Developmental and Systems Analysis of Marital and Family Communication in Clinic and Non-Clinic Families" (doctoral diss., Harvard Graduate School of Education; University Microfilms International, 1983); A. F. Henderson, "College Age Lesbianism as a Developmental Phenomenon," *Journal of the American College Health Association* (1979); Henderson, "Homosexuality in the College Years: Developmental Differences between Men and Women," *Journal of the American College Health Association* (1984); A. F. Henderson and R. Kegan, "Learning, Knowing and the Self," in Field,

Cohler, and Wool, eds., *Motive and Meaning*; S. Powers, S. Hauser, J. Schwartz, G. Noam, and A. Jacobson, "Adolescent Ego Development and Family Interaction," in H. D. Grotevant and C. R. Cooper, eds., *Adolescent Development in the Family* (San Francisco: Jossey-Bass, 1983); R. Selman, *The Growth of Interpersonal Understanding: Developmental and Clinical Analyses* (New York: Academic Press, 1980); R. Selman and L. H. Schultz, *Making a Friend in Youth: Developmental Theory and Pair Therapy* (Chicago: University of Chicago Press, 1990); A. P. Demorest and R. Selman, "Observing Troubled Children's Interpersonal Negotiation Strategies: Implications of and for a Developmental Model," *Child Development*, 55 (1984): 283–304; M. Basseches, "Toward a Constructive-Developmental Understanding of the Dialectics of Individuality and Irrationality," in D. A. Kramer and M. J. Bopp, eds., *Transformation in Clinical and Developmental Psychology* (New York: Springer-Verlag, 1989); A. Hewer, "From Conflict to Suicide and Revival: Disequilibrium and Reequilibration in Experience of Psychological Breakdown and Recovery" (unpublished qualifying paper, Harvard Graduate School of Education, 1983); A. Hewer, "Equilibrative Processes in Social and Moral Cognition Observed in Relation to Changes in Psychopathology" (doctoral diss., Harvard Graduate School of Education, 1986); V. Kelley, "Ego Development in Men and Women and Psychotherapeutic Self-understanding," (doctoral diss., 1983; abstract in *Dissertation Abstracts International*, 44/11B:3530; Ann Arbor: University Microfilms International, no. 84-05002); M. B. Carlsen, *Meaning-Making: Therapeutic Processes in Developmental Psychotherapy* (New York: Norton, 1988); B. L. T. Aardema, "The Therapeutic Use of Hope" (doctoral diss., Western Michigan University, 1984; Ann Arbor: University Microfilms International, no. 85-05196); R. O'C. Higgins, "Psychological Resilience and the Capacity for Intimacy" (doctoral diss., Harvard Graduate School of Education, 1983).

13. The case of Rita is an amalgam of the case of Amy in L. Rogers and R. Kegan, "Mental Growth and Mental Health," and the case of Beth in L. L. Lahey, "Males' and Females' Construction of Conflict in Work and Love," doctoral disscertation, Harvard Graduate School of Education, 1986.

14. The first and second of these are drawn from the work of Kiyo Morimoto and William Perry, respectively (personal communication), former directors of Harvard University's Bureau of Study Counsel; the third is drawn from my own clinical work.

15. M. Robbins, *Midlife Women and the Death of Mother* (New York: Peter Lang, 1990).

16. For constructive-developmental perspectives on religion, faith, and religious experiencing see J. W. Fowler, *Stages of Faith: The Psychology of Human Development and the Quest for Meaning* (San Francisco: Harper and

Row, 1981); S. D. Parks, *The Critical Years: The Young Adult Search for a Faith to Live By* (New York: Harper and Row, 1986); W. Conn, *Christian Conversion: A Developmental Interpretation of Autonomy and Surrender* (New York: Paulist Press, 1986); M. B. Moehl, "Religious 'Knowledge': A Psychological Analysis of Atheism and Theism" (doctoral diss., Harvard Graduate School of Education, 1988); R. Kegan, "There the Dance Is: Religious Dimensions of a Developmental Framework," in J. Fowler and A. Vergote, eds., *Toward Moral and Religious Maturity* (Morristown, N. J.: Silver Burdett Company, 1980); R. Marstin, *Beyond Our Tribal Gods: The Maturing of Faith* (Maryknoll, N.Y.: Orbis Books, 1979); S. S. Ivy, "The Structural-Developmental Theories of James Fowler and Robert Kegan as Resources for Pastoral Assessment" (doctoral diss., The Southern Baptist Theological Seminary, 1985).

8. Learning

1. I thank Carol Aslanian, Director of the College Board's Office of Adult Learning Services, for these statistics.

2. See Gerald Grow, "Teaching Learners to Be Self-Directed," *Adult Education Quarterly*, 41 (Spring 1991): 125–149; S. Brookfield, ed., *Self-Directed Learning: From Theory to Practice*, New Directions for Continuing Education, no. 25 (San Francisco: Jossey-Bass, 1985); S. Brookfield, *Developing Critical Thinkers* (San Francisco: Jossey-Bass, 1987); P. C. Candy, "Reframing Research into Self-Direction in Adult Education: A Constructivist Perspective" (doctoral diss., University of British Columbia, 1987; Ottawa: National Library of Canada, Canadian Theses Microfiche, no. 0-315-40011-0); L. S. Gerstner, *On the Theme and Variations of Self-Directed Learning* (doctoral diss., Columbia University Teachers College, 1987); J. Mezirow, "A Critical Theory of Adult Learning and Education," *Adult Education Quarterly*, 32 (1981): 24; M. S. Knowles, *Self-Directed Learning: A Guide for Learners and Teachers* (New York: Cambridge Book Co., 1975).

3. Grow, "Teaching Learners to Be Self-Directed," pp. 133–134.

4. W. G. Perry, Jr., and C. P. Whitlock, *Harvard University Reading Course* (Cambridge: Harvard University Press, 1967); W. G. Perry, Jr., and C. P. Whitlock, "A Clinical Rationale for a Reading Film," *Harvard Educational Review* (Winter 1954).

5. S. Kierkegaard, *The Journals of Kierkegaard*, trans. A. Dru (New York: Harper, 1959).

6. L. Daloz, "Martha Meets Her Mentor," *Change Magazine*, July–August 1987.

7. S. D. Parks, *The Critical Years: The Young Adult Search for a Faith to Live By* (New York: Harper and Row, 1986).

8. M. F. Belenky, B. M. Clinchy, N. R. Goldberger, and J. M. Tarule, *Women's Ways of Knowing* (New York: Basic Books, 1986).

9. K. Bruffee, *Collaborative Learning: Higher Education, Interdependence and the Authority of Knowledge* (Baltimore: Johns Hopkins University Press, 1993).

10. Ibid.

11. Ibid.

12. R. Bellah et al., *Habits of the Heart: Individualism and Commitment in American Life* (Berkeley: University of California Press, 1985).

13. Charles Seashore, "In Grave Danger of Growing: Observations on the Process of Professional Development" (unpublished paper, Washington School of Psychiatry Group Psychotherapy Training Program, 1975).

14. Kathleen Taylor, "Transforming Learning: Experiences of Adult Development and Transformation of Re-Entry Learners in an Adult Degree Program" (doctoral diss., Union Graduate School, 1991), p. 71.

15. Ibid.

16. Ibid.

17. Ibid.

18. Ibid.

19. Ibid.

20. Ibid.

21. Laurent Daloz, *Effective Teaching and Mentoring: Realizing the Transformational Power of Adult Learning Experiences* (San Francisco: Jossey-Bass, 1987), p. 215.

22. Taylor, "Transforming Learning," p. 90.

23. Ibid., p. 92.

24. Ibid., p. 58.

25. Ibid., p. 59.

26. Ibid., p. 67.

27. Ibid., p. 97.

28. Ibid., pp. 60–61, 95.

29. Baird Brightman, "Narcissistic Transformation in the Training Year," *International Journal of Psychoanalytic Psychotherapy*, 10 (1984): 293–317.

30. The research of Thomas Hodgson is fascinating in this regard. Among other things, Hodgson did subject-object assessments of adult undergraduates' "prior learning portfolios," that is, work-related autobiographies written for academic credit. He then correlated his subject-object assessments with the actual credit awards (anywhere from twelve to thirty-five semester credits) faculty granted to the autobiographical projects. He found a statistically significant relationship between increasing

credit awards and increasingly complex subject-object structures. And he found that the mean subject-object score for the group that received the *fewest* credits did not reach the fourth order threshold, while the mean subject-object score for the group that received the *greatest* number of credits had reached the fourth order threshold. See T. O. Hodgson, "Constructive-Developmental Analysis of Autobiographical Writing" (doctoral diss., University of Massachusetts, 1990).

31. Taylor, "Transforming Learning," p. 103.
32. Ibid., pp. 105–106.

9. Conflict, Leadership, and Knowledge Creation

1. For further consideration of this essentially "dialectical" point, see the discussion of the transformation from the fourth to the fifth order in L. Lahey, E. Souvaine, R. Kegan, R. Goodman, and S. Felix, *A Guide to the Subject-Object Interview: Its Administration and Interpretation* (Cambridge: The Subject-Object Workshop, 1988); E. Souvaine, L. Lahey, and R. Kegan, "Life after Formal Operations: Implications for a Psychology of the Self," in C. N. Alexander and E. J. Langer, eds., *Higher Stages of Human Development: Perspectives on Adult Growth* (New York: Oxford University Press, 1990); and M. Basseches, *Dialectical Thinking and Adult Development* (Norwood, N.J.: Ablex, 1984).

2. My thanks to Ariela Bairey, who gave me a background in this field. See J. W. Burton, *Conflict and Communication: The Use of Controlled Communication in International Relations* (London: MacMillan, 1969); Burton, *Resolving Deep-Rooted Conflict: A Handbook* (Lanham, Md.: University Press of America, 1987); J. W. Burton and F. Dukes, *Conflict: Practices in Management, Settlement and Resolution* (New York: St. Martin's Press, 1990); L. W. Doob, ed., *Resolving Conflict in Africa: The Fermeda Workshop* (New Haven: Yale University Press, 1970); Doob, "Adieu to Private Intervention in Political Conflicts?" *International Journal of Group Tensions,* 17 (1987): 15–27; L. W. Doob and W. J. Foltz, "The Belfast Workshop: An Application of Group Techniques to a Destructive Conflict," *Journal of Conflict Resolution,* 18 (1973): 237–256; R. J. Fisher, "A Third-Party Consultation Workshop on the India-Pakistan Conflict," *Journal of Social Psychology,* 112 (1980): 191–206; Fisher, "Third Party Consultation as a Method of Conflict Resolution: A Review of Studies," *Journal of Conflict Resolution,* 27 (1983): 301–334; Fisher, *The Social Psychology of Intergroup and International Conflict Resolution* (New York: Springer-Verlag, 1990); Fisher, *Conflict Analysis Workshop on Cyprus: Final Workshop Report* (Ottawa: Canadian Institute for International Peace and Security, 1991); H. C. Kel-

man, "The Problem-Solving Workshop in Conflict Resolution," in R. L. Merritt, ed., *Communication in International Politics* (Urbana: University of Illinois Press, 1972), pp. 168–204; Kelman, "An Interactional Approach to Conflict Resolution and Its Application to Israeli-Palestinian Relations," *International Interactions*, 6, no. 2 (1979): 99–122; Kelman, "Interactive Problem Solving: A Social-Psychological Approach to Conflict Resolution," in W. Klassen, ed., *Dialogue toward Inter-Faith Understanding* (Jerusalem: Ecumenical Institute for Theological Research, 1986), pp. 293–314; H. C. Kelman and S. P. Cohen, "The Problem-Solving Workshop: A Social-Psychological Contribution to the Resolution of International Conflict," *Journal of Peace Research*, 13 (1976): 79–90; Kelman and Cohen, "Resolution of International Conflict: An Interactional Approach," in S. Worchel and W. G. Austin, eds., *Psychology of Intergroup Relations*, 2nd ed. (Chicago: Nelson-Hall, 1986), pp. 323–342.

3. This "union of opposites" Jung called "enantiodromia," depicted by the snake who eats its tail, the joining of the poles making a single whole. Interestingly, Jung associated the union of opposites with midlife.

4. L. Chasin, R. Chasin, M. Herzig, S. Roth, and C. Becker, "The Citizen Clinician: The Family Therapist in the Public Forum," *American Family Therapy Association Newsletter* (Winter 1991): 36–42; R. Chasin and M. Herzig, "Creating Systemic Interventions for the Sociopolitical Arena," in B. Berger-Gould and D. H. DeMuth, eds., *The Global Family Therapist: Integrating the Personal, Professional and Political* (Needham, Mass.: Allyn and Bacon, 1993); S. Roth, L. Chasin, R. Chasin, C. Becker, and M. Herzig, "From Debate to Dialogue: A Facilitating Role for Family Therapists in the Public Forum," *Dulwich Centre Newsletter*, no. 2 (1993): 41–48; C. Becker, L. Chasin, R. Chasin, M. Herzig, and S. Roth, "From Stuck Debate to New Conversation on Controversial Issues: A Report from the Public Conversations Project," *Journal of Feminist Family Therapy*, in press.

5. C. Argyris, *On Organizational Learning* (Cambridge: Blackwell Business, 1993); C. Argyris, *Overcoming Organizational Defenses: Facilitating Organizational Learning* (Boston: Allyn and Bacon, 1990); C. Argyris, R. Putnam, and D. M. Smith, *Action Science* (San Francisco: Jossey-Bass, 1985); C. Argyris, *The Applicability of Organizational Sociology* (Cambridge, England: Cambridge University Press, 1972); S. Srivastva and Associates, *The Executive Mind* (San Francisco: Jossey-Bass, 1983); C. Argyris, *Increasing Leadership Effectiveness* (New York: Wiley, 1976); Argyris, *Inner Contradictions of Rigorous Research* (New York: Academic Press, 1980); D. A. Schon, *The Reflective Practitioner* (London: Temple Smith, 1983); D. A. Schon, ed., *The Reflective Turn: Case Studies in and on Educational Practice* (New York: Teachers College Press, 1991); C. Argyris and D. A. Schon, *Theory in*

Practice: Increasing Professional Effectiveness (San Francisco: Jossey-Bass, 1974); Argyris and Schon, *Organizational Learning: A Theory of Action Perspective* (Reading, Mass.: Addison-Wesley, 1978); D. A. Schon, *Intuitive Thinking?: A Metaphor Underlying Some Ideas of Educational Reform* (Cambridge: Division for Study and Research in Education, Massachusetts Institute of Technology, 1981); Schon, *Educating the Reflective Practitioner: Toward a New Design for Teaching and Learning in the Professions* (San Francisco: Jossey-Bass, 1987); W. R. Torbert, *The Power of Balance: Transforming Self, Society and Scientific Inquiry* (Newbury, Calif.: Sage Publications, 1991); Torbert, *Managing the Corporate Dream: Restructuring for Long-Term Success* (Homewood, Ill.: Dow-Jones Irwin, 1987); Torbert, *Learning from Experience: Toward Consciousness* (New York: Columbia University Press, 1972); Torbert, *Creating a Community of Inquiry: Conflict, Collaboration, Transformation* (New York: Wiley, 1976).

6. Personal communication.

7. For an illuminating discussion and exploration of the mental demands implicit in Argyris's "action science," see E. Souvaine, "Creating Contexts for Effective Action and the Development of Meaning-Making" (unpublished qualifying paper, Harvard Graduate School of Education, 1985).

8. See Lahey et al., *A Guide to the Subject-Object Interview*; Souvaine et al., "Life after Formal Operations"; and Basseches, *Dialectical Thinking and Adult Development*.

9. R. A. Heifetz and R. M. Sinder, "Political Leadership: Managing the Public's Problem Solving," in R. Reich, ed., *The Power of Public Ideas* (Cambridge: Balinger, 1988).

10. R. Kegan and L. Lahey, "Adult Leadership and Adult Development," in B. Kellerman, ed., *Leadership: Multidisciplinary Perspectives* (New York: Prentice-Hall, 1983).

11. K. Mannheim, *Essays on the Sociology of Culture* (London: Routledge and Paul, 1956); M. Foucault, *Power/Knowledge* (New York: Pantheon Books, 1980).

12. N. C. Burbules and S. Rice, "Dialogue across Differences: Continuing the Conversation," *Harvard Educational Review*, 61 (1991): 393–416.

13. Z. Bauman, "Strangers: The Social Construction of Universality and Particularity," *Telos*, 28, no. 23 (1988–1989) (quoted in Burbules and Rice, "Dialogue across Differences").

14. P. Lather, "Post-Modernism and the Politics of Enlightenment," *Educational Foundations*, 3, no. 3 (1989) (quoted in Burbules and Rice, "Dialogue across Differences").

15. Z. Bauman, "Strangers"; Burbules and Rice, "Dialogue across Differences."

16. Ibid., p. 398.

17. Ibid., pp. 398–401.
18. Ibid., pp. 402–407.
19. Arlin identifies a stage of cognitive development beyond the fully formal operational "problem solving," which she calls "problem finding," in which thinkers seek out and are nourished by contradiction. Are Arlin's "problem solving" and "problem finding" stages cognitive reflections of the fourth and fifth orders, respectively? See P. K. Arlin, "Cognitive Development in Adulthood: A Fifth Stage?" *Developmental Psychology*, 11 (1975): 602–606; Arlin, "Piagetian Operations in Problem Finding," *Developmental Psychology*, 13 (1977): 247–298; Arlin, "Adolescent and Adult Thought: A Structural Interpretation," in M. L. Commons, F. A. Richards, and C. Armon, eds., *Beyond Formal Operations: Late Adolescent and Adult Cognitive Development* (New York: Praeger, 1984); Arlin, "Wisdom: The Art of Problem Finding," in R. J. Sternberg, ed., *Wisdom: Its Nature, Origins and Development* (New York: Cambridge University Press, 1990).
20. Belenky et al. identify a "way of knowing" beyond "procedural knowing" which they call "constructed knowing," in which we become more aware of and responsible for the constructed nature of our procedures. Are "procedural knowing" and "constructed knowing" expressions of the fourth and fifth orders, respectively? See M. F. Belenky, B. M. Clinchy, N. R. Goldberger, and J. M. Tarule, *Women's Ways of Knowing* (New York: Basic Books, 1986).

10. On Being Good Company for the Wrong Journey

1. N. Chodorow, *The Reproduction of Mothering* (Berkeley: University of California Press, 1978).
2. Ibid., pp. 167–169.
3. *New Yorker*, August 20, 1990, p. 58.
4. *New York Times*, March 1, 1992.

Index